D0948205

The Foundations of Mind

Oxford Series in Cognitive Development

Series Editors
Paul Bloom and Susan A. Gelman

The Foundations of Mind

Origins of Conceptual Thought

JEAN MATTER MANDLER

OXFORD
UNIVERSITY PRESS

2004

OXFORD
UNIVERSITY PRESS

Oxford   New York
Auckland   Bangkok   Buenos Aires   Cape Town   Chennai
Dar es Salaam   Delhi   Hong Kong   Istanbul   Karachi   Kolkata
Kuala Lumpur   Madrid   Melbourne   Mexico City   Mumbai   Nairobi
São Paulo   Shanghai   Taipei   Tokyo   Toronto

Copyright © 2004 by Jean Matter Mandler

Published by Oxford University Press, Inc.
198 Madison Avenue, New York, New York 10016

www.oup.com

Oxford is a registered trademark of Oxford University Press

Library of Congress Cataloging-in-Publication Data
Mandler, Jean Matter.
The foundations of mind : origins of conceptual thought /
by Jean Matter Mandler.
     p.   cm. — (Oxford series in cognitive development)
Includes bibliographical references and index.
ISBN 0-19-517200-0
 1. Cognition in infants.   2. Concepts in infants.   I. Title.
II. Series.
BF720.C63 M36 2004
155.42'2323—dc22   2003017304

9 8 7 6 5 4 3 2 1

Printed in the United States of America
on acid-free paper

For Peter and Michael

For whose sake I wish I had understood these issues 40 years ago

Preface

This is a book about meaning, in particular conceptual meaning and how it arises in the human mind. Sadly, psychologists have more or less abandoned the study of meaning in recent years. This trend is due in part to the diversion of research to the study of the brain. An unfortunate side effect of otherwise exciting research on brain functioning is an increasing tendency to explain everything in terms of the way the brain works, skipping the mind altogether. But the brain cannot tell us about meaning. That is the province of the mind, and if psychology does not pay attention to the way the mind processes meaning, it is in danger of losing its central core.

In this book I address the foundations of the conceptual mind—how we come to be able to interpret the world and to think about it. Although much of my inspiration came from studying Piaget, the story I tell (informally known as How to Build a Baby) is a markedly different account of infancy and the foundations of mind from his. No one today can claim to replace Piagetian theory in its entirety. Perhaps that is because we now have so much more data and in that sense know so much more than Piaget did. All the ins and outs we have come to appreciate make it much more daunting to encompass the development of mind from its inception to its culmination in adulthood. Nevertheless, it seems possible to start at the beginning and ask: Is this the right way to go? This book is the result of years of research that insistently has said: No, the infant does not start out in the way that Piaget assumed. Infants appear to be conceptual beings from the start, without going through an extensive sensorimotor period lacking any conceptual thought. I attempt to show not only that this is so but also what some of the earliest thoughts might be like.

My position will be controversial, not least because it makes a clear distinction between percepts and concepts. I recently attended a conference on conceptual knowledge that brought together cognitive, developmental, and comparative psychologists, anthropologists, neuropsychologists, and neurobiologists. At the last session of the conference, the participants were asked to define what they meant by conceptual knowledge. The answers were dismaying. There were roughly as many opinions about how to define *conception*, *perception*, and their relationships as there were speakers. It seems incredible that we have been in the mind business for hundreds of years and have not yet agreed on some definitions of the terms we all use in our work. We still reside in a Tower of Babel, and until we knock it down or leave it, I doubt that progress will be made.

I do not expect consensus soon. I do ask, however, that anyone writing on these issues try as clearly as possible to set out their conditions of use of the terms *perception* and *conception*. Needless to say, the particular terms we use do not matter. As I discuss in chapter 3, the distinctions I make are sometimes referred to as procedural and declarative, sometimes as implicit and explicit knowledge. In spite of different terminology, each of these sets of terms captures some of the distinctions I believe we need to make if we are to understand how the conceptual mind develops.

These distinctions also explain some persistent controversies in development, such as why it is that infants can see the difference between a dog and a cat by 3 months of age but do not distinguish them on some tests until months later, why infants pass number tests that they fail as preschoolers, or why they seem to have knowledge about physics that apparently deserts them a few years later. These discrepancies are often attributed to task-dependent knowledge, but that seems to me too narrow a way to describe them. Many tasks can be solved in more than one way, and it is important to know whether implicit perceptual knowledge or explicit conceptual knowledge is being used to do so. This book explores these issues, illustrating them extensively in the areas of categorization, inference, and memory tasks.

In these pages there is relatively little discussion of cultural influences on infant conceptual development. Infants are to some extent shielded from such influences by their lack of language. Of course, even without language, culture has at least some effects. As we will see, concepts of cars and motorcycles are an early achievement of urban California infants that would not be found in infants raised in a forest culture. Conversely, urban California infants are slower to develop knowledge about animals and plants than about artifacts, which might not be true for forest- or farm-raised infants. However, the ability to recall past events, categorize objects and spatial relations, and learn the important basics of language are all governed by universal factors common to infants in all cultures. It is when the foundations have been laid down and the naming practices of the culture begin to teach the infant which details are important that we begin to see more cultural influence. This issue is illustrated in chapter 11, in which learning relational concepts and the words that express them are the main focus. There is also little discussion in this book of parental influences on infant learning. This is due mainly to my conviction that the earliest conceptual learning and memory development are more a function of what infants observe and analyze than of what parents try to teach. It is possible that I underestimate parental influence in this regard, but in any case I hope readers will come to appreciate just how much infants can achieve on their own.

The first three chapters of this book describe the methods we use to study infant conceptual development, the brilliant but ultimately unsatisfying theory of Piaget on sensorimotor development, and the necessity for a dual representational system to account for infants' cognitive functioning. Chapters 4 and 5 describe the heart of my theory of concept formation in infancy, describing perceptual meaning analysis, the image-schemas that arise from it, and how these can be combined into the concepts that infants form. Chapter 6 explains why the first concepts about objects cannot be at the basic level and makes clear why we must distinguish between perceptual and conceptual categories. Chapters 7 and 8 summarize much of the data collected in my laboratory on the kinds of global concepts that infants first form and then how these concepts are used to make the inferences that build up the knowledge base. Chapter 8 also reprises the theory introduced in chapters 4 and 5. Chapter 9 discusses the lifetime continuity from infant to adult in concepts of objects and compares acquisition with conceptual breakdown in semantic dementia. Chapter 10 describes the growth of recall in infancy as still another example of early conceptual functioning. Chapter 11 adds language to the picture and shows how its acquisition accounts for increasingly differentiated object concepts. It also discusses the way that, in contrast to object concepts, language reorganizes preverbal spatial relational concepts. Finally, chapter 12 reprises the role of consciousness in the various accomplishments described in earlier chapters and summarizes the most important conclusions arising from the research and theory the book offers.

I wish to thank Laraine McDonough for cherished collaboration over the years in which the research described in this book was carried out. Without her, much of the experimental work would not have been accomplished, and her lively conversation and questioning made me think more deeply about issues than I might otherwise have done. She, along with Katherine Nelson and George Mandler, did yeoman service in reading an earlier draft of the book. George also kept me going when I sometimes tired of putting it all together and was always available to talk out problems and issues. I also wish to thank Patricia Bauer, who collaborated with great dedication and skill on much of the research on deferred imitation reported here, along with many undergraduates who put in countless hours of work. Last but not least, I thank the National Science Foundation for supporting this research for many years. In particular, Joe Young was an encouraging and supportive director of the cognitive panel that funded my work.

Contents

The Foundations of Mind

I

How to Build a Baby
Prologue

. . . in which I introduce the idea that infants have a conceptual life and are not just sensorimotor creatures. The term concept *is defined and differentiated from other kinds of representation in infancy. Doing so requires making a distinction between procedural and declarative knowledge, and these terms are briefly discussed as well. I describe the techniques we have used to study the formation of concepts in infancy and pay my respects to Piaget, who inspired me to think about how to build a baby deeply enough that I could see where he went wrong in his own theory of the birth of conceptual thought.*

Anyone who has conducted research on perception or cognition in infants has likely encountered colleagues, science writers, and others who have expressed disbelief at his or her findings. Evidence for perceptual and cognitive capacities in infants strains the beliefs of many people because it conflicts with prevalent conceptions about infants and intuitions about cognitive development. . . . When data conflict with intuition, however, intuition is rarely the best guide for advancing understanding.
(Spelke, 1998)

Concepts Within the Larger System

One of the most prevalent intuitions about early cognitive development is that young infants have virtually no conceptual life. Instead, babies are described as sensorimotor creatures who understand the world solely through their perceptual and motor systems. They recognize things they have seen before, they can move themselves and manipulate objects, but they have no concepts and so cannot think, recall the past, or imagine the future. This view, of course, is a legacy of Piaget. I discuss his theory of how thought begins in chapter 2. Here I merely note that the sensorimotor character of infancy has been so widely assumed that to many it may seem beyond dispute. Yet one of the central points of this book is that this assumption is misleading. I will develop the position that infants begin forming a conceptual system very early in life and that this system does not gradually develop out of a prior sensorimotor period, at least not in the sense that Piaget intended or as the term is usually used.

To document the beginnings of the conceptual system requires clarity of definition. With a few notable exceptions, such as Smith and Medin (1981) and Nelson (1985), terms such as *concept* and *category* usually go undefined in the literature, even though psychologists use these expressions all the time. Another central purpose of this book is to make as clear a distinction as possible between the conceptual and the perceptual systems. Because these terms are usually used without much consideration of their wider implications, they have different meanings for different people. For example, the first time I said that there has been almost no research on the infant conceptual system, I was told that this was an exaggeration, because a great deal of research had been carried out on the "object concept" and the "number concept." But the status of these "concepts," in spite of a decade or more of research, is still not clear. As I use the term, a *concept* refers to declarative knowledge about object kinds and events that is potentially accessible to conscious thought. As far as a "number concept" is concerned, 5-month-olds are sensitive to addition and subtraction of small numbers (Wynn, 1992), but their success is probably due to an implicit tracking mechanism rather than to conceptual knowledge of cardinality (Simon, 1997). A system of object files governed by the perceptual system (Kahneman & Treisman, 1984) may deliver information in implicit form that enables infants to keep track of small numbers of objects (Uller, Carey, Huntley-Fenner, & Klatt, 1999). There is also an implicit ability to estimate magnitudes that human infants share with many species (Whalen, Gallistel, & Gelman, 1999). These are important innate abilities that undoubtedly are related to later mathematical achievements (Carey, 2001; Gelman, 1991), but at present there does not appear to be strong evidence for conceptual knowledge of number at this young age.

It may be even more difficult to assess the status of the "object concept" because the phenomena that have been demonstrated in the literature are a mix of implicit (unconscious) and explicit (conscious) processes. Infants learn many things about objects in the first months of life, and only a few of these fall under the rubric of conceptual knowledge.

For example, the sensorimotor system delivers the implicit information that objects are three-dimensional and solid and do not implode as they move behind barriers. On the other hand, some of the object permanence tests showing that 6-month-olds represent specific information about hidden objects, such as that an object behind a screen is on top of a track rather than in front of or behind it (Baillargeon, 1986), seem difficult to account for in terms of implicit sensorimotor knowledge; the infants must remain aware of information no longer in view. (Interestingly, however, a few of the demonstrations of object permanence that involve objects disappearing behind screens and reappearing again, such as Baillargeon & DeVos, 1991, might be accomplished on the basis of the implicit object-tracking mechanism previously mentioned.) So in my terminology the notion of *the* "object concept" is an oversimplification. Infants learn a lot of implicit nonconceptual information about objects, but in addition they also conceptualize them in a more explicit way.

Another example of a serious lack of definition of commonly used terms is the claim that the first concepts about objects to be formed are "basic-level" (that is, concrete concepts such as dog or chair). Not only is the term *basic-level* undefined in this claim but so is what is meant by a concept. That makes such a statement extremely difficult to disprove. However, as I discuss in chapters 6 and 7, when concepts are more clearly defined and differentiated from perceptual schemas, it becomes easy to show that it is highly unlikely for most first concepts to be at such a concrete, specific level. Infants do form very specific perceptual schemas of what dogs and chairs look like. The problem comes when a leap is made to the assumption that this perceptual schematization must be the foundation upon which concepts are built. This traditional view assumes that the first step in conceptualizing a dog, for instance, is to know what a dog looks like. However, it is quite possible to know what a dog looks like and not have any idea of what it is and, as I will show, equally possible to have a concept of animal without a commitment to any particular kind of shape or features. We cannot make this leap as a matter of course but must examine what infants actually do. Is it the case that they form perceptual schemas of the objects that surround them and use this perceptual base as the glue to hold associations together? Do they understand dogs as the same kind of thing because they look alike and then associate various properties with this kind of object? This is an entrenched view, but when we examine what infants are doing in detail, it does not do a good job of describing the data.

This view of the foundation of the conceptual mind as consisting of associations accruing to perceptual schemas pervades our thinking not only about infancy but also about the preschool years. Young children are said to be perceptually bound, to know only the superficial aspect of things, not to have any organized, coherent system of knowledge about the different kinds of things that exist in the world. Although this view of young children has been attacked from time to time (for example, by both Margaret Donaldson and Rochel Gelman in 1978 and in 1991 by Michael Siegal and also by Susan Gelman and Henry Wellman), it remains the dominant view when it comes to understanding the first concepts and early thought. Why is this so? Perhaps because it is easy to get children to depend on the superficial perceptual aspects of things—just give them problems in domains they don't understand well or with which they have had little experience. That is, do just what you would do to adults if you wanted to make them appear disorganized and confused.

I raise this issue to illustrate the pervasiveness of the view that the early percepts of infants can be called concepts because perceptual and conceptual knowledge are on some kind of continuum, with one merging into the other. Although everyone agrees that seeing is not the same as thinking, when it comes to laying out the differences between the two, some psychologists say it probably can't or shouldn't be done. This attitude is puzzling, but I imagine it is due to the definitional problem just discussed. Because we are usually not clear about what we mean when we say that something is conceptual, it indeed becomes very difficult to separate from a perceptual representation. As I discuss in chapter 3, my approach to this problem is to posit a dual representational system. This idea is quite common nowadays, but it was not always so. During the behaviorist period and the days of the grand learning theories of Hull and Spence, a single representational system was assumed. Of course, behaviorists would have rejected the notion of representation, so they talked instead about a common set of mechanisms that was assumed to apply to all processing. (We may be heading back to this view today, as connectionism has gained sway in the field.) Even earlier, in the days of the British empiricists, a distinction between percepts and concepts was made but again not in terms of different representational systems. For example, Locke posited simple ideas derived from perception and complex ideas derived by combining simple ideas. Thus, there was a common "mind stuff," and the distinction between percepts and concepts was a matter of degree.

In my opinion, the only solution to the long-standing problem of how to relate perception and conception is a dual representational system, each governed by its own mechanisms and types of processing. Certainly a good case can be made for such a distinction, as more and more evidence accumulates of differences in both psychological and brain processing in procedural and declarative representation. At the same time, it must be admitted that this solution brings new problems, in particular, how the two systems interact with each other, for instance, how object files or implicit magnitude estimations are related to the explicit number system learned in childhood. This issue comes up again in chapter 3, where I discuss how the whole system is put together, but I raise it here to point out that the distinction between percepts and concepts is separable from the issue of whether the mind requires a single or dual representational system. One could in principle accept a distinction between percepts and concepts yet reject a dual representational system as the way to handle the distinction. As the following pages make clear, however, I do not believe such an approach to be viable in the long run. Needless to say, acceptance of a dual representational system does not require one to accept the format for conceptual representation that I describe in chapters 4 and 5. Whether to talk about concepts in terms of symbol systems or image-schemas is still another choice to make as one decides how to build a baby.

However these issues are approached, it is important to take a stance one way or the other. If one decides to work on concept formation, the nature of the conceptual system itself cannot be ignored. One cannot just accumulate data about what babies can discriminate without worrying about the status of this knowledge. For example, some kinds of knowledge result from the slow accumulation of information represented in the form of sensorimotor habits that are not accessible to conscious thought. Accessibility, by a long-standing definition (Tulving & Pearlstone, 1966), means the ability to come to conscious thought. Therefore, to say "accessible to consciousness" is redundant. (Nevertheless, I use this redundancy periodically because the term *accessibility* has often been used so loosely that it may fail to convey this crucial aspect of its meaning, and sometimes it is even defined differently; e.g., Spelke & Hespos, 2002.) Other kinds of knowledge are generalizations from individual analytic observations; these are probably accessible to conscious thought from the start. Because accessibility is one of the major differences between perceptual and conceptual information, in order to build one's baby in a consistent fashion, the kind of learning that is taking place in a given situation must be one of the early decisions in describing any data set. This decision, however, leads at once to the next choice point. If the information in question is accessible, is it represented differently from inaccessible information, or is it merely stronger or more integrated in some way? The answer to this question has implications for the way in which the information is stored and for whether or not it is retrievable. Therefore, even though the distinction between percepts and concepts and a single or dual representational system are independent of each other, each must be considered before we can create a theory of how the conceptual mind is constructed.

So we embark on a journey to explore the conceptual foundations of mind. There is still much to be learned, and several parts of this book are speculative. I do describe a good many experimental results, but until my lab began studying these issues about 20 years ago, there was a rich anecdotal base but little experimental data about how or when the earliest conceptions of things such as animals, vehicles, plants, and furniture are formed. The reason for that is the legacy I mentioned before: If babies do not begin to develop a conceptual system until the end of the sensorimotor stage (at roughly a year and a half), why try to study concepts before that time? It usually doesn't pay off in science to search for the nonexistent. In addition, if one wanted to study the transition from a sensorimotor creature to a conceptual one, the research problems were formidable because few nonverbal methods were available. The most common solution to this problem was to use the first words as the measure of the underlying conceptual system, more or less ignoring the fact that mapping of language onto a nonverbal conceptual system must be an uncertain and imperfect process. At any rate, the majority of the work on early concept formation was conducted with children old enough to talk and at the least relied on verbal instruction. To study preverbal children, however, means that even the instruction procedure must be wordless.

Techniques to Study Concept Formation in Infancy

At the time I began this research, only two nonverbal methods were available to study concept formation in infancy, and a relatively small number of experiments had been conducted using either of them. The first was a technique developed by Henry Ricciuti (1965) as a nonverbal precursor to object sorting. This technique, which we call object-manipulation or sequential touching, was explored further by Katherine Nelson (1973a) and then used more extensively by Susan Sugarman (1983). The technique relies on young children's spontaneous tendency, when given an array of objects, to touch sequentially those that are alike. However, the technique was mostly used to assess sensitivity to various perceptual contrasts, and the significance of the concentrations in touching that were found was evaluated on an intuitive basis. In my lab, collaborating at various times with Robyn Fivush, Steven Reznick, and Patricia Bauer, we developed several statistical tools for assessing the significance of the runs of sequential touches to items from a common category that infants produce in this situation, and so we could be more confident that the runs were not occurring by chance. We have used this technique to study infants' responsivity to various conceptual contrasts at differing levels of generality.

The other technique we began to use was derived from the familiarization/preferential-looking task. In this task, infants are first shown a series of stimuli from one category and then an exemplar from another category; how long they look at the new stimulus is measured. Our variant, called the object-examination task (first used by Ross, 1980), gives infants little replicas of real-world objects to explore instead of having them passively look at pictures, and examination time is measured.[1] For example, we let an infant examine a series of little animals and then see if they dishabituate upon being given a vehicle (that is, examine it longer than the last animal). This technique can be used with infants too young to manage the sequential-touching technique. Sequential touching requires presenting infants with a number of objects at once. Such a plethora of goodies is too much for infants younger than about 15 months; they tend to freeze up and not interact with the objects. But you can accomplish a similar end by giving them the objects one at a time and measuring how long they then examine an object from a different class. Laraine McDonough and I adapted this technique from the work of Ruff (1986) and of Oakes, Madole, and Cohen (1991). We have used it with infants as young as 7 months, and I see no reason that it could not be extended to 6-month-olds. Unfortunately, we have not yet discovered a good technique to use before that age, because younger infants do not yet manipulate objects. As I discuss in chapter 7, habituation–dishabituation or familiarization and preferential-looking techniques using pictures as stimuli may put infants into a passive mode that masks conceptual activity, and in any case active examination of stimuli is not the same as looking time. For the moment, then, we may have to be content with the techniques we have devised for ages 6 months and upward.

Another technique for studying preverbal understanding that was available, although it had been used only with older children, was deferred imitation—that is, imitating some observed event after a delay. This was originally suggested as a means of assessing nonverbal recall by Piaget (1952). He merely observed it anecdotally with his children, but I, and Patricia Bauer in conjunction with Cecilia Shore, adapted it as an experimental technique (Bauer & Shore, 1987; Mandler, 1986). At about the same time, Andrew Meltzoff (1988a) also began using the technique to study recall, and we all have used it extensively to study what preverbal infants recall from events they have observed and how long they retain the information. It is an interesting way of uncovering the kinds of conceptualizations that preverbal infants have formed; you can't ask them, but because of their strong tendency to imitate, they will act out what they remember having seen. Indeed, it was this work on nonverbal recall that made us realize how conceptual babies are. You can't recall anything you haven't conceptualized, yet as discussed in chapter 10, babies as young as 9 months can remember and reproduce after a delay events that they have observed on only a single occasion.

The other technique we use to study the early conceptual life of the infant is an adaptation from our imitation work that we call generalized imitation. Instead of using imitation to study recall of the past, Laraine McDonough and I have used it to uncover the limits on the inductive generalizations infants have made (e.g., Mandler & McDonough, 1996a). We model an event for the infants, again using little replicas, such as giving a dog a drink from a cup. Then we give the infants the cup, but instead of providing the dog, we substitute two other objects (say, a bird and a car) and see which, if either, object they use to imitate drinking. This technique allows us to explore concept boundaries, effectively asking infants to answer such questions as "What sort of things drink?" We are especially happy with this technique because it taps directly into the major way of acquiring knowledge in infancy: observing events and making inductive generalizations from those observations. This is how infants acquire a repertoire of "facts." They necessarily observe only a limited number of instances of any association and so must generalize. How far they generalize tells us what they consider to be the same kind of thing.

The experimental results from these techniques have led us to a different picture of early conceptual life than is found in the textbooks. One of the major things we have learned is that early concepts tend to be global in nature and not at the basic level. Infants have an idea of what an animal is but are hazy about the differences between one animal and another. They have an idea of what a container is but are hazy about the differences between a cup and a pan. Another thing we have learned is that their concept formation is less influenced by perceptual similarity than is often assumed. Right from the beginning, infants form concepts in a way that looks remarkably like using defining features rather than overall perceptual appearance. We do not yet know for the most part what those "defining" features are, but we are beginning to discover them. For the animal domain, for example, it appears that certain aspects of movement may be defining, such as the ability to move by itself and to interact contingently with other objects.

Going Beyond Piaget

I conclude from these and other considerations discussed throughout this book that babies are much more thoughtful than they have typically been given credit for. They observe the world and theorize about it, albeit in a primitive way. Right from the beginning, or at least from a few months of age, babies function in ways that merge continuously into those of older children and adults. They form concepts, they have notions of different kinds, they generalize from their experiences on the basis of the concepts they have already formed, and they are reminded of absent objects and events by this or that cue and recall them. These capacities mean that from the start babies are forming a declarative knowledge system, one that they use to give meaning to what they see and that a year later will help them acquire language to talk about what they see. This is a rather different baby from the one described by Piaget.

So at many places in this book I am critical of Piaget's theory of development. At the same time, I happily admit that many of my ideas about infancy were greatly influenced by his work. Only after I had deeply absorbed his system could I begin to find its flaws. Many psychologists have pointed out the grave difficulties that any stage theory poses, but one in particular caught my attention. If one assumes a new stage builds on the accomplishments of the old, one must specify the transition rules by which the transformation comes about (Kessen, 1962). This cannot be just a promissory note. Concepts do not spring forth full-grown like Minerva from the head of Jupiter. They have a history—roots that need to be traced in order to define and understand them. Piaget clearly understood the need to trace this history but was not able to fully accomplish it. It was working through the various options he proposed for the transition from the sensorimotor stage to conceptual life that led me to the contradictions buried in his attempts. I discuss these at some length in chapter 2.

I raise the issue here mainly to note my great debt to Piagetian theory. Indeed, the theory I describe in this book shows the influence of many of Piaget's ideas. Three in particular are important. First is the notion that concepts are not innate but constructed. Second is the idea that concepts are based at least in part on perceptual knowledge. Piaget recognized a sensory source for thought, even though he relied more heavily on motor learning. Third, Piaget thought that conceptual schemas were built out of a process similar to what I call perceptual meaning analysis.[2] However, because he thought this kind of analysis had to be worked out on the level of action, he was forced to assume that it was a late-developing process. Control of the hand is a slow development in infancy; if the conceptual mind depends on it, then it must be slow to develop as well. Nevertheless, Piaget's analyses of the actions his infants carried out when they were learning how to imitate complex behaviors, such as blinking their eyes or sticking out their tongues, are excellent examples of perceptual meaning analysis. He also gave these examples special status but did not relate them to the process of reflective abstraction he described later in his career. Reflective abstraction (if I understand it correctly) refers to the workings of a thoughtful mind analyzing and systematizing aspects of the knowledge it has gained to date. Piaget would have been unlikely to credit infants with this ability, but it was his descriptions of the analytic work his infants engaged in when trying to imitate complex behavior that first gave me the notion of perceptual meaning analysis. I did not realize my debt at the time I first wrote about it (Mandler, 1988), but it has become increasingly apparent to me. All of this is by way of acknowledging the debt I owe Piaget for making me think seriously about what might be going on in infant minds. We come to different conclusions, but he was the source of my inspiration.

Having said that, it is time to move beyond Piaget. What he missed, in part because, like the rest of us, he was often blinded by his own theory, was that more was going on in infancy than perceptual and motor learning. Infants are beginning to analyze and construe their world and not just when they are physically acting on it. Piaget, like many others, was also misled at times by infants' lack of language and the difficulty they have in getting word meanings straight in the early stages of language acquisition. Misuse of words is seductively easy to equate with conceptual misunderstanding, but it is just as likely to be due to trouble in mapping language onto existing concepts.

Some infant accomplishments came to light only once the experimental study of infant cognition took off about 20 years ago. As I write this, I am struck by what a short time ago that was. In 20 years we have already accumulated a vast amount of information about what babies know before they speak. I said at the beginning of this chapter how little we yet know about infant cognition, and that is true, yet the rate of our knowledge accumulation is extraordinary. Surely infant cognition has been one of, if not the most, productive parts of developmental psychology in recent years. What we are learning about infants is that perception and action are not enough to explain what they know. They are interpreters of the world around them from an early age. We don't yet know how early, although Werner and Kaplan's (1963) estimate of 3 months as the onset of contemplation of the world cannot be much more than 3 months off the mark! The very young infant who cannot yet act upon objects is never-

theless construing the actions of others. This means that conceptualization is already on the march, perhaps even earlier than 3 months of age.
I describe this process in detail in chapters 4 and 5.

Before turning to a critique of the notion of a purely sensorimotor
baby, I give here a rough sketch of the kind of alternative system I propose in this book. It is explicated in detail in chapters 3, 4, and 5, but this
brief introduction may help to orient the reader while I discuss the traditional sensorimotor view in chapter 2. I propose an organism that is
born with the capacity to form two very different kinds of representation. One of these, largely sensorimotor in character, uses perceptual and
kinesthetic information to form perceptual schemas of objects and motor
schemas that control actions. This kind of learning is procedural; that is,
it operates outside the bounds of consciousness, and the schemas it creates are not accessible to conscious thought.

At the same time, or possibly briefly lagging slightly behind at the beginning, a mechanism of perceptual meaning analysis extracts and summarizes a subset of incoming perceptual information from which it creates a store of meanings or simple concepts. These meanings are typically
descriptions of what is happening in the scenes the infant observes, for instance, "self-motion" or "containment." Such meanings arise from attentive, conscious analysis of spatial information and are markedly different
from perceptual and motor schemas. I have suggested that these meanings
are represented in the form of image-schemas, although there are other
formats that could serve this function. In any case, image-schemas are
not themselves conscious (they are merely a representational format), but
they enable conceptual interpretations to take place in conscious awareness. Not all thought takes place in conscious awareness, but in the preverbal infant what conscious thought does take place needs to be couched
in images.

Thus, image-schemas have three main functions: first, to create an
explicit, declarative conceptual system that is accessible to conscious
thought; second, to structure and give meaning to the images that we are
aware of when we think; and third, to provide the underlying meanings
or concepts onto which language can be mapped. It should be noted that
image-schemas are spatial representations that are quite different from
conscious images (see chapter 4) and that the concepts we use to think
typically are combinations of image-schemas (again, see chapter 4). In

this formulation, the capacity to conceptualize the world and to bring aspects of the perceptual world to conscious awareness is present from birth. What develops are concepts themselves, not the ability to form or access them.

With these considerations in mind, we can now take a closer look at the notion of the infant as a purely sensorimotor creature. My position (Mandler, 1988) is that instead of there being a prolonged sensorimotor period that only gradually gives birth to conceptual life, an accessible conceptual system develops simultaneously and in parallel with the sensorimotor system, with neither being derivative from the other.

2

Piaget's Sensorimotor Infant

. . . in which I draw out the implications of there being a purely sensorimotor stage in early human development, as described by Piaget. Some of the flaws in this idea are shown by Piaget's own observations and by the difficulties he had in figuring out how a transition from a sensorimotor stage to a conceptual one might come about. I suggest that some of this difficulty arose from his failure to distinguish clearly between symbols and concepts. I also dwell at some length on one of the most interesting of Piaget's notions about infancy, namely, that imagery develops from imitation, because his work on this topic foreshadows my own theory of how concepts are created, discussed in chapter 4. Finally, I touch on some distortions in views of infancy that have arisen when inferring conceptual incompetence from motor incompetence.

If we are going to have a cognitive science, we are going to have to learn to learn from our mistakes. When you keep putting questions to Nature and Nature keeps saying "no," it is not unreasonable to suppose that somewhere among the things you believe there is something that isn't true. (Fodor, 1981)

What a Sensorimotor Infant Would Be Like

Amid his acute observations and brilliant theorizing, Piaget made a risky assumption that plagued developmental psychology for many years thereafter. He mistook infants' motor incompetence for conceptual incompetence. Because of this, he posited an initial stage of development in which infants learn to perceive and to act but cannot yet think. As I described his view some years ago:

> According to Piaget, the sensorimotor child . . . does not
> have a capacity for representation in the true sense, but only
> sensorimotor intelligence. Knowledge about the world consists
> only of perceptions and actions; objects are only understood
> through the child's own actions and perceptual schemas. It is a
> most unProustian life, not thought, only lived. Sensorimotor
> schemata . . . enable a child to walk a straight line but not to
> think about a line in its absence, to recognize his or her mother
> but not to think about her when she is gone. It is a world very
> difficult for us to conceive, accustomed as we are to spend
> much of our time ruminating about the past and anticipating
> the future. Nevertheless, this is the state that Piaget posits for
> the child before 1½ . . . (Mandler, 1983, p. 424)

Let us put this a bit more formally. What is missing from this sensorimotor version of an infant? The crucial lack is a conceptual system. First,
because there is no conceptual system, the sensorimotor infant cannot recall anything, either events it has experienced or the characteristics of
objects it has observed. It can recognize familiar objects when they are
present, in the sense that it responds to their familiarity and it knows how
to interact with them, but once they are out of sight, they are gone. The
infant has no capacity to bring to mind (form an image of) something
absent because that requires a concept—an accessible representation of
the object. Searching for a hidden object is impossible if one cannot remember that there is something to search for. The infant might "know"
that objects fall if not supported, that an object cannot be in two places
at once, or that one object cannot pass through another. These bits of
knowledge could be represented as expectations about what objects do
and do not do when they are in sight, and so they would fall within the
capacity of a sensorimotor infant. But a conceptless infant, although possibly able to briefly retain the information that a disruption has occurred
in whatever it was doing when the object disappeared, could not recall the
object itself when out of sight. An indispensable requirement for searching for an object, as Piaget (1952) recognized, is the capacity to recall it
when it is hidden. A conceptless infant might cast its sensors around following the disappearance of an object, but that is different from remembering a specific object.

As an aside, I note that the possibility of "nonspecific" recall is one of the ambiguities in research on the "object concept" mentioned in chapter 1. In Renée Baillargeon's experiments, in which young infants must briefly remember that an object that has disappeared behind a screen is still there, it is possible they recall that *something* is there, and even where it was located, without being able to recall the object itself. As we will see in chapter 10, the ability to recall may be just beginning near the end of the first 6 months. Indeed, 4½- to 6½-month-old infants do better in these hiding experiments if an object similar to the hidden one remains in view at the side of the screen (Baillargeon, 1993). The exact mix of sensorimotor expectations, conceptualization, and memory demands required by these tasks has yet to be specified.

The second thing lacking in sensorimotor infants is that they can recognize objects only in a very limited sense and cannot do what is meant by recognition in the adult literature. When Mama appears, sensorimotor schemas such as sucking at the breast may be activated, arousing warm emotional feelings and consequently a smile. But Piaget's sensorimotor infant does not know who Mama is, in the sense of remembering any of the previous interactions they have had or anything about her other than that she looks familiar. The sensorimotor infant could not even tell you (if it had language and were asked) that it had seen Mama before, because it does not have the ability to recall her, a process that is involved in recognition in adults (G. Mandler, 1980). A sensorimotor organism could be *primed* by the appearance of Mama. Priming can instigate learned motor habits, emotional responses, and perhaps a sense of familiarity, but not recognition in the sense of being able to say (or know), "I have seen you before" or "I know who you are." In chapter 10, I discuss the issue of how one can distinguish recognition from priming and why the infant recognition literature provides data only on priming (or what I term "primitive" recognition), not "adult" recognition.

Because even the simple form of thought that adult recognition represents would not be available to a purely sensorimotor baby, other forms of thought, such as reasoning by analogy and making deductions, would be completely out of the question. A conceptless organism is a thoughtless one. But are there processes related to thought the infant could do? For instance, could the sensorimotor infant make inductive generalizations? I think so, because a simple form of inductive inference consists of generalizing to "similar" stimuli, which is a general organismic capacity. However, to do inductive generalization without a conceptual system would mean that the infant would be dependent for such generalizations solely on its perceptual system; it could generalize from one stimulus to another only if they were perceptually similar. It would not be able to do inductive generalization on the basis of concepts. So, for example, it would not be able to generalize from a fish to a bird on the basis of their both being animals.[1] Therefore, the baby could generalize from the family cat to the neighbor's cat, but whatever behavior it had learned to display in the presence of cats would probably not transfer to dogs, and even less likely to fish or birds. It would have no idea, of course, that all of these objects are animals, because that is a conceptual classification. We will see in chapter 8, however, that even in infancy inductive generalization is based on concepts more than on perceptual appearance.

The purely sensorimotor infant could also learn to anticipate the next item in a sequence. Conditioned expectations are a simple form of learning common to most, if not all, organisms. For instance, the infant might learn to anticipate the end of mealtime by raising its chin to have its bib removed. This does not mean the sensorimotor baby could imagine the coming event, however, because imagery is another capacity that is dependent on a conceptual system. In addition to the difficulties already mentioned, the sensorimotor baby cannot imagine either the past or the future. Piaget and Inhelder (1971) made it clear that imagery is constructed from conceptual knowledge and is not just a picture that results from perception. As Piaget put it, when discussing 10-month-old Jacqueline's anticipatory behavior: "When Jacqueline expects to see a person where a door is opening or fruit juice in a spoon coming out of a certain receptacle, it is not necessary for there to be understanding of these signs and consequently prevision, for her to picture these objects to herself in their absence. It is enough that the sign sets in motion a certain attitude of expectation and a certain schema of recognition of persons or of food" (Piaget, 1952, p. 283).

This example casts the sensorimotor baby as the infant counterpart of the absent-minded professor. When I am deep in thought at my computer, I sometimes come to and find myself in the kitchen and wonder what I have come for. I can't bring it to mind but cast my eyes around in the hope that the sight of whatever it is that I wanted will bring recollection with it. This ploy sometimes works: Aha, I came for coffee! The absent-minded baby, on the other hand, can't recollect under any circumstances, although when presented with appropriate cues could know what to do next. I think it is something like this that Piaget had in mind: a baby that is controlled by current stimuli accompanied by implicit (imageless) expectations.

I believe that Piaget was correct in his assumption that imagery requires a conceptual system. We don't have a great deal of evidence, but what there is indicates that one cannot form an image on the basis of perception alone. Concepts are required to mold perceptual data into imaginal form. This is reflected both in theory and in data. Kosslyn (1980), for instance, found it necessary to posit a propositional store of conceptual information in addition to a visual buffer in order to explain image creation. An early and impressive demonstration of the conceptual nature of imagery was an experiment by Carmichael, Hogen, and Walter (1932). They showed people nonsense line drawings that were given different labels. For example, a figure consisting of two small circles connected by a horizontal line was labeled either as eyeglasses or as a dumbbell. When the participants were later asked to draw the forms from memory, it became obvious that the labels had influenced the nature of the images they recalled. The figures they drew were recognizably more like eyeglasses or dumbbells, depending on which label they had heard for the figure. This example involves verbalization, but the principle is the same for nonverbal interpretation. However we conceptualize a figure at the time of encoding, whether verbal or not, that conception is what is potentially accessible at a later time. Of course, for preverbal infants there is no choice; the only conscious format available to them is imagery. (I note, however, that contrasting images and verbal recall is a somewhat misleading dichotomy; although not visual, verbal recall can be construed as auditory imagery.) If we have conceptualized two circles connected by a line as eyeglasses, then something that looks like eyeglasses is what we will recall. A number of similar experiments have shown that it is the way we conceptualize something that determines what image of it we later form (Chambers & Reisberg, 1992; Intons-Peterson & Roskos-Ewoldsen, 1989; Piaget & Inhelder, 1971).

Piaget's View of Image Formation

If imagery requires conceptualization and sensorimotor infants do not yet conceptualize, how do they begin to form images? Piaget thought that imagery came about through imitation. He did a careful charting of the development of imitation (Piaget, 1951), showing how his infants became more and more adept at doing the sorts of analyses he thought were required for imitation of anything complex to occur. Once imitation of these complex events was successful, they could be internalized in the form of images. There is some problem here about the causal sequence being described. Imitation leads to imagery, and imagery in turn constitutes the representation of the first concepts. But as we shall see, much of Piaget's description of imitation suggests that the very process of imitation itself requires a conceptual base. That is, infants can probably not succeed in doing complex imitation without a conception of what they are trying to reproduce. But if concepts are required for the imitation that is used to form images, and images are the first concepts, then we have a problem with the direction of causation in this account.

I discuss the relation between imagery and conceptualization further in chapters 4 and 5 and show how a mechanism of perceptual meaning analysis transduces perceptual information into conceptual form by creating image-schemas, a level of representation that is used to form actual images. As we will see there, image-schemas, which are not the same as conscious images, are an essential part of cognitive architecture, mediating between perception and conception. Here I merely want to note what an important idea it was that imagery comes from imitation—or more precisely, from detailed analysis of what one is observing. Could it not derive from mere repetition of sights and actions? Piaget insisted that looking alone is insufficient to form a visual image. He thought that to form an image you have to engage in some extra accommodatory effort, in order to be able to copy what you have seen. He needed to maintain this view, because if mere looking or repetitively doing something were sufficient to form an image, then, in principle, there would be no reason why even very young infants could not have imagery. If they did, then they could, in principle, use the imagery to represent things and to think about things in their absence. So the "imagery through analysis" position is essential to his whole argument about the strictly sensorimotor, non-representational character of infancy.

There is still relatively little evidence as to what is required to form an image. Interestingly enough, one set of data (and I know of no others like them) came from my husband's lab in an experiment that was designed for quite a different purpose than for studying imagery. Mandler and Kuhlman (1961) were interested in studying the overlearning of motor patterns and the conditions under which one can transfer learned motor patterns from one set of stimulus conditions to another. For this purpose they designed what came to be known as the "idiot board." The idiot board was a 10 x 10 array of switches. Subjects had to learn a randomly generated sequence of eight switches. At first, they could operate only by trial and error, but gradually over a number of trials they learned the correct order in which the switches were to be thrown. For present purposes, the interesting part of their data consisted of subjective reports of the development of imagery. They spontaneously noted that by the time they could pull the eight switches with no errors they had formed a kind of kinesthetic image of the pattern that the eight switches formed. They could put their hands in front of them (with no board present) and run through the motor pattern required to hit the right switches in the right order; that is, they had a body-feel for the pattern. Many trials later, when performance became asymptotically fast and smooth, subjects began to report visual imagery of the pattern. They could close their eyes and "see" what the pattern would look like if it were lighted up, even though they had never seen the whole pattern displayed at once. Now this is an excellent example of the formation of imagery through repetitive action, but it is not clear whether it was the repetition itself that was important or the active analysis of the pattern that surely went on during learning.

Although there is little positive experimental evidence like this to show image generation, there is an occasional experiment indicating that repetition alone is insufficient to create an image. Nickerson and Adams (1979) found that American college students cannot accurately image a penny, in spite of handling pennies countless times over. Back in the days when telephones had dials, I used to run an experiment in class in which I asked students to make a drawing of the dial. Most of them had made literally thousands of telephone calls, each time dialing the numbers while looking at the dial. But they typically had only the sketchiest image of what the dial looks like. They didn't know which letters were associated with which numbers, whether it said operator anywhere, or, if so, where. Even though they used this information all the time, they did not analyze it sufficiently to create an image. As a result, they usually failed abysmally to reproduce accurate details.

My tentative conclusion is that Piaget was correct. No amount of looking alone will result in imagery. One must analyze what one is look-ing at (or touching), and analysis requires a conceptual system. Thus, im-agery itself requires a conceptual base. Needless to say, we don't have any direct evidence for imagery in preverbal infants. We cannot tell them to form an image to study its effects on priming, nor can they describe their images for us. However, as we will see in chapter 10, preverbal infants can recall episodes from the past. Because they do not as yet have lan-guage, it is difficult to understand how they could do so without the ca-pacity to image things they have seen.

To summarize the sensorimotor infant: It is a conceptless creature who cannot think independently of action, who cannot recall the past or imagine the future, but who can recognize familiar objects and people (in the sense described earlier of primitive recognition) and act appro-priately toward them. How does this infant turn into a person like us who not only has sensorimotor understanding but also has a conceptual life? It was this development that Piaget thought took up most of infancy. He posited six substages in the sensorimotor period. In the first five stages, the mind is action oriented and action based. Infants understand the world primarily through their own actions on it. But in Stage 6 (18 to 24 months), Piaget not only heard his children verbally recall but also saw evidence for covert problem solving, as opposed to problem solving through overt trial and error. Up to then, he thought his children solved problems only by trying out various solutions physically. Now they began to solve problems mentally. For example, one of Piaget's (1952) observations was of his daughter Lucienne, who tried to kneel on a stool on casters, but it scooted away. She immediately took the stool and put it against a sofa so that it was firmly lodged and she could kneel on it with-out its moving. He also began to observe his children showing anticipa-tion of problems. For example, Jacqueline arrived one time at a closed door with some grass in each hand. She stretched out her hand toward the doorknob but saw she couldn't turn it without letting go of the grass. So she put the grass on the floor, opened the door, and then picked up the grass again. What has happened? How did we get a child who can think, imagine, and recall the past from one who had no capacity to do any of these things?

Piaget's Theory of the Transition to Conceptual Thought

As a stage theorist, the problem that Piaget faced was how a purely procedural organism gains the capacity to conceptualize and to access concepts for purposes of thinking about things when they are absent—that is, to form a declarative knowledge system. Piaget thought that this was a long, slow process. Most of his discussion of the transition from sensorimotor to conceptual representation was couched in terms of the acquisition of symbols to refer to concepts (Piaget, 1952). He had relatively little to say about the formation of the conceptual system itself (which, in contrast, is the focus of this book). Rather, he emphasized how the infant could create signifiers to bring concepts into a train of thought—for instance, to call forth an image to represent what was to be thought about. For conscious thought—and on this we are in agreement—one must rely on images or words (Piaget considered both of these symbols) to present to awareness what is being conceptualized. Piaget may also have agreed that much thinking takes place at the conceptual level without coming to consciousness. What remains obscure in his system is whether the first concepts are sensorimotor schemas that are merely made accessible by the development of symbols but otherwise remain the same as before or whether the process of symbolization creates a separate less action-oriented (more conceptual?) layer (as, for example, suggested by Bruner, 1974–75). In either case, Piaget's discussion of the transition focused on the development of symbols to *refer* to concepts rather than the concepts themselves.

In the earliest stages (toward the end of Stage 1 and during Stage 2; that is, from about 1 to 4 months), the most primitive precursors of later symbols appear. Piaget called them signals: One perception indicates to the infant that another perception is to follow. For example, the sight of the breast indicates that milk will enter the mouth, and the baby salivates in response to it. The signal is a basic associative device, typically described in the conditioning literature as a conditioned stimulus (CS) or a discriminative stimulus. Needless to say, the response of the baby to a CS, or signal, does not mean that the baby is thinking. This kind of associative learning is a strictly procedural mechanism that does not require awareness or thought.

Nevertheless, Piaget suggested that these early conditioned signals are the basis on which later signifiers of meaning get developed. In a primitive sense, the sight of the breast that sets off anticipatory sucking means that food will follow, and the baby salivates in response to that expectation. However, there is no evidence that such signals can be reproduced by the baby in their absence. The physical sight may mean food in that situation, but the infant can't represent it in the form of an image or other symbol for purposes of thinking about food. In other words, signals are exterior to the mind of the infant, not interior. Some would say they do not belong to the infant.

The next step in the development of signifiers, according to Piaget, comes around 6 months of age. The primitive signifiers of meaning have become more sophisticated and are also self-produced. Piaget observed a phenomenon at this time that he called motor recognition. When Lucienne caught sight of two parrots that used to be in her cradle but were now across the room, she shook her legs at them, using the gesture she had used when she played with them in her crib. Piaget suggested that the infant was expressing her recognition of a familiar toy and "naming" it, so to speak, by performing an abbreviated version of her accustomed action on it.

Should we consider this kind of action to be a symbol? To be sure, it is a gesture and therefore not solely mental, and it was only observed to take place in front of the object for which the symbol might be said to stand. (I note, however, that it is not obvious that an observer would notice or attribute significance to similar foot shaking if it took place when the object was absent.) Piaget recognized that this occurrence was different from the anticipatory sucking that occurred at the sight of the breast. The baby didn't seem to be expecting anything, nor did she attempt to act directly on the parrot. But he assumed that the gesture was elicited by the object and to that extent was still context-bound. He assumed the gesture would not be used outside the context of the object and therefore it did not have the flexibility of use that we associate with true symbols, nor could it be used to represent the parrot in its absence. This is why he referred to the phenomenon as motor recognition, not as a symbol capable of mediating recall.

I have previously related this phenomenon to the beginning of signs, or signlike actions, in young native American Sign Language (ASL) speakers (Mandler, 1988). There have been a number of reports in the literature on deaf children learning sign language, indicating that they produce their first signs earlier than hearing children speak words: as early as 6 months and on average about 8 months. There is controversy as to how to interpret this phenomenon. However, there is a good deal of evidence that deaf children acquire this early stage of language learning sooner than hearing children (Folven & Bonvillian, 1991; Meier & Newport, 1990). This appears to happen because babies gain control over their fingers before they gain control over their vocal apparatus, making gestural symbols easier for infants to produce than verbal symbols (Goodwyn & Acredolo, 1993). It doesn't mean that deaf children are more conceptually advanced than hearing children, and later stages of language acquisition seem to take place on a common timetable.

Elissa Newport once gave me an evocative description of the contexts in which early signs are used. Her daughter, Susanna, grew up bilingual in English and ASL. The first recognizable sign she produced was the gesture meaning "finished." It had been used many times by her parents at the end of meals, and between 5 and 6 months of age she began using it herself at the end of a meal. Although clearly imitative in origin, it might not have had any conceptual import at that point and may have been no different from putting her face up to be wiped—that is, the kind of motor anticipation I have already discussed. But at 7 months Susanna began using this gesture when she didn't want any more to eat, turning her head away from the looming spoon while she executed it. Because it occurred before the end of the meal, it was unlikely to be merely anticipation of the next step in a routine; it seems to have become decontextualized to some extent to communicate "No more!"

This example suggested to me the same phenomenon that Piaget described as motor recognition, and that perhaps we should interpret his phenomenon in a new way. Both observations suggest the use of a familiar gesture to represent a meaning. In one case, kicking at a parrot, the baby was using a habitual gesture of her own. In the other case, the baby was imitating a gesture routinely made by her parents at the end of meal-time. But in both cases, a gesture was being used to stand for something. Whether it could be used to refer to something in its absence, we do not know, but I see no particular reason to assume that it could not. Because, as we will see in chapter 10, 6 months is about the earliest age for which we begin to find evidence for recall, it is possible that such gestures could be used to represent absent objects. It is of interest that similar examples are reported in hearing children at a slightly later age (Acredolo, Good-wyn, Horobin, & Emmons (1999). Acredolo and her colleagues did not study children younger than 11 months, so we do not know whether such symbolic gestures may be common in many younger infants or whether they are more likely to be found in infants exposed to sign lan-guage because of the emphasis on gesture in their homes. The finding of Acredolo et al. (1999) that parental encouragement in the use of sym-bolic gestures increases their use by hearing preverbal infants suggests the latter hypothesis. It is also consistent with the notion that such gestures might be used to express concepts in conscious thought.

However, at best, Piaget would call these early abbreviated actions *indications*—one thing indicates to the baby that another thing is about to happen. He claimed it is a part–whole kind of relationship, in which a part can activate or prime a larger schema, allowing some kind of antici-pation of what will happen next. The indication is similar in kind to the earlier signal, the main difference being that it is less bound to an indi-vidual procedure and more complex. The development of indications was said to continue throughout Stages 4 and 5 (that is, from about 8 to 18 months) without there yet being a true representational capacity. Noth-ing much is changing in this account for this long stretch of time. In-stead, the interesting representational developments are taking place in a different arena—namely, imitation.

Piaget speculated that it was some special aspects of imitation that created images, which he considered to be the first true symbols. Because this is the high point of his story of the birth of symbols, I will detour a bit to discuss what he thought were the crucial developments in imita-tion. The characteristic of imitation that interested Piaget most was that it could not take place without active analysis of the model; that is, he be-lieved that imitation is not a passive process (except perhaps in its very earliest stages) but requires the imitator to analyze what the model is doing. Note the emphasis on active analysis of what is being perceived, an issue I will consider at length when discussing perceptual meaning analysis in chapter 4.

The tendency to repeat actions until well understood (the circular reactions) is axiomatic in Piaget's system. But he thought that mere repetition was insufficient to form an image. Only when the sight or sound of the model had been analyzed would an image result. I mentioned earlier the problem in Piaget's formulation of the relationship between images and concepts. Now we see another aspect of the problem. Active analysis is required to imitate, at least to imitate anything complex. When analysis has taken place and imitation carried out, it eventually becomes what he calls "interiorized" in the form of an image. The problem is that infants imitate from a very early age. That implies analysis. Why, then, does it take a year and a half to begin to form images from that analysis?

Piaget's reconciliation of this paradox is that imitation in the early stages does not require the active analysis that more complex imitation does. In the first months of life, he saw little gestural imitation (although quite a bit of vocal imitation). Nevertheless, as early as Stage 2 (around 4 months of age), infants can imitate clapping hands. That would seem to require analysis. The infant must make a connection between its and the adult's hands, which are not only larger but also present a different view than one has of one's own hands. However, according to Piaget, this kind of understanding comes for free. "When the child . . . becomes capable of co-ordinating the movements of his hands with his vision, he acquires simultaneously the power of imitating certain movements of other hands, by assimilating them to his own" (Piaget, 1951, p. 14). In spite of this promising beginning, Piaget didn't observe any complex imitation until Stage 3, and even then he claimed that infants are able to imitate only those gestures or sounds that they have already produced themselves and so are familiar to them; he believed the capacity to analyze new sights is still undeveloped. In poring over the various examples he gives, however, one finds a number of cases in which his children engaged in comparison processes. For example, when his 4-month-old son waggled his thumb and Piaget imitated him, his son laughed "and compared our two hands several times" (Piaget, 1952, p. 24). Success in imitating a new gesture may be less important as a measure of conceptual activity than the comparisons made along the way.

In any case, although Piaget traced the course of imitation from its earliest onset, his emphasis was on Stage 4 and beyond, when it could no longer be doubted that his children were attempting to analyze and reproduce models of new and complex things. Actually, he found that this development began in the transition from Stage 3 to Stage 4. For instance, Jacqueline could not imitate opening and closing her hand at 7 months. She was able to imitate grasping and even waving "bye-bye," each of which is similar to components of opening and closing the hand. At 8 months, Piaget found her opening and closing her hand spontaneously one day, and watching it with great interest. That night she imitated his opening and closing his hand for the first time. Piaget suggested that even though opening and closing her hand was practiced constantly as a part of grasping, until the child analyzed it herself as an action in its own right, it could not be imitated. This sounds reasonable to me and suggests that the analysis of various states that occur during execution of a motor procedure enables a descriptive account of it to be stored in an accessible fashion—that is, to be stored in a declarative knowledge system. Once there, the description can be accessed and voluntarily manipulated. I also see no reason why Piaget's own criteria for image formation are not also satisfied by this example, which would mean that even within his framework imagery might begin by 7 to 8 months.

The problem that interested Piaget the most in Stage 4 imitation—and it is a fascinating problem—was how his children learned to imitate movement of body parts that they could not see on themselves, such as sticking out the tongue or blinking the eyes. Presumably infants cannot use visual similarity matching because they can't see their own tongues and, even given the presence of mirrors, cannot see themselves blink. Piaget found that his children couldn't manage this kind of imitation until sometime between 8 and 12 months. He gave a detailed account of the development of this skill. Jacqueline had not yet imitated tongue protrusion at 8 months. About that time, Piaget saw her biting her lips one day, and he imitated her. The infant was very interested and watched Piaget carefully. A few days later, Piaget stuck out his tongue and she bit her lips. All his lip movements were imitated by this same action, as if the results of her analysis to that point suggested that the mouth was involved but not exactly how. So she used a schema she already had and was currently practicing.

At about 9 months, Jacqueline stuck out her tongue one day and said "ba ba" at the same time. Piaget imitated her, and over the next few days she mixed up the two responses (that is, did them together) but finally stuck out her tongue without making the sound. Piaget described this sequence of events by saying that the baby used the sound as an auditory index to link two schemas via reciprocal assimilation. She could see Piaget's tongue and hear his sound. She could feel her own tongue movement and hear her sound, which was recognized as the same sound as his. Piaget speculated that the common sound enabled her to make the connection between the sight of Piaget's tongue and the feel of her own; that is, an integrated sight–sound schema and an integrated sound–feel schema enabled her to forge a new sight–feel schema via the common auditory link.

Whether this hypothesis is correct or not, the observations themselves testify to the analytic work the infant was engaging in. (Needless to say, this kind of imitation contrasts greatly with the automatic or released response of a newborn sticking out its tongue in reaction to an adult sticking out the tongue [Meltzoff & Moore, 1977] or making other looming gestures toward the infant's mouth [Jackson, 1979]. As far as we can tell, the newborn responses are involuntary and do not require conscious analysis of what is to be done.) Piaget gave a similar account of his children learning to blink their eyes as an imitative response. Piaget began to try to get Jacqueline to blink her eyes at around 9 months. He got nowhere, although the baby was interested and felt Piaget's eyes with her fingers. Shortly before 1 year, she opened and closed her mouth in response to his opening and closing his eyes. Shortly thereafter, when she was rubbing her eyes one day, Piaget imitated her. She watched him rub his eyes, and then she rubbed her mouth. The next time she rubbed her cheek and then her ear. These responses continued for several days until finally she rubbed her eyes in response to his doing so. That same day he blinked his eyes and she rubbed hers. There appears to be learning here through successive approximations to locate the correct part of the face. Piaget made similar observations with Lucienne. Around 11 months, she opened and closed her hand in response to Piaget's blinking his eyes, followed by opening and closing her mouth. At 1 year, she did both at the same time and also covered and uncovered her face with a pillow.

Piaget saw the overt trial and error but did not emphasize what I would about this situation. It seems to me that his children were expressing a concept of opening and closing. They had the right idea but couldn't locate the right part. The concept was abstract: opening and closing per se—not opening or closing a particular object but a more abstract representation of the act itself. This kind of concept is discussed at length in chapter 5, where I describe how babies might analyze perceptual displays in such a way as to produce analogical representations in the form of image-schemas. Piaget did recognize that there was a kind of analogical understanding going on, but I would add that analogical learning of this sort implies the presence of a working conceptual system. I do not see any way to engage in analogical thought or comparison without some means of representing the analogy.

But Piaget required there be no overt trial and error before he could feel confident that the child had formed an image of something. This he did not observe until Stage 6. At that time he saw his children imitating new behavior so complex as to indicate accommodation to the object taking place internally, rather than by external trial and error followed by recognition. More important, it was also in Stage 6 that he first observed deferred imitation, which, as mentioned in chapter 1, implies some sort of conceptual representation, in that the external model is not present. It is a form of recall. As we will see in chapter 10, however, this form of recall is present by 9 months of age and perhaps a month or so earlier. It joins other pieces of evidence indicating conceptual thought in the period when, according to Piagetian theory, it is not yet to supposed to exist.

Aside from the increasing strain that new data have placed on Piagetian theory, there remains a mystery at its heart. Although Piaget brilliantly combined the two main themes in Western philosophy on the nature of symbol formation—similarity versus association—he was unable to cross the gap between them. Discussions of symbolization become exceedingly complex, but at heart they rely either on a similarity relation between a symbol and its referent, in which the symbol accrues meaning by resembling it, or on an associative relation, in which one thing comes to stand for or refer to another by virtue of an association between them. Piaget emphasized that the growth of the symbolic function was a long, slow development during the sensorimotor period. For most of that development, he relied on an associative account. Thus, babies begin to show anticipatory responding to signals near the end of Stage 1, and in that sense the signal of the breast, for example, comes to stand for the nourishment that will follow. The next development is motor recognition in Stage 3, in which an associated movement is used to stand for the object typically acted on. Then in Stages 4 and 5 come the indications, in which anticipatory responding to stimuli becomes more elaborate and less bound to the immediate stimuli. But none of these developments constituted true symbols for Piaget. For that, Piaget switches from an associative account to a similarity one. The increasingly elaborate sensorimotor reactions (apparently especially those involved in imitation) become "speeded up" and "interiorized" in the form of imagery. It is these images, which resemble what they model, that are said to be the first true symbols (Piaget, 1952).

What remains murky is how the associative developments taking place in the first year and a half of life relate to the development of imagery. I speculate that by internalization Piaget meant that actual sensorimotor chains of some length could be anticipated mentally, and that the speeding up of such mental chains coalesced into some kind of image. But if this was the route he had in mind, then he forwent imitation as the basis of imagery. Speeded-up sensorimotor responses do not require the analysis that he showed was necessary for complex imitation; they require only associative strengthening. Nothing in the associative account would preclude imagery from occurring, perhaps quite early in the sensorimotor period. Only a view that says that imagery is the result of complex analysis implies a late onset. Of course, as I have discussed, we do not know the origins of imagery; it may not require complex analysis. If not, then once again there is nothing to suggest that babies are imageless in the first year of life.

If babies can form imagery, in principle there is no reason why they should not be able to re-create the past by forming images of it. I suppose I should not have been surprised, then, that a decade ago when Piaget's view still dominated the field, Meltzoff's and our data on deferred imitation in 9- and 11-month-olds (Mandler & McDonough, 1995; McDonough & Mandler, 1994; Meltzoff, 1988a) were vehemently rejected by some members of the developmental community (see the discussion section of Mandler, 1990). Because before the end of the first year infants could reproduce novel events observed in the past, they provided dramatic evidence of a preverbal conceptual system.

Even though imagery could provide a means of recalling the past, it is less clear, however, how in itself it provides meaning, especially meaning of an abstract kind. Imagery can reproduce what an object looks like, but how does this provide its meaning? This, of course, has been the traditional objection to imagistic representational systems, such as that proposed by Paivio (1978). The argument goes that a "conceptless" picture of a scene does not specify which aspects are the ones to be thought about. For example, in an image of pouring milk from a pitcher into a mug, is the color of the mug relevant to the meaning, or the fact that the pitcher is 10 inches high, or that the pitcher is held in the left hand and the mug in the right?

Many of the arguments made against imagistic representational codes had this notion at their core: A picture or image can stand for or refer to something but only if the picture or image is conceptually interpreted. The aspect of this issue relevant here is what it means for Piaget's hypothesis that pictures are the first meanings children use for thought. A picture must be interpreted or construed if it is to represent a meaning, just as a perceptual array itself must be interpreted or construed if it is to be considered meaningful. Because a conceptual system is needed to construe both perceptual information and images, images by themselves are insufficient to provide a conceptual system. I think this argument is correct, but I argue in chapter 4 that a different form of imagistic representation (image-schemas) avoids the difficulties that have plagued imaginal representational systems. Perhaps Piaget was just a bit ahead of his time.

Motor Incompetence Versus Conceptual Incompetence

I mentioned at the beginning of this chapter that Piaget confused motor incompetence with conceptual incompetence. This is easy to do. It is a habit of mind that unfortunately we tend to use to pigeonhole people with motor disabilities (how can Stephen Hawking be so brilliant?).

Similarly, it is sometimes hard to believe that a person who struggles to produce words after a stroke is not necessarily also suffering an intellectual defect. Babies are classic examples of motor incompetence, although their incompetence is so charming we sometimes discount its implications. But if we do make note of it, we often make the same assumption that Piaget did. Infants aren't brain damaged, and so if they fail to pick up a desired object in front of them that they watched you cover, or if they fail to retrieve a desired object when it is sitting on top of another, it must be because they are still missing some fundamental conceptual understanding about objects and their permanence. In Piaget's theory of the infant mind, it takes some months before infants know anything much about objects, such as that they are three-dimensional, solid, and unitary. He thought it took even more time to learn that objects continue to exist when out of sight. Indeed, it was the failure first to search for hidden objects, then the failure to find them, that was his chief evidence that infants could not represent absent objects and therefore have not yet developed a conceptual system that would enable them to do so (Piaget, 1954).

One of Piaget's (1954) observations was of his son Laurent about to pick up a matchbox in front of him. When he was just about to reach it, Piaget put it on top of a book. Laurent immediately withdrew his hand and then grasped the book instead. To Piaget, the infant seemed not to understand that when the matchbox was placed on top, it was still a separate object, and that the two objects had not become merged into a single new one. This set of observations is reliable (Hofsten & Spelke, 1985). However, Adele Diamond neatly demonstrated that the difficulty infants have in this reaching task is due to motor incompetence and therefore not necessarily due to lack of conceptual knowledge (Diamond & Gilbert, 1989; Diamond & Lee, 2000). Even at 7 months, infants often fail to retrieve objects because they are not yet able to inhibit reflexive reactions to touching an object; if they brush another object when reaching for a target object, they tend either to pull back the hand reflexively or else to grasp the object they brushed against. What Diamond showed was that infants have no problem grasping an object in a box if the object can be reached by a straight path. However, if the edge of the box is slightly in the way, so that 5- to 7-month-olds touch the edge while reaching for the object, they either withdraw the hand or grasp the edge of the box instead. As Diamond and Gilbert (1989) put it:

> The problem is not in understanding that the toy is there, but in navigating to reach it. Seven-month-old infants lack the finely calibrated motor skill to retrieve a small object without grazing the edge of the surface it borders, and once they graze the edge they are unable to inhibit reacting reflexively with the grasp or avoidance reaction. (p. 248)

The difficulty with this reaching task is related to the failure to retrieve a desired object when a cover is placed over it (Piaget, 1954). The latter error was Piaget's hallmark of Stage 3 understanding (or more appositely, misunderstanding) of objects. This phenomenon is also reliable: Around 6 months, infants will retrieve a partially hidden object but not a completely hidden one. Piaget interpreted the finding as the infant not understanding that objects continue to exist when out of sight. However, it seems a fairly straightforward extension of Diamond's finding to account for the difficulty infants this age have in obtaining a toy they are reaching for when a cloth or cup is put over it. The infant's hand touches the cloth or cup and either grasps it (instead of the object) or withdraws. In contrast, if the infant does not have to uncover a toy but only to reach in the correct direction, 7½-month-olds remember that, and where, an object is hidden for delays of a minute or so (McDonough, 1999).

In addition to this work, Baillargeon and her colleagues (e.g., Baillargeon, 1993; Baillargeon, Spelke, & Wasserman, 1985) devised several familiarization/preferential-looking tests to show that when infants do not have to reach for an object, they can demonstrate their knowledge that a hidden object still exists. The familiarization/preferential-looking test was originally invented to study infants' perceptual discriminations. However, Baillargeon and Spelke's insight was that the technique could be used to study conceptual knowledge as well. The technique, described in chapter 1, relies on infants' preference for novelty. If infants are presented with a number of stimuli that look alike and then with a stimulus that is perceptually different, if they can see the differences between the old and new stimuli, they tend to look longer at the new stimulus. The idea behind the new use of the method was to replace perceptual novelty with conceptual novelty. The latter was created by using impossible test events—that is, events that could not happen in the real world and therefore events that infants would never have seen before—and pitting them against possible test events. The brilliant aspect of this idea was to make the impossible test event identical to the habituation event. This was accomplished by requiring the infant to remember something hidden behind a screen that made the habituation event no longer possible. The goal was to rule out current perception as the cause of the novelty effect, leaving an explanation in terms of conceptual knowledge.

For example, in the Baillargeon et al. (1985) experiment, infants were habituated to a drawbridge continually rising and dropping in a 180° arc. Then, as they watched, a box was put behind the drawbridge. Following this, infants were given two kinds of trials, those in which the drawbridge continued in exactly the same 180° arc as before (and in the real world would have had to go through the box behind it—thus, an impossible trial), and those with a trajectory going back and forth but only through an arc of 120°—that is, stopping at the point at which it should hit the object (a possible trial). A solely perceptual baby should dishabituate to the new display (the trajectory that stopped where the box would be) and continue to habituate to the original display in which the drawbridge went through the full 180° arc. Exactly the opposite happened. Infants showed no particular interest in the trials in which the drawbridge went through the shorter arc but looked significantly longer on the trials in which the arc matched the habituation display. In principle, one would not need to habituate infants with such a display before changing it in a way that violates their conceptual knowledge. One could simply compare looking times to a normal versus an abnormal situation. However, habituation trials focus infants' attention on the relevant variable and also reduce looking at the habituated stimulus, thus highlighting the longer looking that occurs to it when it becomes an impossible display. (In more recent work, Baillargeon has conducted a number of experiments that do not use habituation and just compare looking times to normal and abnormal displays. The same conclusions are reached; see Baillargeon, 2000.)

I mentioned in chapter 1 the experiments in which infants watch a car running down a track. Then a barrier is put on top of the track and a screen is lowered in front of it so the track is no longer in view. The car is then released and runs down the track behind the screen and comes out the other side. Infants look longer at this event than when the barrier is placed in front of or behind the track, showing that they know not just that the barrier is behind the screen but even where it is located (Baillargeon, 1986). These experiments are especially strong. Because the sight of the car moving behind the screen and coming out the other side is identical for both the possible and impossible trials, infants must remember what is hidden behind the screen if they differentiate them, so providing a perceptual explanation for the results would seem to be a superhuman task.

Much has been made of the fact that perceptual explanations are possible for a few of Baillargeon's findings (e.g., Bogartz, Shinskey, & Speaker, 1997; Haith, 1998). However, no one has explained on perceptual grounds alone the enormous variety of results Baillargeon and her colleagues have provided. Obviously, some experiments provide better evidence for conceptual factors than others, and it is tempting to skewer the weaker ones, but to provide a true attack on her point of view, one would have to tackle the strongest experiments, such as the one just described.

There is by now an extensive body of contemporary research indicating a major discrepancy in performance between tasks that require infants either to uncover a hidden object or to reach for it when it is contiguous with another one and tasks that measure knowledge about objects through violation of expectations. As we will see in chapter 10 where I discuss recall, there are related problems with Piaget's most famous hiding task, the A-not-B task, and even with tasks in which infants are taught how to reach, if the task generates proactive inhibition (Munakata, McClelland, Johnson, & Siegler, 1997). Aside from the strain on the memory system that some tasks impose, most of the difficulties infants experience with these tasks has to do with getting the motor system coordinated with the conceptual system. Until near the end of the first year, infants are not yet skilled in controlling their motor responses. Further, they are poor at planning sequences of motor actions, and at inhibiting those that have already been planned, or both (Diamond, 1990). They also have trouble in spontaneously generating plans of action to retrieve objects (Willatts, 1997). They may also find it difficult to implement coordinated action sequences even when they can generate them.

None of these difficulties implicate an undeveloped object concept. This is an important conclusion because it was the difficulties Piaget's infants had on his various hiding and reaching tasks that most strongly influenced his theory of the late onset and slow growth of conceptual knowledge. Until one understands at least the rudiments of what objects are, it would seem unlikely that much conceptual development could take place. Current research, however, makes clear that from an early age infants begin to conceive of objects in roughly the same way as do older children and adults. At the same time, it must be said, we have no information on the status of that knowledge. Is the information that objects are permanent and independent of the infant's own actions (unless, of course, they smash them) explicit conceptual knowledge or merely implicit sensorimotor knowledge that is not accessible for purposes of thought? I return to this issue briefly in chapter 12, but now it is time to consider in more detail the differences between these two kinds of knowing.

3

Kinds of Representation
Seeing and Thinking

. . . in which I argue for the necessity of differentiating seeing (and acting) from thinking. I discuss why we must reject the argument from parsimony that has been used to claim there is only one kind of representational system in infancy. Then I lay out some of the characteristics that distinguish procedural from declarative knowledge, the most important being that declarative knowledge is selective in its encoding but what is encoded is accessible to conscious awareness. I relate this dichotomy to the distinction between sensorimotor and conceptual knowledge. We also need to differentiate procedural and declarative representation from the processing distinction involved in implicit and explicit memory. I end the chapter with some dramatic examples of common kinds of cognitive functioning that lie beyond awareness.

. . . many cognitive scientists now contend that the complexity of human behavior requires that different kinds of representations be used to handle the diversity of cognitive experience. Thus, people's varied abilities, from perception and motor control to language and problem-solving, may not all rest on the same representational base (e.g., featural representations, structured representations, mental models, image-schematic-representations).
(Gibbs, 2000)

On Parsimony and Related Matters

If the arguments of chapter 2 are correct, it means that infants engage in more than sensorimotor activity. They do not just see but begin to think as well. Given that thought is a quintessential human ability, one might not imagine this to be a controversial statement, but it is considered fanciful and unnecessary in some developmental accounts. (By thought, I mean a conscious, conceptual, and manipulable representation.) For example, both Haith and Benson (1998) and Quinn and Eimas (2000) stated that to ascribe conceptual thought to infants is not only unparsimonious but also unnecessary. Quinn and Eimas said that until language is acquired, infants rely for their object categorization on perceptual information alone, learning "less apparent features" via language. In other words, infants are not capable of categorizing on the basis of meaning until language is learned. This is a radical view in that it ascribes conceptual thought to language teaching, without specifying how language could be learned in the absence of conceptualization. Haith and Benson (1998) did not discuss how conceptualization comes about but still insisted that theorizing about infants should emphasize perceptual accomplishments. As they put it:

> Perceptual interpretations are generally more parsimonious
> than cognitive interpretations, the processes are much better
> documented in the infant literature, and they require fewer
> inferential steps between the experimental manipulations,
> the presumed processes, and the observed behavior. There is
> a more direct tie between events and behavior for such con-
> cepts as familiarity, novelty, and salience, for example, than
> for beliefs, reasoning, and inference. (p. 203)

But if Piaget's theory doesn't work, in what way is it more parsimonious to assume as little conceptual knowledge in infancy as possible? Why is it simpler to assume that babies have only low-level sensorimotor processes and that the higher mental functions must come later? Parsimony will be achieved not by making the baby simple but by finding a theory that can account for all the data in the simplest way. Nor does that mean that because perceptual and other sensorimotor processes are easier to measure and better documented, they constitute the correct explanation for all infant behaviors. It is indeed easier to find a key under a streetlight than in the dark, but if it was dropped down the street in the dark, the streetlight will be of little use!

I don't see how it is possible to build a baby with only one kind of representation. Granted, there is a single brain and at some level a uniform neural substrate, but that is not sufficient reason to assume that all knowledge should be represented in the same way. I use the term *representation* to refer to stored information and consider knowledge and representation to be rough synonyms. They are not exact synonyms in that *representation* emphasizes the format in which something is stored, whereas *knowledge* emphasizes the content of what is stored. Nevertheless, for most purposes, I use the two terms synonymously.

As I discussed in the last chapter, Piaget clearly saw the need for more than one kind of representation—not only the difference between sensorimotor and conceptual representation but also, within the latter, preoperational and operational thought. Yet although many developmental psychologists consider themselves to be Piagetians, they do not always agree that the human mind has more than one kind of representation. It is as if once the human organism is said to reach the preoperational stage, then sensorimotor representation plays such a minor role as to virtually disappear, just as when the organism reaches the concrete operational stage, preoperational thought is also said to disappear. People do not usually quarrel with motor representations as being different from other kinds of processes, but when I also draw a distinction between perception and conception, this is often rejected, even though it is merely a continuation of the same distinction. Perceptual processes are part of the sensorimotor system, and although they influence our thoughts and our thoughts influence the way we perceive, it does not make them the same representational form. Seeing is not the same as thinking.

I am accustomed to hearing two kinds of arguments against deeming perception and conception to be different representational forms. The first argument is primarily a developmental one—namely, that babies begin with only one way of representing knowledge (sensorimotor, which includes perception) and conception gradually grows out of it by associations accruing to perceptual categories (e.g., Quinn & Eimas, 1997). In this view, perception + associated perception = conception, not anything fundamentally different in kind. To posit a second process in addition to perception is said to proliferate mechanisms unnecessarily on an ad hoc basis (Eimas, 1994). This view reminds me of the myth that the earth is held up on the back of a turtle. When asked what held up the turtle, the response was "It's turtles all the way down" (Hawking, 1988). It is a form of extended regress. If there are no concepts, then the associations themselves must be percepts, which in turn leads to the view that concepts are only large sets of associated percepts.

Attributing conceptual thought to babies is also said to characterize human infants too precociously (Fischer & Bidell, 1991). According to

Fischer and Bidell, ascribing conceptual thought to young infants is even a socially dangerous notion because it smacks of innate (and therefore, they imply, immutable) ideas. Of course, precocity does not imply innateness; to say that babies have concepts is precocious only within the context of a theory such as Piaget's. Nor, of course, does the fact that there are innate components to the mind imply immutability. There is little in the database on what infants know that we have accumulated over the past 20 years that implies untoward precocity or undue nativism—the interpretation of the data only violates a theory many of us have long held. As I said in my reply to Fischer and Bidell (Mandler, 1992b):

> The assumption that infants live purely sensorimotor lives is deeply ingrained in the developmental community. We know that babies are learning to recognize and manipulate objects, but we typically believe they have no capacity to represent them conceptually. Many of us were surprised by evidence suggesting otherwise; we had not looked for it in the laboratory because we had assumed there was no point in doing so. . . . I remember saying at the time [of Meltzoff and Moore's 1977 claim for neonatal imitation], "If their interpretation is true, we may have to abandon Piaget's theory of the foundations of mind; that's major trouble!" It may be that the fear of having to start over again is a greater source of resistance to the idea of "precocity" than fear that we will be led into a fruitless nativism. (p 10)

The other argument against making a clear distinction between conceptual and perceptual processes is that perception and conception are so intertwined that it is impossible to tell them apart. The import of this second argument is not entirely clear. It might mean that the mind is so complex we should give up, because we cannot hope to disentangle its various parts. More likely it reflects the fundamental view that there is only one kind of "mind stuff" and that to posit more than one representational system goes off on a false trail. Everyone agrees that thinking is not the same as seeing, but somehow or other we do both in a completely intertwined way. Our British empiricist roots (simple idea + simple idea = complex idea) are deep indeed!

Because everyone agrees that seeing is not the same as thinking, we should at least try to specify how they differ. A thesis of this book is that perception and conception differ in content, representational format, and methods of processing. Evidence for each of these points will be adduced during this and the following chapters. In this chapter I discuss mainly differences in representation, with a few comments along the way about differences in processing, which, needless to say, are closely related. As for content, although it may seem a trivial point, people can point unambiguously to an object they perceive but cannot point to its conceptual meaning. (It may be for this reason that actions and spatial relations seem more abstract and less concrete than do objects; you can't unambiguously point to an action or a relation either.)

Procedural Versus Declarative Knowledge

One way to describe the representational distinction between seeing and thinking is in terms of *procedural* and *declarative* knowledge. These terms were borrowed from computer science, but the distinction is a much older one (Schacter, 1987). It is usually described in terms of the difference between information that can be brought to awareness and information that remains inaccessible, even though it demonstrably influences behavior. In the past, memory was typically treated as conscious recall and recognition, although in the 19th and the early 20th centuries some psychiatrists and neuropsychologists, such as Freud, Korsakoff, and Claparède, emphasized that information can be represented in memory in an inaccessible form. In modern times, much of the work on inaccessible memory has come from the study of amnesia. One of the major aspects of this syndrome is that amnesic patients have difficulty learning or remembering new factual information, although they can learn and remember new motor and perceptual skills (Cohen & Squire, 1980; Milner, Corkin, & Teuber, 1968). The distinction between factual memory and perceptual-motor skills has traditionally been called the distinction between *knowing that* and *knowing how*. We know *that* a dog is an animal or *that* Paris is the capital of France. This is conceptual knowledge that we can think and talk about. On the other hand, we know *how* to ride a bike or play the piano. We can't conceptualize very well what it is that we know in the procedural cases, even though we know how to do it. The point to be emphasized here is that this is just as true for perceptual recognition as for motor skills. Perception is a knowing how rather than a knowing that.

The heart of the declarative-procedural distinction is whether information can be brought to conscious awareness.[1] Only declarative knowledge is accessible to conscious awareness. Procedural knowledge remains inaccessible (nonconscious). We can observe only the products of our procedures, not the procedures themselves. This may seem an obvious point. Everyone agrees that we have no access to the programs that control our muscles when we throw a ball. They also agree that we have no access to our psychological procedures, such as retrieval or speech production. On the other hand, many people believe that they do have access to other motor procedures, such as driving a car, typing, or tying shoelaces, as well as to perceptual aspects of recognition. This belief is mistaken. People can watch themselves performing certain acts and make up miniature theories about how they do them, but that is not the same as observing the procedures themselves that are guiding the actions.

Compiling a complex procedure in the first place often makes use of conscious awareness and declarative knowledge, for instance, in the early stages of learning skills such as driving or typing (Anderson, 1982). But using declarative knowledge to control the acquisition of procedural knowledge does not mean that the procedural knowledge itself is now or ever was accessible. We are never aware of exactly what is being compiled or what brings about an increase in smoothness and speed of performance. For example (unless we are told), we are unaware that as we type the first letter of a word, the fingers that will type the later letters are already beginning to rise (Gentner, 1988), nor is this kind of anticipatory action what we intended to do or were conscious of when we learned to type in the first place. Although we were conscious of searching for a particular letter when we first began to type and were deliberately trying to string together letters, we were not aware of much of what our fingers were doing. Certainly we never planned or were aware that we were raising the fourth finger of the right hand (in preparation for *o*) as we began to type the word *unconscious*.

An example I have often used in class to illustrate the distinction is the claim that people know the procedure they follow when they tie their shoes. They say things such as "You make a loop with the right lace, then take the left lace and wrap it around the loop, and then. . . ." This is about as far as they usually get. Somehow a miracle happens, and the knot is tied. Faced with the incompleteness of their description, people may say, "Well, I haven't really observed the procedure in recent years because I haven't needed to, but I could if I wanted to." We obviously can get along well without "paying attention" once a procedure is running smoothly. We may get along well even without an automated procedure. The example of the telephone dial I discussed in the last chapter is a case in which we have acted on an object thousands of times, touching many different sequences of numbers, without taking in some pretty basic details. However, even when we turn our attention to shoe tying we are not actually observing the procedure. Rather, we are constructing a story from observing the outcome of various steps along the way, what have been called "way stations in consciousness" (G. Mandler, 1992). It is the *story* that is conceptual and accessible, not the procedure. Because we are not in fact observing the procedure itself, the story that is constructed is often inaccurate (Piaget, 1976). Thus, when people say they know the procedure for tying shoes, what they mean is that they know how to do it and can offer a description of sorts, perhaps by providing labels for various parts as they watch themselves carrying it out. (This discrepancy can also work the other way, of course; people can learn elaborate descriptions of how to put spin on a tennis ball but be unable to accomplish it in action.) Just as for learning to type, however, this discussion should not be taken to mean we are not using conceptual knowledge when we first learn how to tie our shoes. We set ourselves certain goals (make a loop) and monitor whether we are achieving them, but these goals and the conceptual monitoring do not bear a one-to-one relation to the motor patterns actually being learned.

But what about perception of what things look like, instead of motor skills? Surely we can describe what things look like, and even if we bungle the description, at least we can draw them. So isn't perception available to us in the same way as is declarative knowledge? Unfortunately not. We are not only engaging in a motor procedure when tying our shoes but also perceiving the tying. If perception consists at least in part of declarative knowledge, why is the description so elusive? It is because our memory system includes huge amounts of perceptual knowledge about what things look like, most of which is not accessible to consciousness because it is stored in procedural form. We can't describe what a face looks like because we don't know it declaratively. Instead of asking someone to describe tying a knot, ask for a description of the face of a close friend. Most people are unable to say on which side of the head the hair is parted, which side of the mouth is higher than the other (or even that the two sides are not the same), how far apart the eyes are, whether the earlobes are droopy or not, and so forth. Not infrequently, they can't even say whether the face wears glasses. We are not aware of this information, yet if it changes we may notice the person looks different without being able to say how. In some cases, the particular bit of information has been consciously analyzed (i.e., a declarative description created). Otherwise we can't describe it. A fortiori, we can't draw it. That takes the analytic training that is either self-generated or taught in art class. Such analysis need not be complicated. Once in a boring seminar I was studying the faces around me and noticed for the first time that the tops of people's ears were usually at the level of the eyes. How interesting! It suddenly explained why I had always thought a colleague's face looked slightly odd. It also made my drawings of faces on a blackboard at least marginally more realistic. No longer do I put the eyes near the top of the face, but down around the ears—exactly where I had been seeing them for 50 years but had never noticed.

The situation is even more extreme than this illustration suggests. There are aspects of faces in general that no one knows how to describe. Fagan and Singer (1979) showed that 6-month-olds can categorize faces as male or female, and do so before they are good at discriminating one male from another or one female from another. But this accomplishment, which we have all managed since near birth, is indescribable (and without artistic training, undrawable). People make up stories about the delicacy of the female face or the strong jaw of the male face, but the actual parameters are still unknown (Abdi, Valentin, Edelman, & O'Toole, 1995). Some speculate that the information we use is complex proportional differences relating to the cheekbones, but I believe my point has been made. The information we have used since early in infancy is not accessible to awareness (see Moscovitch, Goshen-Gottstein, & Vriezen, 1994). This kind of categorization is part of the visual input system; it takes place automatically and does not require attention.

Needless to say, this kind of nonconscious pattern learning is not restricted to the look of visual stimuli. It is ubiquitous in human functioning, and I discuss a number of examples in this book. Later in this chapter I mention schema formation, in the sense of learning expectations about the frequency of events. Another example is learning auditory patterns in language, discussed in chapter 11. People are great pattern learners, patterns that are often abstract in character, a fact we may not appreciate just because so many of them are nonconsciously acquired and operate outside our awareness.

There is one caveat about this discussion. To say that sensorimotor information is not accessible does not mean that you are never aware of the sensations (qualia) involved in perceptual and motor learning. You do see the shoe and laces and feel them in your hand, and your attention might be directed to them. But awareness of what you perceive comes with attention. This does not mean that in the absence of attention to what you are currently looking at or listening to, you are in a zombielike state. Typically, it means that you are attending to something else. As you read this, you are experiencing some pressure on your limbs as you sit, but until I call this to your attention, you are not consciously aware of it; instead (I hope), you are aware of what you are reading.

Another way of describing the difference between procedural and declarative knowledge is a sensorimotor versus a conceptual system. This was Piaget's version of the distinction. Piaget claimed that babies are learning many perceptual and motor skills during the sensorimotor period, but in his theory they have not yet begun to conceptualize the information they are processing. He did not mean that infants are not aware of or do not attend to the objects in their surrounding; he meant they can't conceptualize them, which is why he thought they cannot call them to mind when they are absent. (As best as I can tell, he adopted a spatial view of attention—where the eyes are directed—without assuming that attention leads to conceptualization.) Of course, many infant procedures are not learned in the way that complex motor skills are learned in later childhood and adulthood. It takes conceptual (declarative) guidance to learn how to tie one's shoes or drive a car, even though that means only that concepts are guiding the compilation, not that one is aware of the components being compiled; these are motor movements of unknown specification. In infancy, many motor skills such as grasping objects or crawling appear to be acquired without even the step of conceptual guidance. This possibility may have contributed to Piaget's belief that one can adequately describe all of infant learning without recourse to conceptual representation.

Factual knowledge is conceptual in nature. When we "know" that faces are oval, we have learned either through analyzing perceptual information or through being told; it does not come from just staring thoughtlessly at faces. The analysis (through simplification and redescription) puts the information into conceptual form. Once language is acquired, verbal information arrives conceptually prepackaged. These are the kinds of knowledge that are declarative; they can be thought about and used for purposes of recall, planning, and reasoning. Sensorimotor knowledge, on the other hand, is procedural knowledge. It cannot be accessed directly; it can only be run. It can be thought about only by using the conceptual system to make up stories about its workings.

Such conceptualization does not need to consist of complex or high-level theorizing. In its simplest form, as I describe in the next chapter, it can be noticing that an object starts up on its own; here the understanding is at a quite primitive level. An infant might notice that an object begins movement without anything coming in contact with it and conceive of this as a "self-moving thing." A slightly more sophisticated example might be seeing a rabbit eating a carrot and conceiving of it as an animal eating food. The issue here is not when in the course of processing an event such an interpretation begins. I do not know how to answer that question. But I do know that much of the perceptual information we take in while the interpretation is going on is not processed conceptually and, therefore, is not accessible for purposes of recall or further thought. What is accessible is the conceptual interpretation that has been made of the perceptual input, which may, of course, include interpretation of appearance as well as the meaning of the event.

A good case can be made that most of what we perceive is nonconscious. Mack and Rock (1998) call perception without attention *inattentional blindness*, a state in which it is impossible to report what has been seen or heard. So when our attention drifts in a lecture, we no longer are aware of what is being said and it becomes inaccessible, even though the information can prime later processing. In this sense we *would* be rather zombielike, except that we are nearly always attending to something (even if it be only an internal dialogue). Some sensations seem to demand attention, such as a sudden pain or loud noise, but only if we actually attend to them do we become conscious of them (a phenomenon well understood by expert pediatricians, who know how to distract a baby so that a shot in the arm goes unnoticed).

There are two slightly different aspects of inattentional blindness relevant to infant development. First, anyone (infant or adult) who does not attend to something will not be conscious of it and therefore will not be able to think about it. Second, at least in infancy it may be possible to attend to something and so be conscious of it, but conceptualize it so shallowly or imprecisely as to make it irretrievable later. This may happen when 3-month-olds are shown pictures of dogs or cats in laboratory experiments on categorization (e.g., Quinn, Eimas, & Rosenkrantz, 1993). They have only recently become able to maintain extended periods of alertness (Colombo, 2001). They are old enough to attend to the pictures, but it seems likely that they do not yet have the resources to get very far in conceptualizing what they are looking at during the few minutes of the experiment.[2] Nevertheless, as discussed in chapter 6, they form a perceptual category of what they are looking at, which influences their later perception. In itself, however, this should not be sufficient to enable them to think about the pictures at a later time.

Implicit Versus Explicit Learning

It is important to distinguish between procedural and declarative representation and the related dichotomy of *implicit* and *explicit* processing. The latter set of terms is popular in the verbal memory literature and is favored by people who prefer to emphasize different kinds of processing rather than different kinds of representation (e.g., G. Mandler, 1985). One reason the distinction between explicit and implicit knowledge became a fiercely disputed topic (e.g., Shanks & St. John, 1994) is that many such battles take place on the common turf of language processing. This is not a dispute over how to differentiate linguistic or conceptual representation from motor and perceptual skills. Rather, it is how to describe different ways of processing within verbal tasks themselves. In this arena, the distinction involves the presence or absence of attention and elaboration: Verbal material that is consciously attended to and semantically analyzed is explicit, whereas verbal material that is not attended to or at any rate not consciously understood is implicit (e.g., Dorfman & Mandler, 1994).

Many of the disputes over the distinction between implicit and explicit knowledge stem from this language memory literature, in which it is sometimes difficult to know the extent to which attentive processing has taken place. The problem is that language, even though conceptual in nature, can on occasion be processed implicitly; it is registered but not attended to or elaborated. That is, it is not processed in terms of its semantic content or else is processed so shallowly that it does not become integrated into the existing conceptual system. Such a situation can be seen in Graf and Mandler's (1984) study, in which adults were asked either to study a list of words (a semantic task) or to cross out all the vowels in the words on the list (a nonsemantic task). Then they were given recall and recognition tasks and a stem completion task. In a stem completion task, people are given three-letter word stems and asked to complete them with the first words that come to mind. The first words to come to mind are dependent to some extent on how recently they have been activated, so after working with a list of words, a certain portion of the completions will be words from that list. Subjects given both kinds of instructions tended to produce the same number of stem completions from the list, showing the same activation of the material. However, the subjects given the vowel instructions were much poorer on the recall and recognition tests. People given such nonsemantic instructions (or perhaps not paying much attention when reading an article or listening to a lecture) do process the words they are reading or hearing and so show priming effects, but because of the shallowness of such processing (lack of semantic elaboration; G. Mandler, 2002a), they have trouble with explicit tests such as recall. The implicit priming effects stem from the procedural information being used to perceive the visual or auditory structure of the information in question, such as the phonological or visual shapes of words. This kind of information is presemantic and preattentive and results in perceptual, not conceptual, priming These two kinds of priming appear to be independent of each other and to have different neural underpinnings (see Moscovitch, 2000, for discussion).

Thus, the procedural-declarative distinction is not the same as the implicit-explicit distinction. The procedural-declarative distinction has to do with fundamentally different kinds of information that are represented in different ways. This is a *distinction in representational format*. The implicit-explicit distinction, on the other hand, has to do with whether information can be made accessible, which in turn is a function of whether it has been attended to. This is a *processing distinction*. In the case of procedural knowledge, information is never accessible; we cannot process this kind of information in such a way as to bring it to awareness. In the case of declarative knowledge, the information is stored in a conceptual format and has the potential to be brought to awareness. Whether that happens on a given occasion depends on the particular kind of processing that is carried out. Information heard during a lecture, for example, can be processed either explicitly or implicitly, depending on attention and interpretation (elaboration) during encoding.

This family of distinctions is shown in Figure 3-1, where it can be seen that implicit processing is associated not only with procedural knowledge but also in some circumstances with declarative knowledge. The figure divides representation into two types and shows the kind of processing associated with each representational format. Procedurally represented knowledge is always processed implicitly. Declarative knowledge, on the other hand, can be processed implicitly or explicitly. If attention is not paid to what is being said (or seen), the words (or sights) are processed only implicitly. They are activated (primed) but unable to be recalled. If they are attended to, however, they are processed conceptually. If all goes well, they become integrated with existing conceptual knowledge (that is, elaborated) and hence potentially available for recall.

One of the reasons that some psychologists studying language tasks emphasize differences in processing rather than representational differences is because they assume that all linguistic processing makes use of a common semantic store, and it seems odd to them to talk about different representational systems in such experiments. However, even in verbal tasks, procedural representations are called upon. Of course, these adult experiments are rather far removed from the topic of main interest in this

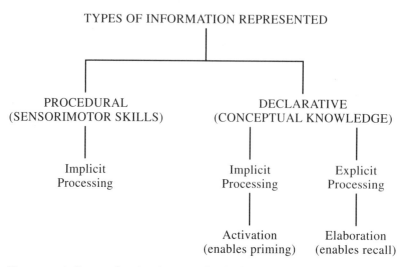

Figure 3-1. A diagram showing that procedural information is always processed implicitly but that declarative knowledge can be processed implicitly or explicitly. Reprinted from Mandler (1998a) by permission of John Wiley & Sons, Inc.

chapter, namely, discussion of some of the ways that sensorimotor perceptual and motor skills differ from conceptual knowledge. One can show interesting differential consequences when words have been processed perceptually rather than conceptually (as in counting vowels versus taking in their semantic meaning), but nevertheless the linguistic sphere does not seem like the ideal place to separate perception and conception.

Representational differences imply processing differences as well, and some of them are illustrated in the discussion of differences in perceptual and conceptual categorization in later chapters. In general, the processing differences between procedural and declarative knowledge can be summarized in the following ways: Procedural knowledge, both perceptual and motor, is inaccessible to consciousness. It is unselective, taking in all the encodable information that is presented to the input system. This information is processed in parallel, so that a great deal of information can be taken in at the same time—more than could be communicated even if formatted properly (Hayes & Broadbent, 1988). In spite of taking in lots of information at once (or because of it?), it is also relatively slow to learn, and learning is accomplished by associative strengthening, typically over a number of trials, as in operant conditioning or perceptual schema formation. Procedural knowledge tends to be context-bound, making it difficult to get at separate parts of the information or to transfer them from one situation to another. It aggregates frequency information—that is, how often something occurs and the sequences in which they occur—and thus is responsible for our expectations about what will happen next. This is also part of language learning, as discussed in chapter 11, as well as forming the scripts and schemas we use to predict the events of daily life.

Declarative or conceptual knowledge, in contrast, is accessible to awareness and is either describable in language or, with a little analytic training, by drawing. It requires attention to be encoded into this format; this means that it is selective (Hayes & Broadbent, 1988; Nickerson & Adams, 1979). The selectivity is due to the limits on conscious attention, which require the system to process information serially rather than in parallel. As Hayes and Broadbent point out, a system that learns selectively takes in only a manageable number of variables, so that what has been learned can potentially be communicated. The system can learn information in a single trial (in small quantities, of course) simply by being told. In comparison to procedural knowledge, it is relatively context free; it is potentially available for many different problem-solving and reasoning situations.

These are dramatic differences in processing, and it is a contention of this book that these differences are associated with equally dramatic differences in representational format. Perceptual and motor learning result in a kind of tuning that changes existing perceptual representations and motor skills. These are the classic cases of not being able to see or act as one did in the past because of the permanent changes that have taken place in the system that processes these kinds of information. Although conceptual learning also can change existing representations, the more frequent result is an addition to existing declarative knowledge without loss of previous acquisitions. Coexistence, rather than replacement, is the general rule for declarative knowledge (although over time unused formulations may be forgotten).

There is an interesting dissociation between conscious and nonconscious expectations that illustrates the difference in selectivity of procedural and declarative knowledge. As just mentioned, procedural knowledge is sensitive to frequencies of occurrence, and it is that sensitivity that creates reasonably accurate expectations of what will happen next. However, we also have conscious beliefs about what those frequencies are, and the two do not always match. Here is a dramatic piece of anecdotal evidence (Mandler, 1984) and then some almost as dramatic experimental evidence.

Some time in the 1970s I decided to cease using masculine pronouns in my lectures when I wanted to talk about people in general. Changing wording is easy enough to do when writing but much more difficult when lecturing, because one is thinking about what to say rather than about the vehicle itself. Nevertheless, I tried to use plural pronouns some of the time and when talking about an individual in an example, to say *he* half of the time and *she* half of the time. Toward the end of the course, I happened to mention that this was what I had done. Immediately, I heard a murmur around the classroom. I stopped and asked what was the matter. Someone raised a hand and said, "What do you mean you gave 'he' and 'she' equal time? You never said 'he' once during the entire course." We discussed this a bit, and then I asked for a head count. How many students thought I had always said *she*? The answer was unanimous. Every student in the class thought I had used *she* 100% of the time. I protested, of course; after all, I had worked hard to equalize my usage of the two pronouns. Then I remembered I had taped my lectures. So, I recruited a couple of students to take two lectures at random and to count the number of times I had used each of the terms. The resulting count shocked us all. I had said *she* only 20% of the time. I was chagrined at how badly I had accomplished my mission, but the students were equally upset at having estimated 20% to be 100% and 80% to be zero—an effect of the magnitude we would always like to find in the lab! What had happened, of course, was that the students weren't paying attention to the language I was using; they were attending to its content. They probably couldn't have reproduced exactly any phrase I had used. They were totally used to hearing *he* to refer to an individual. But in those days one simply did not use *she* to stand for a generic person, and each usage stuck vividly in their minds. When I asked them to make a conscious judgment of my uses of *he*, they examined their explicit memory (the only memory accessible to them), and there they found a great many *she*'s and no *he*'s.

It is as if two different frequency counters are at work here. One counter is set to register the actual probabilities of occurrence of events in the world. (I don't mean this literally; the phenomenon is more likely

due to tuning of perceptual schemas. The point is only that actual frequency of occurrence determines perceptual expectations.) We are not
conscious of this "counter"; that is, we are not aware that we are building
the event and scene schemas that control what we expect to see and hear.
This aspect of schema formation is procedural knowledge. It is automatic
in its functioning, unbiased, and unselective. The other "counter" is selective and biased; it counts only what has been brought to its attention.
This is the kind of information we are able to recall and think about at a
later time. It is neither automatic nor particularly accurate (Greene, 1986;
Hockley, 1984). Looking out at a sea of students, I am thinking about
what I am saying and not about what they look like, what they are wearing, and so forth. None of that information is consciously attended to,
and none of it is recallable. After the class is over, I will be able to recall
only the student who catches my attention by asking a question or reading a newspaper, and even then I am very unlikely to have noticed what
clothing the student wore.

The experimental example is one of a number studying the phenomenon of illusory conjunctions, but this is one of the first and most interesting of them. Hamilton and Gifford (1976) suggested that prejudice
is partly due to illusory correlations between distinctive features of the environment. When distinctive or salient events (defined as statistically infrequent events) co-occur, they are more likely to be associated with each
other than are nonsalient events. In particular, Hamilton and Gifford
speculated that members of a minority group, who are less frequently encountered than members of the majority group and therefore more distinctive, may become associated with socially unacceptable behaviors,
which are also less frequently encountered than acceptable behaviors and
are therefore also more distinctive. To assess this hypothesis, they invented
two groups of people, one considerably larger than the other, differentiated only by the name of the group they belonged to. Then they invented
sets of behaviors, most of which were positive, such as "contributed to a
fund for the blind," and a few of which were negative, such as "was rude
to a shopkeeper." Positive and negative behaviors were assigned in exactly
the same proportion to the minority and the majority groups. College
students were presented with the lists of people and their behaviors and
then rated the members of the groups, indicated the group membership
of the person who did each behavior, and estimated the number of un-

desirable behaviors in each group. The results consistently showed that the minority group was judged to engage in more unacceptable behavior than the majority group. Like my saying *she* in the classroom, each bit of bad behavior was actively noticed and "counted." Similarly, the minority group members were also made more salient than the majority ones by their rarity.

This finding was not due to the fact that the rare behaviors were bad and more noticeable because of their unacceptability. The authors conducted a second experiment identical to the first, except that the rarely occurring behaviors were good and the frequent behaviors were bad. The same results were found, only now the minority group was judged to be better behaved than the majority group. It seems that conscious associations (that is, the sort that can be declared) are formed on the basis of what has been noticed more than on what has actually occurred. We will see a related phenomenon in the control of associations in inductive generalization in chapter 8.

These data, along with the *he-she* example discussed earlier, illustrate some of the complexities in differentiating procedural and declarative knowledge. They clearly show dissociations between expectations based on what we encounter and those based on what we notice, but at the same time they indicate that it is our conscious expectations that are based on what we notice and our nonconscious ones that are based on actual occurrence. The ultimate question, of course, is how these different forms of knowledge fit together. As we have seen in this chapter, perceptual and conceptual knowledge differ in important ways, and as we will see in chapters 6, 7, and 8, it is necessary to distinguish them if we are to understand how the mind develops. But the interrelations between the two are many and intricate and still only partially understood. Indeed, it is fair to say that how we gain conceptual knowledge from perceiving and how these conceptions influence what we see have preoccupied psychology since its inception. In the next chapter, I suggest the beginning of an answer to the first question, namely, how we gain conceptual knowledge from perceiving. It may be easier to tackle this problem by looking at its foundations in infancy than by trying to unravel the intricacies of the adult mind.

4

Perceptual Meaning Analysis and Image–Schemas
The Infant as Interpreter

. . . in which I discuss how infants form concepts from perceptual data. After some initial comments on nativism, I introduce the notion of perceptual meaning analysis, by means of which perceptual information becomes conceptualized, thus enabling nonverbal thought. I suggest that the information derived from perceptual meaning analysis is couched in the form of image–schemas. These are spatial representations (not the same as images) that express fundamental meanings, such as PATH, SELF-MOTION, CAUSED MOTION, and CONTAINMENT. These meanings are combined to form concepts of animate and inanimate objects as well as the events in which objects partake.

. . . no verbal symbols can do justice to the fullness and richness of thought. (Dewey, 1930/1960)

The words or language, as they are written or spoken, do not seem to play any role in my mechanism of thought. The psychical elements which seem to serve as elements in thought are certain signs and more or less clear images which can be voluntarily produced and combined. (Einstein, cited in Holton, 1996)

Nativism Versus Empiricism

We come to the heart of the matter. How do babies construct their conceptual life? As we have seen, Piaget's solution was to assume that as action routines develop, they gradually become internalized and transformed into thought. But if babies do not need a well-developed action system before beginning to form concepts, how do they accomplish it?

What source of information about the world is available for them to use? There are really only two choices—either they use perceptual data to construct concepts or else they have an innate conceptual repertoire at their disposal. This, of course, is the classic divide between empiricism and nativism.

Philosophers such as Locke and Hume assumed that we form images of perceptual displays and then associate them with one another. Some such view has been part of psychology ever since. However, aside from laws of association, philosophy has not had much to say about how the transformation of perceptual data into concepts is accomplished. If images are merely reflections of the way the world looks and sounds, then meaning would be the same for everyone. In any case, mechanisms are needed to account for thought, and mechanisms are the province of psychologists. Psychologists, even while accepting an associative account of meaning, have been more likely to ask how exactly this transformation of percepts into concepts takes place. In my opinion, Piaget came the closest, and in spite of my ultimate disappointment in his account of early conceptual development, I believe he was, in important ways, on the right track. He understood that we need something more than percepts and associations among them to create meanings. Some kind of analysis of perceptual sights and sounds must be carried out if meaning-bearing symbols are to be formed.

Unfortunately, even among psychologists, a fairly superficial empiricism is common. For example, laboratory research has shown that infants can schematize their perception of common objects, such as horses or chairs, and so can recognize novel instances of these categories. Once we know that infants can form perceptual schemas of horses and chairs, do we need any other mechanism than the capacity for associated information to accrue to them? This view (e.g., Eimas, 1994) is appealing in its simplicity, but as we will see in later chapters, it glosses over, rather than solves, some serious problems.

The advantage of a nativist solution is that not all concepts need be empirically derived. If some or all of the conceptual system is innately specified, then there is a natural way of getting conceptualization started. This approach does not mean, of course, that no learning devices are required. No nativist (with the possible exception of Fodor, 1981) believes that infants are born knowing about theoretical physics or recipes for chicken soup. Rather, they believe that the essential elements are in situ, and associative learning can take care of the elaboration and development of these elements into complex thought. Thus, one of the main differences between nativist and empiricist views is not whether learning mechanisms are required but how many inborn constraints need to be fed into those learning devices along with perceptual data.

As Jerry Fodor (1981) put it: "Everybody's a Rationalist in the long run. Everybody accepts the requirement for a primitive conceptual basis . . . everybody accepts that primitive concepts are psychologically simple; everybody accepts that simple concepts are unlearned. What distinguishes Descartes' kind of Rationalism from, say, Locke's—in so far as they differ in their views about concept attainment—is an issue over how big the primitive basis actually is" (p. 315). Fodor's argument marches on to the conclusion that there must be a rich set of innate concepts. Along the way he suggests that both empiricists and nativists agree that there is a distinction between primitive and complex concepts and that the complex concepts get built out of the primitive ones by the operations of some sort of combinatorial apparatus. Both sorts of theories assume that the availability of primitive concepts is a function of environmental stimulation, and both assume that primitive concepts ("ideas") are innate. Notice that this use of the term *concept* is broader than the one adopted in this book.

Fodor provided a valuable service in making clear that there is more overlap in assumptions between nativism and empiricism than is often assumed. Nevertheless, it is also true that empiricism comes in many forms, and in my view, he presented an empiricist version as extreme as his own nativist conclusion that the entire stock of human concepts must be innate. For example, Fodor claimed that all empiricists agree that concepts are built up from a primitive sensory base that consists of simple, unstructured concepts. He thought they disagree only on how to formulate precisely the criterion that picks out the primitive concepts, not on their sensory nature or lack of internal structure.

I consider myself an empiricist but do not subscribe to these views. As I discuss shortly, the requirement that the earliest concepts be sensory and/or lack internal structure is not only unnecessary but also actually incorrect. The conceptual base I describe has its roots in environmental stimulation, as Fodor put it, but only in the trivial sense that all organismic functioning is related to environmental input. And, as we will see, even primitive concepts are structured. As George Lakoff (1987) pointed out, the concept of containment, for instance, is by its very nature structured—there must be an inside and an outside and a boundary between. The components of inside or outside themselves have no meaning beyond the overall structure of the concept.

Even though I deny that all empiricists agree with the assumptions Fodor ascribed to them, nevertheless he is surely right that the traditional split between nativism and empiricism is an oversimplified dichotomy. Some of the most interesting empirical work from the behaviorist period was that showing that even simple organisms are "prepared" to associate different kinds of responses with different kinds of stimuli. The laws of association are not strictly general. For example, it is not the case that the sights and sounds that co-occur with the onset of stomach pains become associated in aversive fashion. Rats associate a shocking stimulus with the pain it produces, but if they eat tainted food and later begin to feel pain, it is associated not with current stimuli but with the food eaten hours before (Garcia & Koelling, 1966). If organisms are more likely to make some associations than others, then they have innate biases—built-in constraints that are not innate concepts but feed into concept-forming mechanisms. Such findings presaged the cognitive revolution of the late 1950s, but the relevant point here is that all theoretical positions consist of some kind of mix of innate proclivities and learning from experience. The more extreme either position is, however, the greater danger it faces of sweeping important problems under the rug. Psychologists of the empiricist persuasion do not always give the notion of meaning due respect. Images or other representations of the appearance of objects are considered somehow to carry meaning in their own right. This mistake is so easy that we all make it at least some of the time. If you look at an object, you can just "see" it is a dog, and of course a dog is a meaningful object to us. Nativists, on the other hand, sometimes sweep inconvenient learning problems under the rug. At any point that it becomes difficult to figure out how concepts such as caused motion or goal could be learned from perceptual data alone, it is all too easy to assume that these are innate concepts that infants are "prepared" to understand. Hence there is a danger of proliferating built-in constraints.

Given that both sides agree that there are both innate and learned characteristics, I suspect that some of the heat in the current psychological debates between nativist and empiricist infant researchers arises because they typically talk about different topics. If we take Elizabeth Spelke (e.g., 1994) and Alan Leslie (e.g., 1994) as two prominent researchers with strong nativist leanings, their theoretical interests have centered on knowledge of a much broader kind than dogs or chairs. They have been concerned with how infants come to learn about objects in general—what, as discussed earlier, Piagetians call the object concept. How is it that infants learn that objects are solid and cannot pass through each other or be in two places at once, and especially that objects retain their properties when they are out of sight? How is it that infants learn about physical causality, that one object makes another move or that objects fall when unsupported? These concepts are not concepts of specific things; rather, they are ontological commitments. To ask whether these commitments are built in or learned is different from asking how an infant learns what a terrier, dog, or animal is. One can be a thoroughgoing nativist on the first issue—believing that we are born to conceive of objects in certain ways—and a thoroughgoing empiricist on the second—believing that all concepts of specific objects (terrier, dog, or animal) are learned from experience.

Although it is mainly the second issue that I address in this book—namely, how specific concepts are learned—I believe that some biases in the conceptual interpretation of perceptual data are built in. However, my approach has been to assume a minimal number of them. It is one thing to theorize that some understanding of objects qua objects must be part of our genetic makeup, but it is quite another to theorize that there are innate concepts of, say, animacy and inanimacy, not to mention dogs and chairs. The latter route leads to a proliferation of innate ideas, such as that taken in Fodor's (1981) tour de force. Genetic space is limited, and I assume it has more important tasks to accomplish than to build in knowledge about dogs and chairs, especially since a person can live a long and successful life without encountering either of these things. It may be too precious to expend even on ontological notions such as animacy. So we need to ask whether fundamental notions like animacy, upon which other concepts are built, can be learned from experience without benefit of any particular innate idea.

I have a further problem with the notion of innate concepts, other than the intuition that we should build in as few cognitive structures as possible. I don't know exactly what it would mean to say that the infant is born with a concept such as animacy. It may be that infants are born with a tendency to react differently to animate than to inanimate things. But we are searching for the origins of *concepts*, not the basis of procedural, sensorimotor responses that are "known" only implicitly. As we saw in the last chapter, these responses do not require contemplation or thought and in some cases do not even require conscious awareness, so they are far removed from the notion of a concept. A person can be innately responsive to animate things without being able to think about what an animate thing is and what it does.

At least some of the persisting arguments between nativists and empiricists (or constructivists) are due to a failure to make a distinction between implicit procedural knowledge and explicit conceptual knowledge. For instance, Spelke (1994) seems not to make a distinction between implicit perceptual knowledge about the way that objects move and concepts about objects that enable infants to reason about them. In writing about causality, she noted that 3-month-olds still have limited ability to perceive objects either by looking or by touching and also limited ability to act on objects. The fact that by this age they already know quite a bit about object motion suggested to her that "perceiving, acting, and reasoning develop in synchrony over the infancy period." This point of view, which merges perception and reasoning, led Spelke to conclude that initial knowledge is innate:

> If children are endowed with abilities to perceive objects,
> persons, sets, and places, then they may use their perceptual
> experience to learn about the properties and behavior of such
> entities. By observing objects that lose their support and fall,
> children may learn that unsupported objects fall; by observing
> people who move in the direction they are facing, children
> may learn that people look at the things they approach. It is
> far from clear how children could learn anything about the
> entities in a domain, however, if they could not single out
> those entities in their surroundings. For example, if children
> could not represent the object-that-loses-its-support as the
> *same object* as the object-that-falls (and as a different object from

the support itself), they might learn only that events in which something loses support are followed by events in which something falls (the object) and something remains at rest (the support). If children could not differentiate a person from an inanimate object, they might learn only that some things look where they move and other things do not. Learning systems require perceptual systems that parse the world appropriately. . . . Some evidence suggests that a common set of principles underlies both perception and reasoning about persons, sets, and places as well (see Carey and Spelke, 1994). If the same initial principles underlie perception and reasoning, however, then the principles could not be learned, because the child would have no other way to parse the stream of experience into the relevant entities. (pp. 438–439)

As this quote indicates, Spelke came to this view because of the assumption that the perceptual and conceptual systems share a common underlying set of principles. Carey and Spelke (1994) suggested that in the realm of inanimate objects, two of these principles common to both perception and reasoning are continuity of motion (objects move only on connected paths) and solidity (objects move only on unobstructed paths and cannot share the same spot at the same time). I would say in reply, to be sure, the conceptual system makes use of a perceptual system that parses the world into objects, sounds, and so forth, but that doesn't mean that the conceptual system follows the same principles as the perceptual system. Perception delivers objects and certainly provides information about continuous paths. However, it can do so without recourse to a conceptual system, and so it does not follow that the principles need be the same as those that govern our conceptual inferences. For example, Leslie (1994) argued that the perceptual system produces spatial descriptions, not mechanical ones such as solidity. As a result, it can produce illusions that the thinking mind rejects, indicating that the principles are not the same. He describes the Pulfrich double pendulum illusion in which the perceptual system shows one solid object moving through another, even while the thinking mind says: No, that can't be. Furthermore, it is not clear that the perceptual system must itself parse animate and inanimate objects as different.

As I plan to show, it may need only to parse both animates and inanimates as objects, letting experience with these objects shape our different conceptions of them.

I described in the previous chapter several ways in which the perceptual and conceptual systems differ. What may make them appear to be governed by the same principles is that infants derive concepts by operating on perceptual information. In that sense, percepts and concepts are closely related. However, to say concepts are derived from percepts does not imply a stage theory in which the infant proceeds from a perceptual (or sensorimotor) stage to a conceptual one. On the contrary, the conceptual system develops simultaneously and in parallel with the perceptual and motor systems. When I first wrote about how the conceptual system arises (Mandler, 1988), I stated that neither the perceptual system nor the conceptual system was derivative from the other. I meant by this to deny the notion of an exclusively sensorimotor stage and to stress that perceptual and conceptual development work in tandem. Because concepts in the first instance are derived by operating on perceptual information, in a weak sense concepts are being derived from percepts. But not in a stagelike fashion! I assume conceptual interpretation of what one perceives happens at least crudely from birth. This assumption does not imply an innate conceptual repertoire. Rather, what is innate is a mechanism that operates on perceptual information. I originally called this mechanism *perceptual analysis* (Mandler, 1988, 1992a). However, because this label implied to some people a solely perceptual process, rather than a conceptual process for extracting meaning, I have changed the label to *perceptual meaning analysis*.

Perceptual Meaning Analysis

It does not seem necessary to build in innate concepts. The extent to which it is necessary to build in innate underlying principles that guide the course of concept formation is less clear, because on this topic both evidence and theorizing are murkier. I assume there are at least a few innate biases in the mechanism involved. I first tackle how concepts might be learned and later discuss whether the mechanism acts the way it does because it is preprogrammed to treat spatial information in some ways rather than others.

I have suggested that a single innate mechanism of *perceptual meaning analysis* in conjunction with the innate characteristics of our perceptual systems can account for much of the early conceptual learning we find in babies (Mandler, 1988, 1992a). The function of perceptual meaning analysis is to analyze perceptual displays into meanings. Of course, these meanings might themselves be considered to be innate ideas, and if so then perhaps simplification would fly out the window. Importantly, however, most meanings that are extracted from perceptual data do not have to be innate. One of the advantages of this approach to conceptual learning is that it allows new ideas to be formed from scratch at any stage of development. It is possible to notice a sight or sound (or event) one has not noticed before, to attend to it, and to analyze it in greater and greater detail. This process can result in new ideas that were not present before because the data were unknown in the sense of being conceptually unanalyzed. This approach to concept formation does not require hypothesis testing, the rock on which Fodor's (1981) theory of concept formation foundered. As Fodor pointed out, to test a hypothesis you must have some idea of what you are looking for, and in that sense the concept to be formed must already be present. Infants analyzing perceptual displays do not do so with hypotheses in mind. They merely apply an analytic mechanism to what they are looking at. This mechanism asks: How shall I interpret that? and not Could that be a . . . ? Nevertheless, there must be a core of possible meanings that human creatures can extract by means of this mechanism. Why is this meaning extracted rather than that meaning? Why do infants analyze some kinds of displays rather than others? Innate biases there certainly seem to be, and I discuss what some of these may be in more detail later in this chapter.

Before proceeding, I should probably point out that there are many different definitions of *meaning* and *concepts*. In my terminology, meanings are either concepts or components of concepts, and a conceptual system is a system of accessible knowledge. Infants interpreting the world are ascribing meaning to what they perceive, and those meanings form concepts. Infants' concepts refer to the world, even though they do so less completely than do those of adults and from the adult point of view are often mistaken. Medin and Heit (1999) suggested that because reference is to some extent a matter for experts to determine and because meaning includes relations between concepts and referents, the study of concepts doesn't provide a full account of meaning. But the view I take of meaning does not have to do with reference as a province of experts. For purposes of understanding infants' concepts—or adult concepts, for that matter—it doesn't matter what the "true" definition of a mammal or a bird is, only what the person thinks it is.

When I first wrote about perceptual analysis (Mandler, 1988), I conceived of the mechanism as a comparator—a device to compare one perceptual display with another—so that similarities and differences could be noted. (In all cases when I talk about perceptual displays and perceptual meaning analysis, audition and touch are meant to be included. Because so much of the available research has emphasized vision, however, the examples I use are almost exclusively visual.) In later writing (e.g., Mandler, 1992a), I played down the comparative notion, in part because adults' comparisons are usually made by means of already formed concepts and so are somewhat misleading as examples of infant analysis, and also because comparison implies too much a process like vicarious trial and error, or VTEing (Muensinger, 1938), in which the organism actually looks first at one thing and then at another. Of course, VTEing does appear to be a kind of analysis—one has only to watch a rat hesitating in the choice point of a maze, its whiskers alert, looking back and forth between one arm of the maze and the other, to be convinced the creature is comparing the two alternatives. But comparison is only part of what perceptual meaning analysis is about, so in later writing I began to deemphasize it.

Nevertheless, comparison is a useful notion to convey the thoughtful, attentive aspect of perceptual meaning analysis. This thoughtfulness can be observed in infants as young as 3 to 4 months—what Werner and Kaplan (1963) called the contemplative attitude. It is presumably related to the increase in shifts in attention between two stimuli presented at the same time that begins to happen around the same age (see chapter 3, note 2). Comparison is what we are doing when we notice for the first time that an apple can be green. I watched my young granddaughter engage in this process one time. She asked for an apple and accepted the one offered to her. Only after some time had passed did she appear to notice that it was not the expected color and said, "I thought apples were red." I do not know what brought the different color to her attention, but when it did, she expanded her concept of apples—they come in two colors.

It is difficult to convince people how often we "look without seeing," not consciously registering what is impinging on our sensorium. We are surprised at experiments such as those of O'Regan, Rensink, and Clark (1999), showing that sometimes even large changes in scenes we are looking at go unnoticed. These authors conclude that "humans' internal representation of the visual field is much sparser than the subjective experience of 'seeing' suggests. Only the parts of the environment that observers attend to and encode as interesting are available for making comparisons" (p. 34). As discussed in chapter 3, inattentional blindness (Mack & Rock, 1998) is probably the fate for much of the perceptual information we process. (The same thing is true for storage in long-term memory: Even when we are trying to memorize a scene, what we find uninteresting or ordinary may be attended but is processed so poorly that major changes to the boring bits often go unrecognized at a later time; Friedman, 1979; Mandler & Johnson, 1976.)

It is easy to pick up an apple and not be aware of its color. Our thoughts are on more important things, and our accustomed sensorimotor habits carry us through our expected routines. As discussed in the last chapter, this nonconscious looking is a very different use of perception from the conscious analysis of what we are looking at. It is the conscious use of perception that typically will teach a child that apples and tomatoes are both red. It is possible—perhaps even the rule—to encounter tomatoes and learn what they taste like, and also to encounter apples and learn what they taste like, without making the observation that they have the same color. At some point the color of one or the other will be actively noticed, and the conceptual expansion takes place. Similarly, it is perfectly possible for a child to drink from a two-handled cup for some time before noticing that it differs from her parents' cups. These kinds of expansion are a result of comparison, albeit one that may occur between a present experience and a remembered one, rather than between two present experiences. It is an example of what G. Mandler has called elaborative processing (G. Mandler, 1979). It is the conscious relating of one item to another that makes them enter the declarative, conceptual knowledge store and therefore possible to recall at a later date.

Of course, the creation of an addition to one's concept of apples (they can be green as well as red) does not mean that no information about apples coming in different colors had been processed before the perceptual meaning analysis took place. We take in a great deal of information about objects whenever we encounter them, all of which influences our behavior to some extent. So my granddaughter did not appear startled to receive a green apple, as she might have been if it were covered in purple stripes. She just did not consciously know that apples can be either red or green until she engaged in a bit of perceptual meaning analysis.

It is relatively easy to illustrate the comparative aspect of perceptual meaning analysis. But at least for infants, comparison is not the most crucial aspect. For them, the crucial thing about perceptual meaning analysis is that it is a concept-making engine, transforming perceptual information into another form. The examples I just gave of apples and tomatoes involve analysis of a somewhat trivial sort and involve only the use of already formed concepts. My granddaughter already had a concept of apple when she perceptually analyzed a green one. It is for this reason that examples of the kinds of comparison that older children and adults engage in are somewhat misleading when used to illustrate infant mental activity. A young baby doesn't have a concept of apple in the first place. The baby only has the ability to attend to and analyze perceptual displays. These analyses result in the meanings that are used to create concepts such as apple. Indeed, before language, perceptual meaning analysis appears to be the only way that concepts can be formed.

It is difficult to describe this concept-forming or meaning-forming process because we use our adult concepts to understand it. But I will illustrate it with a hypothetical example. Assume babies do not at first have a concept of animal. How do they use perceptual meaning analysis to create it? They see many examples of animate things around them. Most of these are presumably people, rather than other kinds of animals, but for present purposes that doesn't matter. In the first month or so, visual acuity is not great, so infants are not getting high-quality foveal information about what the objects moving around them look like. But they can parse the world into objects because of their coherence against the background when the objects move (Kellman & Spelke, 1983), and they also get good information about at least three aspects of the movement of these objects. First, by 3 months (the youngest age studied) they discriminate biological motion from nonbiological motion for both people (Bertenthal, 1993) and other mammals (Arterberry & Bornstein, 2001). Second, by 2 months (again the youngest age studied) they treat objects that act contingently with them as animates, as shown by smiling at them (Frye, Rawling, Moore, & Myers, 1983; Legerstee, 1992; Watson, 1972). Third, infants between 4 and 6 months (again the earliest ages studied) are responsive to the difference between an object beginning to move without anything else coming in contact with it and an object moving when touched by another (Leslie, 1982, 1984).

I see no reason for responsivity to any of these factors to be built in as part of an innate concept of animate thing. We do not need to build in a special sensitivity to recognize people or other animals as animate things because it "comes for free" as a result of the perceptual system's ability to discriminate various motion parameters. Work in robotics suggests that a very few parameters, such as coupled oscillation of limbs and minimization of jerk, account for the appearance of biological motion (Wilson, 1986). I have been told that another factor involves the rhythmic changes that take place in the center of gravity in relation to the medium in which the movement is carried out. In similar fashion, the processing of contingencies between one movement and another is part of the very general capacity of organisms to respond to contingent events. That capacity is the basis for associative learning and indeed must be innate. Something similar can be hypothesized about noticing self-movement. Infants are responsive to motion from birth (Haith, 1980), but because they cannot at first see objects very clearly, especially rapidly moving objects, it is much more likely that they will process whether two objects meet before motion begins than the figural details of either of them. Thus, the early differentiation between animate and inanimate objects may be due to the kind of perceptual system we inherit rather than to some kind of innate concept of what an animal is. We do construct such a primitive ur-concept, one that still influences sophisticated adults with years of biological education (see chapter 9). But that earliest conception of animal seems to be due largely to characteristics of the perceptual system in conjunction with its immature state in the first month or so of life.

Each of these three discriminations—biological versus nonbiological motion, contingent motion, and self- versus other-instigated motion—

is by itself a simple perceptual discrimination. None of them alone, or even a combination of them, constitutes a concept of animal. These pieces of perceptual data need to be redescribed via perceptual meaning analysis into an accessible format in order to qualify as concepts. The claim I am making is that this redescription process can, and probably does, begin early in infancy. Whenever infants gaze (or listen) attentively, they are in a position to analyze what is being perceived into simplified and more abstract representations. And what they attend to tends to be motion rather than figural detail. Bahrick, Gogate, and Ruiz (2002) showed that even at 5½ months infants are more likely to process and maintain information about what people around them are doing than what they look like. In these experiments infants watched videos, all of which showed close-ups of faces doing actions such as brushing teeth or hair. However, neither the objects being used nor the faces of the actors were encoded as well as the activities themselves. Attention sets the stage for analysis, and as I discuss in the next section on image-schemas, I hypothesize that spatial representation is the basic format of these analyses—for example, the paths that objects take as they participate in the variety of spatial relations that we call events.

Consider again the baby who has not yet developed expectations about the world, whose foveal acuity is still poor, but whose attention is attracted to moving objects (Arterberry, Craton, & Yonas, 1993; Kellman, 1993). What might this infant notice about events like the following? She sees an object nearby, she cries, the object begins to move, approaches, looms, and she is picked up. Leaving aside details such as whether she has already begun to form a perceptual schema of the "face" of the object (Johnson & Morton, 1991), she might not be able to analyze much more than that an object began to move independently of the rest of the surround, moved on a somewhat irregular path, did so contingently on her cries, and ended up by interacting with her. This simple description illustrates the three characteristics of animate things I just described. What I believe that perceptual meaning analysis does with an event of this sort is to pick out movement-related aspects of a highly complex scene and put them into a simpler and more abstract form. Even if the baby abstracts only something about the trajectory of the moving object, the way the trajectory begins and ends, and the contingency between the trajectory and her own behavior, she will have gone a long way toward conceptualizing an object as animate. As we have seen, there is ample evidence that from an early age infants do differentiate animate from inanimate objects. Perceptual meaning analysis is the mechanism by which such differentiations become conceptualized.

Notice that although conceptualizations of animate and inanimate things result from perceptual meaning analysis, the mechanism itself does not require comparison of one kind of motion with another. The baby can analyze self-motion, for instance, simply by observing that an object began to move in the absence of any other object touching it. It is because these early analyses may take place without a simultaneous comparison of two objects moving at the same time that I have come to discuss perceptual meaning analysis less as a comparator than as an analyzer. Comparison of more than one kind of thing in a given perceptual display may well make analysis easier, creating the conditions for what Gentner and Markman (1997) call structural alignment, but it is not essential. You do not have to contrast motion without contact to motion with contact to analyze either one. Comparison of a thing with a previously established representation, as in the case of apples discussed earlier, may also make analysis easier, but it, too, is not essential. The analysis itself, however, *is* essential to creating a representation that will serve as a meaning. It is also essential that these meanings can become combined to form complex concepts, although they do not need to be combined all at once; for instance, the infant might analyze contingent interaction before noticing and analyzing self-motion.

Peter Eimas (1994) claimed that the mechanism of perceptual meaning analysis is "special purpose," devised solely to account for categorization data, making it ad hoc and an unnecessary proliferation of cognitive mechanisms. However, perceptual meaning analysis serves a crucial function in the mind: It creates accessible concepts out of perceptual data, thereby allowing the mind to think about both past and future events. It is true that this formulation denies there is only one kind of learning, a single process that operates on every and all kinds of information. Perceptual meaning analysis operates differently from the implicit accrual of information that takes place in ordinary perception, as discussed in chapter 3. And the mechanism does have a specific function, namely, to put information into a conceptual store. It would be surprising if the mind were so simple as to process all kinds of information, both attended and unattended, in exactly the same way.

My theory of perceptual meaning analysis is related to that of Annette Karmiloff-Smith (1992), who also proposed that people form concepts by transforming procedural information. This capacity, which she called representational redescription, may be involved in a transition from a sensorimotor to a conceptual stage of thought, but it is more general than that. According to her theory, procedural information is continually redescribed as it becomes systematized. She suggested that initially in learning any new domain, information is encoded procedurally; in this form it is implicit and encapsulated. It may stay in this format for lengthy periods of time, but as experience continues with the domain, redescription begins to take place, leading to new representations that are stored independently of the procedures themselves. Because these are potentially available to the rest of the cognitive system, Karmiloff-Smith called them explicit but stressed that they are not yet accessible to consciousness; further redescription is required before the information can be brought to awareness or expressed linguistically. Thus, Karmiloff-Smith equated procedural knowledge with implicit knowledge, as do I, but divided explicit knowledge into several levels, the first of which, in the terminology used in this book, would still be implicit (not declarative) because it is not yet accessible to conscious awareness. In her view, still further redescription is required for that purpose. Her first "explicit" level may be roughly equivalent to a level of meanings such as the image-schemas I discuss in the next section. These form the underlying structure of conceptual knowledge but are not themselves accessible to awareness. It should be noted, however, that in my view image-schemas come from analyzing perceptual displays, not from the spontaneous redescription of previously learned perceptual procedures.

Many of the examples Karmiloff-Smith (1992) studied involve systematic aspects of highly familiar information. Indeed, one of her claims was that extensive periods of behavioral mastery typically precede representational redescription. For instance, she showed that French children do not become aware that the word *one* (*un*) stands for both a determiner and a number until several years after they have used the single form for both meanings without error. Similarly, children's drawing routines do not show the flexibility that allows them to be altered upon demand until several years of drawing experience have passed (Karmiloff-Smith, 1993). In this view, then, redescriptions take place on already procedurally encoded information; information is first encoded in implicit, inaccessible form, and only later is redescribed into explicit forms. Representational redescription does not take place through analysis of incoming data, but instead results from system-internal dynamics that make connections not there before.

Thus, Karmiloff-Smith's theory differs from mine in several crucial respects. I claim that all explicit knowledge is potentially accessible, even though it may be processed implicitly under some circumstances (see Figure 3-1). I also claim that information can be encoded directly into the declarative system, rather than arriving there via redescriptions of established procedural knowledge. That is, the redescription of incoming perceptual information into image-schemas takes place online and can take place even on new, unfamiliar sights. This issue is important for understanding concept formation in infancy. I do not believe that concepts are typically formed by redescribing well-established procedural information. There do not seem to be long periods of behavioral mastery in infancy before concepts about objects and events begin to be formed. If anything, Piaget's work showed us that many kinds of behavioral mastery are absent during this period. Rather than early concepts being derived from the redescription of systematized procedural knowledge, I claim that they are developed independently and in parallel with the procedural system. They are derived in the first instance from analysis of perceptual information, an analysis that allows them to be stored in an explicit, accessible format.

Nevertheless, Karmiloff-Smith's work does make evident that something akin to perceptual meaning analysis can take place on already established information and does not necessarily involve new incoming data. At this late stage in my life, I can still remember when I first realized that the word *breakfast* meant to break one's fast. The word was a part of my explicit, conceptual knowledge, but for years it remained unanalyzed into its component parts. Indeed, it could have functioned conceptually for a lifetime without such analysis taking place. Yet at some point (for reasons I no longer remember, although it may have been due to a primary school English teacher who encouraged analysis of words) I did analyze the word and discovered its separate parts. This example may be similar to Karmiloff-Smith's example of children eventually becoming aware of the relation between the single morpheme meaning both *one* and *a*.

The result of the early ability to conceptualize is that the post-Piagetian baby is no longer a purely sensorimotor creature who can act but not think. The new baby seems more congenial than the old one, because she is the kind of baby we adults can understand. As I discuss in the following pages, she is a baby who has formed concepts of animate and inanimate things. She interprets other people as agents. She understands events as sequences in which agents act on objects or in which objects cause changes in other objects. She can recall objects and events and can think about them. Finally, she is beginning to understand the world in such a way that language, which describes these kinds of understandings, can be learned. All these accomplishments are not infrequently used to describe what the 1½- to 2-year-old infant knows. They may also be what Piaget had in mind as the final accomplishments of the sensorimotor period, although he did not use this vocabulary. My point here, however, is not only that these accomplishments occur considerably earlier but also that sensorimotor schemas are not adequate to represent them. Concepts are certainly required to think and to recall the past and perhaps even to understand sequences in terms of agents acting on objects. These notions do not require a lengthy period of sensorimotor understanding to enable them; rather, they develop from a separate base—the analysis of observed data, not established action routines. (In addition to analysis of the events infants observe around them, their own action routines can also be analyzed, as in the example discussed in chapter 2 of Piaget's daughter analyzing opening and closing her hand. The crucial component of conceptualization is the analysis, not the source of the data being analyzed.) Piaget himself understood that at least some of these kinds of accomplishments require conceptual thought; he just didn't have the data that would have told him thought begins so early in life and that therefore their dependence on sensorimotor development was suspect.

Piaget also assumed that the first concepts—in his view, transformations of sensorimotor schemas into a symbolic form—constitute the basis on which language develops, but he did not specify their representational format. Until recently there has been no theory of how the first concepts are represented, perhaps because it has been easier to confine the study of early concepts to the words that newly verbal children use. But concepts and words are not the same thing, and to assess concepts only through the linguistic system, especially a system that is in the process of being formed, will surely distort our picture of what the earliest concepts are like. Even more serious, the first concepts are formed long before language begins, so their origins must be nonlinguistic in nature.

Image-Schemas as a Conceptual Format

It is consideration of linguistic form that has led many philosophers (and psychologists after them) to assume that conceptual representation is propositional in nature. We appear to think in sentences, whose components are concepts couched in propositional format. Not only is this phenomenal experience of thought as equivalent to language at least somewhat illusory but also it is of no use in understanding prelinguistic representation. My introspection says I think in English sentences, but is a Korean baby going to think in English sentences? Obviously not, nor in Korean sentences either. What is needed is a more universal representational format, one that is not specifically language based but still suitable for learning whatever language one's native tongue will turn out to be. In short, what is needed is what Fodor (1975) called a language of thought, although it certainly does not need to resemble natural language as much as Fodor's formulation implies. One would, however, expect it to have some characteristics common to language in general. For example, these characteristics might underlie the universal grammar sought by many linguists. Whether or not there is a universal grammar, however, prelinguistic thought must bear some relationship to the characteristics common to languages everywhere; otherwise, language would be difficult if not impossible to learn.

There are various approaches one could take to the format in which the earliest concepts are couched. I present one here, but I emphasize that even if one disagrees with the view on offer, specifying the vocabulary of concepts is a problem that *cannot* be avoided, no matter what one's theory of conceptual development. I should probably also emphasize how little this issue has been discussed in the literature. Aside from researchers who have discussed the primitives involved in the first causal and number concepts (e.g., Carey, 2001; Gelman & Gallistel, 1978; Leslie, 1988), about the only researchers who have discussed the issue of the representation of the first concepts are those in the field of language acquisition who have talked about preverbal or semantic primitives, such as containment or support (see chapter 11). Although these formulations attempted to specify the contents of conceptual primitives, they left their format unspecified.

The approach to prelinguistic conceptual representation that I have developed was inspired by the work of cognitive linguists, in particular Mark Johnson (1987) and George Lakoff (1987), but also Gilles Fauconnier (1994), Ronald Langacker (1987), and Leonard Talmy (1987). These theorists, although not developmentalists, are interested in the underlying basis of the concepts expressed in language. This quest has a natural affinity with development. Some of the concepts expressed in language must be preverbal, because it is these on which language acquisition rests. A basic claim of cognitive linguistics is that one of the foundations of the conceptualizing capacity (in or out of language) is the ability to form image-schemas. Image-schemas are spatial representations that express primitive or fundamental meanings. *Primitive* in this sense means foundational, not that image-schemas are atomic, unitary, or without structure. For example, containment is a primitive notion, but it requires both an inside and an outside. Common image-schemas are notions such as PATH, CONTAINMENT, UP-DOWN, and LINK. All of them are simplifications of spatial structure. The image-schema PATH is the simplest conceptualization of any object following any trajectory through space, without regard to the characteristics of the object or the details of the trajectory itself—it is merely something moving through space. CONTAINMENT is conceived of as something in any fully or partially enclosed space— that is, a bounded space with an inside and an outside—again without specifying any details of the appearance of the thing or the container.

Cognitive linguists speak about image-schemas as lying at the core of people's understanding of events and of the metaphorical extensions of these concepts to more abstract realms. A simple event of two people walking together hand in hand can be understood by conjoining a PATH and a LINK schema, but so can a marriage. The first example is a physical linkage between two people taking a common path. The second is a metaphorical extension to the realm of abstract paths, in which two people are linked together by following a common path through life (Lakoff & Johnson, 1980).

For purposes of understanding the first concepts, we need to understand how such representations are derived. I have hypothesized that image-schemas are derived from the process of perceptual meaning analysis described in the last section (Mandler, 1992a). Perceptual meaning analysis redescribes the spatial and movement structure of perceptual displays. This perceptual information is derived in the usual case from vision, but it also can be provided by touch, audition, and even one's own movements. (Even though spatial information can be gleaned from both audition and touch, and must be in the case of blind infants, we are visual creatures and get better spatial information from vision than from our other senses. This difference is presumably responsible for the initially somewhat slower conceptual development of blind infants.) Thus, the image-schemas that perceptual meaning analysis creates are analog representations that summarize spatial relations and movements in space.

Note that although image-schemas are used in image construction, they are not visual images but schematic spatial representations. Their analog character means that they are not unitary, as are the words commonly used in propositional representations. Image-schemas may serve the same function as words in infants' thought, but they are not static units in the way that words are. They are dynamic representations that can change their focus (Lakoff, 1987). As we will see in the next chapter, the focus of PATH changes as one considers its start, the path itself, or its end point. Nevertheless, image-schemas are often simple enough for words or brief phrases to be substituted for them, and they could, if one had some reason to want to, be combined into propositions; they are productive. Image-schemas fit most naturally, however, into a mental space form of representation, such as described by Langacker (1987, 2000) for language and by Fauconnier (1994) and Fauconnier and Turner (2002) for reasoning and thought.

I stress that image-schemas are *not* images, because this is often mistakenly believed to be the case. This, in fact, is where the debate between the imagists and the propositionalists that took place in the late 1970s went wrong.[1] It was apparently not understood by either side, including the imagery folk, that analog representations do not have to be perceptual or consist of images. One of the arguments against imagistic representations surfaced recently in a discussion of my views on the origins of concept formation (Carey & Markman, 1999). They say:

> Mandler . . . assumes that early perceptual redescription results in a dynamic analog code ("image-schemas") rather than a propositional code. Her justification for this assumption is that a propositional code uses symbols that themselves must be interpreted. This in turn implies either that the symbols must be innately specified or that there must be some other mechanism for interpreting them. Mandler (1992) believes that an image-schema finesses this problem because 'its meaning resides in its own structure.' Thus, Mandler is suggesting that the process of perceptual redescription provides a course of conceptual representations that obviates the need for positing innate concepts.
>
> The same questions about interpretation that Mandler raises about propositional codes arise in the case of imagistic codes. As Mandler (1988, 1992) argues, because image-schemas are schematic they contain much less information than their corresponding perceptions. But no matter how abstract the image, more is encoded than abstractions such as *path, containment*, and *goal*. To take Mandler's example, suppose all that children represent from an event is *path*—that an object has moved from one place to another. Direction and speed are not represented. In a given dynamic iconic representation, however, the path must have some direction, speed, and so on. How does the child know to interpret that iconic image as representing *path* alone, ignoring speed, location, and local details for direction? Thus, even iconic representation of the sort Mandler proposes requires interpretation of symbols and thus is not, in that sense, an advantage over a propositional system. . . . (p. 234)

The mistake that I believe is made in this quotation is the assumption that image-schemas are a form of imagery and so must retain iconic information about speed and direction that the infant then has to ignore when using the image-schema to represent a meaning. It is correct that image-schemas are abstracted from perceiving objects in space, but they eliminate figural details, including many details of movement. They are not temporary constructions, as are images, but permanent representations of meaning. And although like images they are analog representations, they are not visual ones. I usually refer to them as spatial representations, but that may be misleading, too, because many spatial representations do include information about the direction of moving objects. However, image-schema representations are not just simplified images. Furthermore, they are not conscious and can be neither attended to nor ignored.

It is possible to represent a shape without an orientation, a path without a direction, or stripes without a representation of their number (see Barsalou, 1999, for discussion of this issue). Different neural pathways are involved in handling these different kinds of information. That is, both perception and image-schemas are constructed out of bits and pieces, and the bits and pieces can be represented separately. An image-schema is a little like the representation one is left with when one has forgotten most of the details of an event. You may remember an object moved from one place to another and came to rest by another object, but you have no accessible information about the directions involved. There is solely a spatial relation of one object joining up with another. A precise realization of this kind of notion is exemplified by Terry Regier's (1995) connectionist model of learning spatial terms. The architecture of the model has several information-reducing characteristics somewhat similar to those suggested here. One of these is that it represents paths in terms of starting and ending points and a *nonsequential* static representation of what occurs on the path between these points. Although it seems odd to our ordinary declarative thought, which has trouble thinking about a path without any sequential order, and which typically does include figural details of events (at least for a while), it is not that difficult to design a spatial representational system that selectively ignores various sources of information. Of course, language does this, too! We are quite comfortable with a linguistic representation of a path or of an object abutting another that does not mention direction or orientation, so we ought not to be confounded when an analog representation does so as well.

A more familiar way of considering the sparsity of information in image-schemas is to relate them to topological representations. An image of a container, for example, must have a particular shape, and the material inside it either conforms to the shape of the container or not, but a topological representation of this relation eliminates this information, leaving only the topological relation of a bounded space with an inside and an outside. In this sense, image-schemas are topological: They simply do not include some of the information that might be in an image. They are such a spare form of representation that they approach symbolic representation in which discrete symbols such as <move> or <stop> are used instead. Thus, the reduction of the information in image-schemas approaches the reduction of information in words (or other symbols), but the reduction is not arbitrary, as it is with words or other symbols, and there remain in image-schemas more continuous aspects and more complexity. The image-schema of containment, discussed in detail in chapter 5, can be characterized as consisting of a boundary plus an inside and an outside. The boundary is continuous, and inside and outside are parts of the same image-schema. Thus, the image-schema is not unitary in the way symbols are. However, the most important difference is that the reduction is not arbitrary. It reflects the structure of the spatial information being analyzed. A great deal of information is lost in the process, but the resulting representation can be traced back to its perceptual source. Perceptual information includes topological information, so that the original scene can be described in topological rather than Euclidean terms. Image-schemas are not quite the same as topological representations—for example, ABOVE and BELOW are not topological concepts but are good image-schemas—but both these types of representation refute the notion that imagistic information must include all the types of perceptual information provided by the environment.

This issue may be relatively unimportant at this stage of our understanding of how the conceptual system is put together. An image-schema might be represented by a numerical vector or as a component of a mental space (Fauconnier, 1994). The crucial difference between an image-schema and a symbol, however, is that, whatever its exact format, an image-schema encapsulates a meaning by its structure. The topological notion of a bounded region has structure, and so does an image-schema of containment. That is the nontrivial issue here, namely, how to solve the symbol grounding problem (Harnad, 1991). As Stevan Harnad and others have pointed out, there must be a way for symbols to acquire meaning; otherwise, we are left with a Chinese room in which we can speak Chinese but without any idea of what it says (see Searle, 1980).

The solution, I suggest, is that whether vectors or abstract analog structures are used, meaning is grounded by being extracted from perceptual information and directly represented by its format, not by assigning perceptual information to an otherwise arbitrary symbol. It is soon enough to deal with arbitrary symbols when language begins to be learned!

The image-schema formulation I discuss here has a good many affinities with Larry Barsalou's (1999) perceptual symbols. Indeed, he sometimes uses the term *image-schemas* to refer to them (e.g., Figure 1, p. 578). He describes perceptual symbols as productive componential representations extracted from perception by selective attention and stored permanently in long-term memory. Many of the ideas propounded in this book could fit fairly easily into Barsalou's system. The main difference, I believe, is that Barsalou doesn't make, or at least doesn't emphasize, a distinction in format between perception and perceptual symbols. As a result, perceptual symbols are not as clearly differentiated from perception itself as are the image-schemas I discuss here. Perceptual symbols are more framelike than individual percepts, because the extracted pieces summate and so wipe out incidental detail, but in his system both perception and conception seem to convey pretty much the same information. In contrast, I emphasize the different format of image-schemas; although derived from perception, they characterize information in a different vocabulary that then results in a different kind of processing. The distinction between implicit and explicit processing follows naturally from this difference in the way information is stored. However, without further specification of perceptual symbols, it is not certain whether this is a major or minor disagreement. A more obvious difference in our accounts is that I emphasize the developmental aspects of the processes Barsalou proposes. For example, he does not specify why attention focuses on some features rather than others, or how the cognitive system learns to categorize the world or to form the abstractions that enable inductive inferences. Nevertheless, in spite of some differences in emphasis there is a close affinity between our two approaches.

This discussion raises still another issue: What constraints or biases must one build into the system in order to extract the fundamental spatial information found in image-schemas? Assuming that the essentials of events can be described by spatial descriptions, can all of these be learned merely from observing events, or must there be constraints built into the system to extract some kinds of information rather than others? It seems almost certain that some innate constraints or biases are built in. After all, humans all do end up thinking like humans and not like camels. One way of constraining learning is found in structured connectionist systems, such as Regier's, in which the architecture of the system has characteristics that both facilitate learning and limit it. In the Regier (1995) model, for instance, events are parsed into source, path, and destination. A source buffer contains a representation of a starting configuration of a trajector (a moving object), and at the last time step a current buffer contains a representation of the ending configuration. A set of motion buffers builds up the static representation of the path between the two. These constraints are the equivalent of innate biases to emphasize beginnings and endings of paths. It seems clear that some such biases must be built into the human system as well. At this point we have little idea of how much in the way of innate specifications are required. I suspect the set need not be large. A small number of spatial primitives may be sufficient to form the bedrock of the emergent conceptual system, as well as the language system that rests upon it (see chapter 11).

We can get some clues by examining the earliest conceptual notions that seem to be formed. Let's look at a simple image-schema such as PATH a little more closely, to get an idea of how it might be constructed. From birth, infants see objects moving through space. At first they probably get relatively little figural detail from moving objects, but each can be seen as following a path. They almost certainly would not represent speed and perhaps not anything about location, although infants often see an object beginning to move or coming to rest (both of which frequently often involve abrupt changes in motion), and these aspects of events can also be represented in image-schematic form. In the very simplest form, the image-schema would simply be PATH itself, a trajectory unspecified as to speed, direction, jerkiness or smoothness, or any other figural aspect.

However, because image-schemas are analog, they can have parts, as in the CONTAINMENT schema discussed earlier. In the case of PATH, one could focus on the path of an object, or on its beginning or ending. In this sense, image-schemas can embed. BEGINNING-OF-PATH is embedded in PATH, as is ENDING-OF-PATH. At the same time, each of these is an image-schema in its own right. One can notice (or think) successively about each aspect of an object's trajectory—how it begins, how it moves through space, and where it ends up. Because an image-schema may contain information about the end of its path, that might be represented as another object without any information about the spatial location of either object. Thus, infants can use perceptual meaning analysis to conceptualize and store information about paths and their parts in the form of image-schema representations. It is the image-schemas that constitute their conceptualization of what is being observed and that then enable access for recall and thought at a later time. (As discussed later, we are not conscious of image-schemas when we recall, but we use the information contained in them to structure the images of which we are conscious.)

So our conceptualizing baby is observing what the objects around her are doing, in the sense that she is analyzing the paths the objects take (in addition to whatever figural information she is able to extract). To the extent that she analyzes the paths themselves, she will be able to recode biological and nonbiological motion into ANIMATE-MOTION and INANIMATE-MOTION, discussed further in the next chapter. To the extent that she analyzes the relation of one path to another, she will be able to observe contingent motion and recode it into LINK image-schemas, also discussed in the next chapter. To the extent that she notices the beginning of a given path, she will be able to analyze that the object either starts up on its own or that another object comes in contact with it. This information can be recoded into image-schemas of SELF-MOTION and CAUSED-MOTION. These are the notions that are combined into the first concepts of animate and inanimate things. (Each image-schema represents a single meaning or concept. A great many concepts, however, are complex, consisting of more than one meaning. Animal is one of these.) These recodings into image-schemas provide infants with a meaning for objects such as animate thing. For an infant, an animate thing (by which we should understand animal, not plant; see chapter 9) is something that starts up on its own, moves in a rhythmical and often somewhat irregular way, and interacts contingently with other objects, often from a distance. This is not a bad first definition of an animal, and it appears to be the foundation on which all later conceptions of animals are built. Similarly, an inanimate thing either doesn't move at all, or when it does move, it does so only when something else contacts it, it moves on regular paths, and it does not interact contingently with the infant (or other objects) from a distance. These ideas are expanded in the next chapter, along with discussion of relevant experimental data, but are outlined here to indicate that these spatial notions are sufficient to constitute an early meaning of animal or animate thing and object or inanimate thing.

An important question is why the earliest meanings should be spatial descriptions, rather than, say, a figural description of what a particular kind, such as a person or a chair, looks like. There are at least two likely reasons. The first reason, as I have discussed, may be the limited perceptual capacity of young babies; spatial relations and movements are available to them earlier than are the figural details of objects' perceptual appearance. Although color is registered, shape is apt to be blurry, and infants in the first month often do not even scan the interior of objects and so get few of the details that identify particular kinds for adults (Salapatek & Kessen, 1966). Of course, this situation does not last for long; acuity and other perceptual capacities rapidly improve over the first few months. And that's a good thing, too, because it will become just as important to recognize individual kinds as to characterize their animate or inanimate status. But I assume that infants strive after meaning more or less from birth and use their capacity for perceptual meaning analysis for that purpose almost from birth as well. If so, the first fruits of their analyses will be limited by poor acuity and dependent upon what can be gleaned from movement and the low spatial frequencies involved in spatial relations. Thus, one reason for the spatial basis of meaning is because that's how it starts, and later meanings are built up on the basis of the earlier ones.

Second, and in the long run much more important, the meaning of objects for human beings ultimately depends on what they do or what is done to them, as Katherine Nelson pointed out many years ago (Nelson, 1974). If the world stood still, there would be no conceptual mind—it is events that demand interpretation: What is happening? What is going on? Although it is possible that it is solely the attraction to motion that sets up perceptual meaning analysis in terms of paths and their characteristics, it seems more likely that what infants attend to and analyze for meaning is one of those indirect innate factors, determined perhaps by the needs of the species. What objects do and what is done to them is crucial, whether that be to threaten or nurture, as something to be eaten or to hold water. It is hard to see how we could be the tool-using species we are without some way to capture for ourselves the meaning of containers, supporters, pullers, carriers, and so forth. No one would dispute that what things do is important for meaning, but the position espoused here is stronger than that. What things do is the *core* of their meaning, and for some time in infancy it is the only meaning that is available. Young infants have no notion of the social uses of objects, for example, why one drinks from glasses and not from cooking pots. They have no notion of why we sleep in beds rather than in bathtubs. Even if some recognition of conspecifics is built in (Johnson & Morton, 1991), the meaning of these and other animate things is the way in which they interact with the baby—for better or for worse. Thus, paying attention to what things do seems likely to be an innate bias of a very general sort. It is possible that this bias consists of no more than to attend to moving things over non-moving things (probably a widespread organismic bias). In any case, for the human infant it focuses meaning analyses on the way in which things move and how they move vis-à-vis each other. This is why I have suggested that the earliest meaning analyses and resultant image-schemas involve paths and their associated characteristics of going in or out, going up or down, linking together, and so forth, rather than figural information about what objects look like.

We are spatial creatures to be sure, but are we not also temporal creatures? Do infants not analyze time as well as space? I suspect not. Infants may have no concept of time. Even as adults, we seem unable to think about time independently of space. As Guyau (1890/1988) described it: "We can easily imagine space; we have an inner eye for it, an intuition. Try, on the other hand, to represent time as such; you will only succeed by means of a representation of space. You will have to align successive events, placing one at some point along the line, and the other at a second point. In other words, you must evoke a sequence of spatial images in order to represent time" (p. 99).

Guyau suggested that we conceive of time in terms of a path from then to now, that is, as a path from one location (the past) to another (the present). But we sometimes also conceive of time as a path that flows past us rather than as a path that we move along (Boroditsky, 2000). These conceptions differ somewhat, but both involve PATH. We have specific linguistic terms to refer to time, but these, too, are spatially derived. Many linguists have noted that in all languages studied, temporal terms have a spatial sense as their primary meaning (H. Clark, 1973; Fillmore, 1982; Traugott, 1978). Of course, we have the intuition that we can tell the difference between a spatial path and a temporal path, so they can't be the same thing. I suspect this intuition arises because we do not usually make the distinction between procedural and declarative knowledge. We live in time, we act in time, and we can sense time passing when we engage in our daily sensorimotor routines. But this knowledge is not conceptual. When we think about time, when we try to say what it is to ourselves or others, we fall back on notions of a time *line*, a *passage* from *here* to *there*. In short, we cannot think of time in a nonspatial way. We know that time is not the same as space, but when we think about time it becomes spatialized.

This is an example of the way in which abstract ideas such as time are formed on the basis of our experience with the more concrete spatial realm. In a series of interesting studies Boroditsky and Ramscar (2002) showed that our concepts of time are so spatially imbued that recent spatial experiences can change the spatial way in which we conceive of time at the moment. For example, they found that people departing from a long plane trip were more likely to think of themselves moving along a time path rather than time flowing past them than were people who were waiting to depart. Interestingly, people waiting to depart were in turn more likely to think of themselves as moving through time than were those waiting to pick someone up. These authors concluded that it is not the recent sensorimotor spatial experience causing these differences, because even just thinking about taking a trip is sufficient to affect one's representation of time. Needless to say, I concur; conceptual representations are at issue, not actual sensorimotor experience.

Time is not the only abstract concept we spatialize. Take goals: We have internal goals and act according to them, but when we think about them (when we conceptualize what a goal is) we think of them as *ends*, *places* we are trying to *get to*. We talk about goal *paths*, of following a *path* or a *route* to some end. Obviously, space is not the same thing as meaning, but in addition to living in space and being able to think about living in space, we use space to enable conscious thought about nonspatial ideas. These include not only time but also goals and other abstract concepts such as marriage, discussed earlier, or comprehension (*taking in* or *grasping* an idea). I hope that this conclusion does not seem paradoxical. All it takes is to maintain a firm *grasp* on the distinction between being phenomenally aware of something such as time or space and the *way* we conceptualize it. The inability to clearly express the difference we feel between time and space may seem unsatisfying, but it is a result of the limits of our conceptual system. We cannot conceptualize everything we experience.

Needless to say, infants in the first year of life have not yet used their conceptions of space to understand highly abstract domains such as marriage or comprehension. In principle, however, they already have the means at their disposal to do as adults do when constructing abstract concepts, namely, to use spatial analogies to understand abstract realms (Gentner, 1983; Gibbs, 1994; Lakoff & Johnson, 1980). Indeed, the use of spatial image-schemas to construct abstract understanding can already be seen in the concepts of animal and agency, discussed at greater length in the next chapter.

Concepts of Kinds and Identification of Kinds

The bias to attend to how things move in relation to each other means that the analysis of objects into different kinds of things emphasizes events and the "roles" that objects take in events. Infants must learn to identify particular kinds of things, and as we will see in chapter 6, they are capable of enough perceptual ability to enable them to distinguish one kind from another by around 2 to 3 months of age. In terms of understanding what objects are, however, babies need to know what they do or what is done to them, and their initial understanding tends to be more global and less detailed than the perceptual information they use to identify them. This distinction between identification of a kind and its meaning has not always been made, and when it has not, debate has followed. A good example is one that was raging when I first began to do developmental work. Nelson (1973a) showed that infants used the function of balls to decide which objects were balls. Tomikawa and Dowd (1980) riposted: No, shape and other perceptual factors are crucial in determining what infants will decide are balls. With hindsight, it seems likely that such a debate would not have happened if researchers at the time had distinguished clearly between identifying a member of the class of balls (where shape is important) and determining if something actually is a ball (where rolling is the crucial variable).

The relative roles played by function and perceptual similarity is an old debate in the developmental literature, and I discuss it at some length in later chapters, although in infancy "function" is often quite a primitive conception. Here it is sufficient to note that perceptual identification is obviously crucial to psychological functioning, but the information that enables it to take place is not necessarily part of the concept of a given object, as we saw in the case of recognizing faces in chapter 3. One must be able to identify what something is, but the figural details that support the distinguishing of one thing from another are not necessarily part of the concept. Although this may not be true in most cases for adults, who have had years of time to notice and analyze many details, it is likely to be the rule for infants. For example, as we shall see in chapter 8, infants typically seem to be unaware of the distinguishing parts that differentiate a cup from a saucepan or a dog from a horse; even though they see these differences, they don't actively notice them. An infant is much more likely to conceptualize something as an animate creature than as a dog, even though it may use legs, eyes, and tails as identifiers of animacy. This is, of course, merely another example of the distinction made throughout this book between perceptual appearance, which is in the first instance part of the procedural knowledge system, and conceptual knowledge, which is part of the declarative knowledge system. Infants, like adults, need both kinds of information, but the claim I am making here is that they begin their conceptual life by analyzing what objects do rather than what they look like.

Xu and Carey (1996) suggested that even at 10 months infants do not yet have genuine concepts of kinds of things because they fail tests like the following: From behind a screen a ball comes out and then goes back again. Next, a duck comes out from the other side of the screen and then goes back again. The screen is then raised and either both objects are there or only one is there. Ten-month-olds are not surprised when only one object appears. Van de Walle, Carey, and Prevor (2000) found a similar result when the task involved reaching into a jar to retrieve unseen objects. These authors concluded that 10-month-olds do not individuate objects on the basis of kind information and so their concepts are quite different from those of older infants and adults. Although this conclusion is possible, there are other explanations for the data than that infants lack individuated kind concepts. Infants may not automatically engage in enumeration of objects in an unseen space when spatiotemporal information about number is lacking. This is different from adult responding but not necessarily due to the nature of their kind concepts. Furthermore, the difficulty is eliminated when the processing demands of the tests are reduced (Baillargeon & Wang, 2002; Wilcox & Schweinle, 2002), suggesting interpretative difficulty with the displays rather than lack of individuated concepts.

To summarize this chapter, I have proposed that infants represent information from an early age at more than one level of description. The first level is the result of a perceptual system that parses and categorizes objects and object movement (events). I assume that this level of representation is roughly similar to that found in many animal species. In addition, human infants have the capacity to analyze objects and events into another form of representation that, while still somewhat "perception-like" in character, contains only redescribed fragments of the information originally processed. These redescriptions are spatial and analog in form; we call them image-schemas. Image-schemas, such as SELF-MOTION, form the earliest meanings that the mind represents. The capacity to engage in perceptual meaning analysis and to combine the resultant meanings allows complex concepts to be formed. It also enables new concepts that are not merely combinations of previously formed image-schemas. In both these senses, it is a productive system. This representational system creates a conceptual system that is potentially accessible; that is, it contains the information that is used to form images, to recall, and eventually to plan.

A related level of representation may exist in primates (Povinelli, 2000) and perhaps in other mammals, too, although the format would presumably vary as a function of the particulars of the sensory systems involved. Dan Povinelli's description of chimpanzees ascribes conceptual thought to them but only at the level of what can be perceived. As he puts it, chimpanzees are organisms "fine-tuned to detecting detailed perceptual patterns and statistical regularities without interpreting them within a coherent explanatory framework" (p. 310). The topic of how human infants go beyond statistical regularities and begin to build an explanatory framework is continued in the next chapter.

5

Some Image-Schemas and Their Functions

*. . . in which a few image-schemas are explored at greater length and ex-
perimental support offered for the presence of the related concepts in infancy.
I discuss how an initial concept of animal rests upon the image-schemas of
SELF-MOTION and LINK, involving self-moving objects that interact with
other objects from a distance. The concept of an inanimate object, in contrast,
rests on the image-schema of CAUSED-MOTION. I also discuss the concept
of agency and its dependence on the SOURCE-PATH-GOAL schema.
Turning to relational concepts, I consider image-schema representations of
CONTAINMENT and SUPPORT. Finally, I discuss how image-schemas
support both imagery and preverbal thought, and act as the representational
base that enables language to be learned—the last topic to be explored more
thoroughly in chapter 11.*

*In response to my movement of opening and closing my eyes, J. . . . opened
and closed her mouth . . . , L. . . . opened and closed her hands. . . . The
child's mistake must . . . be due entirely to analogy. When the child sees
other people's eyes opening and closing, he assimilates what he sees, not to
the visual schema related to other people's mouths, but to a general schema,
partly visual but mainly tactilo-kinesthetic, of opening and closing
something. (Piaget, 1951)*

Examples of Image-Schemas

The first conceptual division of the world seems to be that between animals and artifacts (see Legerstee, 1992, for a review). This is not the same
as the animate-inanimate distinction as that is understood in scientific or
philosophical discussions. Infants quickly learn to respond differently to
animals and artifacts, but it is unlikely that they see any relation between

animals and plants or between household objects and inanimates such as rocks or hills. This issue is discussed again in chapter 9, and I raise it here merely to note that the categorical distinctions babies make between animals and the various common artifacts of their experience are relatively restricted in that they can be derived only from analysis of what they perceive. Even though the first concepts such as animal are global in scope, the core of the concept must rest on perceptual information. Infants can observe that animals move about and plants don't, that animals have different textures from plants, and so forth. But they have no way of grouping animals and plants on the basis of their both having life spans or being able to reproduce themselves. So we must look to perceptual information that can be attended to, analyzed, and schematized in the form of image-schemas.

In Mandler (1992a), I identified five image-schemas that appear to be foundational to a first conceptual division of the world into animals and artifacts: SELF-MOTION, ANIMATE MOTION, and LINKED PATHS for animals and INANIMATE MOTION and CAUSED MOTION for artifacts. I discuss these here, first in relation to animals, then artifacts, and then in relation to agents, that is, the conceptualization involved in animals acting on objects. I also specify some of the experimental data that tell us that infants are sensitive to the information involved in these schematic notions, although of course there are no experimental data that directly tell us that perceptual meaning analyses are being carried out. For the most part, the data can directly tell us only that infants make one or another discrimination and categorize on the basis of it. Following this, I discuss image-schema representation of some spatial relations that appear to be conceptualized from an early age, such as CONTAINMENT, SUPPORT, UP, and DOWN. Further detail is provided in chapter 11, where these notions are discussed in relation to language acquisition.

Conceptualizing Animals

Self-motion refers to the observational fact that an object begins to move without anything coming into contact with it. This discrimination is almost certainly within the perceptual capabilities of even very young infants. Leslie (1982) found that 6-month-olds react differently to films of balls that start motion on their own as opposed to being hit by another ball. Spelke, Philips, and Woodward (1995) found that 7-month-olds look longer at displays in which an inanimate object starts to move without contact from another object than when a person does so. Poulin-Dubois, Lepage, and Ferland (1996) found that 9-month-olds were distressed when a machinelike robot (i.e., an object that did not look like a person) began to move on its own. They were also distressed when the robot moved contingently upon verbal commands given by the mother, indicating they did not expect inanimate objects' movements to be influenced from a distance. This is one of relatively few experiments that go beyond perceptual data. One might expect surprise or longer looking at unexpected or unusual events, but the negative affect shown by the infants is a stronger reaction, of the sort one might expect if one's conceptual model of the world is being violated. This is speculative, of course, but suggestive that infants think that only animals move themselves and respond contingently from a distance. If the information about the onset of motion is attended to and represented in the form of an image-schema of SELF-MOTION, it will be schematized in form, without specifying anything about the perceptual details of what "starting to move" looks like. For example, it doesn't specify legs, wings, or fins, although each of these provides quite different perceptual events.

As for animate motion, Bennett Bertenthal (1993) has shown that at 3 months infants can distinguish between correct and incorrect human motion. He used the technique originally invented by Gunnar Johansson (1973), in which lights are placed on the joints of moving objects and the scenes are shot in the dark, thus eliminating all figural information. Bertenthal found that infants discriminated between a display using lights corresponding to the joints of a moving person from one in which the lights moved through an equal amount of displacement but did not correspond to human joints. Thus, at least by 3 months, infants have become sensitive to the parameters of human motion. At the same age they can also categorize mammals as different from vehicles on the basis of moving-light displays alone (Arterberry & Bornstein, 2001), indicating that they have abstracted the even more general biological parameters mentioned in the last chapter. Thus, they have represented something very general about the way that animals move compared with mechanical motion. Again, although we see the responsivity to biological motion in young infants, we do not have direct evidence that this information has undergone perceptual meaning analysis. If it has, the image-schema of ANIMATE MOTION that results is apt to consist of a very simple description of the way animals move, such as "rhythmic, up and down, irregular" or something comparable.

I originally thought that self-motion would be the aspect of animal motion most crucial in defining animals for infants, but I have come to suspect that the third notion, contingency of motion between objects, may be even more important. Responsivity to the contingency of events is present at least from birth and is one of the most powerful factors governing perceptual learning and controlling attention. One of the first kinds of contingency that neonates learn is between two events in the environment, resulting in S-S conditioning (Sameroff & Cavanaugh, 1979). The motor limitations of young infants severely restrict their manipulation of objects, but they are surrounded by people whom they observe interacting contingently both with themselves and with other objects. Perhaps especially important for achieving a concept of animal, these interactions often take place without contact, because people (and perhaps a pet dog or cat) are the only objects that respond to the infant and its vocalizations from a distance.

John Watson (1972) did the seminal experimental work on this topic. He showed that at 2 months of age infants would learn to make a mobile hanging above their crib turn when the movement was contingent on their pressing their heads on a pillow. When the mobile did not turn or turned noncontingently, head presses did not increase. An interesting response of infants trained contingently was that after a few sessions of practice, they began to smile and coo at the mobile. Watson hypothesized that the contingencies made the mobile become a social stimulus. I am not sure how to define the difference between a social stimulus and an animate one (see the section titled conceptualizing agents and goals), except that a social stimulus is one that reacts contingently to one's own movements, as opposed to reacting contingently to the movement of other objects. Infants learn to expect contingent interaction from their mothers very early. Murray and Trevarthen (1985) found that 6- to 12-week-old infants became upset if their mothers, shown on videotape, did not respond contingently to them (see also Muir & Nadel, 1998). Similarly, as young as 2 months, infants become upset if their mother does not respond to them at all but presents only a still face (Tronick, Als, Adamson, Wise, & Brazelton, 1978).

Following Watson's work, Frye, Rawling, Moore, and Myers (1983) found that 3-month-olds reacted similarly to their mother and to a toy when either of these was interacting contingently with the infant, and differently when either the mother or the toy did not interact contingently. This kind of result indicates the power of contingent interaction and suggests it may be extremely important in early assessments of whether an object is animate. It is noteworthy that as long as toys behaved in a contingent manner toward the infant, 3-month-olds did not react differently to them than to a person.

There have also been experiments showing that contingent responding of an object to an infant is sufficient to cause the infant to follow the object's "gaze." That is, if the object turns away from the infant toward something else, the infant will look in that direction. Scaife and Bruner (1975) and Butterworth (1991) showed that by 6 months of age infants will follow an adult's gaze if it moves away from the infant. In this case, of course, there are eyes to look at. More recently, Johnson, Slaughter, and Carey (1998) showed that even a faceless "animal-like" object elicits "gaze" following from 12-month-olds if it interacts in a contingent fashion with infants. Similarly, Movellan and Watson (2002) showed that a completely mechanical-looking robot that interacted contingently with 10-month-olds elicited "gaze" following; these authors also reported that the infants would laugh and "converse" with the robot if it acted contingently.

An interesting question is whether we can extrapolate from these findings to the conclusion that animals that infants merely observe interacting (dogs and cats or flocks of birds) will be conceived of as animals just because they also engage in contingent behavior among themselves. As a bit of anecdotal evidence, when my grandson was 6 months old, he came with his parents from the snowy East Coast to California and saw for the first time gulls at the beach. It was December and probably his first experience with birds at close range. While my son and I talked, for 10 minutes or longer my grandson stared with utter fascination at the gulls soaring and diving in seeming concert—it seemed like a great lesson in animacy. I suspect that mere observation of other objects interacting contingently will be conceived of as animate, but as we will see in the discussion of agency and goal-directed behavior in the section titled conceptualizing agents and goals, this is a complex issue. It is possible that the earliest learning about contingent activity among animals occurs when the infant is one of the recipients. It may be that analyzing self–other interaction (such as the give and take of parent–infant turn taking; e.g., Murray & Trevarthen, 1985) precedes infants' analyzing contingent interactions that other objects take among themselves.

There are several LINK schemas that represent these kinds of contingencies between events involving animates (Mandler, 1992a). The simplest kind is the one-way link, in which one event is regularly followed by another, such as happens in common kinds of associative learning. An infant actively noticing that every time she drops something over the side of her highchair her mother picks it up is conceptualizing a kind of "if-then" relation (suggesting that this is one of the image-schemas on which intuitive understanding of logic rests). This kind of LINK is not exclusive to animates, of course; presumably it underlies our conception of any kind of relation of the sort "if A happens, then B happens." Another LINK schema is the two-way link in which there is back-and-forth interaction among objects, as in the turn taking just mentioned. And there are linked paths, in which objects follow joint trajectories. The last may be particularly important in conceptualizing what hands do with objects, because this is the situation in which an inanimate object, by virtue of being conjoined with an animate one, moves on other than an inanimate path. It may also be vital to conceptualizing continuously contingent paths as goal directed, as in a chase, even when an end point is not reached. This issue is discussed further in the section titled conceptualizing agents and goals.

Even though contingency may be the most important factor in conceptualizing animates, nevertheless self-motion plays a role as well. For instance, Pauen (2000b) showed 7-month-olds an animal-like creature and a ball. Looking time at the two objects was approximately equal. Then the two objects moved together in contingent fashion. Following this display, the objects again became motionless. The infants looked longer at the animal in this third display, suggesting that the infants attributed the observed motion to the animal and not to the ball and that they expected the animal but not the ball to move itself again. When the animal and ball moved together because both were moved by a hand, however, the infants showed no more expectation that the animal would move in the third scene than that the ball would.

To summarize, image-schemas related to animacy form a cluster of notions that describe animals as things that start themselves, move in a rhythmic although not always predictable way, and interact with other objects contingently both directly and from a distance. These clusters of meaning create the overall structuring of the animal domain that organizes and guides infants' learning of other domain-specific characteristics. The learning mechanism that associates these characteristics need not be specific to the animal domain. For instance, Rogers and McClelland (in press) show how a rather simple but quite general learning algorithm makes use of the kind of associative structure described by image-schemas (although they did not use the particular kinds of information found in image-schemas) in learning to categorize animals as different from plants. The same algorithm also learns to differentiate individual animal and plant kinds, but that follows after the global differentiation. As we will see in chapters 7 and 8, infants' learning about conceptual details, such as the ways that dogs differ from rabbits or even from fish, tends to take place later than their ability to conceptualize animals per se.

Conceptualizing Inanimates

From the infant's point of view, inanimate objects either do not move at all or, if they move, do so only when another object comes in contact with them. This distinction between self-motion and caused motion is salient to infants at least by 6 months of age and quite likely earlier (see Leslie, 1984, for data on 4-month-olds). Leslie (1982) showed that 6-month-olds discriminate between objects that are caused to move and those that start up on their own. His data are similar to those of Michotte (1963), who studied causal perception in adults. Leslie (1994) speculated that infants come equipped with a domain-specific module that computes the mechanical properties of objects (Theory of Body Mechanism, or ToBy). ToBy receives inputs from vision and analyzes motion with respect to force dynamics. For this purpose, ToBy is equipped with an innate concept of force. It "paints" force onto the object and kinetic information that the perceptual system provides, leading to the perception of causality. Although a case can be made for innate causal perception, it may not require a built-in module as Leslie posited. Peter White (1988) suggested that because of the particulars of the temporal integration function of the eye, we actually perceive the transfer of motion from one object to another.

White hypothesized that the powerful sense of causality perceived in displays in which one ball launches another (Michotte, 1963) comes from the short duration of iconic storage (approximately 250 msec). This store, which holds visual information prior to attentive processing, is continuously refreshed and is what enables the temporal integration by which we see motion as continuous. Michotte noted that the timing of the launching events he studied is crucial if we are to perceive a causal relation. He found that if the delay between the first ball touching the second ball and the second ball beginning to move is greater than 150 msec, the perception of a causal relation between the two disappears, and the perceiver sees two independent movements. The second ball also has to be present for at least 100 msec before the first ball contacts it; otherwise, a single object showing continuous motion is seen. And if a single ball that pauses briefly is shown, motion is not seen as discontinuous if the pause is less than 100 msec. So if there is one object moving and a pause less than 100 msec, continuity of motion is seen, and if there are two balls and the pause is less than 100 msec, a causal relation is seen. Using these data, White (1988) proposed that when spatial discontinuity tells us there are two objects we perceive a causal relation. However, the continuous motion suggests to us a single object. This conflict is resolved by interpreting the event as involving two objects and the transfer of motion from one to the other (what Michotte, 1963, called ampliation). The impression of causality disappears if the temporal parameters of the moving balls are not within the time frame of temporal integration.

This analysis has always seemed important to me, because it provides a basis for actually *seeing* a causal relation, not just inferring it. This issue bedeviled the British empiricists because they could not see how causality could be directly perceived. Hume pointed out that only constant conjunction could be observed, not the forceful aspect that is at the heart of causality. I agree that force cannot be seen, but White's analysis shows how certain conditions of motion in launching displays of the kind that Michotte and Leslie used make us actually see the transfer of motion from one object to another. Seeing transfer of motion may provide the basis for causal perception. If White's analysis is correct, we may not need a lot of innate machinery to get causal conceptions off the ground. In this view, causal perception is an observational property given by the way the eye integrates information over time. That is the perceptual half of the story. The other half is the causal conception that comes from perceptual meaning analysis of motion "transfer." The result of that analysis appears to be one of the roots of our concept of force; the hit object is made to move because the hitting object transfers its own motion into it. This is undoubtedly only one of the bases of the concept of force. Pushing and being pushed, as well as feeling and exerting pressure, are everyday occurrences in an infant's life. Analysis of them added to analysis of transfer of motion lays the foundations for a concept of causality.

On this view, it is not necessary to build in innate knowledge about force and related mechanical properties (Leslie, 1994). Because Leslie believes, as do I, that the perceptual system delivers kinetic rather than dynamic (force) information, he thought it necessary to build in a module that provides the notion of force innately. But it may be that a notion of causal force is not primary but instead is derived from analysis of the transfer of motion from one object to another, in conjunction with bodily experiences of pushing against resistance and being pushed. Proffitt and Bertenthal (1990) pointed out that there are no data showing that infants are sensitive to dynamical, rather than kinematic or geometrical, constraints. They added that even adults have dynamical (force) intuitions for only the simplest of object motions, so it would be surprising if infants have more sophisticated notions. Although Leslie clearly showed that infants discriminate launching events from those with a spatial or temporal delay, that does not tell us exactly what the infants have extracted from these events. Proffitt and Bertenthal concluded that it is "more likely that, throughout the lifespan, motions are perceptually represented in terms of kinematic parameters, and dynamical intuitions are largely formed from these parameters as they are structured by experience-based heuristics" (Proffitt & Bertenthal, 1990, p. 8).

In addition to launching events, Leslie (1984) studied infants' understanding of the role of hands in making objects move. At least from 4 months of age, infants understand that hands pick up objects, whereas blocks of wood do not, and that if an object is held by a hand, it will be supported, whereas if the hand lets it go, the object will fall (see also Baillargeon, Kotovsky, & Needham, 1995). I am sure there are countless similar demonstrations that will be found to show the rapid learning of many of the details of people's causal interactions with objects. Again, this early learning does not need to involve notions of force. It may well be that the initial understanding of causality is in terms of transfer of motion, with the notion of transfer of force a later addition. Sensorimotor experience of forceful action, at least as far as the infant's own action is concerned, is unlikely to be common before manipulation of objects and perhaps also self-locomotion begin. In addition, perceptual meaning analysis of one's own sensorimotor feeling of force seems to be a more difficult task than analysis of the spatial sights an infant sees.

Johnson (1987) described a number of force image-schemas, such as compulsion, blockage, restraint, and removal of restraint. Although, as just indicated, we do not know exactly when infants begin to analyze— not just experience—the variables that lead to these notions, at some point they clearly do. I have emphasized spatial analyses because I consider these likely to be ontogenetically prior to analyses of experienced force, but that is not to deny the importance of analysis of bodily experiences of force in developing full-blown causal concepts. Johnson (1987) also pointed out that our intuitive understanding of concepts of necessity, possibility, and moral obligation rest on a metaphorical extension of analyses of sensorimotor experience of force to the social and metaphysical worlds (see Sweetser, 1990, for deep discussion of this point). Although these extensions lie beyond infancy, their root sources seem likely to be set down relatively early in life.

Conceptualizing Agents and Goals

From knowing what hands do to understanding agency seems a small step and one that is taken quite early. Amanda Woodward (1998) found that 5- and 9-month-old infants attended more to the goal of a reach than to its spatiotemporal properties. Infants were habituated to a display in which an arm reached to one of two toys side by side. Then the positions of the toys were switched, and infants were shown the arm either reaching to the same position as before (and thus to a new toy) or to the same toy as before. Infants looked longer at the event in which the goal of the reach had changed than at the event in which the arm went along a new path of motion to reach the same object. This kind of finding suggests that infants were attending to the goal of an action rather than its physical properties. However, the result was found only when a hand reached, not when a mechanical claw reached, suggesting the infants were more likely to attribute agency to a familiar "grasper" than to an unfamiliar one.

Are infants merely more likely to associate hands with objects than with positions in space? Woodward and Sommerville (2000) found the same kind of result with 11½-month-olds in a situation more complex than merely grasping an object. They showed a hand touching the top of a transparent box. In a single-action condition, that is all the hand did. In an embedded-action condition, the hand opened the box and grasped a toy. Test trials consisted of the hand reaching toward a new box that contained the toy or to the original box with a new toy in it. There was no preferential looking in the first condition, but when the hand had retrieved the object, infants now looked longer when the hand went to the old box with the new toy. A second experiment tested the same embedded-action condition, except that the toy was outside, not inside the box, so that touching the lid and grasping the toy were no longer causally related. In this case, looking times did not differentiate the two test conditions. These data suggest not only that the infants interpreted the touching action on the basis of what happened afterward but also that they linked actions into "goal plans," in which one action, touching a box, is seen as a means to a goal of opening a box, which in turn is seen as a means to a goal of obtaining an object.

In similar research, Woodward (1999) found that perhaps as young as 5 months and clearly by 9 months, infants differentiate between a person grasping an object and apparently unintentionally dropping a hand onto the object; that is, they distinguish between a goal path and a similar but not purposeful one. Baldwin, Baird, Saylor, and Clark (2001) showed that 10- to 11-month-old infants have learned something about the perceptual structure of intentional action. They showed the infants videos of everyday purposeful actions, followed by test videos in which the motion was suspended either in the middle of the actions or at their ends. Infants renewed their looking at the videos whose structure was interrupted.

Interpreting behavior in terms of goals not only begins early but is pervasive and, at least by 9 months of age, abstract in character. A series of studies by György Gergely, Gergely Csibra, and their colleagues (Csibra, Gergely, Bíró, Koós, & Brockbank, 1999; Gergely, Nádasdy, Csibra, & Bíró, 1995) made use of computer displays similar to the famous Heider and Simmel (1944) film that showed geometrical forms moving and interacting in various ways. That film, as well as the simplified displays used by Gergely, Csibra, and colleagues, gives adults as powerful an impression of goal-directed interactions as do Michotte's films of causal interactions. In their first experiment, Gergely et al. habituated 12-month-olds to computer displays showing two circles, A and B, with a short vertical bar between them. A approached the bar, paused, returned to its original position, and then approached the bar even faster, jumped over it, and came to rest against B. A control group was habituated to the same display, except the bar was placed at one side, rather than between the two circles, so that A's jumping action appeared unmotivated. For both groups, one test display consisted of the same display as seen by the control group during habituation, namely, a display in which A made a jumping arc to B, even though there was no bar in the way. The other test display was a novel action in which A did not jump but simply went in a straight line to B. Experimental subjects dishabituated to the jumping action (even though this is what they had seen during habituation) but did not dishabituate to the new action in which, in the absence of the bar, A went in a straight line to B. That is, the experimental group reacted to the habituated jumping action as if it were novel (presumably because there was no longer a bar to jump over) and to the novel display in which A made a beeline for B as if it were familiar. Csibra et al. (1999) replicated this finding with 9-month-olds but not 6-month-olds. These are quite remarkable results, because the displays consisted solely of moving circles, so there was no figural information at all to indicate an agent following a goal. This means that the infants were interpreting (that is, conceptualizing) goals purely on the basis of interactive motion. Similar data were reported by Johnson and Sockaci (2000), who found that 14-month-olds treated purple blobs as agents if they engaged in goal-directed activity.

In their first experiment (Gergely et al., 1995), there were some cues associated with animacy; A pulsated when it came next to B, and B pulsated in turn. In Csibra et al. (1999), all indications of animacy were eliminated, including self-starting motion. Infants were habituated to A coming from offscreen, sailing over the bar, and coming to rest next to B. The height of the bar varied from trial to trial, and in each case A just cleared it on its path to B. The same kind of result was found as before. When the bar was removed, infants dishabituated to the movement to which they had been habituated but did not dishabituate when A went directly to B. These data imply that by the end of the first year infants have learned something abstract about the kind of route that an object traveling along a path to another object will take. Of course, in these experiments the infants were habituated to A taking the most direct path to B. But it is interesting that they apparently made the generalization that having repeatedly taken a direct route to B, A would do so again, even though the physical situation was changed. This result is consistent with the Woodward experiments.

I originally suggested that an image-schema of AGENCY consists of a schematic spatial representation of an animate object acting on an inanimate one (Mandler, 1992a). But this leaves out the goal-directed aspect of agents, and it appears from both Woodward's and Gergely and Csibra's data that goal paths are an important part of this understanding. Our understanding of goal-directed behavior is a classic example of an image-schema representation. Lakoff (1987) discussed it in terms of a SOURCE-PATH-GOAL image-schema, consisting of a starting point and a path taking one to an end point—a thoroughly spatial conception. Like other simple image-schemas, movement is being used to conceptualize purpose. We reach out for objects, we move across a room to get an object, and so forth. Infants begin to engage in such activities themselves after a few months of age. Before then, it may be the changes of state that infants observe to take place at the ends of paths that draw their attention, thus beginning the process of perceptual meaning analysis. At any rate, infants appear to understand agents' behavior in terms of how they move vis-à-vis other objects, so the SOURCE-PATH-GOAL and AGENCY image-schemas are closely related. An agent both acts on other objects and follows goal paths.

The end of path or goal in the Woodward experiments was picking up an object. In Csibra and Gergely's experiments, it was given to the infants by repeatedly showing one circle, A, following a direct path to another circle, B. In recent work, Csibra, Bíró, Koós, and Gergely (2003) showed scenes of a large circle A "chasing" a smaller circle B. B went through a small hole in a horizontal bar in front of it, too small to let A through. At that point, A veered around the end of the bar and continued after A until both went off the screen. That is, no end of path was seen, only the kind of continuously interacting behavior involved in what adult observers see as a chase. After being habituated to this display, infants were shown test scenes that were the same except that the hole in the bar was now large enough to let either circle go through it. At 12 months, but not at 9 months, infants dishabituated to the test scene in which A still went around the end of the bar rather than through the now large enough hole. Csibra and colleagues suggest that these displays are more difficult than the earlier ones because the end point of the path is not shown.

An interesting question raised by these experiments is whether agents must be animate. Gergely, Csibra, and their colleagues ascribe infants' responses to their displays to a teleological bias, by which they mean a tendency to interpret events in terms of goals and "rational" ways to achieve them. The repetition of a circle A going to circle B by the shortest available route, given the constraint of the bar, made infants interpret the events as A trying to reach B. If the bar is no longer there, the jumping route is no longer the rational (that is, the most direct) way to reach B. Similarly for the chase scene: If A cannot follow B through the hole in the bar, then the most direct route is to go around the bar. If the hole is large enough to let A through, going around is no longer the direct route. There is nothing that says that this teleological stance should be restricted to animate agents, and Csibra and colleagues do not imply this. We should consider the possibility that infants' first assumption is that any object moving on a direct path to another is goal directed. Certainly infants have a lot of experience that both animate and inanimate objects can follow direct paths. A ball rolls on a direct path to another object and knocks it over, or a glass falls off a table and breaks. The telephone rings, and people go to it from wherever they are. Objects taking direct paths to an end (that is, where something happens) are ubiquitous. Experience with both animate and inanimate direct trajectories may lead to the kinds of expectations about direct paths that the infants in Gergely and Csibra's experiments showed, rather than their expectations demonstrating an innate link between agency and animacy. Learning to limit a teleological (or a goal-directed stance) to animates may take developmental time.

So we have something of a puzzle. Is agency a relatively simple extension of early conceptions of animacy (as I suggested in Mandler, 1992a), or does it evolve from independent roots, involving analysis of paths specifically with regard to their ends? Contingent interaction with another object and following a goal-directed path to or from an object are not coterminous. Goal-directed paths are only an intersecting set with contingent interactions from a distance. In the case of a ball going over a bar, following a direct path repeatedly to an object on the other side may evince goal-seeking but not necessarily contingent interaction. Conversely, turn taking involves contingent interaction but does not involve goal seeking. Rochat, Morgan, and Carpenter (1997) showed that even 3-month-olds distinguish one object chasing another in continuously varying paths from objects that move independently of each other, but we do not know whether they did so on the basis of goal-directed behavior or contingently interacting behavior. In neither case, however, was contingent responding to the infants themselves involved. To untangle these issues, it seems important to distinguish between goal-directed behavior, contingent behavior, and contingent responding directed toward the infant.

It seems plausible that the innate responsivity to contingent events that is responsible for associative learning leads to a universal tendency to analyze all events in a teleological fashion. Both children and adults often interpret even inanimate events in goal-directed terms, and in some cultures they do so pervasively. Such an innate tendency, in conjunction with differences in the observed movements of objects in the world, should gradually associate goal-directed behavior more strongly with animates than with inanimates, but at the same time it could leave a residual tendency to ascribe goal-directed behavior even to inanimates. Thus, it should be possible to get the human conceptual system up and running without building in domain-specific knowledge about animate and inanimate objects.

Although more evidence is certainly needed, it remains a plausible hypothesis that a concept of a goal can be derived as a generalization from analyzing objects moving on paths and what happens at their ends.

It is possible that the mechanism of perceptual meaning analysis I have described, which conceptually represents objects in terms of the spatial paths they follow, including their beginnings, endings, and interactions, will be sufficient to account for the notion of a goal, rather than having to build in this interpretation of the world as an innate proclivity. In either case, there is at present no strong evidence that infants' understanding of goal-based behavior is restricted to animals. As just mentioned, this view is contrary to the current notion that knowledge about animals is due to domain-specific learning and innate biases that apply solely to animals (e.g., Carey & Spelke, 1994). If agency is the conceptual interpretation of an object following certain kinds of contingent paths with respect to another objects, it seems more like a domain-general interpretation that with experience becomes narrowed down (for the most part) to animals.

This view, of course, has its critics. Carey (2000, 2002), although generally sympathetic to my overall theory of early concept formation, nevertheless doubts that perceptual meaning analysis of spatial displays is enough in and of itself to account for infants' differential conceptions of animate and inanimate objects. She asks: "Where do the categories represented in the image schematic meanings themselves come from? If one cannot derive causality from spatiotemporal descriptions, or agency from spatiotemporal descriptions (even those that provide the necessary input for attributions of each type of causality), then the problem of how these concepts arise has not been solved" (Carey, 2000, p. 40).

I am suggesting, however, that "categories" (i.e., concepts) of both causality and agency *can* be derived from the spatiotemporal descriptions that perceptual meaning analysis produces. As discussed in the previous chapter, although we believe there is a difference between time and space, when we conceptualize time, we spatialize it. Similarly, when we conceptualize causal contact between objects, we spatialize it in terms of transfer of motion along a path from one to the other, and when we conceptualize goals, again we spatialize them as ends of paths. The story in each case will undoubtedly be complex; for instance, the difference between an end of a random path and an end of a path that is determined by a contingency between two trajectories (as in a chase resulting in capture) needs to be specified in detail. In principle, however, I hypothesize that our concepts of causality and agency can be derived from spatiotemporal analyses and that there need be nothing mysterious about their origins.

Following the previous quote, Carey goes on to say that core knowledge (Carey & Spelke, 1994), derived from innate learning mechanisms, is required to solve the problem of the origin of concepts. I agree that we need a mechanism that goes beyond perception, one that analyzes perceptual displays. In contrast, Carey and Spelke's view involves several still unspecified mechanisms innately attuned to differences between animate and inanimate objects. To my mind, it is preferable that innate propensities lie in the way our visual and motor systems are organized in conjunction with the kinds of information such as motion we are attuned to encode, rather than requiring mechanisms dependent on innate conceptualizations about different kinds of objects. To the extent that conceptual notions can be acquired by analysis of incoming data, innate conceptual specifications are not required. Of course, a mechanism that does the analysis *is* required. In spite of these differences, however, there are many affinities between our views. Carey (2002) talks about dedicated input analyzers that take spatiotemporal data as input and output abstract conceptual representations. That sounds like my mechanism of perceptual meaning analysis. The main difference seems to be that I do not see the need for separate input analyzers (or perceptual meaning analysis) to be dedicated to animate and inanimate domains. Aside from the mechanism of perceptual meaning analysis itself, the most likely candidates for innate status seem to me to be kinds of spatiotemporal data that command the infant's attention and are subjected to analysis, such as the paths of moving objects and contingencies in their interactions.

As mentioned earlier, the kind of learning I have described here is potentially able to be modeled by the network that Tim Rogers and Jay McClelland (in press) used in their developmental connectionist work. The network, based on one devised by Rumelhart and Todd (1993), has a distributed input layer, in which various perceptual features of an object are encoded. This layer feeds into a representation layer that gradually becomes differentiated as learning about the input proceeds. In addition to the representation layer, there is a relation layer that specifies whether a property (e.g., color), part (e.g., legs), or activity (e.g., walk) is being analyzed on a given occasion. This is a localist layer (something like perceptual meaning analysis) in which one relation per trial is encoded and that organizes learning in ways similar to those described here for image-schemas. These two layers feed into a standard layer of hidden units. Finally there is an output layer that learns to reproduce the properties of the input objects. As various aspects of objects in events are observed, the representation layer begins to produce distinctive patterns of weights that represent various conceptual categories. At first these are global in nature (e.g., animal), and with experience they become gradually differentiated (e.g., land animal or fish). In this respect the network's performance mirrors the patterns of conceptual learning in infancy to be discussed in chapters 7 and 8.

Rogers and McClelland used only a few of the characteristics of animate and inanimate things described in this chapter in their modeling. However, in principle, learning that uses the characteristics described here could proceed in the same way and model the known data from infants in a more realistic way. Analysis of animals into activities such as starting oneself, moving rhythmically, and interacting in a contingent fashion with other objects forms a cluster of properties that organizes the animal domain even before the particular perceptual appearance or parts of individual animal kinds are learned. These regularities do not have to be programmed into the network, but because of their existence in the environment, they quickly become domain-specific properties. Other activities, such as being picked up by hands and moving in a mechanical way, form a cluster of properties that specifies an inanimate object. Although these divisions into animate and inanimate things specify neither causal nor intentional properties, they may quite adequately characterize the first knowledge of animate and inanimate domains that infants acquire.

An intriguing aspect of the Rogers and McClelland model is that it effectively differentiates visual input, which takes in a great deal of perceptual information in parallel, from a relatively narrow subset of perceptual information that I would call attended information. For example, this information concerns what the object input on a given occasion is doing, such as walking or singing (although it also represents attributes such as legs or wings on other occasions). Unfortunately, because some of the same attributes are included in both the input and relation layers (which seems like an unnecessary complication), it is difficult to determine exactly how the relation layer interacts with the visual input layer in controlling learning. Nevertheless, it is clear from their modeling of some of our developmental data (Mandler & McDonough, 1993) that the relation layer is doing most of the organizing work. This layer provides information that is crucial to extracting the global notions of animacy and inanimacy—namely, motion and other characteristics of animate versus inanimate categories. Indeed, as Rogers and McClelland point out, they have virtually modeled the working of image-schemas by allowing the model to group together items that have different appearances on the basis of a few abstract shared properties. What needs to be specified in their account are the factors that determine the content of the relation layer, that is, why it contains the particular information it does. From my point of view, this layer reflects perceptual aspects of the world that are attended and analyzed. Although they do not describe it in those terms, it appears to act in that kind of selective way.

Conceptualizing Spatial Relations

In addition to concepts about objects and their interactions, the thinking mind must be able to conceive a variety of spatial relations. Although these are extremely important to our conceptualizations of the world, there are surprisingly few of them (Landau & Jackendoff, 1993). There are infinite degrees of variation in spatial relations, but the mind seems to mark out relatively few as important. Some of these are containment (and the related concepts of opening and closing and going in and going out), support (and the related concepts of contact and attachment), verticality in the sense of vertical motion or position (above and below or up and down), and horizontality (left and right). This is not meant to be an exhaustive list, but these are some of the basic spatial relations that we know infants are sensitive to, and many other spatial relations such as between appear to be derivatives of these. Others are aspects of paths, such as toward and across, that although they have not yet been studied in infants, may also be relatively early conceptions. There are also various combinations that can be made of these simple spatial relations, such as combining support and attachment or attachment and verticality. But because the initial set is small, the combinations are not numerous either. One can have support with or without attachment, containment with or without contact, attachment with or without verticality, and so forth. Languages vary a good deal in how they package spatial relations, but in all of them the variations that are lexicalized tend to be relatively small, even when expressed by open-class verbs (see chapter 11). Please note that this discussion is not meant to equate concepts with words, only that the size of a lexicon presumably reflects the richness or lack thereof of the underlying concepts that support it.

Containment is one spatial relation that has been relatively well studied in infancy. Baillargeon and her colleagues have conducted a number of experiments charting the growth in understanding of containment relations between 2½ and 12 months of age. As young as 2½ months, infants understand that if something is to go into a container, there must be an opening, and that something in a container will move where the container moves (Hespos & Baillargeon, 2001a). Not until 6 months of age, however, do they understand that a wide object will not go into a narrower container (Aguiar & Baillargeon, 1998), in spite of the fact that at 5 months they distinguish loose-fitting from tight-fitting containment (Spelke & Hespos, 2002). Other work showed that not until 7½ months do infants understand that a taller object cannot disappear completely when it is lowered into a shorter container, although as early as 4 months they are successful at the same relationship when the object is lowered behind a screen instead; that is, the finding is specific to the understanding of containment (Hespos & Baillargeon, 2001b). Baillargeon and her colleagues suggest that as early as 2½ months infants have a concept of containment that is basically an open-closed distinction. Gradually they add quantitative variables to it, such as the size relationships that obtain between a container and the contained.

The description of an early concept of containment as centered on an open-closed distinction or as a place where things disappear and reappear (Freeman, Lloyd, & Sinha, 1980) fits well with Lakoff's (1987) description of the CONTAINMENT schema as consisting of an interior, boundary, and exterior. It seems likely that this notion arises from the times when infants' attention is attracted to containment events, and perceptual meaning analysis of objects going into and out of containers can take place. Babies experience a great many containment events: They eat and drink out of containers, they watch their bodies being clothed and unclothed, they are put in and taken out of cribs and playpens, and so on. It has been suggested that our understanding of containment stems originally from our bodily experience of taking in food (Johnson, 1987). However, as discussed earlier for force, that seems a more difficult situation for perceptual meaning analysis than visual analysis of external containers, such as bottles and dishes, along with the acts of pouring liquid or spooning food into and out of containers and similar events. Similarly, one could think of a hand as a representation of a container. As adults, we might use a hand to represent containment if we aren't allowed to give a verbal description, and so we might assume the notion is a bodily conception. However, for infants, especially before they begin to be adept at manipulating objects, seeing hands act as containers must be more a visual experience than a bodily one. Newborns do engage in reflexive grasping, but it takes several months before this activity becomes coordinated with the visual system and infants begin to examine what they are grasping (Piaget, 1952).

Baillargeon and her colleagues have also documented the course of learning about support relations (Baillargeon, Kotovsky, & Needham, 1995). At 3 months, infants expect objects to be supported if they are in any contact with a surface. By 5 months, they expect an object to be supported if a part rests on the surface. By 6½ months, they have begun to differentiate between partial but inadequate support (15% overlap between the object and supporting surface) and adequate support (70% overlap). Similar to the understanding of containment, the first notion of support is overly simple (two objects in contact), and considerations of gravity or weight distribution are only gradually learned over the course of the first year.

How do we know that learning about containment and support is not merely implicit perceptual learning, rather than an early kind of conceptualization? We don't know for sure, although the work of Baillargeon and colleagues suggests that noticing—the occasion for perceptual meaning analysis—is required. If perceptual learning were all that was involved, it should not require the passage of months before some of the details that Baillargeon has documented are figured out. This kind of learning seems to require close attention. For instance, on the basis of perceptual learning alone, it is difficult to account for the finding that infants realize that a tall object can't disappear behind a short screen but do not realize that a tall object can't fit into a short container. One might argue that infants have merely had more experience with objects lowering behind screens, but that seems unlikely; if anything, one would expect them to have considerably more experience with and interest in containers. (Whenever it begins to be conceptualized, an image-schema of containment, like LINK discussed earlier, may be a basis for our intuitive understanding of logic. Lakoff [1987] suggested that CONTAINMENT is not only the basis for understanding P or not P—in or not in—but also for the Boolean logic of classes, as in "if A is in B and B is in C, then A is in C." Needless to say, I am not suggesting that infants have even an intuitive understanding of logic, only that the roots of the intuitions that ground logic may appear quite early.)

Similar questions can be asked about learning the spatial relations of above and below. These spatial relations are discussed in chapter 11 vis-à-vis language learning. Here I note only that as young as 3 months infants can categorize an object as above or below a line (Quinn, 2003). If one presents the object in several positions above the line, infants dishabituate if it is moved below the line. However, to categorize the relation itself—that is, to categorize *aboveness* (UP) or *belowness* (DOWN) across several different objects—takes several more months to achieve. Categorizing a relation independently of the objects instantiating it is a more abstract accomplishment. It is possible that both accomplishments are implicit perceptual categories, but as in the previous discussion of containment, one can ask why there should be a developmental gap in the perception of *aboveness* (or *belowness*) when it is associated with a single object versus multiple objects. Quinn, Polly, Furer, Dobson, and Narter (2002) tested whether 3-month-olds might have been distracted by multiple objects during familiarization, thus missing the above or below relation. To test this, they used a single object in familiarization and a different object in test. This did not help 3-month-olds to abstract the relation of above. Similarly, familiarizing the infants with the test object itself also did not help.

It appears that at 3 months, relations like above and below are perceptually tied to the particular objects that instantiate the relation. When new objects come along, the spatial relations between them must be encoded anew. Like color, above and below appear to be perceptual primitives; they are perceptually given in a display of an object above or below a line, and even 3-month-olds are sensitive to them, perceptually encoding the spatial relation. To go beyond this and abstract aboveness away from the rest of a perceptual display appears to require further analysis beyond what the perceptual system provides, indicating that it is an achievement of the conceptual system. As discussed in chapter 12, it takes developmental time to conceptualize color as well.

One reason it is difficult to resolve differences between perceptual and conceptual responding is that the tests that have been carried out on spatial relations all are of varying perceptual displays. None of them requires representing absent objects. They have merely measured whether infants look longer at kinds of perceptual displays they have never seen before, such as an object going into a container with no opening, or whether infants look longer at a spatial relation that has changed from habituation to test. More than for the data on conceptual categorization of objects, which are discussed at length in the following chapters, the representational status of spatial relations remains somewhat ambiguous. At the same time, as discussed in chapters 11 and 12, to learn language requires conceptualization, and there is considerable evidence (albeit often indirect) that to learn spatial terms requires conceptualization of spatial relations. Comprehension of various terms for containment begin at about 18 months, within less than a year of the accomplishments documented by Baillargeon and her colleagues, and quite abstract notions of containment have been documented between 9 and 14 months (Casasola & Cohen, 2002; McDonough, Choi, & Mandler, 2003).

Some Uses of Image-Schemas in Infancy

Thinking and Imagining

There is ample evidence that infants are capable of thought before they learn to speak. Although Piaget saw no evidence of internal thought processes taking place before Stage 6 of the sensorimotor period (sometime after the end of the first year), since then a good deal of positive evidence for preverbal thought has been uncovered. Much of it is described in this book: I have already mentioned in chapter 2 Piaget's descriptions of analogical thought in his 10- to 12-month-old infants. Beyond this, I delineate the ability of preverbal infants to make inductive inferences in chapter 8 and the ability to recall the past in chapter 10. In addition, the work of Willatts (1997) on problem solving shows that forming multistep problem-solving plans begins to develop around 8 months of age. Inductive inference, recall, problem solving, and planning—these are the achievements of a thinking mind. We still have much to learn about how infants attain these achievements, because until recently we had little data and, presumably because of that lack, little theory. One of the accomplishments of the past 15 years of infancy research has been to produce a database that has sparked new theoretical ideas.

The position I espouse is that infants can create mental work spaces in roughly the same fashion as do adults (Fauconnier, 1994, Fauconnier & Turner, 2002), using image-schema representations of objects and their interactions. Piaget's (1951) account of his infant's opening and closing her hand while trying to figure out how to imitate blinking eyes (quoted at the beginning of this chapter) indicates the use of an abstract image-schematic representation of opening and closing, although it does not tell us how the whole thought is assembled. I assume the assembly is accomplished in the fashion that Fauconnier and Turner (2002) call conceptual blending and that has been extensively documented in adults (e.g., Coulson, 2000). The infant takes a familiar mental space of opening and closing the hand and uses the generic image-schema of opening and closing itself to connect (blend) opening and closing the hand with opening and closing the eyes.

A second example was provided by Janellen Huttenlocher (1974) in a study of early language learning. A 10-month-old had learned to play peekaboo by putting a diaper over her head. One day, Huttenlocher surreptitiously removed the diaper from the toys assembled around the infant and a bit later said to her, "Let's play peekaboo." The child looked around for the diaper, and upon not finding it hesitated a moment, and then picked up a bowl and covered her face with it. This bit of creative analogical thought could be accomplished by the same kind of blending as in the example of blinking eyes. The infant took a familiar mental space of covering and uncovering her eyes by means of the diaper and used the generic (abstract) image-schema of covering and uncovering to connect (blend) the familiar activity with an entirely new form of cover that could accomplish the same end.

As still another example, Ann Brown (1990), taught 1- to 3-year-olds how to obtain an object out of reach with a rake. When transferring to a different situation in which there was no rake but a variety of other implements (including a short rake, a crook, and a pole with a dish mop on the end), they relied on underlying structural similarities of containment and capture rather than perceptual similarity of the available implements to the learned implement. (She also found this in infants as young as 13 months.) I suggest that they understood the rake's actions in terms of the generic image-schemas of taking a path to an object, capturing (containing) it, and bringing it back to the start of the path. These generic schemas enabled them to recognize that a crook could accomplish the same end, whereas a short rake or a pole with a dish mop on the end could not.

Although I am confident that such image-schema analyses of analogical learning can be worked out in detail, it has only recently been accomplished for adult thought. For example, the computational model of Veale and O'Donoghue (2000) shows in considerable detail how Fauconnier and Turner's conceptual blending can be implemented. However, almost nothing has been done within this framework on infant thought (but see Kuehne, Gentner, & Forbus, 2000, for a somewhat different approach). What I have tried to show here is that even in infancy concepts are represented in such a way that they are accessible for analogical learning, problem solving, and recall. Furthermore, the relatively small amount of data on their analogical learning suggests they approach such problems in ways similar to those of adults.

Insofar as recall is involved, imagery is undoubtedly involved as well. It seems plausible that the same image-schema representations used for thought are also used to structure the images used in recall. As discussed in chapter 2, images do not come free as a by-product of perception. We can look at a face for years and still not be able to image it. Visual imagery is constructed from what we know as much as from what we have seen. This is a very old psychological principle (although one we often seem to forget). The Carmichael et al. (1932) experiment that I described, in which the images that people formed were shown to be dependent on the way they conceptualized the stimuli, is more than 70 years old!

Image-schemas would seem to be an ideal format for constructing images. Kosslyn's (1980) theory of image formation involved a visual buffer to reproduce visual information about a given display, plus a set of propositions specifying various conceptual information in more abstract format (propositional, in his theory). Image-schemas might be able to provide both functions at once. If one is imaging a bottle on a table being picked up and milk being poured from it into a cup, various aspects of the conceptual understanding such as containment, above and below, and paths going out and in are already in image-schematic form. As discussed earlier, this format is spatial in nature, not visual, but the spatial relations it describes provide a framework that structures the paths and other spatial relations found in imagery. It is the resulting concrete images that we are aware of when we imagine, of course, not the image-schemas themselves. This notion that the very concepts themselves can structure visual imagery is speculative, but it adds to the view that image-schemas are a crucial part of our mental architecture. They are used not only to create meanings but also to help form the specific images that instantiate the meanings aroused during comprehension or conscious thought. Stanfield and Zwaan (2001) and Zwaan, Stanfield, and Yaxley (2002) provided good examples of the role played by unconscious image-schemas of spatial relations in comprehending sentences and how these image-schemas speed recognition of pictures of the scenes the sentences described. For example, a sentence mentioning a pencil in a cup speeded recognition of a picture of a vertical pencil, whereas a sentence mentioning a pencil in a drawer speeded recognition of a picture of a horizontal pencil. We are not usually aware of such spatial details when we read or hear a sentence, but the conceptualizations that the sentence induces are structured by image-schemas that contain this kind of information.

A Base for Language Learning

A further function of image-schemas is to create the representational base onto which language can be mapped. The capacity of image-schemas to represent relations of various sorts is particularly important in understanding how the relational aspects of language, such as prepositions and modal verbs, are learned (Brugman, 1988; Sweetser, 1990). As will be discussed in chapter 11, it was long assumed by many people that language is mapped onto sensorimotor schemas. But sensorimotor schemas are dynamic structures controlling perception and action, not meanings onto which relational morphemes can be mapped. An interface between sensorimotor activity and its continuously changing dynamics and the discrete propositional system of language is needed (Mandler, 1994, 1996).

There are at least two characteristics such an interface should have. First, it should provide a simplified packaging of preverbal experiences. The experiences themselves are too rich in detail to be mappable in their entirety. Their generalizable aspects need to be distilled, not only to learn language but also to carry out the kinds of thinking previously described. Infants don't wait for language to begin to think, so packaging meanings into useable form is not even primarily a linguistic problem. Second, the interface needs to be in a form onto which a discrete symbol system can be mapped. The richness and the continuous nature of perception must be tamed. One way to do this is to transform perceptual information into a still analog but more discrete form that will enable the mapping to take place. Although many people assume that this criterion implies the necessity for a propositional language of thought (Fodor, 1975), I have tried to show here that a propositional preverbal system is not necessary. It is not necessary for concept formation, image formation, preverbal recall, or simple analogical reasoning, let alone for learning a natural language. Indeed, it is quite possible that propositional representation simply does not exist in the human mind until language is learned (Mandler, 1994).

To summarize the point of view developed in this and the previous chapter, perceptual meaning analysis operates on perceptual information, leading to image-schemas. These image-schemas represent events in a simple, abstract, spatial form. They create the meanings that supply the foundations of the conceptual system and allow language to be learned. The most important characteristic of this system is that it is accessible, first in the form of imagery and later via language, thus making conscious thought and imagination possible. A crucial component of image-schemas is their abstractness. An abstract, or generic, schema, as in the example of opening and closing discussed earlier, is required to generalize from a known example (opening and closing one's hand) to a structurally similar example in a new and perhaps even unseeable domain (opening and closing one's eyes). This kind of analogical learning, ubiquitous in human life, begins in infancy. It also enables the later metaphorical extension of infants' concepts about space to social and metaphysical realms.

6

Some Differences Between
Percepts and Concepts
The Case of the Basic Level

. . . in which the notion of basic-level concepts is deconstructed and found both theoretically and experimentally wanting. I discuss how this notion distorted our views of early concept formation. I suggest we need to go back to the old notion of concepts having conceptual cores plus identification procedures. Different kinds of information are involved in conceiving something and in recognizing it. Insofar as there is merit to the notion of a basic level it may have to do with relative ease of identification rather than a special level of conceptualization. In any case, to understand early concept formation it is important to understand how it differs from perceptual category formation.

Perceptual categories differ from conceptual ones. Perceptual categories are not accessible to conscious manipulation. . . . (Nelson, 1985)

A Critique of the Notion of Basic-Level Concepts

In the 1970s, Eleanor Rosch published a series of influential papers that brought a rush of fresh air to traditional experimental research on categorization (e.g., Rosch, 1973). Her work on categories as prototypes, based on Wittgenstein's notion of family resemblance, was an important corrective to the prevailing rigid views of categorization based on logical classes, and it helped open up the field to new and interesting ways of thinking about how concepts are structured. One of the ideas she developed, however, in my opinion had a somewhat pernicious influence. That is the notion that there is a particular level of categorization that is primary or fundamental—a level that came to be known as the basic level.

By the 1980s it had become ingrained in the literature that the first concepts to be formed are at the basic level. From what has been said so far, one can see that the view presented in this book is on a collision course with such a notion. If the first concepts are global and abstract, they cannot be at the basic level. Of course, such a statement assumes we know what the basic level is. In this chapter I show that not only do we do not know what the term means but also, given any more or less understandable definition, the basic level is not the way to characterize the first concepts.

The term *basic level* is usually meant to refer to a particular kind of concept, such as dog or chair (Mervis & Rosch, 1981). It has been defined as an objectively determined level of categorization that reflects similarity in the shapes of things (Mervis & Crisafi, 1982), but it has also been defined as a knowledge-based category determined by culture and individual expertise (Mervis & Mervis, 1982). These two definitions seem somewhat opposed to each other, in that similarity of shape is a property of objects in the environment but culture and expertise are properties of people determined by experience. In their first article on the topic, Rosch and Mervis (1975) defined the basic level as that level of abstraction at which objects are most naturally divided into categories. They proposed that both artifacts and biological kinds consist of information-rich bundles of attributes that form natural discontinuities in the structure of the environment. Wings, feathers, and beaks are not distributed randomly but instead form a cluster correlated with birds. Basic-level conceptual cuts were assumed to be created at these discontinuities in the world, forming a unique level of abstraction. This level was said to carry the most information and to possess the highest cue validity. *Cue validity*, in turn, was defined as the extent to which an attribute predicts a particular category, for example, the extent to which the attribute wings predicts that something is a bird and does not predict a different category, such as butterflies. Basic-level categories were said to maximize the amount of within-category perceptual similarity compared with between-category dissimilarity.

The idea of a special level of categorization was based in part on work by anthropological linguists on folk taxonomies of animals and plants around the world (e.g., Berlin, Breedlove, & Raven, 1973). Folk taxonomies are similar to the Linnaean taxonomy (which itself was presumably influenced by ancient folk notions), in that animal and plant terms come at different levels of generality. Not all folk taxonomies have a term for the highest level such as *animal* or *plant* (the unique beginner level), and various other levels can be missing, too, but there is one that is always there, namely, the level of the genus, or generic level (Brown, 1984). A sketch of a simple taxonomy, with examples of animals and plants at each level of description, is shown in Table 6-1.[1] The table represents a hierarchy with the most general level of description of animals and plants at the top and more detailed levels of description toward the bottom. Some taxonomies include more levels, such as a family of felines above cats or a varietal level below the species level, such as Pacific sea bass. That is, the number of named levels varies from culture to culture. In a small ecological niche, there is often only one kind of cat or bass, and so the generic level is often at the bottom of the taxonomic tree for that culture (Atran, 1990). In any case, the generic level not only appears in all taxonomies but also, largely because it is often at the bottom of the tree, contains the largest number of terms. (This follows from the branching nature of a taxonomic tree. If all genera included more than one species, then the species level would have the most terms.)

Rosch used the generic level as the basis for her notion of a basic level of concepts such as bass or maple that is somewhere in the middle of some taxonomic trees. Superordinate concepts are grouped above them, as in fish and tree, and subordinate concepts are grouped below them, as in sea bass and sugar maple. Of course, artifacts do not have formal taxonomies, and here apparently intuition (guided by language use) was used to find basic, superordinate, and subordinate levels. For example, within the domain of musical instruments, Rosch, Mervis, Gray, Johnson, and Boyes-Braem (1976) used musical instrument as the superordinate, guitar as a basic level, and electric guitar as a subordinate concept.

Table 6-1. A Simple Taxonomy of Animals and Plants with Examples at Each Level

Unique Beginner	Animal		Plant	
Life-form	Mammal	Fish	Tree	Grass
Genus	Cat	Bass	Maple	Fescue
Species	Persian	Sea bass	Sugar maple	Red fescue

Rosch claimed that basic-level concepts are the most easily discriminated from related concepts because the basic level of such taxonomies has the highest cue validity. The cue validity of a concept is the sum of the cue validities for each of the attributes of the members. The validity of a given attribute—that is, the extent to which it predicts the concept—increases as a function of the frequency with which the attribute is associated with the concept and decreases with the frequency with which the attribute is associated with other concepts. So, for instance, the attribute of having a seat is highly predictive of the concept chair but not predictive of many other kinds of furniture, such as desks and beds. The attributes of chairs give greater cue validity to the concept of chair than do the attributes of rocking chairs. Many of the attributes of rocking chairs also predict dining chairs and easy chairs, so different types of chairs are more difficult to differentiate from each other than chairs are to differentiate from desks and beds.

Unfortunately, this approach to an objective definition doesn't actually define the basic level, because in any hierarchy cue validity increases with category inclusiveness. Any attribute of any animal (beak, gills, fur, and so forth) predicts the animal class, whereas most of them do not predict basic-level classes such as dogs. Thus, more inclusive categories always have a cue validity as great as or greater than their subordinates. Indeed, in a footnote introducing her main body of work on basic-level concepts (Rosch et al., 1976), Rosch notes this problem and says that concept cue validity refers instead to a psychological factor. This admission makes it clear that cue validity isn't out there in the environment in the form of information-rich bundles of perceptual and functional features that form natural discontinuities among concepts of one kind but not another. However, even the psychological version of the argument fails, because the psychological measure of cue validity is also a summation of similar probabilities that increase with inclusiveness. Murphy (1982) showed that you get the same problem if instead of the sum of features you use the average of feature validities, and Medin (1983) showed you get just as many problems if instead of working with cue validity you work with concept validity. Concept validity is the extent to which a concept predicts certain attributes, such as having a seat or rockers, rather than an attribute predicting a concept. Here the problem is that it is always the lowest level subordinate concept that is most predictive. For example, rockers predict the subordinate class of rocking chairs, not the basic-level class of chairs. A number of writers have concluded that this level of conceptualization has never been unambiguously defined (Lassaline, Wisniewski, & Medin, 1992; Mandler, 1997; Tanaka & Taylor, 1991). Needless to say, these various definitions are highly dependent on what one considers to be an attribute. If one considers some of the most fundamental attributes of objects I have already discussed, such as contingent motion, self-motion, and biological motion, then the natural discontinuities in the world would seem to break most sharply at a superordinate level, for instance, between animals and nonanimals.

In spite of these definitional difficulties, Rosch et al. (1976) tested her hypothesis that the basic level was a privileged level of conceptualization with a famous series of 12 experiments that have often been cited as providing convincing evidence for the basic level as the most informative, the most important, and, of interest here, the first to be learned in ontogeny (e.g., see Medin & Barsalou, 1987, who stated that children have a natural affinity for the basic level that may possibly be innate). Unfortunately, this massive attack turned out to be a case of large amounts of smoke suggesting fire, whereas the actual evidence of any conflagration was slim.

The first experiment in this series asked college students to list the attributes of biological and artifact concepts at each of the three levels; for example, they were asked to list all the properties they could think of for trees, maples, and sugar maples and for musical instruments, pianos, and upright pianos. It was hypothesized that the largest number of attributes would be found at the basic level because this was the most informative level. Rosch et al. (1976) found that indeed more properties were listed for what were called the basic and subordinate levels (which did not differ from each other) than for the superordinate level in the realm of artifacts, but not for the animals and plants. In the latter realms, about as many attributes were listed for the superordinate level. This would seem to be clear refutation of the hypothesis that the basic level is "primary" or most informative. American college students know less about basic-level concepts of animals and plants than about superordinate levels. For instance, they know a fair amount about trees and fish but not what distinguishes maples from other trees or bass from other fish. I assume this finding will resonate with many readers, who, like the subjects in these experiments, may be urban folk and relatively unknowledgeable about many details of the natural world.

It may also be noted that for both biological kinds and artifacts many superordinate characteristics tended to be left unsaid. Participants apparently didn't think to mention such taken-for-granted attributes of superordinate classes as animate, starts itself, man-made, rectilinear, and so forth. As Wendell Garner (1974) showed many years ago, verbal descriptions are highly dependent on the context of the surrounding items. For example, a square drawn in black ink on a card is apt to be described as a square. But in the context of red ink squares, it is apt to be described as a black square. In the present case, it seems likely that when asked to list attributes of many related concepts, participants would focus on those that differentiate one category from another, not the attributes they have in common. That is, the task implicitly asks what differentiates one concept from another, not how much you know about concepts at one level or another.

Similar discrepancies in the treatment of biological and artifact categories were found for listing the movements that are typically made when interacting with these objects, for instance, petting animals or sitting on furniture. Differences were found among levels of categorization for the artifact domains but not for biological ones. Given this further evidence, one would expect that now the hypothesis would surely be rejected, because the biological domains on which it was based (animals and plants) refuted it and the levels ascribed to artifacts did not have any independent basis. Instead, the hypothesis was retained, but the basic level for the biological concepts was changed. Plants were dropped altogether, and bird and fish, but not mammals, were reclassified as basic level concepts.

In the next two experiments, the amount of overlap in shape and the recognizability of one object superimposed on another were studied. It was found, not surprisingly, that the basic- and subordinate-level objects from the furniture, clothing, vehicle, and animal domains had more overlap in the shapes of various exemplars than did superordinate categories. Pictures of two dogs superimposed on each other were still recognizably dogs, but a dog imposed on a butterfly created an unrecognizable mess.

The next three experiments studied speed and accuracy of processing but did not include any biological categories. In one, it was shown that superordinate names such as furniture did not speed signal detection of an object; only subordinate and basic-level names were helpful. Similarly, it was found that picture recognition is primed by words at the basic or subordinate level but not at the superordinate level. These results led to the conclusion that the basic level is the highest level at which an image of an object can be formed, although no experiments on imagery were performed. Rosch et al. (1976) noted that people who say they have an image of a superordinate class do so by imaging an exemplar. But no information was obtained about the details of what people actually imaged when given a basic-level word. For myself, when asked to image a chair, I image a specific chair. It is vague in detail to be sure, but recognizably a particular kind of chair, for example, a straight-backed chair with no arms; that is, it depicts a subordinate category. If asked, I would say I was imaging a chair; unless probed, I wouldn't say I was imaging an "armless dining chair" because that is not how we use language in everyday speech. We cannot conclude from these data, as some authors have done, that the basic level is the highest level at which we can image an object because there is not sufficient evidence for it; subjective experience suggests that for many categories the subordinate level may be the norm. We need to remember that what is in front of us is always a subordinate exemplar of a category (assuming there is more than one kind of category member). We may not interpret it that way; indeed, we often don't. We see a straight-backed armless chair and interpret it as a chair. But when we image a chair, it will be one type of chair or another.

Overall, these experiments found no significant differences between subordinate- and basic-level concepts, with the single exception that it takes longer to identify detailed subordinate concepts; it takes longer to decide that a picture represents a claw hammer than it does to decide it represents a hammer. What did show up clearly was that for artifacts, but not biological kinds, basic-level and subordinate concepts both behaved differently from superordinate concepts. The conclusion that Rosch et al. (1976) reached was that the basic level, even though it differed from the subordinate level on only one of their measures, was the most informative—sometimes expressed as the highest level at which some characteristic can be asserted. It is hardly surprising that superordinate terms like furniture are not as useful in priming picture recognition as more detailed terms, but at the same time that does not provide convincing evidence for a special "basic" level, especially given the lack of differences between subordinate and basic-level terms. What remains most troubling, however, is the failure to find any special level in the biological categories on which the hypothesis was originally based. Rosch suggested that for American college students, most of whom have grown up in an urban culture (as opposed to the rural cultures studied by the anthropologists interested in folk taxonomies), there is a different basic level for plants and animals. In a sense there is nothing wrong with this conclusion, aside from the inelegance of having the life-form level of fish and birds now become the basic level while mammals remain at the life-form level, but the point of the experiments was to determine whether there *is* a special basic level across conceptual domains. What appears to have happened instead was that the basic level was assumed to be real and the only question was what objects fulfill it.

This dilemma led to a good deal of discussion in the literature about how normal folk in our culture may differ from those in other cultures and also how experts can have different basic-level concepts than normal folk. Many American college students are deprived of detailed experience with different kinds of animals and plants, and so they must necessarily conceptualize at a more general level. Others, who have become experts in a field, may do the opposite; from daily interaction with the fine points of a topic, they may typically conceptualize at a more detailed level than other people. For instance, an airplane mechanic might treat a Cessna as a basic-level concept, with types of Cessnas as subordinate concepts, whereas for many of us airplane is "basic," in the sense that we have little knowledge about how one kind of plane differs from another (except perhaps in size). The expertise approach seems reasonable in that as we make finer and finer distinctions in a domain, the level of detail we can handle in normal thought and/or communication undoubtedly changes. But insofar as this approach is seen as a resolution of the failure to confirm the hypothesis on offer, it leaves much to be desired. Not only have we assumed as fact the theory that was to be proven but also this cultural or "amount of experience" definition of the basic level abandons the original search for an objective, universal definition of what a basic-level concept is. Brent Berlin (cited in Lakoff, 1987) went so far as to say that there really is a universal basic level of categorization determined by general physiological and psychological factors, but that some cultures underutilize these capacities. At this point, the basic level begins to sound a bit like phlogiston.

Because it has proved impossible to find an objective definition of basic-level concepts, people tend to fall back on nominal definitions, listing the common names for things used in everyday speech in Western society. Examples cited in the biological realm are familiar mammals (dog, cat, horse, etc.) and bird and fish, with the plant domain usually ignored. In the artifact realm, common kinds of furniture, clothing, and tools, such as table, shirt, and hammer, are often cited. These all have familiar and frequently monosyllabic names. Other artifact domains typically remain unmentioned, at least in part because we have no information at all about what might be basic level in many of them, such as buildings or reading materials. A further problem is that we have no basis for comparing levels across domains because they vary in number of levels; for example, should we consider mammal to be like chair and table, as was proposed for bird and fish, or is it more comparable to furniture?

To my knowledge, the only domain in the realm of artifacts that has been studied in detail other than in Rosch's own work is musical instruments. Rosch et al. (1976) posited that the basic level consists of concepts like piano, violin, and drum. They tested this by contrasting responses to terms like *musical instrument*, *piano*, and *grand piano*. Palmer, Jones, Hennessy, Unze, and Pick (1989) examined responses to musical families in addition. Using Rosch's criteria, they claimed that the basic level for both grade school children and ordinary adults is not at the level of piano, violin, and drum, as Rosch had claimed, but at the level of keyboard instruments—strings, woodwinds, and percussion instruments—that is, at the level of musical families. Speed of recognition and number of attributes listed were greatest at the family level. This was also true for adult musicians, although the authors speculated that for a musician's particular instrument it might not be true. Overall, then, the only artifact domain systematically studied did not fare better than biological domains had in Rosch's original work.

I have gone into detail on this topic to set the stage for one of the most common claims for the basic level having a special status in terms of conceptualization. That is that basic-level concepts are the first to be learned. This claim is often justified by noting that basic-level names are the first (object) words that children learn. The reason for this is said to be that concepts at this level are the most discriminable from each other and therefore should be the easiest for children to understand for purposes of language acquisition. It is certainly the case that common terms like *dog* and *chair* are more frequent in early vocabularies than terms like *animal* or *furniture*, which are often rather late. The question is how one should interpret this fact.

Roger Brown (1958), in a famous article titled "How Shall a Thing Be Called?" noted that there seems to be a special level at which things are named. He noted that we tend to use the word *dime* for a particular coin, rather than call it *money*, or *coin*, or *1958 dime*. He speculated about some of the reasons for this, although somewhat surprisingly did not mention communicative needs. Surely, much of the reason we use one level of specificity rather than another when talking is to take into account the needs of the listener, as well as whatever task is at hand. There may be some universal level of specificity, but it seems somewhat unlikely. If we need 25 cents for the telephone, we will say *quarter*, but if we need a coin to toss to see who gets to use the telephone first, we probably will say *coin*. Nevertheless, clearly many if not most of the common terms we use to refer to objects are at a finer level of detail than the unique beginners of domains and at the same time are not at a very detailed level of specificity, such as *1958 dime*. This is an important fact about the human mind, although how much it has to do with communicative pressure and how much to do with a particular level of specificity at which we formulate thoughts is not clear. In any case, the issue here is why children tend to learn this level of language first. The main reason, of course, is that they don't have any choice. They must learn the language that is spoken to them—the language of everyday speech. As Brown pointed out in his article, however, the level of specificity in the language spoken to young children is unlikely to be the level at which they conceptualize the world. He suggested that their conceptualizations are apt to be more general—that is, to be at a global rather than detailed level—and children would have to learn to hone these down to their accepted meanings.

So children's first words are taken from the vocabulary they hear. If those words match their level of thought, so much the better, but we cannot use their first words to tell us about their concepts without further ado. Considerable work is required to determine the extent to which the words children learn match their preverbal concepts. One set of relevant findings is the literature on extension of the first words. A common finding from this literature is that many of the first words are overextended in their usage (Clark, 1983; Rescorla, 1980). Children use so-called basic-level terms, such as *dog*, to refer to other animals. Underextensions occur too, but they appear to be rarer, although this may be in part a measurement problem; it is easier to measure overextension than underextension in production. If basic-level terms matched the underlying concepts children use to learn language, then one should not expect overextensions, but it is exactly what one would expect if young children's concepts are broader than the language they usually hear.

Ideally, one should not even rely on production for this determination. Children's early vocabulary is considerably smaller than is appropriate for their communicative needs, and so one might well expect over-extensions as children make a small vocabulary cover the many topics they wish to comment on. This would tell us little about their underlying concepts. Comprehension data would be much better for this purpose, although surprisingly there are still relatively few such data. One study by McDonough (2002a) compared both comprehension and production and found that even at 2 years, 29% of both production and comprehension was overextended in the domains of animals, food, clothes, and vehicles. These data are discussed in more detail in chapter 11. The point here is that limited vocabulary cannot account for the full range of overextension data. Young children appear to be unclear about the boundaries of many basic-level terms. They typically know the general domain being referred to but often do not have detailed specifications. So they have a double problem: They must figure out the extension of the word being used in the framework of not being sure what the differences are that make parents and others use different words—not an easy task!

If the first words do not answer the question of what the first concepts are, how can the hypothesis that the first concepts are at the basic level be tested? This notion was new when Rosch et al. (1976) first introduced it. Although Inhelder and Piaget (1964) had suggested that superordinate categorization was a late development, in the first part of the 20th century a common view was that concept development went from the general to the specific. Certainly Werner (e.g., 1957), who was one of the major developmental figures of the time, encouraged the view that development proceeded by a process of differentiation of global concepts into more detailed ones. In any case, at the time when Rosch proposed her theory, there were few developmental data contrasting superordinate and subordinate levels of categorization and virtually none on young children. Piaget and Inhelder had used sorting tests that require instructions, which meant that children must be at least 3, and preferably older, before they produce clean data. This is unduly late in development to study the earliest concepts, but the rationale may have been that if even at 3 years children produce confused or illogical conceptual groupings, there is no point in testing younger children's concepts, which would be equally or more confused.

Rosch et al. (1976) conducted only two developmental experiments, which they reported in the series of experiments previously discussed. Unfortunately, these experiments could not answer the question of the nature of the earliest concepts. Aside from the fact that the youngest children were 3, the studies themselves left much to be desired. One study used a sorting task in which children were asked to sort items either into basic-level or superordinate categories in the domains of clothing, furniture, vehicles, and, somewhat surprisingly, faces.[2] It was found that even as late as the first grade (mean age, 6 years, 5 months), children still had difficulty doing superordinate classification, in spite of the fact that the items were very common ones. Indeed, except for faces (which aren't objects and for which there are no norms), the objects used were the kind of items that children this age generate by themselves when asked to name all the clothing or furniture they can think of (Lucariello, Kyratzis, & Nelson, 1992),[3] so the fact that they did not sort them correctly into their superordinate classes suggests something went awry with the method. In part, the problem may have been that the criterion for correct responding was very strict. Sorting was considered incorrect if a superordinate class was subdivided. Apparently the instructions did not tell the children how many piles to use for their sorts, and if, for example, they put shirt and pants in one pile and shoes and socks in another, this was scored as an error.

A more serious problem, perhaps, was that the task used a confounded design. If one wants to test whether basic-level classification is easier than superordinate classification, one should not use sorting shirts, chairs, and cars as the basic-level test and sorting clothing, furniture, and vehicles as the superordinate test. Shirts, chairs, and cars may all be at the basic level, but they are equally exemplars of three different superordinate classes, so if children do well on the task it could be due to using basic-level information (all shirts look very much alike), superordinate information (all shirts are clothing), or most likely both. That is, they would have two sources of information available for the basic-level test and only one source for the superordinate test. To test the basic level, as Rosch and Mervis (1975) did with adults, one would have to contrast shirts with pants and shoes, or chairs with tables and beds. However, this confounding of basic-level and superordinate information characterized all the sorting tests in the developmental literature of the time, including the work of Rosch and Mervis (e.g., Daehler, Lonardo, & Bukatko, 1979; Mervis & Crisafi, 1982; Saxby & Anglin, 1983). That this confound really matters is shown in the next chapter; when we unconfounded the basic-level and superordinate contrasts in the fashion just described, we found that young children do better at a superordinate classification task than at a basic-level one (Mandler, Bauer, & McDonough, 1991). We used the sequential-touching task, which, as described in chapter 1, is a version of a sorting task designed for children too young to follow sorting instructions. We found excellent categorization of animals and vehicles by 1½- to 2½-year-olds. But when we used true basic-level contrasts by contrasting, say, dogs with rabbits or cars with motorcycles, we found very little basic-level categorization at 1½ years, and not until 2½ years did the majority of the children categorize at this level. Only when we used a confounded design such as Rosch et al. (1976) used, contrasting dogs with cars, did we find basic-level categorization on this task in the second year (Mandler & Bauer, 1988).

The other developmental experiment that Rosch et al. (1976) used was a match-to-sample test with 3- and 4-year-olds, again studying superordinate and basic-level contrasts, this time with animals and vehicles. Although performance was at ceiling by 4 years, the 3-year-olds were roughly at chance on the superordinate contrast of animals and vehicles. This is a surprising finding, suggesting as it does that 3-year-olds can't tell the difference between animals and vehicles. In any case, it does not jibe with data that Patricia Bauer and I collected, using the same task but with much younger children. We found a high rate of superordinate matching to sample by 1½- to 2½-year-old children (Bauer & Mandler,

1989). The poor performance of the children in the Rosch et al. (1976) study on the superordinate task may have been due to misunderstanding of the instructions and/or to the use a pretraining procedure that emphasized perceptual matches (which was a common procedure in similar studies of the time). Whatever the reason, it is highly unlikely that the children's difficulties with the superordinate contrast were due to lack of understanding that animals and vehicles are different kinds of things.

Rosch was sensitive to the difficulties I have mentioned in giving a developmental interpretation to her data, because she later noted that the principles of categorization she promulgated had to do with explaining categories coded by the language of a given culture and did not constitute a theory of development (Rosch, 1978). Yet both Mervis and Rosch (1981) and Mervis and Mervis (1982) explicitly claimed that basic-level categories are the first to be acquired, and by this they did not mean culturally or linguistically variable concepts but rather a specific kind of concept, such as chair or bird (that is, of objects that have similar overall shapes, elicit similar motor patterns in responses to them, and so forth). More important for the field, this is the interpretation that came to be standard in the literature, and the claim that basic-level concepts are the first to be learned was commonly found in the developmental texts of the 1990s (e.g., Bjorklund, 1995; Siegler, 1991). At the same time, it was often pointed out that children's basic-level concepts may differ from those of adults. For instance, Mervis and Mervis (1982) talked about "child-basic" concepts, which can be either broader or narrower in scope than adults. Unfortunately, this makes a hash of the notion that there is a special level of conceptualization that is the easiest to learn because it maximizes within-category similarity and between-category dissimilarity. Instead, it suggests that "child-basic" means any concept that children learn.

So what are we to make of the claim that there is a level of conceptualization that differs from other levels? My sense is that the basic level has come to be understood as culturally determined and/or a question of expertise. Given the great diversity of cultures and of expertise within cultures, it is not clear that this leaves any core notion worth saving. In any case, it means that basic-level concepts cannot be the first to be formed. Both cultural knowledge and expertise require extensive learning and so cannot provide entry-level concepts. As we will see in chapters 7 and 8, what is usually called basic is a level to be attained, not a starting point.

Basic-Level Categorization as a Part
of Perceptual Categorization

There is, however, another way to interpret the meaning of the term *basic level* that may have more merit. Rosch, like most of her colleagues at the time she was writing, did not make a distinction between perceptual and conceptual categories. When she discussed basic-level concepts and how to measure them, most of the criteria had to do with the physical features of objects. Although object functions were considered to be legitimate features, nevertheless, most of the features discussed were parts of objects or other physical aspects. Thus, the correlated cluster of features that make birds a coherent class was said to be such things as beaks, wings, and feathers—all physical features. The criterion in many of the experiments was recognizability, which has to do with object identification rather than conceptual understanding. The specification of cue validity in terms of maximizing within-category similarity and between-category dissimilarity is another example. Although similarity can be conceived of in terms of object function, in almost all realizations of this notion it had to do with physical similarity and how easy or difficult it is to tell one object apart from another. So the tests used in Rosch et al. (1976) tended to emphasize physical similarity, in particular, similarity of shape. Perhaps what Rosch was measuring was some level of perceptual categorization at which it is particularly easy to form a perceptual prototype or schema of what objects look like. This idea has not been systematically tested, although one set of experiments using artificial stimuli suggested that the advantage in learning new basic-level concepts lies in similarities in shape (Murphy & Smith, 1982). But to my knowledge no one has examined whether it is easier to learn to categorize a real-world category of dogs, for example, than of collies or terriers.

Perhaps the issue of the difference between perceptual and conceptual categorization was bypassed because of the critique by Smith and Medin (1981) of the classical view of concepts. Following Miller and Johnson-Laird (1976), they proposed that concepts have a core meaning consisting of necessary and sufficient features and also a set of identification procedures by which one recognizes instances. Nevertheless, it seemed to Smith and Medin that so much of the work of conceptualization involves the identifying features that core features might be doomed to irrelevance. However, Frege's (1952) notion of sense (core meaning) and reference (identification) is too fundamental to give up (see chapter 11). Among other things, understanding the meaning of an object involves putting it into some context, to know something about what it does or what is done to it, and neither of these is centrally involved in being able to recognize it. Although one can recognize an object faster and more accurately in a familiar context than in an unfamiliar context (Loftus & Mackworth, 1978; Mandler & Johnson, 1976; Palmer, 1975), the basic processes involved in object recognition are not associative but perceptual. And if we consider this issue from the point of view of newborns beginning to categorize and conceptualize their world, there is evidence that two different processes are involved, if for no other reason than that infants can learn to perceptually categorize objects before they have any notion of their meaning. As I discussed in chapter 3, perceptual schema formation is a primitive process that takes place in an automatic fashion and that does not require any conceptual understanding to be accomplished. Because of several decades of work on implicit versus explicit processing, we are in a better position today to explicate the mutual workings of conceptual cores and perceptual identification procedures.

In recent years, in large part because of the work of Quinn and Eimas and their colleagues, we have begun to learn a good deal about just how early young infants begin to form real-world perceptual categories. Instead of using line drawings of geometric forms or artificial faces, which had been the most frequent way to study categorization in infancy, Quinn and Eimas began to work with pictures of real animals. In one study (Quinn, Eimas, & Rosenkrantz, 1993), 3-month-olds were familiarized with pictures of cats or dogs. They learned to categorize such stimuli in as few as six 20-second trials, each of which consisted of two pictures of exemplars of one of the categories. The test trial consisted of a new exemplar of the familiarized category paired with an exemplar of the other category. Categorization was assumed if infants preferred to look at the exemplar of the new category.

It may be of some importance that there was an asymmetry in the results. Infants were better categorizers when they were familiarized with cats than when they were familiarized with dogs. Quinn et al. (1993) speculated that this was because dogs are more variable in appearance. Because of the greater range in values of various physical dimensions of dogs, a cat is a possible dog, but it doesn't work the other way around: A dog makes a bad cat. This hypothesis was confirmed by work of Mareschal, French, and Quinn (2000). They measured various features of the faces of the animals used in these experiments, such as eye separation, ear length, and nose width. Dogs were indeed more variable than cats, and furthermore the values for the cats were often a subset of those for the dogs. Therefore, dogs were more difficult to categorize than cats. If variability is too great, no commonalities that organize category learning may be found. For example, Younger and Fearing (2000) showed that for 4-month-olds to form perceptual categories of cats, horses, or cars in the laboratory (few of which may have been experienced in the real world) they must be given concentrated experience with one category at a time. When two of these categories were trained together, the variability was such that basic-level categorization no longer took place.

In addition to dogs and cats, Eimas and Quinn (1994) showed that in the same number of trials 3-month-olds learned to categorize horses as different from zebras or giraffes and cats as different from tigers, although not from lions until 6 months of age. Behl-Chadha (1996) showed that they could also categorize tables, chairs, and beds. So it is obvious that with a very few exposures even quite young infants can learn to categorize real-world objects of the kind that are usually called basic level. None of these investigators (nor I) think that these categorical feats have conceptual content. Three-month-olds in our culture don't have any experience with horses and giraffes or any basis to conceptualize differences between these categories. What they do have is a highly efficient perceptual learning mechanism.

As discussed in chapter 3, forming a perceptual category—or, more accurately stated perhaps, forming a perceptual schema—is a low-level sensorimotor accomplishment that is part of the basic workings of the perceptual system. It is an automatic process that does not require conceptual thought. It accumulates information about the physical dimensions of what is being perceived and over the course of repeated exposures builds a prototype. Infants as young as 3 months form perceptual prototypes of objects in roughly the same fashion as adults (Bomba & Siqueland, 1983; de Haan, Johnson, Maurer, & Perrett, 2001). The perceptual system pulls out the main factors or principal components of the patterns being presented. This kind of process is easily modeled by a connectionist autoassociative model, in which prototypes are formed by summing connection strengths across individual events while also retaining some information about individual exemplars (McClelland & Rumelhart, 1985). These models act like factor analyses, finding and making use of the correlations present in the stimuli. Quinn and Johnson (1997) used a simple version of such a network to model the kind of perceptual learning they found in 3-month-olds. (Although these "top-down" models for perceptual learning seem persuasive to me, other connectionist models that rely on a more traditional "bottom-up" approach—building up representations from simple to more complex units have also been proposed [Cohen, Chaput, & Cashon, 2002]. These models seem diametrically opposed. Perhaps all we can say at this point is we don't yet know for sure exactly how perceptual learning proceeds.)

Whether top-down or bottom-up, that perceptual categorization is a relatively low-level process is illustrated by the fact that pigeons are great perceptual categorizers. I have nothing against pigeons, but they do have bird brains, and from the data from pigeon labs I see little evidence of their forming conceptual categories. It seems to me that the view of Ed Wasserman (1995), who claims that pigeons can form abstract concepts, epitomizes the problem of not distinguishing perceptual and conceptual accomplishments. It has been known for some time that pigeons, which have a highly developed visual system, are capable of forming abstract categories such as trees (Herrnstein, 1979). But perceptual categorization, which pulls out the principal factors in patterns, is often abstract. As we have seen, 3-month-old infants categorize biological motion, which is abstract, to say the least. Trees should be easy; they form dendritic patterns that are highly dissimilar to blocky man-made buildings and similar objects, so it is not really surprising that distinguishing trees from buildings is a task that even a bird brain can accomplish. Abstract does not equal conceptual.

Wasserman (1995) claimed that pigeons have abstract concepts because they can learn to differentiate displays consisting of a grid of 16 small pictures, all of which are the same, from displays of 16 small pictures that are all different—thus evidencing "concepts of sameness and difference." A glance at the two kinds of array, illustrated in the top portion of Figure 6-1, shows a striking perceptual difference. I'm not sure exactly how to describe it (because it is not well conceptualized!). Young

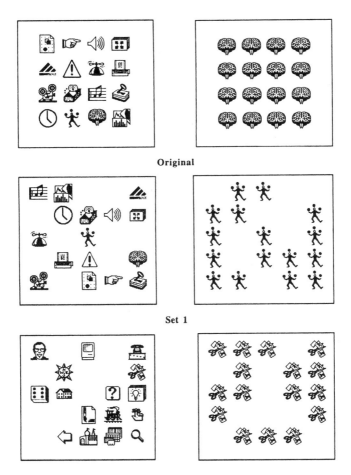

Figure 6-1. Examples of the repetitive versus variable stimuli Wasserman (1995) and Young and Wasserman (1997) used to claim that pigeons have abstract "concepts." Figure from Young and Wasserman (1997), copyright © 1997 by the American Psychological Association. Reprinted with permission.

and Wasserman (1997) suggested one possibility might be linear orderliness. To get around the possibility that the pigeons might be responding to perceptual differences in linearity, Young and Wasserman used arrays like those found in the middle and bottom portion of Figure 6-1. The perceptual difference between these displays is even more difficult to describe conceptually, but there is directional alignment in the variable displays that is absent in the repetitive ones. Some responsivity to differences in this or other aspects of the variability seems likely to account for the discrimination. (Young and Wasserman employed a measure of entropy detection.) It is of interest that pigeons require many hundreds of trials before this kind of discrimination is made. I must say these data confirm my notion of a bird brain. Whatever the pigeons are responding to does not appear to be anything like a human concept of same-different but rather an abstract perceptual variable. Almost certainly it is not the basis for infants' ability to do the same-different superordinate match-to-sample tasks described in Bauer and Mandler (1989). The pigeon data tell us that birds respond to abstract perceptual parameters, but *abstract* is not a synonym for *conceptual*.

The infant categorization data make clear that it is possible to separate conceptualization from perceptual category formation. What 3-month-olds are doing in categorization experiments of the sort conducted by Quinn et al. (1993) is learning how to identify objects, which they can do independently of any ideas about them. For instance, they have no trouble learning to recognize and categorize two-dimensional dot patterns, as long as these stimuli have some regularities amenable to factor analysis (Bomba & Siqueland, 1983). This ability is a very important part of the human mental apparatus, but it is not concept formation. Because this kind of categorization has to do with object identification, it seems plausible that the findings of Rosch and her colleagues tapped largely into perceptual knowledge rather than conceptual knowledge. As we have seen, her tests tended to be perceptual identification tests, such as speed of identifying objects given more or less specific primes or the extent to which shapes of objects overlap at one level of specificity compared with another.

The experiment by Murphy and Smith (1982) mentioned earlier in this chapter supports this notion. These authors pointed out that factors other than the number of distinctive attributes might have caused the finding that people are fastest to identify objects at the basic level. For instance, there are often not clear perceptual features differentiating basic-level and subordinate items (such as peach and cling peach). To get around this problem, they used artificial categories that looked like schematic versions of tools. They found that what they decided were superordinate, basic-level, and subordinate concepts behaved much like they did in

Rosch et al.'s (1976) experiments. In another experiment, they tried to show that this result doesn't have to do with the basic level being in the middle of a hierarchy and therefore receiving activation from both above and below. In this second experiment, they found that basic-level concepts were faster to identify than subordinates, because the way they constructed the stimuli made the subordinates look more like each other and so it was more difficult to reject false instances. So they switched the hierarchies they used around, making size differences the top level, functional relatedness the middle level, and overall shape differences (which they considered to be the basic level) the lowest level. Now they found that shape differences made for the fastest reaction times, size next, and functional differences the slowest. These results suggested that the advantage of the basic level is that objects compared at this level have the most distinctively contrasting shapes.

Having said this, however, it must be noted that we have no data to tell us whether perceptual categories (perceptual schemas) are easiest to form at some middle hierarchical level rather than at more detailed levels. We don't know this about adults, and especially important, we don't have any relevant information about babies. It may be that it is just as easy for 3-month-olds to learn to discriminate dachshunds from German shepherds as dogs from cats. It obviously depends entirely on the salience of the perceptual differences. Perhaps the very different shapes of the two breeds of dogs would be as salient as the features that distinguish dogs and cats, but until the relevant research is done we won't know. The general point to be made is that Rosch may have uncovered an important fact about object identification, but the pertinent data have not been systematically collected. Some of the data in Rosch et al. (1976) are relevant to this perceptual hypothesis, but they were not designed to test it.

Quinn and Eimas (e.g., 1997), along with a good many other psychologists, made the assumption that because even very young infants easily categorize dogs and cats or tables and chairs, then these categories provide the foundation on which concept formation rests. Infants see dogs and cats, tables and chairs, and they categorize them. Therefore, all they need to do to begin to form concepts is to associate various activities with these categories, and conceptual life is off the ground. This is a very old view, but as I have tried to show in this and the preceding chapters, to see is not the same as to think. In the present chapter, we have seen that insofar as concepts are concerned there are no data to support the hypothesis that basic-level concepts are the first to be formed. It is very difficult even to be sure exactly what a basic-level concept is, but even if we merely enumerate them—dog, cat, table, chair, and so forth—all we know from the data we have discussed to this point is that babies can perceptually categorize them. However, they can also form broader perceptual categories equally young or perhaps even younger (Quinn & Johnson, 2000), and very likely narrower ones as well, so the notion of a basic level seems to tell us very little about development.[4]

There Are Multiple Forms of Categorization

If we insist on searching for "a" theory of categorization to cover all categorization phenomena, we will remain hopelessly mired. The current situation is reminiscent of scientists of the 18th century who did not distinguish between heat and temperature (see Smith, Carey, & Wiser, 1985). There is more than one kind of categorization, a fact that is ignored when someone says, "Categories are. . . ." I don't need to mention any article in particular for the reader to recognize the frequency of statements such as "A current discussion in the literature is whether categorization is based on. . . ." Or "Mandler has argued that infants first form global categories and only later form basic-level categories." This oversimplification occurs in spite of the fact that a number of authors have emphasized that the kinds of information used to categorize in a given task depend on the information available, instructions, and a variety of contextual effects (e.g., Deak & Bauer, 1996; Gelman, 2003).

Conceptualization is only one kind of categorization, as the preceding discussion and earlier chapters make clear. Both perceptual and conceptual categorization operate on similarity—in the case of the former, on similarity of physical appearance, and in the case of the latter, on similarity of kind. The type of similarity being used needs to be specified. However, even similarity is not a definitive requirement for categorization. Another form of categorization, called categorical perception, groups stimuli along a perceptual dimension as a function of differential sensitivity in the perceptual system at various points on the dimension. For example, when we group *b* sounds as different from *p* sounds, we are engaging in this kind of categorization; we hear abrupt shifts from one phoneme to the other in spite of continuous variation in voice onset time. This is an automatic un-learned process, and I do not discuss it in this book because it is not par-ticularly relevant to understanding early conceptual development. Still another form of categorization, however, is relevant, and that is cate-gorization by association rather than similarity. Some years ago, Robyn Fivush, Steven Reznick, and I (Mandler, Fivush, & Reznick, 1987) found that 14- and 20-month-olds have formed categories of kitchen things and bathroom things (although the categorization was marginal at 14 months, a finding replicated in Mandler & Bauer, 1988, suggesting that these as-sociative categories may be slower to develop or perhaps are less salient for infants). The items in these categories are extremely varied and have little or no perceptual similarity by which to categorize them. It could be done either by spatiotemporal associations or by conceptualizing the ob-jects as part of the events that take place in these locations. We called them contextual categories to emphasize that they were neither percep-tual categories based on perceptual schematizing nor the more frequently studied taxonomic categories based on kind.

As these findings and the research described in the next two chapters make clear, we cannot build our baby with only one kind of categoriza-tion process. Contextual categories (and even categorical perception) can be seen as an existence proof for more than one basis for categorization. In the light of this, it does seem surprising that the notion of multiple forms of categorization is not infrequently rejected out of hand by some developmental researchers (Eimas, 1994; Madole & Oakes, 1999). Eimas (1994) expressed unhappiness about my calling upon more than one kind of categorization, saying that it is ad hoc and special purpose:

> . . . development of conceptual representations and even of the naive theories in which they are ultimately embedded is a con-tinuous process that does not require the application of special-purpose processes of development. What is necessary instead is the application and re-application of processes that are available to all sentient beings (as far as we know), that are innately given, that are operative early in life, and that remain operative throughout the course of our existence. . . .The initial function of these processes is to form perceptually driven categorical

representations, whereas their later function is to enrich these initial representations informationally and to do so to an extent that they begin to take on the characteristics of concepts. . . . The apparent qualitative difference between perceptually and conceptually driven representations [is] in actuality for us one of degree of informational richness and complexity. (pp. 85–86)

I agree with some of this quote but come to a very different conclusion! Of course, the development of conceptual representations is a continuous process and depends on innate abilities. That does not mean the human mind is restricted to only one kind of process, however. In addition, although the quote does not specify the meaning of informational richness and complexity, a concept cannot be merely a richer percept. Among other things, this would not account for the early appearance of nonperceptual concepts such as animal or furniture, let alone concepts such as toys or bedtime. As I pointed out in chapter 3, the notion Eimas espouses is the classic British empiricists' notion that concepts consist of percepts plus associations (that is, ideas + associations = complex ideas). But at best this approach would produce only a rich "concept" of dog, not do the abstractive work that results in concepts like animal.

Madole and Oakes (1999) take a position similar to Eimas. They suggest that making a distinction between perceptual and conceptual categories confuses our attempts to understand psychological reality. Instead, they claim there is only one kind of categorization, although it can select different features at different ages. What changes with development is that infants become increasingly attentive to "abstract features of objects." They do not define abstract features but mention that taxonomic category and function are two. How class membership can be a feature of an object—or for that matter perceived—is not clear. Both these positions suffer from a good deal of overgenerality. It is high time for more detailed accounts of concept formation to be formulated.

A final point before proceeding to research findings: Categorization differs depending on whether one is deliberately doing a categorization task. When we are consciously trying to form a new concept or decide on how to group a set of stimuli, we may engage in hypothesis formation and testing. But that is not the way that most categorization takes place.

Perceptual schemas are formed automatically and so are clearly not in the realm of hypothesis testing. But what about concept formation? In infancy (and I suspect in most situations in life), concepts are formed by the application of selective attention and analysis. But these processes are not hypothesis testing either. A baby might observe a snail emerge from its shell and move forward in an irregular path across the floor, and then categorize this thing as an animal. But what hypotheses were tested here? This is more a case of generalization on the basis of one of the simple rules acquired by perceptual meaning analysis (animals are self-moving things) than hypothesis testing as that term is normally used.

One often reads in the literature that babies are little scientists (Gopnik, Meltzoff, & Kuhl, 1999). Although I agree with this in that infants are curious explorers of the world, the implication that might be taken from this kind of statement is that they spend a lot of their time forming concepts by making hypotheses and then testing them. Outside of school tasks set to make us do that or being in a profession that requires this sort of activity, most of our concept formation is "intuitive" in nature, involving attending to selected aspects of a situation, noting by analogy (similarity) their relationship to something we already know, and coming to a categorization on that basis. This approach is humanly reasonable, but it does not bear much resemblance to hypothesis formulation followed by testing. The next chapter summarizes some of the research showing the course of development of early kinds of "intuitive concepts."

7

Some Preverbal Concepts

. . . in which I describe how we were unable to find evidence for most of the "basic-level" concepts such as dog or chair that have been assumed to be the first ones formed. In contrast, we found ample evidence of global concepts, such as animal, vehicle, and furniture. The data suggest a double dissociation in different categorization tasks in infancy, implying that more than one process is at work. One process involves identification of objects and the other involves interpreting their meaning. I discuss why categorization tasks involving pictures may evoke in young infants identification more than interpretation, and why tasks involving objects tend to fully engage conceptual processes.

. . . as our experimental techniques get better, infants seem to get smarter. (Fodor, 1987)

Global Concepts

Our beginning experiments investigating early concepts originated in the hypothesis that "basic-level" concepts, based on perceptual similarity, could not account for all that infants and young children are categorizing. We had already seen in our work on contextual categories (Mandler et al., 1987) that perceptual similarity is not a necessary condition for categorization. Next we tackled the question of whether it is sufficient. We asked whether there are cases in which items are not categorized even though they are similar in appearance. In the last chapter I discussed how all of the developmental tests of early concepts used confounded designs, in which the categories that were being contrasted were taken from contrasting superordinates, such as dogs and cars. Bauer and I used the sequential-touching task to show that when dogs were contrasted with horses instead of cars, not until 20 months did children reliably categorize them (Mandler & Bauer, 1988), and even then only half the children did so.

We went on to study this issue in detail by systematically varying the perceptual similarity of the classes being contrasted (Mandler et al., 1991). In the first study we gave 18-, 24-, and 30-month-olds four sequential-touching tasks, each of which provided a different kind of contrast. One was a superordinate contrast of animals versus vehicles, in which the items differed considerably both within and between classes. There were also three within-domain contrasts, in which within-category similarity was the same and high in all, and only between-category similarity varied. One was a low-similarity contrast because the categories came from different life-forms—dogs versus fish and cars versus airplanes.[1] The next two were both proper "basic-level" contrasts, one of which we considered to be a medium-similarity contrast—dogs versus rabbits and cars versus motorcycles. The other we considered to be a high-similarity contrast—dogs versus horses and cars versus trucks. The percentage of children who categorized at both the superordinate and basic levels is shown in Table 7-1.[2] As can be seen, the data were quite regular. At all ages the majority of children made the superordinate categorization of animals versus vehicles, thus showing categorization of items with low similarity both within and between classes. The majority also categorized the land and air categories of dogs versus birds and cars versus airplanes (high within-class similarity, low between-class similarity). For the basic-level tasks, when the between-category contrast was of medium similarity (dogs versus rabbits or cars versus motorcycles), a majority of the 18- and 24-month-olds did not categorize, and for the most difficult task, in which the between-category contrast was high in similarity (dogs versus horses or cars versus trucks), performance was even worse.

Thus, similarity of items such as dogs or cars was not in itself sufficient for categorization to take place. For the basic-level and life-form contrasts, categorization depended not on similarity among the items to be categorized but on the contrasting class. The greater the similarity be-

Table 7-1. Percentage of Children Categorizing at the Superordinate
and Basic Levels

	18 Months	24 Months	30 Months
Superordinate contrast: Animals vs vehicles	73	67	77

Life-form contrast:
    Dogs vs fish
    Cars vs airplanes
	75	65	75

Basic-level medium-similarity contrast:
    Dogs vs rabbits
    Cars vs motorcycles
	40	45	70

Basic-level high-similarity contrast:
    Dogs vs horses
    Cars vs trucks
	30	40	45

tween the contrasts, the worse the performance. Would an explanation in terms of both within- and between-category similarity be sufficient to account for the data? The chief difficulty with such an approach is the fact that the children in these experiments were *15 to 27 months older* than the age at which infants have been shown to distinguish the same or similar basic-level contrasts perceptually, even though between-category similarity is equally high (e.g., dogs and horses; Eimas & Quinn, 1994). Why then did so few of the children categorize at the basic level? And why were the life-form and superordinate contrasts relatively easy for them? A more nuanced explanation would take into account the fact that children interpret stimuli conceptually and that the nature of their interpretations affects their categorization. It seems that the children were making some conceptual distinctions and not others. The distinctions they did make were between land and water animals and between road and air vehicles.

We weren't sure how to test vehicles further, because the children did not seem to pay attention to number of wheels, and developmental lore suggested that young children might not treat boats as vehicles. (As it turns out, in Experiment 3 we included a boat among a superordinate category of vehicles, and children did treat it like other vehicles, but we didn't know that at the time.) However, for the animal domain we could fairly easily determine whether young children have made a tripartite division of the animal domain into what might be called animals that walk, swim, and fly—or alternatively, animals that are found on land, in the water, and in the air. We had already shown they categorized dogs as different from fish, so in Experiment 2 we tested a group of 2-year-olds on a contrast of dogs and birds. They did very well, with 80% of the children showing categorization. Overall, the data from these experiments indicated that in the second year, children have made some conceptual subdivisions in the animal and vehicle domains, albeit at a very general level.

In this series of experiments, we also examined categorization of plants, kitchen items, furniture, tools, and musical instruments. In an experiment with 24-month-olds, we found categorization of kitchen items as different from furniture, and animals as different from plants, but no categorical distinction between tools and musical instruments. The latter finding does not mean that children this age don't know anything about tools or musical instruments. Many children hammered with the hammer, tooted on the horn, and pretended to play the piano. But they did not react to tools and instruments as classes, choosing instead to do such things as fix the piano with the pliers. This behavior can be contrasted with the systematic within-class touching of furniture and kitchen things. The children could just as well have spent their time putting the cup and plate on the table, but instead they were more likely to manipulate the kitchen items or the furniture together. The lack of such behavior with tools and instruments suggests that although children this age have learned appropriate responses to this or that musical instrument, they have not yet formed an overall conception of how these objects are related to each other. In addition to these global tests, in another experiment we investigated four within-domain contrasts in the domains of plants, furniture, utensils, and musical instruments. We found little or no evidence of categorization in tasks that contrasted cacti with trees, tables with chairs, spoons with forks, or stringed instruments with horns.

These data indicate that by 2 years children have categorized various domains at a global level but even at this relatively old age have not yet developed a firm grasp of many of their subdivisions. At this point we began to use the term *global* rather than *superordinate* to refer to concepts such as animals or plants. To the extent that early concepts are sweeping in their scope but without subdivisions, it doesn't seem appropriate to speak of superordinate concepts. Although our data indicated that plants, furniture, and utensils were in this state, even the youngest children tested in these experiments did show a tripartite division of animals and at least a binary division of vehicles. Of course, these data made us intensely curious about younger infants. How early are these distinctions learned? If we had tested slightly younger children, would we have found no subdivisions at all in the animal and vehicle domains? Or are these major distinctions in place from a much earlier age?

First, we had to figure out a way to test younger children. Although Starkey (1981) had some success in using the sequential-touching task with 9-month-olds, his stimuli were identical geometric forms. Categorization of realistic objects, each of which is varied in appearance, is a more difficult task (Gopnik & Meltzoff, 1992), and before about 16 months, putting eight such stimuli at once in front of infants often overwhelms them.[3] Even after much thought, we could not think of a better method than some version of the familiarization/preferential-looking test, in which infants are familiarized with one or more stimuli and then tested to see if they dishabituate to a new stimulus. We weren't particularly happy with this choice, because in our experience after about 8 months of age infants tend to be restless when given series of static pictures to look at. We decided to use the variant called the object-examination test, described in chapter 1, in which infants are familiarized with objects from one category and then given an object from a contrasting category. How long they examine this object in comparison with a new object from the familiarized category is the measure used. This task lets infants engage in relatively normal and voluntary activity with one object at a time; they can examine it, turn it around, or make it move. We find that even young infants are thoroughly engaged when handling an object, which must surely be a plus in terms of activating conceptual thought processes. One indication of infants' interest is that subject loss is virtually nil, which contrasts considerably with many picture-looking studies in which infant participants are often lost due to resistance of one form or another. Figure 7-1 shows a 9-month-old in this task and illustrates the intense concentration that we often see in infants engaged in manipulating our little models.

The problem with the task, of course, is that in many instances it is possible to categorize objects with similar shapes sheerly on the basis of perceptual similarity, and the resulting data are therefore ambiguous about

Figure 7-1. An example of the intense involvement infants often show when participating in the object-examination task. Reproduced from Mandler (1997) by permission of Psychology Press.

concept formation. We know from the work discussed earlier that infants can rapidly construct perceptual schemas from pictures of dogs, horses, and cats (Eimas & Quinn, 1994; Quinn et al., 1993). So if infants dishabituate to a dog after seeing a series of cats, that does not tell us that they have concepts of dogs and cats that differ. This would create a problem when so-called basic-level categories such as dogs and cats or tables and chairs were contrasted. We thought, however, that it would not be a problem when global categories such as animals and vehicles were contrasted because the exemplars do not look alike. This assumption caused us more trouble than it was probably worth, because it was roundly attacked by researchers committed to the view that all infant categorization is perceptual in nature (Haith & Benson, 1998; Quinn & Eimas, 1997).

Nevertheless, we claimed, perhaps optimistically, that our little plastic models of animals, such as an elephant, turtle, rabbit, and bird, could not be categorized on the basis of shape alone. So if infants categorized these on the object-examination test when contrasted with a motorcycle, bus, cement truck, and train engine, it would be on the basis of conceptual rather than perceptual similarity. We thought it likely that if we gave infants contrasts between dogs and rabbits or dogs and fish, they would categorize them on the basis of shape differences, but that if they categorized animals versus vehicles we would be able to make the case for conceptual categorization. What we did not expect was the actual result we found, namely, that animals were discriminated from vehicles, but dogs were *not* discriminated from rabbits or fish.

The first series of experiments we did using the object-examination task (Mandler & McDonough, 1993) was with 7-, 9-, and 11-month-olds. We studied the global contrast of animals versus vehicles and several within-domain contrasts taken from those we had studied previously on the sequential-touching task (Mandler et al., 1991). For the easy (land versus air or sea) contrasts that 18-month-olds had categorized, we used cars versus airplanes and dogs versus fish. For the more difficult set of land contrasts that 18-month-olds had trouble with, we used cars versus motorcycles and dogs versus rabbits. The percentage of 9- and 11-month-olds who examined the exemplar of the novel category longer than an exemplar from the familiarized category for each of the contrasts studied is shown in Table 7-2.[4] It can be seen that the infants did well on the global contrast of animals versus vehicles and also on both within-domain contrasts in the vehicle domain, but they did badly on both of the within-animal contrasts. We were especially surprised by the last result, because the shapes of the dogs and the fish (shown in Figure 7-2) seemed to us so different that we expected categorization to take place simply on the grounds of perceptual appearance. Given this within-domain failure, we were also surprised that the infants were successful on the within-domain vehicle contrasts, which seemed comparable in their perceptual differ-

Table 7-2. Percentage of Infants Who Examined the Novel Category Longer

	9 Months	11 Months
Animals vs vehicles	80	100
Dogs vs fish	30	60
Dogs vs rabbits	40	60
Cars vs airplanes	100	90
Cars vs motorcycles	100	70
Birds vs airplanes	85	75

Figure 7-2. The dogs and fish that 7- to 11-month-
old infants do not categorize as different on the
object-examining task.

ences to the within-animal contrasts. The last experiment in this series
was a perceptual control test. We tested 9- and 11-month-olds on a contrast between birds and airplanes, all with outspread wings. These objects, shown in Figure 7-3, were highly perceptually alike, but at both
ages infants treated them as belonging to different categories (see the last
row of Table 7-2).

   These data presented several puzzles. In particular, it is difficult to find
a perceptual explanation for the pattern of successes and failures, because
neither within- nor between-category perceptual similarity consistently

Figure 7-3. The birds and airplanes that 9- to
11-month-olds do categorize as different on the
object-examining task.

affected categorization. On the global task of animals versus vehicles, within-category similarity of the exemplars is relatively low, yet the infants categorized these items. On the other hand, within-category similarity of exemplars was high in the case of dogs, fish, and rabbits, but the infants did *not* categorize these classes. It was (presumably) equally high in the classes of cars, motorcycles, and airplanes, but here the infants *did* categorize. As for between-category dissimilarity, it was presumably high in the global contrast of animals and vehicles, which could account for success, but it was extremely low for birds versus airplanes, on which they were also successful. In general, there is no easy perceptual explanation for these findings. The birds–airplanes contrast in particular was as strong a test as we could think of to disconfirm our hypothesis that global categorization of animals and vehicles is not due to perceptual factors alone and therefore, by default, due to some appreciation of similarity in conceptual meaning. Perceptual similarity was very high both within and between the two classes, but still the birds and airplanes were treated as different.

More recently, the conclusion that perceptual similarity is not what accounts for this kind of categorization in 10- to 11-month-olds was confirmed in a series of experiments by Sabina Pauen (2002), which systematically varied between-category similarity of little models of animals and furniture. In low-similarity conditions, the items were realistic and varied greatly in shape, color, and surface patterning. In high-similarity conditions, each item had legs, curved as well as rectilinear parts, and black-and-white dots that could be interpreted as eyes in the animals and knobs or decorations in the furniture. In addition, the furniture items were designed so that each item has the same overall shape as one of the animals, the same colors as another animal, and the same surface pattern as another of the animals. Pauen found that even when there was high between-category similarity among the items, 10- and 11-month-olds categorized the items appropriately, and did so as much as when between-category similarity was low. Her work used two different versions of the object-examination task, and on both, whether perceptual between-category similarity was high or low, the infants treated animals and furniture items as members of distinct global categories.

The finding of categorization for the global domains and lack of within-domain categorization for animals fits our hypothesis of infants developing broad, global concepts before learning more detailed ones. The finding inconsistent with this hypothesis, of course, was the good performance on contrasts within the vehicle domain, where infants seemed to have no difficulty in categorizing cars, motorcycles, and airplanes all as different. Because a perceptual explanation seemed unlikely for the reasons given before, we assumed that infants have already learned more about vehicles in the urban southern California community where the data were gathered and hence may be more advanced in their conceptualization of vehicles than animals. I return to this issue later and also in the next chapter.

One question that remained open from this first series of experiments was whether the global categories of animals and vehicles that we uncovered might be better described as animate versus inanimate things. With only two domains being studied, it would be impossible to say whether infants have developed concepts specifically of these domains or of the larger realms of which they are instances. The second series of experiments we conducted (Mandler & McDonough, 1998a) was designed to explore other domains and to check whether the advanced categorizing behavior we had found within the vehicle domain was true in general for artifacts or was restricted to vehicles. In the first experiment in the new series, we used the object-examination test to study 7-, 9-, and 11-month-olds' responses to the contrast of animals versus furniture and furniture versus vehicles. These contrasts would enable us to see if finer distinctions were being made than animate versus inanimate and also if a task that crossed the animate-inanimate divide was easier than one contrasting two domains within the inanimate realm. Infants were successful at both tasks. Significant age differences were not found (although there was somewhat less categorizing among the 7-month-olds). This finding tells us that in the second half of the first year, animals, vehicles, and furniture are all distinguished from each other as different kinds.

Next we investigated three global contrasts: plants versus vehicles (a distinction between the realms of living things and artifacts), plants versus animals (a distinction within the realm of living things), and kitchen utensils versus furniture (a distinction within the realm of artifacts). We studied only 11-month-olds, because the plastic plants and some of the utensils were fragile. Younger infants more often mouth the stimuli, and we were afraid that parts might break off and be swallowed. The 11-month-olds were equally successful at all three tasks. We could not find sturdy plants, but we were able to collect a set of sturdy kitchen utensils, so we tested 9-month-olds on these contrasted with furniture. They failed to categorize on this task. This suggests that 9-month-olds, who successfully categorize furniture as different from vehicles, might be responding to a more global category of "things in the house" rather than furniture per se. This may seem like a somewhat odd conceptual category, but as I discuss in chapter 9, a category of indoor things has been found in studies of the breakdown of the semantic system in adults (Warrington & McCarthy, 1987). Such a category would be another based on associative processes, like the kitchen and bathroom categories discussed in chapter 6.

To summarize these data, by 7 months infants appear to have developed global concepts of animals, vehicles, and furniture. Their data, although not significantly different from those of 9-month-olds, still appear somewhat tenuous, so at this point it is probably best to say that between 7 and 9 months infants show evidence of these concepts. By 11 months (at least), infants have developed global concepts of plants, and they have also begun to differentiate a global concept of indoor things (or perhaps household things) into furniture and utensils. Thus, infants in this age range are not only making conceptual distinctions between the animate and inanimate realms but also carving out domains within each of those realms. A summary of these results is shown in Table 7-3.

Table 7-3. Ages by Which Various Global
Contrasts Are Differentiated

Age	Contrast
7 to 9 months	Animals vs vehicles Animals vs furniture Furniture vs vehicles
11 months	Animals vs plants Plants vs vehicles Furniture vs utensils

Note. Plants were not tested before 11 months.

A Dissociation Between Global Concepts and Detailed Perceptual Schemas

Following this series of experiments on global concepts, we turned our attention again to the issue of whether any more specific concepts are developing in the first year. In the next experiment, we investigated the within-furniture categories of tables, chairs, and beds (Mandler & McDonough, 1998a). We studied 7-, 9-, and 11-month olds, but at none of these ages did we find categorization. In addition, we made another attempt to find some differentiation in the animal domain. As discussed earlier, we know that by 18 months infants have formed a tripartite division of the animal domain. When we first investigated 7- to 11-month-old infants in this regard, we had tested dogs versus fish and found no categorization. We now tested dogs versus birds, both with outstretched wings and with wings folded against the body. Now we found clear-cut categorization. I do not know why this difference was found between birds and fish, but I presume it has to do with the fact that the infants were unfamiliar with fish. Perceptual explanations for the difference seem unlikely, because the birds with wings folded against the body have an overall shape not that different from the fish we used. This is only an adult's informal judgment of the stimuli, of course, and it may be that some specific feature such as beaks makes a difference. Whatever the basis, however, we now know that as young as 7 months, infants distinguish dogs and birds.

What remains is to find out if any mammals are conceptually distinguished from each other. We chose to test this with dogs and cats, in part because of the Quinn et al. (1993) data discussed earlier, which tell us that infants as young as 3 months can see the differences between these two mammal kinds, and in part because these are the two land animals with which infants in our culture tend to have the most experience. We familiarized 7-, 9-, and 11-month-olds either with dogs or with cats and then tested them with a new member from the familiarized category and a member of the other category (Mandler & McDonough, 1998a). The results were that neither 7- nor 9-month-olds categorized dogs or cats, but 11-month-olds did. (In contrast to Quinn et al., 1993, who found that 3-month-olds categorized pictures of cats more easily than dogs, we found no such asymmetries in our object-examining data.) Thus, when we used the animals with which infants in this age range are most familiar, we found that between 7 and 11 months they learn this distinction. Hence, on the basis of the available data, it appears that the earliest conceptual distinction among mammals occurs toward the end of the first year.[5]

By now I expect the reader to be asking why it is that such different data accrue from familiarization/preferential-examining tests using objects and familiarization/preferential-looking tests using pictures. Formally, the two tasks are almost isomorphic. Both involve a relatively small number of familiarization trials to one category, followed by a new member of that category and an exemplar of a new category. We have seen that infants as young as 3 months distinguish dogs and cats on the picture-looking task. But not until between 9 and 11 months do they do so on the object-examining task. Three-month-olds also categorize tables as different from beds and chairs on the picture-looking task (Behl-Chadha, 1996) but even at 11 months do not do so on the object-examination task. Is it merely that the latter task is more difficult (8 months more difficult, so to speak)? There are several reasons to think that such an explanation is unlikely, aside from the fact that the tasks are so similar. First, the global categorization that infants accomplish on the object-examination task is not always shown on the picture-looking task. Behl-Chadha (1996) had difficulty showing a discrimination between furniture and vehicles. She also used more trials, in comparison to the "basic-level" contrasts, to show discrimination of mammals from furniture (although this wasn't necessary for discriminating furniture from mammals, suggesting that the furniture exemplars were perceptually more similar and so easier to categorize). Second, in my lab we failed to get global categorization in the same familiarization/preferential-looking task using pictures. Before we discovered the object-examination task, we tried to show global categorization by using the standard picture technique. We familiarized 10-month-olds to pairs of detailed drawings of animals, vehicles, clothing, or furniture and then paired two new test pictures, one from the familiarized category and one from a new category, that looked as much alike in overall shape as possible. Figure 7-4 shows the test pairs we used following familiarization with either animals or vehicles. Figure 7-5 shows the test pairs we used following familiarization with either furniture or clothing. Note particularly the contrast of airplane and bird in Figure 7-4, which 9-month-olds categorize with ease on the object-examination test. The infants did not discriminate between any of the test pairs in this picture study.[6] Third, a few other studies have also shown difficulty in categorizing pictures of animals at the global level, accompanied by evidence of categorization at a within-domain level (Roberts, 1988; Roberts & Cuff, 1989).

Figure 7-4. A failure of global categorization using pictures: the test scenes used following familiarization with either animals or vehicles.

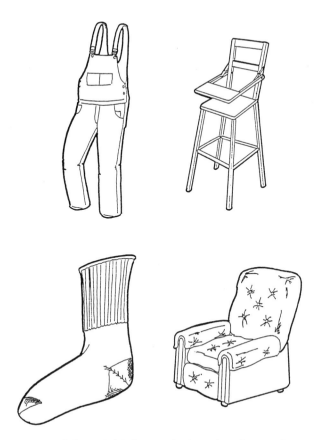

Figure 7-5. A failure of global categorization using pictures: the test scenes used following familiarization with either clothing or furniture.

These data form something like a double dissociation, the classic test for more than one process being at work. The dissociation consists of good performance at a global level on the object-examination test and poorer performance at a more detailed level, along with good performance at the detailed level on picture-looking tasks and poorer performance at the global level. The dissociation is not perfect. Although Behl-Chadha (1996) had trouble getting infants to categorize furniture and vehicles, she did find that 3-month-olds discriminated pictures of mammals from vehicles. Similarly, we have usually found some discriminations within the vehicle domain on the object-examination test. So the differences in data from the two tests are only suggestive. This is not surprising, given that by the time infants are old enough to handle objects, they should be able to make use of either perceptual or conceptual processes on categorization tests. Even adults, dominated as they are by conceptual processes, react to salient perceptual differences if that is all that is on offer. So to say that infants respond on the object-examination test by using their conceptual knowledge is not to say they will not respond to salient perceptual differences. It is the failures on the object-examination test that are more informative than successes: Infants seem not to find the differences between various mammals or various pieces of furniture to be salient in spite of the perceptual differences.

Part of the problem in identifying the causal factors involved in picture-looking and object-examination tests is that many comparisons from the two kinds of test have not yet been carried out. If more domains had been investigated in both paradigms, there might be a clearer answer. Nevertheless, within the limits of the available data and with a moderate degree of consistency, "basic-level" distinctions are more apt to be discriminated on picture-looking tests and global distinctions on object-examination tests.

Why should this be, given that the tests are virtually isomorphs of each other? There are a number of possible answers. First, there are (probably minor) differences in technique, such as that the picture-looking studies have presented the test pairs simultaneously rather than sequentially. Second, the photographs used in the picture studies have typically provided more finely grained perceptual detail than the little models we have used, even though the models we use are not toys but realistic replicas. Third, objects elicit intense interest and active exploration from infants, which contrasts with the more passive looking found in picture studies. Longer looking at a perceptually novel item does not require conceptualization because it can be the result of habituation to an automatically formed perceptual category; that such a category can be formed online in a few trials is shown by Quinn et al.'s (1993) or Eimas and Quinn's (1994) work on perceptual categorization in 3-month-olds. As discussed in chapter 3, learning a perceptual schema or category is part of the visual input system and is not gated by the attentional system. Fourth, picture-looking experiments may not motivate infants greatly, although this is less likely to be true for very young infants. Paul Quinn tells me that his 3-month-olds are alert and interested. Nevertheless, there is often a fairly high subject loss in picture-looking experiments. Manipulating objects, on the other hand, thoroughly engages infants of all ages; we never lose subjects through lack of interest or restlessness. Their full attention (and thus, I propose, their conceptual system) is engaged by the task. Glance again at Figure 7-1 to see how enthralling the task can be.

Fifth, and probably most important, are the dependent measures used in the two tasks. At first glance, the dependent measures, too, seem very similar: following familiarization, an increase in looking time to a different category versus an increase in examination time to a different category. In both cases, categorization is clearly involved, but there are important if subtle differences in the two measures, suggesting that different processes are being measured in picture-looking and object-handling tasks. *The object-examination studies measure only those periods during which infants actively examine the stimuli rather than total looking time, which is the measure used in the picture studies.* Attentive examining constitutes only a portion of total looking time (Richards & Casey, 1992), which means that gaze itself is not a reliable measure of attentive processing. We know this is true of adults, who can attend to a location without looking at it (Posner, 1988), and apparently it is true even of young infants (Johnson, Posner, & Rothbart, 1994). It is important that object-examination studies measure just those periods of intense examination that involve perceptual meaning analysis, as discussed in chapter 4—that is, periods of analytic observation in which conceptualization is taking place. In this regard, the mere fact that in the object studies infants actually interact with the objects may emphasize their conceptual, event-related aspects more than when they look at pictures.

This view is supported not only by the data indicating that attentive looking is only a portion of looking time but also by the analyses carried out by Holly Ruff and her colleagues (Ruff, 1986; Ruff & Saltarelli, 1993). They showed that when objects are manipulated, examining measures a more active attentive process than does looking (see also Oakes & Tellinghuisen, 1994), and as we have seen, it is examining, not just looking, that is scored in the object-examination test. For example, periods of mouthing, banging, and passive looking are excluded. Thus, familiarization/preferential-looking tasks are actually measuring different processes when pictures and objects are used, resulting in different data in the two cases. The differences illustrate how different conclusions can be reached as a result of slight changes in method and scoring. We have found there is really only one way to measure examining properly and that is to train coders well and keep a close watch over scoring. If scorers are not alerted to the problem, it is easy to revert from measuring examining to measuring looking, which is more obvious. When that happens, clean data begin to become noisy.[7] It may also be noted that the implication of these findings is that gaze alone is not a reliable measure of attention. A shift in gaze might seem a better marker for the presence of attentive processing, but even that is suspect. A movement or sound in the periphery, for example, may make infants move their eyes in that direction, but that does not guarantee that attentive processing will follow. So the fact of perceptual categorization in itself is not sufficient to inform us what infants are attending to. They could be thinking about what they are looking at or about anything else.

On the whole, the data from the object-examination task in the first year fit well with the data we collected from the sequential-touching task in the second year, a task that is as close as we can get at this age to instructed sorting (clearly a conceptual task). Global distinctions between animals and vehicles were found in both tasks. Birds were distinguished from dogs in both tasks, while different kinds of mammals were not distinguished in either task. Fish were not distinguished from dogs in the first year but were by the middle of the second, with differentiation among mammals lagging behind. A global distinction between furniture and utensils was found by 11 months on the object-examination task and also with older children on the sequential-touching task. At the same time, distinctions within the furniture domain were found on neither. The one discrepancy was that infants were good at categorizing cars and motorcycles on the object-examination test but were poor at categorizing these items on the sequential-touching task. The sequential-touching task is more difficult than object examination, but as we will see in the next chapter, a vehicle advantage sometimes appears on other tasks as well.

We thought originally that familiarity might account for the more advanced performance our infants showed on vehicles. In the southern California urban population we studied, many children have little daily interaction with animals (other than people, of course), but they almost all spend a great deal of time in cars and observe many and varied vehicles on the road and grouped together in parking lots. However, the failure to categorize different kinds of furniture, with which they are surely equally or more familiar, and which they also see grouped together, makes such an explanation unlikely. It is possible that a combination of everyday experience and attraction to moving objects accounts for the difference.

As for learning about animals, the small amount of evidence available indicates that humans and other animals may not be at first well differentiated (Quinn & Eimas, 1998) but become so by about 7 months (Pauen, 2000a). Three- to 4-month-olds generalize from pictures of humans to cats and horses, but not vice versa. Quinn (in press) suggests that infants' extensive experience with humans makes them already expert categorizers of people and that their representations of people may be more exemplar based. Although these data are perceptual categorization data, it seems plausible that the early conceptualization of animals is a generalization from infants' observation of the humans that surround and interact with them. That is, infants may learn the major aspects that differentiate humans from artifacts and then on the basis of these characteristics generalize animals as being similar. The characteristics I have stressed as important to understanding animals (here being used in the broadest sense) are self-motion, biological motion, and contingent interaction with others at a distance. Surely infants have the most daily experience with these characteristics exemplified by humans, but they are easy to recognize in other animals as well. One of the reasons that infants are able to conceptualize animals as a class is the way they interact with other objects in events. The data described in this chapter indicate that infants from 7 to 11 months of age have not formed any particular conceptions of the differences among dogs, fish, and rabbits but instead are operating at a more general conceptual level in terms of "how animals behave."

At the most general level, animals are similar in a number of ways. For instance, they are all self-starting, and this is equally true of humans and other animals.[8] This and other event-related characteristics enable infants to categorize dogs, fish, and birds as being of the same kind. To the extent that they are most interested in what a creature is doing, it may be irrelevant to them whether the creature moves itself via legs, fins, or wings. At the same time, their sensitivity to self-motion should at some point direct their attention to self-moving parts. This seems the most likely basis on which 9-month-olds differentiate our little models of birds and airplanes. Bird wings and airplane wings certainly look more like each other than like legs or fins, at least in the little models used in our experiments, but apparently carry different meanings for infants (as well as for us).

This analysis, suggesting as it does that the way objects move or how they behave in events is important in giving them meaning, also implies that infants treat our little models representationally. We see convincing evidence for this in the next chapter, but it is apparent even here. To the extent that the way objects move is involved in the categorization we found, such analysis must have already taken place and been represented. The models we used were not moving, and so there was no current motion perception that infants could use.

Interpretation Versus Identification

Needless to say, an equally important implication of these data is how infants recognize the various models we use as instances of a class. It is all very well and good to say that the meaning of animals for an infant has to do with the way they behave in events, but because the models are not acting in events, infants must use perceptual appearance to identify the objects as exemplars. Meaning will take you only so far. Unfortunately, we have little information on the physical features infants use for this purpose. Shape is only partially useful as a clue to animalness. Although animals tend to have curvilinear rather than rectilinear form (van de Walle, 1999), as Pauen (2002a) showed, this is not a sufficient cue, and in any case the overall shapes of animals vary widely. Faces are probably a better bet. Quinn and Eimas (1996) found that faces were the most important aspect of 3-month-olds' ability to discriminate pictures of cats from dogs, and Quinn and Johnson (1997) suggested that faces are the basis for categorizing animals as different from nonanimals. This finding may be due to the detailed face information in the pictures they use, or perhaps to an innate bias to attend to faces (Johnson & Morton, 1991). Even 2- to 3-month-old infants can follow the general direction of adults' eye gaze (Hood, Willen, & Driver, 1998). Johnson, Slaughter, and Carey (1998) found that 12-month-olds would follow shifts in direction

of amorphously shaped objects if the objects had eyes or if they interacted contingently with the infant.

Although faces do seem useful for identifying something as an animal, the bases used for identification must be broader than that. First,
faces cannot account for infants' ability to categorize furniture as different from vehicles, and curvilinearity cannot account for their ability to
categorize animals as different from plants. Second, no specific set of
features seems to be necessary. Our birds all have beaks, not noses or
mouths, and some have no other facial markings but are categorized as
animals; some of our planes have distinctive Flying Tiger facial markings
but are categorized as vehicles. Similarly, Pauen (2002) found that 11-
month-olds categorized animals as different from furniture even when
all items had legs and eyelike features. The answer probably is that infants
learn to associate structured sets of features with certain kinds of activity. For example, legs and faces must become associated with things that
move themselves, and eyes as well. At first, infants may pay attention to
only one feature at a time, but at least by 7 months they are responsive to
correlations among features as well (Younger & Cohen, 1986).

In the real world, infants see objects with certain features taking various roles in events. They understand what they are by virtue of those
roles, but features will become associated with those roles. In the object-
examination and sequential-touching tasks, infants don't see the activities
but can use the features to determine what sort of things the little models are. Note, however, this ability to identify objects on the basis of one
or more of their features does *not* mean that the basis of the categorization is the features themselves, as Haith and Benson (1998) suggested.
These authors said that because physical features are required to recognize an exemplar as a member of a category, it is these features that define the category (that is, the identifying features are the same as the
defining features). They suggested that infants form a category in the
first place on the basis of physical features and then infer other characteristics as a result of the categorization. Given the great difficulties adults
have in forming disjunctive categories (Bruner, Goodnow, & Austin,
1956), it seems unlikely that infants could do so by aggregating over the
highly varied features found in superordinate categories (for example,
legs or fins or wings, fur or feathers or scales, and so forth). This has been
the major argument for why superordinate categories should be late in de-

veloping: They don't have common physical features (Rosch & Mervis, 1975; Smith & Medin, 1981). Furthermore, as discussed in chapter 6, identifying and defining features do differ. It is for that reason that the ability to recognize (identify) something does not require meaning. Meaning accrues from what things do, not what they look like. The converse follows as well, although perhaps more weakly. To know the meaning of something doesn't say much about what it looks like (probably providing no more than a few constraints).

So infants do not categorize animals as different from vehicles or furniture on our object tests because animals look alike. They also see that dogs don't look like birds, and if that is what is on offer even 7-month-olds treat them differently on the object-examination test. But they are equally willing to categorize them together in spite of their different appearances if what is on offer is a contrast between animals and vehicles. That they must do on the basis of similarity of meaning, not similarity of perceptual appearance. This is not to say that they do not respond to salient perceptual differences on this test. They clearly do. Gretchen van de Walle (1999) showed that when 9-month-olds were presented with a set of red horses, they responded with renewed interest when presented with a yellow horse but not when presented with a red pig. In this experiment, which contrasted different kinds of mammals, a categorical distinction to which infants this age are typically not responsive on the object-examination test, they responded on the basis of color instead. This is a nice confirmation of our claim that infants have not yet formed different "basic-level" concepts in the animal domain. It equally shows that they can use perceptual similarity, perhaps especially when there isn't any other basis on which to respond.

Hence, at any age and on any task, perceptual appearance may be used to categorize objects, especially if perceptual similarity is emphasized and/or meaning is de-emphasized.[9] For example, Waxman and Markow (1995), using the same object-examination test we used in Mandler and McDonough (1993), found that 12-month-old infants categorized cows as different from dinosaurs but were not responsive to the differences between animals and vehicles. However, they gave only half the number of familiarization trials we used. Because other investigators have confirmed our finding of global categorization of animals on the object-examination task before 12 months of age (Oakes, Coppage, &

Dingel, 1997; Pauen, 2002), it seems likely that the different performance of the infants in Waxman and Markow (1995) was due to this change in technique. Providing only a few familiarization trials may be sufficient to allow perceptual categorization of highly similar items such as cows but insufficient for noticing the subtler, less "in your face" information that the highly varied items being presented are all animals.

However, because infants can categorize on both the object-examination and sequential-touching tests on the basis of either conceptual or perceptual differences, this makes them less than ideal to demonstrate conceptual responding. Partly for that reason, McDonough and I turned to another kind of test in recent years, one that is less ambiguous in terms of the processes that are required to solve it. In the next chapter I discuss our test for preverbal inductive inferences. There we will see not only clear evidence for conceptual categorization but, on this more stringent test, failure at some "basic-level" conceptual distinctions for which the object-examination test had provided positive evidence (such as differentiating dogs from cats at 11 months).

8

Conceptual Categories as Induction Machines

. . . in which the inductive generalizations infants make are uncovered and explored using the technique of generalized imitation. We found that the inductions that infants make reflect their underlying concepts — the generalizations tend to be global like the concepts themselves. I explain why infants do not use "basic-level" concepts for inductions. Only during the second year do infants begin to narrow their generalizations down to something like the "basic" level. The generalized imitation technique also proves useful as a way to get preverbal infants to tell us exactly how they are construing the world. I end with a summary of the differences between percepts and concepts revealed by the research reported in this and the previous chapter.

Locke . . . was alone among the classical empiricists in maintaining that the principles of the "association of ideas," based upon contiguity, similarity and the like, do not provide a general explanation of the processes of human reasoning. (Greenwood, 1999)

Inductive Generalization

I have offered a good deal of evidence to show that when familiar conceptual categories are used to form the stimulus sets in object-examination and sequential-touching tests, infants' responses tend to be conceptual in nature. Some of the evidence was indirect, however, showing more that perceptual explanations are inadequate to explain the behavior in these experiments than providing positive evidence that categorization of a different kind is taking place. As van de Walle's (1999) work shows, infants sometimes do respond perceptually on the object-examination test. What we need at this point is positive evidence for conceptual categorization, rather than saying that other explanations can't account for the data. Ideally, we would like to see conceptualizations in use in tasks that we can be sure require what used to be known as the higher cognitive processes. These include making inferences, problem solving, recall of the past, imagining the future, and, in most accounts, learning language. All of these functions, essential for human life as we know it, require conceptual interpretation or construal of events. Thus, any of these processes that can be documented in infancy (and with the exception of imagining the future, they all can be) attests to the conceptual nature of the categories being used. In this chapter I discuss inductive inference. Recall of the past is discussed in chapter 10 and language learning in chapter 11.

Although the previous chapters provide a good deal of evidence for conceptual categories in infancy, we don't know much about them. Are they sufficiently stable to provide a basis for inductive generalization? Perhaps they are closer to what Piaget (1951) called "preconcepts." In Piaget's description, the first concepts (and, for that matter, concepts throughout the early preoperational period) are hazy, unprincipled, and shifting in meaning from day to day. If this were an accurate assessment, then the earliest concepts would not be useful as a basis for inductive inference. Most generalizations would be contradicted tomorrow, which should certainly discourage the tendency to generalize, or else the conclusions made would be a jumble of inappropriate or contradictory information. Although this is possible, nothing we have seen so far suggests that the conceptual system being constructed is so unstable. Indeed, the data presented indicate a sensibly smooth accumulation of knowledge and a good deal of systematicity. How does this come about?

The traditional empiricist doctrine of how inductive generalization begins is that it is an innate responsivity to physical similarity (e.g., Quine, 1977). Because it was assumed that infants, like animals, have no concepts, there was no other possible basis to get things started. Physical similarity itself was described in terms of sensory qualities, such as color, shape, and texture, that can be directly perceived without being mediated by a conceptual system. Quine called this early responsivity an immediate, subjective, animal sense of similarity. According to this view, which Frank Keil (1991) dubbed the doctrine of "original sim," before children

develop abstract concepts or theories about the world, they are influenced only by the laws of perceptual similarity. In short, they can make
associations and generalizations only on the basis of what things look like.
The more two things resemble each other in appearance, the more likely
it is that an inductive inference from the properties of one to the other
will be made. In this kind of view, upon seeing the family cat eat, the infant comes to expect that other cats will eat as well. The generalization
happens because a category of cats can be formed on the basis of the innate sense of similarity. The work of Quinn et al. (1993) provides support for this part of Quine's assumptions, because it shows that as young
as 3 months infants can indeed form a perceptual category of cats. The
story goes on as follows. With experience the infant observes other animals eat, such as dogs and birds, and eventually (perhaps with the help
of language) makes the more difficult inference that all animals, even
though they don't look alike, nevertheless all eat.

There are several difficulties with this view of the foundations of inductive inference. First, it does not make clear why the infant does not
infer that *all* objects eat: Without an animal category boundary, there is
no stop rule. To be sure, the infant has negative evidence, never having
seen cars or chairs eat, but in all likelihood it has never seen turtles or ele-
phants eat either. At best there might be a perceptual similarity gradient
around the objects initially observed to eat, but this would surely map
very imperfectly onto such a diverse domain as animals. For example,
airplanes might be included with birds rather than with motorcycles (see
Figure 7-3). So even if generalization continued from cat to other mammals, it is not obvious how it could extend to more distantly related animals or that it should stop at their boundary. A second problem with this
approach is that it does not tell us how anything conceptual ever emerges.
As Keil (1991) has pointed out, no one espousing the traditional view has
shown how generalization on the basis of physical appearance gets re-
placed by more theory-based generalization. How, for example, does the
concept of animal itself arise? On the traditional account, it is by noticing commonalities among animals, such as that each of them eats. But
then the explanation flirts with circularity. One gains the conceptual category of animal through induction but needs to have the animal category
to stop wildly inappropriate inductions from being made.

These difficulties show up in Quinn and Eimas's discussions of how perceptually based categories such as cats become concepts (e.g., Quinn & Eimas, 1997). In their view, conceptual knowledge of the world consists of "informational enrichments of the original perceptually based categorical representations of young infants." Concepts can be derived in this way because "they do not differ in kind from perceptually based categories." However, Quinn and Eimas also say that "inferential knowledge cannot be perceptual in nature; it is a consequence of knowledge already represented—an emergent structure." Nowhere do they say how this emergent structure that allows inductive inference comes about. This seems to be a fairly empty solution to the issue of how we end up with theory-based generalizations from a set of perceptual categories. About the most Quinn and Eimas say about it is that much of the knowledge accumulation is language based. Another problem with this view, as we will see in the studies of induction described next, is that we cannot leave the infant in a state in which it has perceptual categories of different levels of generality (but no concepts) and still be able to explain why one level of categorization is used for induction and another not. In particular, Quinn and Eimas's point of view, like that of Quine, should predict that the first associative enrichments should accrue to the "basic-level" perceptual categories that even very young infants form.

However, as we have seen, infants also form global conceptual categories such as animals, vehicles, furniture, and plants, and they seem to do so without much regard to perceptual similarity. For this reason, Mc-Donough and I thought that the first inductive generalizations might also not be particularly influenced by perceptual similarity of the objects. The technique we used to study this issue is one we call generalized imitation. We model actions with little models of animals and vehicles and see if infants imitate the actions afterward on different exemplars from these domains. This technique allows us to assess how widely infants generalize properties of various classes that they observe. For instance, we might model giving a dog a drink from a cup, and then give the infant the cup, but instead of giving them the dog, we give them, say, a cat and a car, or a cat and a bird, to see if and how far they generalize drinking.

The technique of generalized imitation relies on two characteristics of infant behavior. First, infants spontaneously imitate events they have observed. Second, their imitations are determined by what they have understood from their observations, as amply documented by Piaget (1951).

Hence, although imitation does not require awareness of "standing for" relations, or what Judy DeLoache (2000) calls "representational insight," it is based on conceptual representation of what the infant thinks is going on in the scenario being modeled. The data described in the previous chapter certainly implicate representational responding, but apparently it remains surprising to some. This may be the result of a different usage of the term *representational* to include awareness of symbolic "standing-for" relations. For example, several researchers (Madole & Oakes, 1999; Nelson, 2000) have suggested that in light of research by DeLoache (e.g., 1989) showing that even 2½-year-olds have trouble using a scale model of a room to find a hidden object in the real room being represented, it is unlikely that year-old infants would treat little models as representations. It is important to note, however, that treating objects representationally (in the sense of understanding them as symbols) is a multiplex skill that develops over a number of years. For example, DeLoache and Burns (1994) showed that although 24-month-olds cannot use a photograph of a room to help them *find* a hidden object, suggesting difficulties in the representational function, they can nevertheless use a photograph to tell them where to *put* an object in the represented room. This example not only indicates the complexity of the emerging ability to understand and make use of physical representations as symbols but also suggests a gradual rather than abrupt development.

To see the similarity between a little model and its real-world counterpart and then use the model to imitate an observed event is only the beginning of the kind of representational activity of which children will eventually become capable. It does not require the dual representation that DeLoache has shown is needed to understand that one object is meant to refer to another. It requires only expressing a conceptualization by acting out an observed event (instead of describing it in words).

Another illustration of the (simple, not dual) representational nature of infants' imitations is the fact that they tend not to imitate events they think are incorrect (Bauer & Thal, 1990; Killen & Uzgiris, 1981). Mandler and McDonough (1996a) found that 14-month-olds rarely would imitate incorrect actions such as giving a car a drink or keying a dog; they would imitate an appropriate action using an unfamiliar exemplar of a class (e.g., giving an armadillo a drink), but they would not do something inappropriate to the class. The reluctance to key an animal is noteworthy, given that many 14-month-olds have at least seen windup animal toys. Perhaps because they are still learning basic information about different kinds of objects, infants at the young ages we have studied do not seem to engage in playful bizarre behavior, as older infants sometimes do. In addition, Bauer and Thal (1990) found that even 21-month-olds were less likely to imitate when event sequences were modeled in the incorrect order, and when they did imitate, they often reproduced the sequences in the correct order instead. These kinds of findings indicate that infants do not just follow the leader and ape whatever a modeler does. It appears that if they don't like (agree with?) the story the experimenter is telling, they either ignore it or fix it up.[1] Note that we also find domain-specific imitation at 9 to 11 months, which is an age at which parents are more apt to give their children stuffed animals to play with than realistic models of animals and vehicles. Therefore, an explanation sometimes offered for domain-appropriate imitation in terms of parents teaching "appropriate" play behavior seems unlikely.

The only other explanation for what appears to be representational behavior would be that the infants thought the little models were real, for instance, that the dog was a living creature. Nelson (2000) has suggested that perhaps that is the case, citing the observation that 18-month-olds sometimes try to sit on a toy chair. I can think of a number of reasons for 18-month-olds to engage in that kind of behavior, including exploring the relationships between representations and reality, but there is no evidence whatsoever that infants think our replicas are real—that the little model of the dog, for example, is alive and might move by itself. Infants in our studies pick up and manipulate these lifeless objects, and because the ability to distinguish an animate from an inanimate thing is one of the first conceptual accomplishments in infancy, it simply doesn't seem possible that a year-old infant would make that mistake in the imitation situation. That is, it must be the case that infants see that the model looks like a dog but that it is not a real dog capable of moving or biting when the infant picks it up. Nevertheless, it activates the concept of a dog. This enables infants to understand the scenario being acted out by the experimenter as applicable to the real world. Their propensity to imitate the scenario is an indication of an early willingness to understand and tell stories about the world.

I have gone into this issue in some detail, because imitation is sometimes regarded as symbolic behavior but, as I have just indicated, that depends on how the term *symbol* is used. (See Huttenlocher & Higgins [1978] for a thorough discussion, ending with a rather restrictive definition.) Sometimes the term is used so loosely as to be virtually shorn of meaning. For example, in a recent article Younger and Johnson (in press) say that not only are artifacts, such as flags and street signs, symbols but so are language, concepts, and ideas. They present data indicating that not until around 18 months do infants use a little model symbolically to refer to a realistic event shown on a video. Before that age it doesn't seem to occur to infants to relate a model car sitting in front of them to a video of a car driving along a street. This is not surprising, given the work of DeLoache and her colleagues. Troseth and DeLoache (1998) found that 2-year-olds did not use information provided by a video of a hiding event to help them find the hidden object, as long as they knew it was a video. When they thought they were looking through a window at the actual hiding space, they did make use of the information. So the conceptual understanding of the video was there, just not the representational insight. However, because of the extremely broad notion of "symbol" that Younger and Johnson used, they overgeneralized from their data to conclude that before 18 months "toys, animals or vehicles are unlikely to evoke conceptual representations of . . . real kinds . . ." This is a conflation of representational insight and conceptualization.

When discussing Piaget's theory of symbol development in chapter 2, I used his terminology and described images and words as symbols that can be used to refer to concepts in conscious thought. That is a common usage, but it is important to differentiate it in some way from activities that require representational insight. For example, in traditional usage, speaking is a symbolic activity, but speaking does not require representational insight. (Otherwise infants wouldn't talk until considerably later than they do.) Imitation is like speaking, except that instead of using words to describe an event it acts it out. The important aspect of generalized imitation for purposes of understanding conceptual development in infancy is that it uncovers accessible conceptual representations (what the infant thinks about the world), and it is for this purpose that we have used it.

In our first set of experiments using this technique (Mandler & Mc-Donough, 1996a), we studied 14-month-olds and modeled actions appropriate either to the animal domain or to the vehicle domain. We modeled giving a dog a drink from a cup or sleeping in a bed, and we modeled turning a key against a car door or a car giving a child a ride. Following each modeling, a generalization test was given. The modeled item was put away, and a *different* animal and vehicle were brought out and put on either side of the prop that had been used (e.g., the cup). We measured which object, if either, the infants used to imitate what they had seen modeled. These results were evaluated against baseline data collected before modeling, in which the infants were given the test objects and allowed to play with them. The baseline period gave us a measure of any spontaneous tendency to act out the events without having seen a model do so.

We assessed the role of perceptual similarity by using animals and vehicles that we judged to be physically either similar or dissimilar to the modeled objects. These are shown in Figure 8-1. For example, when we used a dog for modeling, half the infants received an animal similar to the dog for the generalization test (a cat or a rabbit) paired with a vehicle. The other half of the infants received an animal dissimilar to the dog (a bird or a fish) paired with a vehicle. When a car was used for modeling, half of the infants received a similar vehicle (a truck or a bus) paired with an animal for their generalization test. The other half received a dissimilar vehicle (a motorcycle or an airplane) paired with an animal. In this way, we could test the breadth of the generalizations the infants made. That is, we tested whether infants generalize from a dog to a cat or a rabbit more frequently than to a bird, fish, or vehicle, and whether they generalize more from a car to a truck or bus than to a motorcycle, airplane, or animal.

The results, shown in Figure 8-2, were straightforward. Infants performed some of the actions spontaneously in the baseline period but rarely with the objects from the inappropriate domain. Performance of the actions increased markedly after modeling, and again infants strongly preferred to perform the actions on the exemplars from the appropriate domain, rarely crossing the domain boundary. Furthermore, as long as the test exemplar was from the same category, it didn't matter whether it looked like the dog they had seen or not; they were just as likely to imitate giving a drink to a cat, rabbit, fish, or bird, and after seeing a car being keyed, to key a truck, bus, motorcycle, or airplane. Thus, there was no effect of the physical similarity or dissimilarity of the exemplars within a domain on generalization. Of course, the vehicles on the whole were perceptually more similar to each other than to animals, and vice versa, although inspection of Figure 8-2 suggests this is not always the

Figure 8-1. Examples of the animals and vehicles used in our first study using generalized imitation. A dog and a car were always used as models, but the exemplars used to test generalization varied in their similarity to the modeled items. For example, a similar test item to the dog might be a rabbit, which could be paired with any of the vehicles for the test contrast. A dissimilar test item to the car might be an airplane, which could be paired with any of the animals for the test contrast. Reprinted from Mandler and McDonough (1996a) with permission from Elsevier.

case; the airplane and bird looked a lot alike. Nevertheless, even if perceptual similarity contributed to the choice of another animal when an animal function was modeled, it did not influence the within-domain choices. It is also of interest that the infants generalized keying to jet planes, given that the only vehicles they are likely to have seen keys used with are cars. Their domain-wide generalization suggests overgeneralization that in some instances may later need correction.

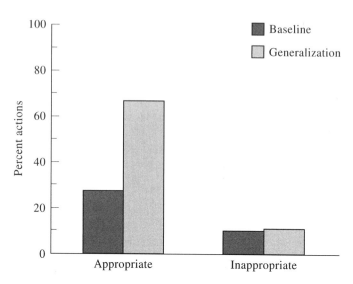

Figure 8-2. This figure shows the extent to which infants spontaneously engaged in the appropriate or inappropriate actions with the test animals and vehicles, such as a bird and a plane, at baseline (before any modeling was done) and with the same items after modeling with the dog or car. Reprinted from Mandler and McDonough (1996a) with permission from Elsevier.

We replicated this experiment, using highly atypical test exemplars (e.g., an armadillo and a forklift), so we could be sure the infants had not seen the particular exemplars before (Mandler & McDonough, 1996a). The same pattern of results was found: 72% of the actions were performed on an appropriate exemplar versus 13% on an inappropriate exemplar. We then used a more difficult test. We modeled the actions on *both* the correct and incorrect exemplars. For instance, we modeled turning a key against the car door but also modeled turning the key against the dog's side. This is a stringent test because our modeling the actions on inappropriate exemplars essentially tells infants that in this game it is okay to do odd things. The results, however, were very similar to those obtained before; there was only a slightly greater tendency to use the inappropriate object even when it had just been modeled. So even when encouraged to imitate inappropriate properties, relatively few infants did so. As discussed earlier, the refusal to imitate incorrect modeling is an indication of the representational nature of their responding. It is also note-

worthy that infants can demonstrate their knowledge of animals and vehicles on such impoverished stimuli as we use. The little models aren't
moving and have many fewer features than their real-world counterparts,
but the infants have no problem in using them to demonstrate their underlying meaning. They have never seen a child ride on the roof of a car or
a dog being put to sleep in a bed, yet they accept these expressions of
transportation and sleeping and reproduce them in their imitations. This
can lead to some interesting twists on reality, as when an infant watched
us give a child a ride on a car and then was given a bird and a plane, making both the child and the bird ride on the plane (but not vice versa).

We extended the generalized imitation method to 9- and 11-month-
olds (McDonough & Mandler, 1998). We had to use a somewhat simpler
technique, for example, letting these younger infants first have an exact
replica of the modeled target object and then providing them with only
one generalization item (either correct or incorrect) at a time. Again the
data mirrored the results of the first two experiments just described. The
infants rarely performed the modeled action on an incorrect exemplar,
even though it was the only one on offer. They were significantly more
likely to reproduce the action on an appropriate object. However, fewer
9-month-olds imitated than the 11-month-olds or the 14-month-olds in
the previous experiments, even when given an exact replica. We can't be
sure, therefore, whether 9-month-olds are at the lower age limit for this
kind of inductive generalization or whether at this young age imitation
of complex events, especially when props are needed to carry them out,
is too difficult to provide a viable technique to examine any such generalizations that are taking place.[2]

In more recent work, we studied domain-neutral ("accidental") properties, along with a set of the domain-specific properties studied earlier
(Mandler & McDonough, 1998b). In addition to the properties of drinking and being keyed, we modeled "going into a building" and "being
washed." Either a car or a person was modeled going into a garagelike
structure, or these items were washed with a sponge. The patterns of generalization were quite different for domain-neutral and domain-specific
properties: 14-month-olds generalized across domain boundaries in the
case of going into a building or being washed but did not generalize
drinking and keying across domains. In the case of domain-neutral properties, not surprisingly they tended to stay within the modeled domain

for their first choice; for instance, if we modeled washing a car, they would first wash the test vehicle before going on to wash the test animal. However, they tended to imitate with *both* test items, in contrast to domain-specific modeling, when they usually restricted their imitations to the modeled class. This result once again demonstrates that infants are not merely treating our little models as toys but are treating them representationally. If they were considering the situation merely a game of "follow the experimenter," then they should behave the same way toward domain-specific and domain-neutral properties, but they do not. Instead, they treat the objects and actions appropriately.

In these studies, we investigated knowledge about behavior that is characteristic of whole domains, such as that animals eat or vehicles give rides. These data demonstrated that infants are making broad generalizations about these domains, but they do not preclude the possibility that they are learning properties associated with more specific classes as well. Indeed, one of our colleagues suggested that we were not giving the basic level a fair shake. Perhaps infants find it even easier to generalize "basic-level" properties. A little reflection suggests that this is a complex and somewhat unlikely proposition, however. Surely, the notion that basic-level concepts are the first to be formed would imply learning that a given animal such as a dog eats, not that it eats bones, and that a bird sleeps, not that it sleeps in a nest. Yet it is the details that differentiate one "basic-level" class from another. A child could not differentiate the behavior of dogs and birds by the fact of eating or sleeping, but rather by where they sleep and what they eat.

The global approach enables infants to begin building a conceptual system, but obviously they are going to have to learn much more precise information about objects than their superordinate category membership. They will need to learn how one animal behaves differently from another (domestic cats are generally safe but dogs are iffy) and the many cultural differences in the use of artifacts (we drink from cups and glasses, not from cooking pots, even though cooking pots are good containers). This means that at some point they are going to have to pay attention to the relationship between the finer details of what animals and kitchen utensils look like and their typical behaviors or functions. Nevertheless, our hypothesis about learning "basic-level" properties was that they, too, would at first be overgeneralized in the same way that more general properties such as drinking and sleeping were generalized to fish and keying to airplanes (Mandler & McDonough, 1996a). Another way of stating this hypothesis is to say that because at first infants construe objects such as dogs as animals, not as dogs, they will overgeneralize dog behavior to other animals, or because they construe objects such as cups as containers, they will overgeneralize drinking from cups to drinking from other containers as well.

We carried out a series of experiments investigating whether there are any generalizations that are restricted to the "basic" level. The first of these is reported in Mandler and McDonough (1998b). We investigated the performance of 14- and 20-month-olds on two artifact functions— beds are used for sleeping and cups are used for drinking—and two natural kind functions—dogs eat bones and flowers are to be smelled. We found that the 14-month-olds overgeneralized all these functions. For example, when we demonstrated giving a little model of a person a drink from a teacup and then gave the person to infants along with a coffee mug and a frying pan, they were as likely to choose the frying pan as the mug to imitate drinking. It is as if infants are conceptualizing these utensils as containers and have not yet narrowed them down to their common social uses. Similarly, they were as likely to put a little person to sleep in a bathtub as in a bed, to smell a tree as a flower, and to feed a bone to a bird as to a dog. Even at 20 months, the infants were still making some of the same overgeneralizations. They were beginning to narrow the artifact characteristics appropriately, but they were still overgeneralizing the natural kind characteristics (presumably because of fewer interactions with animals and plants than with artifacts). These data are shown in Figure 8-3. It can be seen that not until 20 months did most infants restrict their generalizations appropriately, and even then pretty much only for artifacts.

We have since replicated these findings with other properties (Mandler & McDonough, 2000). We wanted to be sure the finding was general. The 14-month-old infants did not seem as engaged in the within-domain tasks as they had when we were contrasting global domains, and as can be seen by comparing Figures 8-2 and 8-3, they had a lower level of responding than in the previous generalization experiments. So we studied the performance of 14-, 19-, and 24-month-olds on four new household artifact functions: washing dishes in a sink rather than in a bathtub, sitting on a chair at the dining table rather than on a toilet, brushing hair

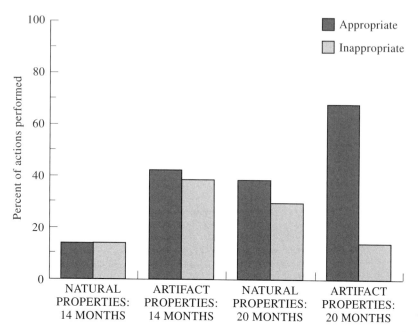

Figure 8-3. Generalization of "basic-level" properties by 14- and 20-month-olds. The natural properties modeled were a dog chewing on a bone (tested with another dog and a bird) and smelling a flower (tested with another flower and a tree). The artifact properties modeled were drinking from a cup (tested with a mug and a frying pan) and putting a child to bed in a crib (tested with a bed and a bathtub). Adapted from Mandler and McDonough (1998b) with permission from Elsevier.

with a hairbrush rather than a toothbrush, and hammering with a hammer rather than a wrench. We found higher levels of responding among the 14-month-olds in this experiment but almost exactly the same results as before: a lack of discrimination between these various alternatives. In contrast, the performance of the 19- and 24-month-olds was excellent.

The previous experiment had indicated that 14-month-olds construe household objects in rather general ways, considering any small container as being drinkable from and various large household containers as being places to sleep. The new findings suggested that infants at this age also construe large household containers as being places to immerse objects, flat-surfaced furniture as places to sit, any kind of tool as suitable for hammering, and any kind of brush as suitable for making hair look nice. Of course, these descriptions are adult glosses and may be incorrect in their particulars. I use them to capture the overly general character of what infants have understood about these objects. The data suggest that when in their play 1-year-olds drink from a cup or put a doll in a bed or bang a peg with a plastic hammer, we may attribute too much knowledge to them to say that they understand that cups are for drinking, beds are for sleeping, or hammers have a specific function. Their understanding may be more global and less detailed than such descriptions suggest. It is not until 19 months that we found a narrowing down of general characterizations to the more detailed specifications implied by the notion of basic-level concepts.

We tested the possibility that 14-month-olds might understand some of the functions we studied in a different way than the glosses of "being drinkable from" or "making hair look nice" suggest. Their understanding might be based on more neutral physical descriptions of the various activities. For example, any flat surface of a certain height affords sitting, and any small, elongated object can be run across the hair. Therefore, we conducted a second experiment with 14-month-olds, in which the same four properties were modeled but the choices provided by the test objects were conceptually more differentiated ones (Mandler & McDonough, 2000). Instead of using a tub as an out-of-category distractor for washing dishes, we used a bed. Instead of a toilet as a distractor for sitting at a table, we used a small, flat-topped car. Instead of using a toothbrush as a distractor for grooming hair, we used a spoon, and instead of a wrench as a distractor for hammering, we used a cup. Now 14-month-olds had little trouble choosing the correct object for their imitations.

So 14-month-olds are not clueless about the functions of household objects but do seem to generalize too broadly within the household domain. Even though the bed (with a headboard and footboard and slightly raised sides) formed a kind of container, it was rarely used to imitate washing. Similarly, although the spoon had roughly the same size and shape as the hairbrush and could be put to the hair as easily, the infants rarely used it to imitate brushing hair. The data tell us that infants are not using simple physical descriptions (such as "large container" or "hand-sized, elongated object") or the affordances implied by these physical descriptions to determine the function of household objects. They may confuse a sink and a tub as a place to wash dishes, perhaps because they have seen washing of some sort take place in both, but they do not confuse a sink and a bed in spite of their overall container-like shapes. And even though they seem not to have noticed the different uses of various brushes, they know that spoons are not used for grooming hair, in spite of their rough similarity in shape. Thus, by 14 months infants have developed some fairly broad but not yet detailed conceptualizations of the functions of various household artifacts.

Because the inappropriate objects in this experiment came from very different categories than the appropriate objects, they were also perceptually somewhat more dissimilar to the objects used in modeling than was the case in the previous experiment. This may have made it easier for the infants to reject them as objects to be used in the generalization task. Still, a chair doesn't look all that much like a toilet or a cup like a frying pan. It seems that 14-month-olds simply do not pay much attention to the details of the objects they interact with and therefore are not sensitive to the role these details play in the activities in which the objects take part. This is just another way of saying that at 14 months infants are not yet paying attention to "basic-level" distinctions, which crucially depend on parts such as whether a container has a handle or a tool has a flat surface suitable for hammering. They can see these differences, of course, but they do not appear to attend to them with respect to the target actions.

These experiments, in conjunction with our prior study of basic-level generalization (Mandler & McDonough, 1998b), suggest that over-generalized conceptions of both household artifacts and animals may be the rule at 14 months of age. At the same time, in several experiments we have found that infants seem to know more about vehicles than they do about either animals or household artifacts. Infants differentiate cars from motorcycles and airplanes on the object-examination test, while failing to differentiate different kinds of furniture or different kinds of mammals (Mandler & McDonough, 1993, 1998a). And even though 14-month-olds show they have generalized vehicle properties across the entire domain, as illustrated by their using keys on airplanes and forklifts, when given the choice, they are more likely to choose another member of the same kind of vehicle for their imitations than a different kind of vehicle (Mandler & McDonough, 1998b). The same selectivity is not shown for animals, suggesting again that infants are differentiating the vehicle domain earlier than some others.

So we did another experiment to examine whether this seemingly more advanced understanding of different kinds of vehicles includes understanding that some vehicle properties are restricted to particular vehicle kinds (Mandler & McDonough, 2000). We were able to find two specific properties that we expected year-old infants to know: wearing helmets when riding a motorcycle but not when riding in a car and putting gas into a car but not into a child's wagon. Although not strictly "basic-level" properties, because helmets are also used with bicycles and gasoline is used with several kinds of vehicles, they fulfill the spirit of such properties in that they are more closely associated with some kinds than with others. (This looser association of "basic-level" properties with their respective basic-level categories seems to be fairly widespread. With the obvious exception of biological properties, many behaviors and actions associated with a given kind, such as a dog rather than a cat being on a leash, or drinking from cups rather than from pans, are occasionally extended to other kinds. In the present cases, however, infants would only have seen gasoline being put into cars, although just possibly into motorcycles too. As for helmets, it is California State law that children wear helmets when riding bicycles or tricycles.) We also included two "basic-level" animal properties—that birds but not rabbits sleep in nests, and that rabbits but not birds eat carrots—not only to ensure the replicability of our prior finding that even at 19 to 20 months children overgeneralize properties specific to particular animal kinds but also to assess the age at which this kind of mistake disappears.

Once again, we found overgeneralization for the 14-month-olds on both animals and vehicles. Again, by 19 months the children were much more likely to correctly generalize "basic-level" characteristics of vehicles than "basic-level" characteristics of animals, but by 24 months they were successful in both domains. This finding tells us that the good performance by 19- and 24-month-olds on vehicles and household artifacts was not merely due to an increase in a general ability to perceptually match the test stimuli to those used in modeling. If that were the case, they should have performed as well with animals as with vehicles, but they did not. If anything, the perceptual differences among the animals were greater than the differences among the vehicles.

This rejection of perceptual matching ability as an explanation for the data in these experiments is not meant to preclude the hypothesis that improved accuracy of generalization with age is due in part to increased attention to perceptual detail. The data merely suggest that less attention is paid to the details of what animals look like than what vehicles look like and that this relative indifference to detail about animals persists longer. At present we have no information about the frequency with which children experience the characteristic properties of animals and vehicles or even whether they are comparable in what they demand in the way of understanding. However, the data add to the frequent if not always significant finding in our prior experiments of earlier conceptual differentiation of vehicles into separate kinds than takes place with animals. It is possible that the social, interactive nature of animals is attention-demanding enough to lessen attentiveness to details of their physical appearance.

The conclusion that perceptual similarity cannot account for the patterns of inductive generalization we have found in infancy fits well with the literature on inductive inferences in early childhood, showing that inductive inferences are controlled more by conceptual class membership than by similarity (e.g., Gelman & Markman, 1986). In the studies with preschoolers, children are told some new property of an object and then are asked to decide the categorical range over which the property is valid. The main difference between the data on infancy described here and the latter work is in the size of the conceptual categories being used to constrain the inferences. Nine- to 14-month-olds' categories tend to be quite global, and consequently their generalizations are global as well. In the second year the categories they use begin to be narrowed down toward more specific levels. By age 4, children already have many categories at a subordinate level, and their inductive inferences are even more frequently made at this level (Gelman, 1988). The narrower the category, the more likely that exemplars will be similar to each other. We have found no evidence for original sim; rather, it appears that paying attention to similarity when making inductive inferences is something that develops with experience.

How to Get Preverbal Children to Talk to You

Before summarizing the induction data, I will describe one other set of experiments. These experiments can be classed as induction experiments like those just discussed, but I believe they have an even more important function, namely, providing a way for preverbal children to tell you how they interpret the events they watch being modeled. Consider the following scenario: We model a dog drinking from a cup and then give the infant a different dog and a cat. Which object will the infant choose when imitating this event? If conceptual class membership is crucial, and the infant has interpreted the event as "an animal drinking," then the infant might be as likely to choose the cat as the dog. (Incidentally, such an outcome would once again show that perceptual matching does not play a great role in this kind of imitation performance.) But now consider the following scenario: After modeling a dog drinking from a cup, we give the infant a different dog and a bird. Now which object will the infant choose? If the infant chooses the bird as often as the dog, then the original conclusion that the infant has construed the event as "an animal drinking" would be supported. But what if the infant now chooses the dog? In conjunction with the first scenario, this outcome would suggest that the infant's construal was not "an animal drinking" but something like "a land animal drinking."

By systematically varying the available choices, we should be able to home in on the infant's conceptual construal of what the infant has seen. This is a slow technique, perhaps, but an effective way to get preverbal infants to tell you what they saw when they observed the modeling event. We have done a few experiments using this technique (Mandler & McDonough, 1998b). We demonstrated for 14-month-olds a little model of a dog being given a drink or being put to sleep in a bed and then tested understanding of these events by giving the infants the relevant prop along with a different dog and either a cat, rabbit, bird, or a novel animal such as an anteater. We also modeled a car being keyed or giving a little model of a child a ride and then tested understanding by giving the infants the relevant prop along with a different car and either a truck, motorcycle, airplane, or a novel vehicle such as a forklift.

We found that the infants were indifferent as to which land animal they used for their imitations of a dog drinking or sleeping. When given another dog and a different animal to choose from, they were as likely to choose a cat, rabbit, or a novel mammal such as an anteater as the dog. On the other hand, they strongly preferred to use another dog for their imitations rather than a bird. These data tell us the infants interpreted the events as happening to a land animal. (They did frequently go on to give the bird a drink or put it in the bed too, suggesting they were telling us, "I saw you give a land animal a drink, but birds drink too.") The picture was different with the vehicles. Here the infants were more selective in their first choices. They tended to choose the correct vehicle category for their first imitation, although they were less discriminating when it came to a novel vehicle, such as a forklift. They still tended to go on to use the other vehicle for their second choice, with the exception of the airplane, which was largely rejected for keying or giving rides. This is an interesting finding, because infants are quite willing to key an airplane or have it give rides when the alternative object to use for their imitation is an animal. Clearly, the choices available determine how strict or loose an infant's interpretation will be. As discussed earlier, this kind of behavior is very common; our interpretation (and therefore how we describe something) is a function of the surrounding context (Garner, 1974). The most important aspect of these data, however, is that they provide confirming evidence that differentiating vehicles into subclasses occurs earlier than for the other domains we have studied.

The animal data also demonstrate compellingly that the behavior of 14-month-olds in the inductive generalization studies is not carried out merely on the basis of perceptual matching and imitation, as suggested by Rakison and Poulin-Dubois (2001). There is no doubt that infants this age see the differences in appearance between dogs, cats, and rabbits. If they were engaged in perceptual matching rather than conceptually interpreted matching, they should choose the stimulus *most similar* to that exemplar during the test. They do not, choosing a cat or rabbit as often as a dog when having observed a dog acting, and therefore we must discard the perceptual-matching explanation for these data. In more recent work, Poulin-Dubois and Vyncke (2003) agreed that perceptual matching cannot account for the data from these tasks. These authors found that 14- and 18-month-olds generalized a dog or a cat drinking from a cup and sleeping in a bed equally to other four-legged mammals and to people, a finding difficult to explain on the basis of perceptual matching.[3]

The technique of systematically varying the distractors that I have described in this section is a most promising one. It is time consuming to zero in on the exact interpretation because each variation in distractors needs to be done in a separate experiment, but it provides a way of finding out more exactly than we have done before how infants are interpreting the events they observe. The data indicate that infants are indifferent as to whether they use a dog, cat, or rabbit to imitate an event modeled with a dog because they consider them all to be the same kind of thing. They can see the perceptual differences among these items, but their imitations are based on their conceptual interpretations of what they have observed, not the physical appearance of the items per se. This point is sometimes difficult for us adults to appreciate because we are so used to thinking of dogs, cats, and rabbits as different kinds. But there is little difference in principle between our considering chairs both with and without arms to be the same kind of thing and an inexperienced infant considering a dog and a cat to be the same kind. Along with this indifference, however, is a somewhat finer appreciation of vehicles. This result is a little disconcerting, but infants in southern California, where these experiments were conducted, spend a lot of time on the road in cars, from which, of course, they observe a great many other kinds of vehicles.

Overall, the various induction data discussed in this chapter are consistent with our previous categorization findings. Our findings from the object-examination task, the sequential-touching task, and the generalized imitation task all converge on the conclusion that infants initially form broad, relatively undifferentiated concepts of animals, furniture, and plants (with evidence that vehicles become differentiated earlier than the other domains). Furthermore, these tasks all indicate that these domain-level concepts are not organized around individual features or overall perceptual appearance, but rather around some possibly quite primitive notion of kind. Needless to say, I do not conclude from these data that young children *cannot* restrict inductions to subcategories in either natural kind or artifact domains; indeed, I assume that one of the functions of the names that parents use with children is to teach them that there are smaller categories than the domain level that are important and that constrain some kinds of properties. Nevertheless, it appears that before the onset of language, the earliest inferences tend to be remarkably broad.

In addition, these data tell us something very important about the way infants form associations. They indicate that property association and generalization are controlled not by the common features of objects or by the perceptual appearance of the objects that infants have actually observed but instead are organized by the concepts they have formed. In the initial stages, the boundaries of these concepts are quite broad. The world has been divided into a few global domains of different kinds of things. The meaning of these broad classes, such as animals or vehicles, does not arise from commonality of physical features. Rather, infants observe the events in which animals and vehicles take part and use their interpretation of the events to conceptualize what sort of thing an animal or a vehicle is.[4] Animals are things that move themselves and act on other things, vehicles are things that give animals rides, and so forth. The most important aspect of this meaning creation is that it is the meaning of the class as a whole that determines what gets associated with what, not just the individual objects or features of objects actually experienced. So, for instance, drinking is associated with "self-movers" and with containers, not just with the dogs one has seen drink or the cups one has drunk from. Note that this view does not claim that no associations between dogs and drinking or cups and drinking are formed, only that initially the associations are broader than that.

Thus, even though infants must use various physical features to tell animals such as dogs and cats apart, they do not rely on them when they are construing the meaning of an event or even when generalizing from it. When we model an event with a dog, and give infants a choice between another dog and a cat or another dog and a rabbit to use for their imitations, they are as apt to choose the cat or the rabbit as the dog. They do not give a drink to a Flying Tiger airplane in spite of its prominent mouth. They use a key on forklifts and airplanes, associations which they of course have never observed. And infants presumably have not seen people sleeping in bathtubs or drinking from frying pans, yet they generalize broadly to these pieces of furniture and containers. All of these phenomena provide evidence that associations are not controlled by individual features or objects but instead by object kind.

What I am emphasizing here is that it is the conceptualization of something—for example, as animate—that controls the association of self-motion with limbs, not the other way around. This may seem an unduly subtle point, but I believe it is an underappreciated aspect of associative learning. Even pigeons, when they associate completely different stimuli with a common event, develop a common meaning or representation for those stimuli, one that is used to create new untrained associations (Zentall, 2000). So we should not be surprised that infants can use common motion events to form conceptual categories such as animals, which then control learning of new associations.

Needless to say, the view that meaning rather than physical features controls associativity does not deny that perceptual similarity can influence the likelihood of making a generalization, particularly making inferences *within* conceptual domains (e.g., Gelman & O'Reilley, 1988). Even adults often have little information to differentiate one animal species from another except physical appearance. To the extent that is so, they must rely on perceptual similarity and dissimilarity to regulate their inferences. Similarly, when infants are faced with truly novel objects about which they have no kind information, they will generalize on the basis of object shape (Welder & Graham, 2001). But they use differences in shape to distinguish one kind from another, which is not the same as asserting that associations or generalizations are made on the basis of these differences. As Paul Bloom (2000) noted, in the absence of other information, shape can provide information about the underlying structure or function of a kind of object. In contrast, Welder and Graham (2001) showed that when 16- to 21-month-old infants are given labels that provide familiar kind information, they generalize on that basis rather than on shape.

Why Infants Don't Use "Basic-Level" Concepts for Inductions

Given that infants can see the features and details that differentiate one "basic-level" kind from another and use them to perceptually categorize objects, why don't they use concepts at this level of specificity for their inductive generalizations? Part of the reason is that infants typically don't attend to many of the details of the animals, plants, and other objects they encounter in their daily lives. That they don't is amply attested by the data presented here. We don't yet have enough data to be sure, but it seems likely that the excellent performance on differentiating animal kinds such as dogs and cats that 3-month-olds show in the familiarization/preferential-looking paradigm (Eimas & Quinn, 1994; Quinn et al., 1993) results from a kind of concentrated exposure to multiple exemplars of categories that must be rare in everyday life. When does an infant see 12 different cats in the space of a few minutes? Is this kind of concentrated experience similar to ordinary perceptual learning? For instance, it might call forth attention to details that does not occur in an infant's normal environment.

In ordinary life, we should not expect infants to pay a great deal of attention to the details of objects around them, unless they are engaged in analyzing them. Perhaps even more important, which perceptual features people encode from objects depends on how they have conceptualized them. Archambault, O'Donnell, and Schyns (1999) showed that when an object in a scene has been labeled at a general level (as a cup or as a computer), adults notice fewer details than when it has been labeled at a more specific level (John's cup or Peter's computer). They take more trials to notice a change in the cup when it has been identified only at a general level. Similarly, Tanaka and Taylor (1990) showed that experts were just as fast at accessing subordinate representations in their area of expertise as "basic-level" representations. These experiments suggest that the *level* of conceptualization at which objects are represented affects perception of them: The more general the level, the less detail will be encoded. Hence, if infants have encoded an object as, for instance, something to drink from, they may actually take in less detail of its physical appearance than if they had encoded it as a cup. As O'Regan (1992) put it, "Seeing does not involve simultaneously perceiving all the features present in an object but only a very small number, just sufficient to accomplish the task at hand" (p. 482). If an infant's task is to decide if something is "to drink from," then the most likely features to be encoded are those indicating containment, not superficial details such as handles. Similarly, if an infant has interpreted animals as things that move themselves, then the wide variation in their physical appearance may even discourage infants from encoding their individual details.

There may also be advantages to using broad categories to form early inferences. Narrow categories maximize the accuracy of predictions, but their use would also mean that many things would go uncategorized and therefore remain uncomprehended. It is probably more efficient in the long run to make overly general predictions (all animals drink) and learn some exceptions (. . . except for fish) than not to have any idea of what a new animal exemplar is at all. Indeed, Medin, Wattenmaker, and Michalski (1987) found that this is what adults often do when learning new categories and making inferences. They found that people often develop overly general rules and then restrict them by adding clauses that eliminate counterexamples.

This approach begins in infancy. When infants observe people and perhaps a dog or cat drink, they make the generalization that "self-moving, contingent interactors" drink. Thus, they are not dependent upon the details of what a particular object looks like to decide what it is or to make predictions about what it will do. If they see it behave in a particular way, no matter how weird its form may be, they can conclude many things about it. This is one of the advantages of forming concepts of things on the basis of a broad characterization of what they do rather than what they look like (Nelson, 1974).

Another advantage of not attending to detail is similar to that speculated for language acquisition, namely, that limited information-processing skills make the task easier (Elman, 1993; Newport, 1990). The notion is that mastering language requires learning to structure a huge database. A restricted capacity that limits the amount of information being considered can make learning possible without overloading the system. The same argument is applicable to the conceptual system. Infants can begin to interpret what is happening around them and thereby gain a degree of predictability about the world without having to process all of the huge amount of information with which they are confronted. A lack of attention to detail, accompanied by attention to a few salient characteristics of events, gives infants a better chance of not falling into local minima and being trapped by mistaken hypotheses that are driven by local detail rather than being broadly true (Carey & Markman, 1999).

Summary of Some Differences Between Percepts and Concepts

I have argued for the necessity of distinguishing between conceptual and perceptual categories. Some such distinction is necessary because both kinds of categorization occur in young infants. Infants certainly do make use of similarity of surface appearance in forming perceptual categories and do so with ease and from an early age. But infants also form conceptual categories at least by 7 months of age and do so in a way that largely ignores surface similarity. I would characterize the bases of the earliest concepts as theory-like, in that a small set of abstract distinctions is being used to define animals, vehicles, plants, and furniture as different kinds. I call these distinctions "defining" because they are necessary and sufficient for the simple inferences that infants make; what something looks like doesn't matter as much as whether it has these particular characteristics. These characteristics are more abstract than perceptual features. For example, even though motion can be considered a perceptual feature, what that motion actually looks like is not included in the notion of self-motion; that is no longer perceptual but rather a more abstract spatial notion. Interestingly, the characteristics that seem to act like necessary and sufficient conditions for the infant may do so because the conceptual base is so meager. If the only way an infant conceptualizes an animal is as a self-mover, then if something can't move by itself, how could it be an animal? I once horrified a reviewer for *Cognition* by making this comment, but it does suggest how concepts can be built up around a core that acts like a definition in spite of the more variable accretions of later experience that temper and qualify the initial formulation. The result would be the kind of radial categories built around core notions that typify adult cognition (Lakoff, 1987).

Even in this approach, perceptual information is vital. If I am correct that the earliest concept of animal is something like a self-mover that interacts with other objects from a distance, the underlying basis for these notions is information given by the perceptual system. In addition, as discussed in chapter 7, infants must use perceptual appearance to identify an object as a member of a given conceptual class. However, infants do not rely on the features they use to identify objects to constrain their inductions. Keys are associated with car doors in babies' experience, yet they generalize this association to motorcycles, forklifts, and airplanes, for which they have no evidence. Cups and glasses are associated with drinking, but the association is generalized to frying pans, again in spite of the lack of evidence. It appears that it is not just doors or cars that are being associated with keys but vehicles, and it isn't just cups or mugs being associated with drinking but containers. Thus, the data I have described suggest that physical features and the similarity relations they produce are used for identification purposes rather than to constrain the associative learning that builds the knowledge base.

It is for reasons such as these that I have argued for the necessity of differentiating perceptual and conceptual similarity in concept formation. At least in the early stages of development when the basis of the human conceptual system is being laid down, there is evidence that perceptual similarity isn't much used in its formation. It *is* being used for perceptual categorization, but that is different from conceptual categorization, which depends on other kinds of information than what objects look like. There are at least six ways in which this difference manifests itself in the infancy period, some of which last throughout life (Mandler, 2000b).

First, perceptual categories work on different kinds of information than do conceptual categories. This first difference may be considered a matter of definition. There is an important distinction to be made between people's summary representations of what things look like and their summary representations of what things are. Perceptual categorization computes *perceptual* similarity. At least early in infancy, it does so independently of knowledge about function or kind; indeed, it can occur even in the complete absence of meaningfulness. It might be more appropriate to say that it is not categorization at all but perceptual schema formation, reserving the term *categorization* for conceptual categories. If we did, some of the arguments in this area of research might fall away. Conceptual categories compute *conceptual* similarity, which in the realm of objects has to do with class membership or kinds. The concept of a kind may include a perceptual description, but its initial core is the assignment of the object to a domain, which itself is characterized by a few abstract characteristics, typically having to do with event or role information.

Second, the two kinds of information are stored in different ways. Perceptual categorization, as discussed in chapter 3, is part and parcel of the perceptual system. We don't so much *have* perceptual categories as *use* them when we perceive (Smith & Samuelson, 1997). I much prefer the term *perceptual schema* to get across this notion. When a perceptual schema is formed, it changes the way the perceptual system operates so that all future similar perceptual input is necessarily influenced by it; the perceptual system can't perceive in quite the same way as before. A connectionist model handles this situation very well. In some sense the information that distinguishes any two learned perceptual categories is represented by patterns of activity across hidden units, but the main thing that has happened by the learning is that the connection strengths among all the units have changed.

Of course, to some extent this is true of conceptual information too. New concepts can influence our understanding of situations and how we interpret data. Nevertheless, there is a major difference in the characteristics of the storage. We *have* concepts in the way we don't have percepts. We learn new ideas and new facts and salt them away in an accessible database. Although as this database changes, it usually affects how we process related information, this does not always happen. It is possible to learn new information and have it remain unconnected to related information previously learned—a very different situation from the perceptual case. The accessible database is a storehouse—a place where, if all goes well, we retrieve information from the past and facts that we need to use for thinking and planning. This is the luxury system, a repository of knowledge that enables us to carry on high-level thought processes, and it is this aspect of conceptual knowledge that I have been concerned with in this book, rather than the way in which our conceptual knowledge influences our perceptual interpretations.

The third difference is due to the second. As a result of the nature of procedural information, we do not have access to the contents of our perceptual categories, whereas the contents of concepts are accessible for purposes of thought, problem solving, recall, and so forth. There is virtually no direct information on accessibility in infancy, and so I generalize from adults. There is ample evidence that for adults perceptual categories are impenetrable; as discussed in chapter 3, we have no access to the information that enables us to categorize a face as male or female. Whatever this information is, it cannot be considered part of our concept of a face. We use this information to identify males and females, but we do not "know" what it is and so cannot think about it. Given lack of accessibility to this kind of information in adulthood, it seems somewhat unlikely it would be accessible in infancy. We can form concepts about what faces look like, but that is not the same as the perceptual categories themselves. As for the converse, that concepts are accessible to infants as well as to adults, the ability to imitate past events as infants can do at least from 9 months of age (Mandler & McDonough, 1996b; Meltzoff, 1988a) requires not only conceptualization but also accessibility, as shown by the inability of amnesic adults to do such imitation

(McDonough, Mandler, McKee, & Squire, 1995). This issue is discussed further in chapters 10 and 12.

Fourth, perceptual categories contain more detailed information (at least in infancy) than do conceptual categories. A perceptual procedure that can tell dogs from cats in a few brief trials is probably operating on a great deal of detailed perceptual information (even if confined to the face region) in order to extract a summary representation. The perceptual system delivers masses of information in parallel. Conceptual information, on the other hand, is filtered through conscious awareness, which is a limited-capacity system, and only limited amounts of information can be processed at a time (G. Mandler, 1975). This may be one of the reasons that so many early concepts are relatively crude and lacking in detail, as illustrated by infants' ability to conceptually differentiate animals from vehicles but not most animals from each other.

Fifth, there is a different course of acquisition for perceptual and conceptual knowledge. There are still not many data on infants' acquisition of perceptual categories at different levels of generality, but we do know that even very young infants are proficient categorizers at what is usually called the basic level. For conceptual categories, on the other hand, even older infants are more proficient at making a few broad distinctions that separate one domain from another than they are at making the finer distinctions required to categorize at the basic level.

Sixth and most important, perceptual and conceptual categories serve different functions. Perceptual categorization is used for recognition and object identification. Conceptual categories, on the other hand, are used to control inductive generalization and, as we will see in chapter 10, for recall of the past as well. Infants, just like adults, make their inductive generalizations on the basis of kind, not on the basis of perceptual similarity. Of course, adults *do* make use of perceptual similarity in their inductions, but they use it to help determine kind, not as a basis for induction in its own right. No matter how much something may look like an animal, if we think (for whatever reason) it is *not* an animal, we will not ascribe animal properties to it. The same is true for children. Carey (1985) showed that even young children will not induce animal properties (such as having a spleen) to a toy monkey; Massey and Gelman (1988) made a similar point.[5] Our data show that infants, too, are constrained by their notions of kinds, as crude as these may be.

I have couched these differences between percepts and concepts in terms of different kinds of categories. That may not be ideal. There are many who prefer to talk about categorization as a process or even as a kind of experimental task. Nevertheless, it is important to make the contrasts just discussed salient, whether done so in terms of different kinds of categories or as aspects of the different ways in which procedural and declarative knowledge are processed. Regardless of terminology, we have seen crucial differences between perceiving and conceiving, in terms of serving different functions, reliance on different kinds of information, different degrees of selectivity in the information that is taken in, differences in accessibility, differences in storage, and different developmental time courses.

9

Continuity in the Conceptual System
Acquisition, Breakdown, and Reorganization

. . . in which a case is made for continuity in conceptual life between infancy and adulthood. I first summarize what we have learned in previous chapters about the infant's conceptual system. Then I show that it dovetails in many ways with neuropsychological data on breakdown of the conceptual system in adult semantic dementia. Lastly, I briefly summarize the Vygotskian and Piagetian views that stressed reorganization rather than enrichment and differentiation to account for conceptual change, and suggest reasons to reject such accounts.

Be it known that, waiving all argument, I take the good old fashioned ground that the whale is a fish. . . . (Ishmael, in Moby Dick*)*

The Initial Organization of the Conceptual System

It is time to summarize the large body of data we have accumulated over the past decade on the initial organization of the conceptual system. I will try to make of the various results as coherent a picture as possible. The initial, and perhaps most important, conclusion that can be drawn from the data is that because the first concepts about objects are global in nature, the acquisition process tends to emphasize differentiation. First, broad concepts such as animals or vehicles are formed, then subdivisions such as land, air, and sea animals, and then dogs, horses, and so forth. In this way the acquisition process organizes the conceptual system hierarchically. The system will eventually become a complex heterarchy, because of the many cross-references and connections that arise with experience. However, the fundamental underlying structure of the conceptual system about objects is necessarily hierarchical.

I discussed in the last chapter some reasons why global concepts are the first to be used for making inferences. Equally important is that their presence guides the acquisition of the finer details that are associated with smaller classes. This organizing factor makes the learning process coherent. While learning the details that differentiate a sheep from a goat, the young child remains clear about their relationship to other classes: They are both kinds of animals. If children first learned a concept of a dog but did not see any relationship between it and a rabbit or a cow, or if they learned a concept of a chair but did not see any relationship between it and a table or a bed, then the organization of the conceptual system would be wide open, without any principled basis for its development. This is perhaps the implication of theories that posit "basic-level" concepts as the first to be formed. One would expect that learning that proceeds only by synthesizing small classes into larger ones would be a slower and more uncertain process. It would lack the benefit of the broad conceptual divisions already acquired that organize each bit of new learning within a coherent framework. Such a lack might predict greater variability in conceptual organization than we actually observe.

We have seen that by 7 months infants begin to form broad concepts of at least three classes: animals, vehicles, and furniture. Some of the literature discussed in chapter 5 suggests that this conceptual process begins considerably earlier, but to date there are no definitive data that inform us about the *conceptual* status of the discriminations that younger infants make. Even at 7 months the only data we have suggesting conceptual categorization are from the object-examination test and, as we have seen, the data from the 7-month-olds on these differentiations are not strong. The data are more clear-cut for 9-month-olds (for example, categorizing birds as different from airplanes) and can also be supplemented with the data from the inductive generalization test, which offer the most convincing evidence of conceptual responding to global categories. However, the data we have from the latter test at 9 months are only on the distinction between animals and vehicles. So even though 7-month-olds differentiate the inanimate realm into at least two categories (vehicles and furniture), it is still not entirely clear whether infants first begin with a more basic animate-inanimate distinction.

More evidence is needed before deciding if there is initially an animate-inanimate conceptual distinction or a somewhat more differentiated set of initial conceptual categories, such as animals, indoor artifacts, and outdoor artifacts. In either case, it does not appear necessary to start the conceptual differentiation process by building in innate conceptual divisions between animals and artifacts, as several researchers have suggested (e.g., Gelman, 1990; Spelke, 1994). As discussed in chapter 5, the available data suggest that this distinction is learnable from the spatial and movement information presented by the visual system. Nevertheless, whether learned or innate, the distinction is one of the major underpinnings of the conceptual system.

By 9 months, infants discriminate the global concepts of animals, vehicles, and furniture. They fail, however, to discriminate kitchen utensils from furniture on the object-examination test (Mandler & McDonough, 1998a). At 11 months, they make all of these distinctions and also a distinction between plants and both animals and vehicles. (We do not have data on plants before 11 months, so the lower limit of this learning is unknown; again, it could be quite early.) As we have seen in chapters 7 and 8, conceptually differentiating these various domains into subclasses is a continuous process taking place over the course of the next year and a half.

An important issue is whether there are different rates of learning within the animate and inanimate domains. Caramazza and Shelton (1998) suggested an evolutionary basis for an animate-inanimate distinction because the domain-level categories of animals, plants, and artifacts can be affected by cerebral damage independently of each other. They suggested that this might be due to "specific adaptations for recognizing and responding to animal and plant life," which result in specialized mechanisms for recognizing and categorizing members of the realms for which these specific adaptations have evolved. However, if there were dedicated mechanisms for processing animals and plants, one would expect learning different animal and plant kinds to be especially easy. On the contrary, our data suggest that conceptualizing animal and plant kinds is more difficult for infants than conceptualizing kinds of artifacts. The kind of learning infants do appears to be the same for animals, plants, and artifacts, but at least in our culture, it is slower for animals and plants. This difference is not what one would predict from an evolutionary hypothesis that emphasizes special adaptations for learning animals and plants. More seriously for an evolutionary argument, perhaps, even American adults are very poor at distinguishing different kinds of plants and animals, especially nonmammals. As Rosch et al. (1976) discovered, most American college students have little idea about the properties that distinguish one fish from another or one kind of deciduous tree from another, in terms of both what they look like and other characteristic features. These properties need to be emphasized by the culture or else they go unnoticed.

Rather than there being an evolutionary basis for the division between animals and artifacts, I have suggested that it depends on infants' tendency to attend to motion. That tendency, which is widespread among mammals, seems to me more likely to have an evolutionary basis and one that would have wide ramifications for the way that mammals behave. However, that is not the same as saying that evolution has fashioned a special propensity for learning about animals and plants. Caramazza and Shelton (1998) emphasized the categorical organization of the conceptual system, which I think is correct, but there appear to be sufficient grounds for this organization to be learned rather than built in. A distinction between animals and artifacts can be generated from the perceptual information that is available to infants. If this is the case, then one would expect more similarities than differences in learning about the different domains. Aside from faster differentiation of the artifact domains we have studied, which seems plausibly due to infants' greater experience with the various instances, overall the course of learning looks very similar.

We see a hierarchy in the making especially clearly in the case of the division of animals into subtypes. Our data suggest that animals are first conceptually divided into land animals and birds, with fish being a slightly later division. These data are at least partly culturally determined. In the urban society of San Diego, even though the city is by an ocean, fish as living creatures do not loom large in the daily lives of infants. Over the first year or two, children in our culture are gradually exposed to a variety of mammals. With some, such as dogs and cats, they may have daily experience. They see the differences between these two animal kinds from an early age. However, on the object-examination test, they do not categorize them as different until between 9 and 11 months, and in terms of generalizing from one to the other, they still treat them as equivalent at 14 months. This means that for a long period dogs and cats are treated as perceptual variants on each other, while at the same time their animal (or land animal) status is firmly established.

The process of conceptual differentiation is not systematic, nor its results scientifically tidy (Mandler, 2002). For example, it seems unlikely that infants see any relationship between animals and plants. If there is a foundational conceptual division, the distinction is probably not between living and nonliving things but between animals and nonanimals. The animate-inanimate distinction is an adult theoretical construction that children eventually learn rather than a species-characteristic way of viewing the world. Hatano et al. (1993) found that both culture and language influenced Japanese, Israeli, and American children's judgments of the relationship between animals and plants. The children all understood that animals and plants are different types of things but differed in whether they considered plants to be alive. Self-starting movement, biological movement, and contingent interactions from a distance are crucial to conceptualizing animals, and these do not characterize plants. We do not have data comparing the two domains earlier than 11 months, but at that time infants differentiate them. So it seems likely that there is a more fundamental distinction than the animate-inanimate one, namely, the distinction between animals and other things.

Other differences from traditional object hierarchies also appear. For instance, our data show that artifacts are divided into furniture and vehicles from an early age. Although this seems to be a straightforward distinction, it, too, may be an overly adult characterization. It may be more accurate to say that infants divide artifacts into indoor and outdoor things (or perhaps indoor and outdoor artifacts). Some years ago, when we were exploring the sequential-touching task, Bauer, McDonough, and I found a category of manipulable household items that our subjects differentiated from vehicles (unpublished data). We discovered this category when we tried to assess responding on the sequential-touching test when there was only one taxonomic category available. We contrasted vehicles with what we considered to be an unrelated set of things. The items in the sets we used (a lamp, hairbrush, teacup, and wristwatch or a chair, guitar, spoon, and shoe) seemed to us to come from different conceptual domains. To our surprise, our 17- and 20-month-old subjects showed clear categorization of these items when they were contrasted either with cars or with a superordinate set of vehicles. In retrospect, what we considered to be an unrelated group could all be considered household items (or perhaps manipulable things typically found indoors). It wasn't until I read Warrington and McCarthy's (1987) case study of YOT, a patient with selective loss of categorical knowledge who seemed to have a category of indoor things, that it occurred to me we might have inadvertently provided the children with a "real" conceptual category.[1] My hunch is that there will be lots of these—categories that do not fit neatly into the taxonomic systems taught at school but that make sense from the point of view of what matters to the 1- or 2-year-old. Other examples are the categories of kitchen things and bathroom things discussed in chapter 6, which children as young as 14 months differentiate on the basis of different locations or the contexts in which different activities take place (Mandler et al., 1987).

Similar comments can be made about food. It is highly unlikely that infants in our culture see any relationship between food and living things. Food is an early-developing conceptual category. Unfortunately, it is difficult to study by the methods we have been using. It might be called an attractive nuisance, because infants dwell on representations of food, even when made of plastic, to the exclusion of most other items presented to them. That very fact suggests that a food category is an early accomplishment, but we have few details. What little we do know about it, however, suggests that although infants differentiate food from animals and plants, and words for food are prominent in their earliest vocabulary (Nelson, 1973b), infants are slow to categorize different kinds of food, such as fruits, meats, and vegetables. Although there are few data from preverbal infants, the overextension data on language understanding in the second year suggest considerable haziness about different types of food (McDonough, 2002a). Indeed, it has been suggested that the initial organization of this domain is by type of meal (breakfast, lunch, and dinner) rather than by taxonomic structure of the foods themselves (Lucariello & Nelson, 1985).

One proposal for the first subdivisions of animals and nonanimal things into more detailed conceptual categories is laid out in Table 9-1.

Table 9-1. Possible Hierarchical Organization of the Conceptual System in the First Year

Animals		Artifacts					Food
Land	Air	Indoor things		Outdoor things			
		Furniture	Utensils	Vehicles	Plants	Buildings*	

*Hypothesized.

In it, animals, nonanimal things, and food are considered foundational. I have put an asterisk by the category of buildings to indicate we have no data and this is merely a prediction. I would expect a conceptual category of buildings to be learned fairly early, even though infants are on the whole uninterested in large immovable objects (Nelson, 1973b). There are not a lot of data, but I mentioned in the last chapter that 14-month-olds understand that both animals and vehicles can go into buildings (Mandler & McDonough, 1998b), which is the kind of abstract relational characterization one expects from a conceptualized domain. In addition, infants should have enough experience to differentiate homes and supermarkets from a fairly early age. We also have relatively little data on food, but because of the special status food has in an infant's life, I have assumed it is conceptualized as different from other nonanimal things from an early age.

In this proposal there is no overarching animate-inanimate or living-nonliving distinction, but only three divisions of the world, each separate from the others. Of course, this division is speculative. It is possible that food might be considered just another nonanimal thing, in which case the initial division reduces to an animal-nonanimal distinction. What we do know is that the categories of animals, furniture, and vehicles are differentiated from each other at least by 9 months of age and plants by 11 months. Even earlier, land animals are distinguished from air animals. At 9 months, kitchen utensils are not yet conceptually differentiated from furniture but are by 11 months, giving some support to the grouping of both of them under a category of indoor things that initially is undifferentiated but soon begins to be subdivided. Some other categories, such as tools and musical instruments, appear to be still later acquisitions, although we have not investigated these categories as thoroughly.

Breakdown of the Conceptual System

The literature on semantic dementia suggests that breakdown of conceptual knowledge about objects goes from the loss of specific details to more general categories in quite an orderly fashion. Hodges, Graham, and Patterson (1995) have provided one of the most systematic studies of the pattern of breakdown. Their patient, JL, showed a gradual progressive loss of the features that enable discrimination between specific category instances, such as dogs versus horses or cars versus buses. At first, slightly more general knowledge was spared. JL sometimes indicated that an object was a flying animal, or a tool, or something to sit on. The last distinction to go was the animal-nonanimal distinction. So the pattern was first to lose the ability to identify specific classes; then broader divisions within the domains of animals, plants, vehicles, and other artifacts; and finally to lose the animal-nonanimal distinction itself.

Patients have also been reported who selectively lose animate or inanimate concepts. Typically, only subsets of these two great realms are impaired (to my knowledge, there is no case in which all animate concepts remain in the absence of all inanimate concepts, or vice versa), but the subsets themselves tend to follow major categorical divisions. Consider the patient studied by Warrington and McCarthy (1987) mentioned earlier, who was more impaired on comprehension tests of artifacts than on food or animals. Further tests showed that the impairment in artifact knowledge was greater for manipulable household objects than for large outdoor objects (vehicles and buildings). When the domain of household objects was examined in still greater detail, by dividing it into office supplies, interior house parts (such as doors), clothes, utensils, and furniture, she could tell these subdomains apart; for example, she might confuse a pencil with an envelope but would not confuse it with a fork. So she retained the major subdivisions of furniture, utensils, clothes, and so forth, but she did confuse items *within* these subdomains of the larger domain of household items.

Other patients fail the chimera test, in which parts of animals or tools are combined to make chimeric objects and people are asked to say whether they are real objects (Riddoch & Humphreys, 1987). For example, a patient might consider acceptable a head of a horse on a tiger or a set of scissor blades on a screwdriver handle. Findings such as these also indicate a genuine loss of specific category details, leaving the broader domains themselves relatively intact. The size of the impaired and intact domains varies from patient to patient, but in all of them it is the details that are lost first, typically followed by loss at the higher levels of organization.

Such data, of course, implicate a hierarchical organization of the conceptual system. Indeed, this has been a common interpretation of the findings in this area of neuropsychological research at least since Warrington (1975) proposed it. A further approach to explaining category-specific impairments, begun by Warrington and Shallice (1984), is that such impairments are due to differential loss of sensory versus functional information. They suggested that sensory information such as perceptual appearance is more important in differentiating living things from each other, and functional information such as what one does with objects is more important for differentiating one artifact from another. By itself, this view does not dispute a hierarchical organization to the conceptual system. However, more recently, a version of this view has been used to downplay the importance of hierarchical organization itself. It has been suggested that the loss of detail and the sparing of superordinate knowledge reflects the fact that superordinate knowledge can be sustained even in a degraded semantic net, because such a net is better able to support general than specific distinctions. In this view, the semantic system need not be organized hierarchically. Hodges et al. (1995) described this point of view in the following way: "if one's knowledge about an elephant consists of a network of semantic features, then, even when a substantial number of these have been lost or blurred, it is possible that the remaining information would permit the classification of an elephant as an animal (rather than a man-made object), because almost any 'animal' feature distinguishes it from a nonliving thing" (p. 464).

This approach to the organization of knowledge suggests that superordinate information is not fundamental in the way the system is put together. Instead, spared superordinate judgments of animalness or birdiness stem from the use of the remaining features in an undifferentiated network of features that is gradually disintegrating. In this view, you do not need to put categorical information into the system to get categorical impairment; in that sense, superordinate knowledge is emergent rather than foundational. So, for example, Farah and McClelland (1991), who took this point of view, suggested that the organizing principle for semantic memory might be visual versus functional information instead. They further suggested that this might be a more reasonable division of the semantic system than a distinction between animate and inanimate, because different brain areas are dedicated to representing information from sensory and motor channels. A related point of view, although one that emphasizes distributed cognition rather than different brain areas, has been put forth by Tyler, Moss, Durrant-Peatfield, and Levy (2000); in this view, categorical structure emerges from distinctive functional features correlated with perceptual features.

One can certainly devise a model in which no hierarchical information is put into the system directly, yet breakdown occurs along categorical lines. Farah and McClelland (1991) showed that weighting visual and functional information differentially was sufficient to model various semantic memory deficits. However, even if this approach can account for the data on breakdown, it has considerably more difficulty in accounting for acquisition. Superordinate class membership is woven into the way that the conceptual system is formed. In the first instance, animals are objects that move in different ways than artifacts do and are seen to move themselves rather than being moved by others. For both animals and artifacts, conceptualization is organized around what things do or is done to them, so functional information is crucial for both. At the same time, visual information, in the sense of the details of appearance, is less relevant for conceptualizing both living things and artifacts. Hence, it is not clear how a division of conceptual knowledge into visual versus functional can account for early concept acquisition. It is also unclear how such an approach would handle the pattern of early inductive inference I have described. Functional information, in the sense of what things do, is at the root of concept formation and inference and applies equally to animals and artifacts.

It may be that patterns of breakdown cannot by themselves answer the question of the organization of the conceptual system, not only because the hierarchical position and the degraded feature position often make similar predictions but also because breakdown along visual versus functional lines could occur even in a hierarchically organized system. This is where the developmental data can be useful. The argument I have made is that every time an infant or young child learns a new distinction within a conceptual realm, as part of the very learning process the object is understood as a member of a superordinate class. Insofar as the meaning system is concerned, the infant looking at dogs and cats does not at first conceptualize them as two different kinds but only as two different-looking self-movers. When they do become conceptually distinct, it is as two animals that vary in their names or the sounds they make, and so forth, but their animal membership is never in question. Furthermore, our data imply that the associations that enrich conceptual categories occur via the superordinate and are not merely associative pairings of, say, mouths and eating or even dogs and eating. The association is between animals and eating. Therefore, the superordinate domain is not emergent but is crucial in constructing more specific concepts in the first place.

The acquisition data predict that for each of the categories in Table 9-1 lower level distinctions will be lost before higher level ones. Because of the nature of the learning process, in which each new distinction is learned as a subdivision of a superordinate category, the superordinate distinctions should be the most firmly established, and therefore one would expect a pattern of "first in, last out." One can lose details about tigers (for example, whether they are African or Indian animals) while still retaining enough information to differentiate tigers from other animals, but if one no longer knows what an animal is, it would seem virtually impossible to retrieve the fact that tigers are Indian animals. Thus, both the breakdown data and the acquisition data are consistent with a model in which the conceptual system is learned and organized hierarchically from the top down.

Although the way in which the conceptual system is first learned and organized predicts the order in which semantic information is lost, there are two other aspects of breakdown that may also be illuminated by developmental data. The first of these is why animal kind differences are more apt to be disrupted under brain damage than are artifacts (see Saffran & Schwartz, 1994, for a summary). The second is why there should be an association, frequently observed in the neuropsychological literature, between damage to animals and plants (Warrington & Shallice, 1984). The latter finding suggests that animals and plants belong to a common higher level category of living things, so that if the category of animals, for example, were damaged, it might be more likely that plants rather than artifacts would be damaged as well. However, this association does not always show up, because for some patients the category of animals is damaged by itself (Caramazza & Shelton, 1998). The acquisition data, as discussed earlier, are more consistent with a separation of these two categories than with their being part of a larger "animate" distinction.

It is tempting to suggest that any association between animals and plants in conceptual breakdown and also the greater prevalence of breakdown in animal than artifact concepts might be due to the fact that animal and plant concepts are more difficult to learn in the first place. However, the answer may be more fundamental than that, perhaps involving a common factor that influences both acquisition and breakdown. In our society, most of us have much less experience with animals or plants than with artifacts. This begins in infancy. I do not mean to imply that animals are unfamiliar or that familiarity is not an important factor in the breakdown of semantic knowledge (e.g., Funnell & Sheridan, 1992). But familiarity is not the same as the continuous interaction with objects that takes place, day in and day out, over the course of decades. It may be this kind of daily interaction that is crucial in maintaining the conceptual system. We may judge (as I do) that both dogs and spoons are highly familiar, but it is the latter that most of us deal with on a daily basis. In that sense, knowledge of animals and plants in modern society may be more fragile. This is an area that cries out for cross-cultural neuropsychology studies. It seems possible that the loss of the animal category would be less frequent among people whose lives involve daily interaction with animals.

At the same time, the suggestion originally made by Warrington and Shallice (1984) and amended and modified by Borgo and Shallice (2001), that categories whose identity depends more on sensory qualities than on functional or associative ones may be most at risk, is of interest vis-à-vis the acquisition data. Perhaps the relatively slow acquisition of animal and plant kinds that our data indicate is not so much due to lack of interactive experience with them as to the fact that infants do not rely on perceptual appearance to determine conceptual kind. We have repeatedly found that what things look like does not particularly influence infants' conceptual choices in the tasks we have used. Because their attention is directed to what things do or what is done to them, perceptual differences among different kinds of animals or plants (or, for that matter, food) do not seem to play a major role in developing and consolidating these conceptual categories. Infants in our culture are for the most part not given much information about the difference between what one animal and another does (and virtually nothing about what one does with one plant versus another). Not surprisingly, then, even 18-month-olds act as if one mammal is equivalent to another. If one does not have extensive interaction with different animals or plants, the primary database one has about what distinguishes one from another is perceptual. That may not be a sufficient basis to create impervious conceptual distinctions between one kind and another.

Conceptual Growth Versus Conceptual Reorganization

One of the most common views of conceptual development in the literature is that major reorganizations in concepts take place during childhood. Piaget and Vygotsky are the most famous exponents of this view, but it is held in one form or another by many current developmentalists, such as Carey (1985). I consider Piaget's and Vygotsky's views on reorganization briefly here, in light of what we have learned about the initial stages of concept formation. More extensive (and in some cases more severe) critiques can be found in Fodor (1972), Gelman (1978), Keil (1989), and Siegel and Hodkin (1982).

For Piaget (Inhelder & Piaget, 1964; Piaget, 1951), infants and children from age 2 to age 4 or 5 are inchoate thinkers, primarily because they do not yet have anything like an adult hierarchically organized conceptual system. The very notion of a preoperational stage is that there is little systematicity to concepts or their use in thought. To convey something of their reputed instability and unorganized nature, Piaget called them pre-concepts. Vygotsky (1934/1962) held a similar position, perhaps even more extreme in that he was unwilling to call children's concepts "real" concepts until they reached puberty (and so entered Piaget's formal operational period). Both Piaget and Vygotsky followed the classical model of concepts prevalent in their time, in which concepts have formal definitions outlining the necessary and sufficient conditions for their instantiation. However, Vygotsky was stricter in applying this view of concept formation. He also emphasized language in forming "real" concepts much more than did Piaget. As Keil (1989) describes it: "For Vygotsky, only as one comes to internalize language does one have the ability to represent concepts in any other way than via concrete instances and the simple associative principles that operate over these instances. By his account, internalized language frees children from relying on memories of specific instances and enables them to use more abstract, principled representations" (p. 7).

Both Vygotsky and Piaget, however, relied on verbal data more than would be done today to support their hypothesis about the instability and disorganization of early conceptual thought. For example, both used verbal overextension to demonstrate the instability of early concepts. Piaget's (1951) example of Jacqueline's use of the word *panana* to express both "grandfather" and "I want that" illustrates the perils of overinterpretation of early verbal data. Certainly, one could interpret this usage to exemplify a completely different concept from those of adults (grandfather + I want), but a more plausible interpretation would be that a limited vocabulary made Jacqueline use the word for her soft-touch grandfather as a makeshift to express either that she wanted something he would give or perhaps to justify her request. Similarly, it is apt to be a misinterpretation to take the chained uses of early words found in overextension data, in which a single word expresses different meanings on different occasions (Clark, 1983), as evidence that the conceptual system itself is changing. As Rescorla (1980) and others have noted, sometimes the new language learner is making do with a small vocabulary to comment on different aspects of the world.

Both Piaget's and Vygotsky's views portray a fundamental change during development in the way that conceptual knowledge is represented. According to Vygotsky, the first pseudo-concepts (syncretic conglomerations) are formally different from the more organized ones of slightly older children (complexes), and the latter are formally different from adult "real" concepts—only "real" concepts are hierarchically organized. Of course, Vygotsky recognized that younger children represented the world mentally and that their pseudoconcepts overlapped adult "real" concepts sufficiently to make communication possible. But, he said, because younger children's concepts lack abstract logical structure, commonality between children's and adults' concepts is somewhat illusory.

Vygotsky based this view of early conceptual development on the use of what have come to be known as Vygotsky (or Hanfmann and Kasanin) blocks. A series of blocks that vary in color, shape, size, and height is put in front of a child. Each block has a nonsense name hidden on the bottom indicating a category to which it belongs; typically four categories involving height and size are used. One of the blocks is turned over, revealing its category name. The child is asked to discover what other blocks belong to this category and to discover the other categories as well. Modern readers will not be surprised that young children do poorly on this ecologically insensitive task. Most children have no idea of how to go about systematically exploring, combining attributes, and eliminating possibilities, a difficulty apt to be compounded by the artificiality of the concepts to be acquired. Of course, any single test places limits on the conclusions that can be drawn from it, but this test not only uses an unrealistic model of concept formation as hypothesis testing, it also involves an unknown number of other variables than concept formation itself. Many years ago, when I considered using an adult version of this test, I tried it out with various colleagues. At least one famous science professor at the University of California San Diego (who shall remain nameless) failed to solve it. I note also that when Bruner et al. (1956) used quite similar tests with Harvard undergraduates, many of them failed to discover the relevant concepts, and they were often haphazard in their strategies. Although these findings are of interest in themselves, they suggest that this kind of test is unlikely to be useful in uncovering the nature of preschoolers' concepts.

In any case, Vygotsky concluded that children's earliest concepts are unorganized congeries (heaps) without any systematic basis.[2] He said that the groupings a child makes become more related to objective reality as development proceeds in the early years, but nevertheless the complexes of this stage (similar to the "collections" of Inhelder & Piaget, 1964) remain far from abstract or logical groupings and are still perceptually concrete: "An object included because of one of its attributes enters the complex not just as the carrier of that one trait but as an individual, with *all* its attributes. The single trait is not abstracted by the child from the rest and is not given a special role, as in a concept. In complexes the hierarchical organization is absent: All attributes are functionally equal" (Vygotsky, 1934/1962, p. 64).[3]

In this view there is a fundamental change in development with the way concepts are represented. It is a view diametrically opposed to that presented in this book and one virtually impossible to reconcile with the data discussed in this and previous chapters. We have seen that even infants have abstract stable concepts (e.g., animal), well grounded in the reality they have experienced, and that follow principled definitions (animals move themselves), albeit not ones they can express verbally. (If they could, I would expect to hear insistence on characteristics for which adults take more modified views.) In Vygotsky's view, children are incapable of abstract conceptual thought. The fact that we as adults can communicate with children has misled us into thinking that there is more continuity between their concepts and ours than really exists. In contrast to such a view, what I have shown in this book is that there is a great deal of continuity in conceptual development. There is change, to be sure, but most of what has been documented here and in the literature consists of enrichment and differentiation rather than fundamental reorganization.

Needless to say, I agree with Vygotsky's point that children's hypothesis testing is vastly less systematic than that of adults. Furthermore, enrichment and differentiation by themselves guarantee important differences between adult and child concepts. Where I disagree with both Vygotsky and Piaget is that the underlying organization of the conceptual system changes from a haphazard and shifting system to a stable and principled one. Organization characterizes concept formation from the beginning, just as it characterizes every other aspect of human intellectual functioning. Of course, it could be that one organized system changes into another kind of organized system. But as we have seen in this book, insofar as objects are concerned, the outlines of the adult conceptual system can be discerned from an early age. The data Vygotsky (and Piaget) collected on developmental changes in conceptual tasks that led them to posit reorganization are more apt to be due to increasing ability to handle hypothesis testing and increasing likelihood of consciously reflecting on relationships among concepts (for example, the implications of class inclusion; see Smith, 1979), rather than to reorganization of the conceptual system itself.

As we have seen, Vygotsky's view of conceptual development is that it proceeds from the concrete to the abstract. In his version of this traditional opinion, language is what provides the ability to think abstractly. I confess I have never understood this position, which gives language the capacity to instill abstractness. If the mind could not consider abstract concepts without language, how could language itself induce this ability?

Nevertheless, it is still a common view (e.g., Madole & Oakes, 1999). (I note, however, that although language cannot by itself produce abstractness, it can be used to direct and constrain thought, helping to make it rigorous, a point that Vygotsky emphasized.) In some other views, abstractness is not ascribed to the development of language. In Piaget's view, it is the increasing systematicity of thought, accompanied by an increasingly powerful logic (for example, being able to reason about class inclusion), that accounts for a shift from concrete to abstract conceptualization. However, as Keil (1998) pointed out, there is very little evidence for the view that conceptual development proceeds from the concrete to the abstract. He notes "one has to ask why the idea of a concrete-to-abstract shift is so pervasive when the data seem to be so equivocal" (p. 397). His own work, which fits well with the data presented in this book, suggests that, if anything, there is a trend from the abstract to the concrete; that is, concept development tends to proceed through differentiation of quite abstract ideas, becoming more concretely detailed during the childhood years (Simons & Keil, 1995).

In an important series of studies, Keil (1979) documented the process of differentiation between kindergarten and grade 6 in children's conceptions of various ontological categories (for example, physical objects, living things, artifacts, events, ideas). Children were asked such questions as what can be thought of, what can be an hour long, and what can be heavy, tall, alive, asleep, or sorry. The systematic nature of the replies evinced hierarchical relations among different categories of objects and separation of objects from events and ideas at all these ages. At the same time the hierarchies became more differentiated with age. Keil's data resemble ours in infancy in that conceptual development proceeds by differentiation from broad (and sometimes overinclusive) concepts to increasingly finer distinctions. Keil's task is a difficult verbal one that requires reflection upon one's knowledge, and some of the answers from the youngest children did appear to confuse objects and ideas, a confusion that seems likely to have more to do with understanding how language is used than about the world. In any case, if we look at their responses to objects, the youngest children differentiated living from nonliving things and gradually through the school years made finer distinctions between animals and plants, between both these and artifacts, and all of the above from aggregates such as water. By 9 years, the hierarchical trees generated from the responses looked like those of adults, with the exception that most 9-year-olds did not differentiate predicates applicable to animals from those applicable to humans. For example, they tended to say that girls and rabbits could both be awake and sorry.

The point I wish to emphasize here about Keil's data is the similarity in the organization of children's and adults' knowledge. His data provide a great deal of evidence for differentiation of the hierarchical system but little evidence for major organizational changes between childhood and adulthood. How, then, can we reconcile his data with those of Carey (1985), who proposed a major change in conceptual organization with development? Carey based her thesis of conceptual reorganization primarily on the fact that adults' conceptions of animals are biologically based, whereas those of young children are psychologically or behaviorally based. Although other data such as Keil's are not entirely concordant with this position, it does appear that infants and young children do not yet have a theory of biology, whereas older children do. However, adding new knowledge, even knowledge that affects the way in which we understand a domain, does not necessarily constitute fundamental restructuring of the knowledge base. We can change our formal criteria for what makes something an animal without losing the underlying notions that continue to structure the conceptual system. We may even move whales out of the fish class into the mammal class, which is certainly a shift, but the notion of land, air, and sea creatures formed in infancy remains.

There are two ways to look at how one's knowledge changes when one learns that a whale is not a fish, but a mammal. We may come to think about it differently—for example, to care for it more or consider it in some way more human than the fish in the sea. The other view is Ishmael's, quoted at the beginning of this chapter. Ishmael proclaims to be little influenced by Linnaeus's view. What matters it, he asks, that whales birth like mammals or suckle their young? That isn't as crucial to understanding a whale as that it lives entirely in the ocean and never comes on land. That's what makes it a fish. So Ishmael knows about the biological specifications for mammals, but in terms of his conceptual system, that isn't as important as the fact that the creature lives in the sea and only in the sea.

Fish swim in the water, mammals walk on land, and birds fly in the air. These are conceptions that we learn preverbally and that continue to underlie our day-to-day thinking about the world forever after. This does not dispute the fact that we know that whales are really mammals, and in that sense there is reorganization of the conceptual system. It only says that such reorganization does not remove the previous organization, which can coexist and perhaps play an even larger role in our daily thought processes than the newer system that gets added to it. As Scott Atran (1990) pointed out, "tree" and "grass" continue to be thought of as natural kinds, even though scientifically they are not, because they look as if they should be. I wager that many adults still think of a whale as "a fish with a few exceptions." In short, it seems more likely that as older children or adults we *add* biological criteria rather than reorganize the whole animal domain on their bases.

I suspect the same thing happens to many categories. For example, the early organization of food by type of meal seems to last throughout life. We retain throughout adulthood the kind of early-acquired slot-filling organization that Katherine Nelson described, as shown by the order in which adults generate exemplars from superordinate categories. We learn a number of new organizations of foods to be sure—food groups such as meat, vegetables, fruit, and grains, and even their organization by type of shop or by supermarket shelves. But the original organization appears to remain alive, well, and useful.

As Keil (1989) put it: "Theory differentiation may be much more common than genuine theoretical revolution." Theoretical revolution does happen in science, but it may be a rare event in ontogeny. One example of restructuring that Carey discussed is the relatively late learning of a genuine concept of animacy, one that includes both animals and plants as living things. I discussed earlier the likelihood that a concept of animacy as such does not exist in infancy; the criteria infants use to establish animalness are quite different from those they might ascribe to plants. This may be not only an example of a genuine restructuring of knowledge but also an example of adding a higher node to the hierarchically organized knowledge about objects; in short, it appears to be a synthesis rather than a differentiation. Even here, however, we can ask how deep this kind of reorganization is. It is not obvious that most people make much use of this high-level concept of animacy in their thinking. There is a good reason that the animacy item (How are a tree and a fly alike?) was the most difficult item on the similarity scale of the Wechsler-

Bellevue IQ test. Most people cannot answer this question, I think, because the formation of a common concept encompassing them is for many people a bit of a school exercise rather than a major restructuring of their conceptual system. As I said, we can add new ways of thinking about objects throughout life, but that may not change the underlying structure of the knowledge base.

The object concepts under consideration in this book, however, are not the most likely candidates for major reorganization with development. More likely candidates are abstract concepts such as mental concepts (e.g., Gopnik & Wellman, 1994), in which there may be a shift from a nonrepresentational to a representational theory of the mind, or theoretical concepts such as weight. Smith et al. (1985) showed major developmental changes in understanding weight, although even here the developmental change that takes place (taking density into account) appears to be mainly a question of differentiation. Perhaps the most frequent examples of conceptual reorganization, however, are relational concepts. As I discuss in chapter 11, reorganization of spatial relational notions by language and constant use is likely to take place more extensively than for objects. Before turning to language and its effects on conceptualization, however, I will discuss one further line of evidence for conceptual thought in preverbal infants, namely, the ability to recall the past.

10

Recall of the Past

. . . in which I bring forth still another line of evidence for conceptual thought in infancy. I say a few words about recall of absent objects, but the focus of the chapter is on recall of past events as measured by deferred imitation. I explain why infant recognition experiments, in contrast to deferred imitation, do not provide positive evidence for declarative memory. I go on to address the surprisingly contentious issue of how, without verbal evidence, we can be sure that deferred imitation does not merely measure implicit or procedural retention of information. I lay out the criteria and evidence that enable us to state with some confidence that from at least nine months infants can recall the past. This kind of recall is not necessarily autobiographical, however, discussion of which leads to a final few words on some possible causes of infantile amnesia.

The past survives under two distinct forms: first, in motor mechanisms; secondly, in independent recollections. (Bergson, 1911)

So far I have discussed two kinds of evidence for conceptual thought in infancy: categorization on the basis of kind and inductive inference. There is still another type of evidence, just as powerful as those already discussed, namely, the ability to recall events from the past. To understand infants' ability to recall, just as for categorization and inductive inference, we will find that it is necessary to make a distinction between procedural and declarative knowledge. Although the term *recall* often goes undefined in the literature,[1] most of us use a commonsense definition of bringing something to mind or, as Piaget (1951) more eloquently put it, the "evocation of absent reality." Somewhat more formally, to recall means to access (bring to awareness) information about something that is not perceptually present.

Recall has traditionally been classed as one of the higher cognitive functions because it requires a re-presentation of something not available to perception. The ability to re-present an absent object or event from the past also implies having represented it conceptually at the time of encoding. It is obvious in the case of verbal recall that an event being described has been conceptualized because overt recall consists of describing the event in words. But even for nonverbal recall in which we picture to ourselves what happened, conceptualization is required. As I discussed in chapter 2, people do not create images from uninterpreted perceptual records but from perceptual information that has been interpreted or construed (Chambers & Reisberg, 1992; Kosslyn, 1980). I gave an example of the effects of interpretation on recall of a visual image in the Carmichael et al. (1932) experiment. The same drawing was recalled in a different way, depending on whether it had been conceptualized as, for example, a dumbbell or eyeglasses. Conscious recollection is a re-creation of an interpreted past. Unless it is conceptualized, an event cannot be stored in long-term memory in such a way as to make it retrievable at a later time.

That recall requires the declarative knowledge system is not particularly controversial when considering verbally expressed memories. When people describe a past event, the verbalization itself makes it clear that the knowledge is explicit. How then are we to determine whether infants can recall the past when they have no language to express what they have experienced? Following observations of Piaget (1951), Andy Meltzoff, Cecilia Shore, Patricia Bauer, and I all began about the same time to use deferred imitation as a measure of nonverbal recall (Bauer & Mandler, 1989; Bauer & Shore, 1987; Mandler, 1986; Meltzoff, 1988a). The rationale behind this research is that to *reenact* an event after it has happened requires the same type of conceptualization and retrieval as to *retell* what happened. Of course, neither kind of reproduction of the past is complete. Enactment will not produce exactly the same information as verbalization, because it will show what happened rather than describe it, and verbal descriptions leave out many details of the activities being enacted.

Piaget used deferred imitation as a measure of nonverbal recall, on the grounds that if children can reenact something they have seen after a delay, they must be able to evoke absent realities. Indeed, he considered deferred imitation to be one of the main pieces of evidence that a (conceptual) representational capacity had evolved. When children reproduce a novel event that is no longer perceptually present, they must be able to re-present it to themselves. In a famous example, he described how his 16-month-old daughter Jacqueline watched with fascination a visiting child throw a temper tantrum when he could not get out of his playpen, an event that was new and interesting to her. The next day, when she was put in her own playpen, she was apparently reminded of the event because she proceeded to reenact the sequence of behaviors the boy had carried out. Like him, she stamped on the floor of the playpen (but lightly) and tried to move it as he had done. She also repeated some of these gestures when she saw him again 2 weeks later, laughing as she did so. These were some of the observations that Piaget used as evidence that the transition from the sensorimotor stage to a conceptual stage had begun.

Recall of Absent Objects

Another task that Piaget (1954) used to assess the achievement of conceptual representation was search for hidden objects. His rationale was that to search for an object that cannot be seen implies that the object is being represented in its absence. I discussed this aspect of Piaget's theory in chapter 2 in the section on confusing motor incompetence with conceptual incompetence. The two most famous of these tasks were, first, covering an object in full view of infants and seeing if they would search for it and, second, the A-not-B test. In this task an object is repeatedly hidden at location A and then, again in full view of the infants, moved to location B; where they look for it is measured. After hundreds of studies, we have come to realize that these hiding and finding tests (especially the A-not-B task) are complex and depend on several different processes (e.g., Baillargeon, 1993; Diamond, 1985, 1990). However, the simple covering task, as long as reaching requirements and the difficulties they entail are minimized, is potentially able to tell us something about how long infants can remember where an object has been hidden.

In most of Baillargeon's studies on violations of expectations that require the infant to remember an object behind a screen, the time frames over which infants must remember what is hidden are quite short (typically 8 to 10 seconds). However, the technique is appropriate for studying recall beyond the confines of working memory. Baillargeon and Graber (1988) extended the time frame for which 8-month-olds had to remember a hidden object to 70 seconds. They showed an object on a stage and then hid it behind one of a pair of screens. After a 70-second delay, a hand removed the object from behind either the correct screen or the incorrect screen. The infants tended to look longer when the object was retrieved from behind the incorrect screen.

Although the age at which memory for object location is demonstrated tends to be earlier when reaching is not required, it is nevertheless possible to show recall of an object's location even with a reaching paradigm and fairly substantial delays. McDonough (1999) showed that 7½-month-old infants could recall the location of a hidden object after a 90-second delay, when recall was measured by reaching toward the location where the object was hidden. Infants' attention was diverted from the hiding place during the delay. Still, recall was hampered when infants were taken out of the room for the delay or when they were engaged in interesting activities in another part of the room during the interim. Interestingly, the participants in these experiments were all in the age range of 7 to 8 months, but of these the younger were significantly less likely to succeed than the older ones. It may be that if given only a brief presentation, 7 months is about the lower limit of the ability to recall where an object has been hidden.

The other major strand of work on finding hidden objects has involved the A-not-B error. By 8 to 9 months, infants have no problems in finding a hidden object. Piaget believed this is only the activation of familiar action patterns and not knowledge that the hidden object is still there. He thought this, in the face of counterevidence such as successful search, because of the A-not-B error. After retrieving a toy at A several times and then watching it be hidden at B, infants often reach for the toy at A instead of at B. Piaget explained this phenomenon by saying that infants of this age think that objects are partly the results of their own actions on them, and in that sense objects do not have an independent existence. If the infant reached for and found the object at A, then that would happen again.

Although recall failure was considered as a possible explanation for the errors on this test (e.g., Harris, 1986), a number of other explanations have been proposed, such as the difficulty being due to conflicting search strategies (Wellman, Cross, & Bartsch, 1986). In any case, it gradually became obvious that the test is not a good method of studying recall. For one thing, even 10- to 11-month-olds often fail it, in spite of the fact that the object is out of view for only a few seconds. This simply does not dovetail with the ability to find a single hidden object after 1½ minutes as just described and even less with evidence of truly long-term recall of events by these ages, discussed in the next section. Furthermore, the error occurs even when transparent covers are used, so the baby sees the object at B. Even when covered, babies will sometimes reach to A while staring intently at B, or uncover A but not even bother to look there while going toward B (Diamond, 1985). Because of such behaviors, Diamond suggested the error occurs because of a failure to resist the habit of repeating the just previous successful response, that is, because of response perseveration. Still another possibility is the failure to inhibit an already planned reaching response.

We see such discrepancies between what the conscious mind knows and the body wants to do even in adults when an expectation has been set up. A nice demonstration of this is an experiment redoing one of Bower's experiments on infant tracking, using adults as subjects. Bower, Broughton, and Moore (1971) reported that infants who watch a train run along a track, go behind a screen, and then reappear at the other end after a period of trials learn to anticipate where the train will emerge from behind the screen and move their eyes to the spot. Then, if the train is stopped in plain view before going behind the screen, the babies still move their eyes to the other end of the screen where the object had previously emerged. Does this mean the babies thought the train could be in two places at once or that a moving object is a different object when it becomes stationary? Bower (1981) thought so, but that is not a necessary explanation. When the same experiment was carried out with adults, they did the same thing (Chromiak & Weisberg, 1981). Once the conditioned expectation was set up, their eyes also moved to the end of the track when the train stopped in full view. One almost wants to say that the *adults* didn't do the same thing, but their *eyes* did. Motor routines have a life of their own.

In addition to the problem that repeated A trials create in most of the object-hiding experiments, there may also be a problem in updating memory when infants are required to remember the *last* place where something was hidden (or the last action when lots of different actions have been performed on the same object). In Diamond's version of the A-not-B task, the object was hidden over and over again in the same two places. This is the kind of situation that causes proactive inhibition (e.g., Slamecka, 1961). For example, if you ask people to learn paired associates repeatedly, they gradually begin to have trouble remembering them, and this increases over trials. If you change the stimuli to another type, you get release from proactive inhibition. Proactive inhibition is also likely at work in other kinds of hiding tasks that have been used with infants. For example, in the Munakata et al. (1997) experiment mentioned in chapter 2, 7-month-olds were trained how to retrieve an object placed on the end of a cloth by pulling the cloth to them. The experimenters did this to eliminate inadequate motor skills as a component of the test. Then they tested infants on four kinds of trials: an object present or absent on the cloth and a screen in front of it that was either opaque or transparent. Because each infant received a very large number of trials (7 of each type, for 28 in all— a huge number of trials for this age), it seems likely that massive proactive inhibition would set in. Not surprisingly, if you can't remember what kind of trial the current one is, you will do worst on trials with opaque barriers, because you can't actually see if an object is there or not.

Baillargeon (1993) suggested a different form of perseverative response from a motor one; once a solution has been computed to a problem, people of all ages tend to continue to use it whenever possible, thus leading to capture errors (Reason, 1979). Erickson and Mattson (1981) asked college students, "How many animals of each kind did Moses take on the ark?" Most students answer, "Two," without realizing the question asked about Moses, rather than Noah. Baillargeon did a similar task with her 2-year-old son. She asked him a list of questions, such as "What is an animal with a hump?" "A camel," he said. "What is something warm you wear on your feet during winter?" "Boots," he said. Later she asked him, "What is an animal with a hump?" "A camel," he said. "What is something warm you wear on your head during winter?" "Boots," he answered. It may be that motor perseveration is less important in these reaching studies than the bringing forth of a previously computed solution.

All of these difficulties make it clear that the A–not–B task is not as valuable for studying the development of recall of location as the simpler object-hiding tasks, in which a single object is hidden. As long as Diamond's (1990) strictures about motor problems in grasping are kept in mind, it is potentially an informative technique. Unfortunately, there has not been nearly as much recall data collected on this simpler task as on the A–not–B task. Overall, there are a great deal more data on recall of events than recall of location.

Recall Versus Recognition of Events

When we began our research on deferred imitation of events, we had never heard any objections to it as a form of recall. Nevertheless, when our data showed that infants under a year could reenact events they had seen in the past, the method began to be called into question. The problem seems to have been that Piaget did not report deferred imitation in his children until about 16 months, and that was about the same time that he documented verbal recall as well. So his claim that deferred imitation is a measure of early conceptual memory didn't arouse controversy, but ours—studying the same phenomenon in younger babies—did. We ran into two objections (actually two variants of a single argument): One was that our infants were too young to recall and that our research was another example of the precocious infant syndrome (claiming too much for babies; see chapter 3). The other was that if babies could do it, then deferred imitation couldn't be a measure of recall after all. Perhaps the ability to enact an event seen in the past does not require the same kind of higher cognitive functions as verbal recall. Perhaps enactment could be done in some automatic way without bringing the absent information to awareness. When I presented some of our data at a conference in the late 1980s, one of the participants commented that without verbal evidence, unless we could show that amnesic adults could not do deferred imitation, we could not begin to contemplate calling it recall (see discussion section of Mandler, 1990).

The requirement that recall be verbal is clearly too restrictive, even for adults. Although most recall studies in the laboratory have asked for verbal recall, in everyday life much if not most of our recall is not verbalized, and at least for some of us it seems to involve more imaginal thought than language. But what should we use in the place of verbal report when we study babies? How can we be sure that we are studying recall and not some simpler kind of retention? The colleague's remark suggests that deferred imitation might be carried out by activating a previously learned sensorimotor procedure or perhaps by a form of repetition priming of the kind that remains intact in amnesia.

I address this concern in the following section, but first I need to digress a bit to the related issue of recognition. One of the pitfalls we must avoid in infancy research is to confuse recall with recognition. The problem is compounded because there is more than one type of recognition. As discussed in chapter 3, it is possible to recognize something by pattern matching in the procedural sense without being aware that one has seen it before. Indeed, much of our perceptual life never reaches awareness, even though its effects can be seen in our behavior.

In adult research, the term *recognition*, unless otherwise modified, implies consciousness or awareness of prior occurrence. It is assumed that adults are aware that the item in question has been experienced in the past. Adult recognition is studied by asking for a yes–no or old–new judgment as to whether the item has been experienced before. The ability to make an old–new judgment requires *awareness* of prior occurrence or pastness; its loss is one of the hallmarks of amnesia. Amnesics retain the ability to be influenced by past experience and to learn at least certain kinds of new skills, but they have lost the awareness that these experiences are familiar to them (Cohen & Squire, 1980; Graf, Squire, & Mandler, 1984; Warrington & Weiskrantz, 1982).

In contrast, the literature on infant recognition has, unsurprisingly, not even raised the issue of conscious awareness of prior occurrence. Instead, it has been solely concerned with whether infants are "familiar" with a stimulus in the sense that they behave differently to it than to a stimulus they have not seen before. Familiarity with a stimulus is typically measured by habituation, and lack of familiarity by dishabituation. These measures do not tap the same process that is required in a yes–no recognition task in which people are asked specifically about awareness of the past. Habituation to a stimulus indicates what Jacoby (1983) called perceptual fluency or perceptual identification, and it carries no implication of conscious awareness of the past.

Adult recognition experiments, in which participants are asked to make a conscious judgment as to whether they have seen a given item before, require more than familiarity as measured by habituation or shorter looking times. Adults not only can say they have experienced something before but also can often recall the context in which it was experienced, which in turn affects their recognition judgments. Awareness of the past is taken to be a different state from priming by previously presented items, which can occur in the absence of conscious awareness of their having been seen. Thus, amnesics show normal priming, even though they are not aware they have seen the material before (Warrington & Weiskrantz, 1974). Obviously, babies cannot be asked questions, so a habituation–dishabituation method is used instead. However, this technique is the infant equivalent of an adult priming study, not an adult recognition memory study. The fact that babies respond differently to previously presented material than to new material shows that information has been stored but does not provide evidence for awareness of the past experiences. For this reason, I suggested calling infant recognition memory *primitive recognition* to avoid any implications of conscious, declarative memory that the item has been experienced before (Mandler, 1984). (Today, I would call this phenomenon *implicit recognition*, rather than primitive.) Babies *may* be consciously aware that they have seen something before or that it looks familiar (indeed, after the first few months, this seems likely to happen at least some of the time), but because explicit remembering is not required to account for dishabituation, we should not assume that they are aware of what they have seen.

We must be cautious about interpreting the experiments on infant recognition, such as those on face recognition (e.g., Cohen & Strauss, 1979; Fagan, 1970) or those on the control of conditioned responses by familiar stimuli (e.g., Rovee-Collier, 1989), as demonstrating the same processes uncovered in explicit recognition experiments in adults. Adults are required to say yes or no when asked if they have seen an item before, but infants are required only to habituate (or produce a habitual response). Infants *may* recognize things in the adult sense, rather than in the implicit sense of priming, but at present we have no positive evidence that they do. Therefore, it is problematic to use infant habituation and dishabituation or conditioning data to affirm the continuity of recognition memory from infancy to later ages.

This difficulty in testing infant recognition can be put another way. In the case of recall, we can assess whether infants are able to reenact an event sequence that we know adults cannot do without the ability to consciously recall the past (McDonough et al., 1995). If infants can do so, we are reasonably safe in ascribing recall to them even in the absence of verbal evidence. In the case of recognition, however, at present we do not have *any* measures in infant research that distinguish conscious recognition from unconscious priming. Habituation and dishabituation techniques can show only that a stimulus has been primed, not that it has been consciously recognized. Operant conditioning techniques can show an increase in reinforced responding as a function of experience (and a concomitant decrease with lack of exposure to the stimulus over time), but again such data cannot provide evidence for conscious memory of the conditioning sessions that built up the responses in the first place.

At one time it was thought that smiling might be used to indicate awareness of familiarity, but unfortunately there are other equally plausible causes for smiling. Piaget suggested that mastery produces satisfaction and therefore smiling. There is also the comfort that comes from familiarity (perhaps especially for young organisms continually faced with unfamiliar sights), whether or not they are aware that the persons or objects are familiar. In sum, recall is a more straightforward measure than "recognition" to document the development of explicit memory. Studies of implicit recognition are important and interesting, but they are at present impossible to compare with studies of explicit recognition in adults. So I return to the topic of recall, first discussing some of the data produced by the technique of deferred imitation and then returning to the issue of what the technique measures.

Deferred Imitation of Events

In the experimental version of deferred imitation that we have used, we model an event sequence for infants, typically using two or three objects as props. After a delay of a few minutes, a day, week, or even a year, we bring the infants back into the situation, show them the props that were used, and see whether they spontaneously reproduce what they had previously observed. As in the studies of inductive generalization described in chapter 8, before modeling we give the objects to the infants to see what they do with them spontaneously, providing a baseline against which to assess performance after a delay. If after a delay they reproduce more of the events than they do at baseline, this is prima facie evidence for recall of what was modeled. Just as for the generalized imitation and categorization experiments, the technique is instructionless. As a result, however, it may somewhat underestimate memory. As we saw in chapter 8, infants take imitation seriously in the sense that they try hard to reproduce what they have seen modeled. But after a long delay, they may think of other things to do with the objects than reproduce what was modeled earlier, even if they remember it.

Many different kinds of events have been studied with this technique. For example, in one of our early studies we used three kinds of event sequences, each three actions in length (Bauer & Mandler, 1989). There were novel causal sequences that the children would not have seen before, such as making a frog jump. We put a small board on a wedge to make a teeter-totter, put a toy frog on one end of the board, and hit the other end to make the frog sail through the air. If this result is to occur, of course, the sequence must be performed in the modeled order. We also used novel sequences that could be done in any order, such as making a picture by putting a sticker on a chalkboard, leaning the board against an easel, and scribbling on the board. In addition, we used familiar sequences representing common home routines that are mixtures of causally and conventionally connected actions, such as cleaning a table by spraying it with a spray bottle, wiping it with a paper towel, and throwing the towel away into a basket.

In this study we worked with 16- to 20-month-olds, some of whom were able to reproduce both the causal and familiar sequences after delays of 2 weeks. Others reproduced one or two parts, and of course some children did nothing. The arbitrary sequences were more poorly recalled, as is typically the case for both infants and adults. Previously, Bauer and Shore (1987) found that children this age could reproduce similar sequences after delays of 6 weeks. At about the same time, Meltzoff was studying infants' ability to imitate a single action. He found that at 14 months they could imitate a novel action, such as lighting a panel on a box by touching it with the forehead, after a delay of a week (Meltzoff, 1988b). He also showed that 9-month-olds could imitate single actions, such as depressing a recessed button on a box, after a delay of 24 hours (Meltzoff, 1988a). The infants were not allowed to perform the actions themselves and only observed the experimenter carry them out.

As mentioned earlier, these results surprised some people, because according to Piagetian theory, infants this young should not have a conceptual system sufficiently developed to enable them to recall events. Even more startling to some, perhaps, are more recent data showing that even 6-month-olds can imitate a single action after a 24-hour delay (Barr, Dowden, & Hayne, 1996; Collie & Hayne, 1999). This is a difficult task for such young infants and requires more repetition of the modeling than is necessary for older infants. Nevertheless, the newer data suggest that at least minimal recall is possible by 6 months of age. This may be the lower boundary on retrieving information from declarative memory, as suggested by the difficulty that even 7-month-olds have with finding hidden objects (e.g., McDonough, 1999). It is possible that imitating an action on a prop (such as pulling off a large and prominent mitten from a toy bear's paw, as in Barr et al., 1996) may be supported by recognition memory in a way that finding a hidden object is not, which might account for its appearance a month earlier than found for the object-finding task. That is, infants may not need to recall the action if they recognize the mitten from the previous session and reach for it.[2] I believe there are as yet no data on delays longer than 24 hours with infants this young, but by 11 months, single actions can be reproduced a year later (McDonough & Mandler, 1994; see also Klein & Meltzoff, 1999, for confirmation of long-term recall of single actions by 12-month-olds).

Beginning around 9 months, infants begin to be able to reproduce event *sequences* after a delay (Carver & Bauer, 1999). Deferred imitation of a series of events is important not only because event sequences seem more comparable to the kinds of recall of the past that adults engage in than does the memory for a single action but also because the ability to reproduce an ordered string of actions from a single observation is particularly convincing evidence that recall, as opposed to implicit processing, is taking place. To my knowledge, no one has succeeded in demonstrating deferred imitation of a multistep sequence before 9 months of age. It is uncertain whether 9 months represents a lower limit on the ability to engage in ordered recall, or whether it is the difficulty of the imitation procedure that accounts for it. Both limitations may be operative. Indeed, one of the reasons imitating ordered sequences is difficult, regardless of delay, is because of the need to keep in mind a series of actions; the difficulty in imitation itself may be due to difficulty in recall rather than some other kind of limitation. However, by the time they are 11 months old, infants can encode and recall two-step sequences 3 months later (Mandler & McDonough, 1995), and at 13 months they can maintain recall of two-step sequences for another 8 months (Bauer, Hertzgaard, & Dow, 1994). Such data indicate that before the end of the first year the recall capacity is robust and produces long-lasting memories that are sufficiently detailed to enable reproduction of event sequences the infant has observed.

What Deferred Imitation Measures

As the results of some of our early experiments began to accumulate in the late 1980s, we did not at first consider the conclusion they invited—that infants can engage in long-term recall—to be controversial. As mentioned earlier, Piaget's use of deferred imitation as a measure of recall was well known, and in addition there was already one piece of evidence for *verbal* long-term recall from the same age period. Myers, Clifton, and Clarkson (1987) brought back to their lab five 33-month-olds who had taken part in an extensive experiment between the ages of 6 weeks and 9½ months. One of these children was able to recall verbally a picture of a whale used in the experimental procedure that he had last experienced at 9½ months, in spite of the fact that he did not know the word *whale* at that young age (first producing the word 6 months later). If long-term verbal recall is shown for experiences occurring at around 9 months, then we should not be unduly surprised by demonstrations of long-term *nonverbal* recall at the same age. Nevertheless, verbal recall for events in infancy is rare, so mostly we have to rely on nonverbal measures. Deferred imitation fits a set of criteria that we derived in part from the conditions of adult verbal recall experiments (Mandler, 1990). In each case the criteria are meant to differentiate a nonverbal reenactment task from other memory tasks that might be carried out on an implicit basis.

The first criterion is to eliminate an explanation of successful performance in terms of a conditioned response or a learned stimulus-response association. Operant conditioning is one of the simplest kinds of learning, found even in planaria and other invertebrates (Fantino & Logan, 1979), and so it cannot require declarative, explicit memory; it is not one of the higher cognitive functions. So how are we to interpret data on operant conditioning from human infants? They are obviously vastly more complex organisms than planaria, but still that does not entail that in their case conditioning involves declarative memory. Two-month-olds can learn a foot-kicking response and retain it over a period of weeks (e.g., Rovee-Collier, 1989). Nevertheless, when kicking occurs to the trained stimulus after a delay, that does not provide evidence that the infant has *recalled* the earlier kicking episodes, because conditioned responding can occur in the absence of explicit memory. Rovee-Collier described these data as showing "cued recall" (discussion section of Mandler, 1990, p. 514), but this is an unusual (and unusually generous) usage of the term *recall*. The kicking response shows the patterns of generalization, extinction, forgetting, and reinstatement that are typically found in operant conditioning in rats (e.g., Campbell, 1984). This does not rule out the possibility that infants might recall the earlier kicking episodes, but it is not necessary for them to do so for the conditioned response to generalize, extinguish, or be reinstated. Furthermore, these responses are quite context-bound, being disrupted by even minor changes in the surroundings (Butler & Rovee-Collier, 1989; Hartshorn & Rovee-Collier, 1997), whereas recall as measured by deferred imitation is barely affected by changes in the surrounding context (Klein & Meltzoff, 1999).[3]

Similar problems can arise in the interpretation of conditioned expectations about the sequence in which events occur. In a sophisticated set of experiments, Smith (1984) showed that 3- to 5-month-olds learn to anticipate the next event in a series of events in a very few trials, especially if the sequences form well-structured patterns. She presented a picture in one of four locations (A, B, C, or D) in front of the infant. The picture was moved from location to location eight times. For example, the infant might see the sequence ABBACDDC. Various kinds of sequences having different structure as well as random series were presented. She tested learning by stopping a sequence at various points and observing whether infants' eyes went to the next location that would be expected in that sequence. Infants learned the various structured sequences in as few as six trials. Unfortunately, she chose to call this ability "recall of temporal order." Her data are impressive in terms of the speed with which very young infants learn elaborate patterns of ordered events, but, like the ability to categorize pictures of dogs and cats in a few trials or to learn abstract patterns of ordered sequences of phonemes (discussed in the next chapter), this is an example of procedural memory and provides no evidence of conscious recall of the learning episodes or even of the learned pattern itself. Once again, what our eyes do does not necessarily speak to what we consciously know.

Conditioned expectations of event sequences occur in many organisms and early in life in the human (e.g., Haith, Wentworth, & Canfield, 1993). Like conditioned foot kicking, such expectations do not constitute recall, and we need to be sure that when infants reproduce a behavior they have observed that it is not done on the basis of conditioning. One way to avoid this difficulty is to use novel events that the infants have not seen before and also to use actions that they have only observed but not carried out themselves. Conditioned foot kicking and other conditioned motor responding require multiple trials to be built up, as does conditioned expectancy learning. It may be fairly rapid, as in the Smith experiment just described, but to my knowledge multistep sequences always require practice to become automatized. This is another reason why imitation of novel event *sequences*, as opposed to single actions, is important in arguing that deferred imitation is a measure of recall.

Another criterion required to say that recall has occurred is to eliminate recognition as the basis of successful performance. Both finding a hidden object and reproducing an event by deferred imitation fit this criterion, because in neither case is the relevant information there to be recognized. There are cues in both cases (the occluder in object hiding and the props used to enact the events in imitation), but the issue is not cued recall versus noncued recall. All recall is cued by something; one is either reminded by something or specifically asked to recall, in which case one is given relevant contextual information about the target ("Where were you on the night the crime took place?"). The crucial aspect that distinguishes recall from recognition is that the to-be-recalled information is not perceptually present. Again, when an event sequence is reproduced, neither the actions nor the sequence in which they are carried out is perceptually present.

Finally, of course, there must be a delay between the event and its reproduction that exceeds the perceptual span, so that one cannot read off the information from primary memory. I include this fairly obvious criterion because sometimes rather remarkable powers have been ascribed to the perceptual span. For instance, Marshall Haith (1998) suggested that infants in some of Baillargeon's experiments in which a hidden object moves behind a screen for 8 to 10 seconds could maintain a perceptual representation of the trajectory. I assume he had in mind something like our ability to track a moving object that momentarily is hidden from view. However, sensorimotor tracking of an object behind barriers requires a fairly rapid trajectory and is disrupted in infants if the object is hidden for as little as 2 seconds (Mullen & Aslin, 1978). Obviously, finding a hidden object after 90 seconds or deferred imitation after a day cannot be subject to this kind of perceptual interpretation.

These three criteria were designed to eliminate a sensorimotor (procedural) account of deferred imitation, because as Piaget asserted, a sensorimotor system is unable to represent objects or events when they are no longer present. A sensorimotor or other procedural system can enable implicit (primitive) recognition of objects or events, gradual learning of actions on objects and sequences of such actions, and anticipatory expectations about the sequence in which already learned events take place. In contrast to deferred imitation, none of these activities requires conscious recall of the past.

When I presented our data on deferred imitation and gave this analysis of the declarative basis of deferred imitation at the conference mentioned earlier, it was questioned by Janet Werker (see discussion section of Mandler, 1990). She said that the very essence of sensorimotor learning is that an object or an event is understood in terms of the possible actions that can be performed on it, and so recall may not be required. Piaget (1951) made a similar point when he said that young infants, having already developed a schema of clapping hands, can assimilate the sight of another person clapping hands and so reproduce the gesture on the spot merely by assimilating the movement to a familiar schema. However, Piaget was referring to immediate imitation of a familiar action in the presence of a model demonstrating it, not to delayed imitation of novel actions. Werker's point, as I understand it, is more radical. She suggested that reproducing an event can be directly triggered by an object, rather than requiring mental representation of what is to be done. The suggestion is that a perceived object automatically elicits the action to be performed on it, even if it is an action the infant has not done before. This argument implies that observational learning of a series of actions is a kind of procedural learning that can take place in a single trial and does not require bringing absent information to mind. It requires only repetition of the context in which the observational learning took place, and the actions will automatically be forthcoming.

I wish that observational learning were so easy! If it were, I could learn much more than I do from watching a chef cooking on television or the technician installing my computer. With the possible exception of automatically elicited imitative behavior in early infancy (Meltzoff & Moore, 1983; Piaget, 1951), observational learning requires attentive, conscious analysis of what one is trying to learn, and it requires recall if one tries to reproduce it at a later date. Even with intact recall processes, a single presentation is usually insufficient to enable accurate reproduction of a novel event sequence. Werker's comments seem more appropriate to the kind of mutual imitation that parents engage in when they play repetitive imitative games with their children, such as peekaboo, or the sort of situation (clapping hands) Piaget was talking about. Even these typically involve repetitive practice, but in any case the model's and the child's actions are being carried out virtually simultaneously. Recall hardly seems necessary in this situation, in which the behavior is being elicited by the parent on the spot—the behavior is present, not absent. Again, this kind of situation is quite different from imitation after even a short delay, let alone 24 hours or several weeks.

The many instances of generalized imitation described in chapter 8 testify to the conceptual construals infants use to imitate events. However, even if one grants the conceptual nature of imitation, one still might think it possible to reproduce events at a later time without calling upon recall processes. That is, there are two parts to deferred imitation: how the information is conceptualized in the first place and then the process of retrieving it. The definitive test for the latter may be the one called for at the same conference: to ascertain whether amnesics can or cannot do deferred imitation of sequences like those we have used with infants. The rationale for this test is the following: The claim is that recall is a necessary condition to reproduce a novel event sequence after a delay. Amnesics cannot recall. Therefore, they should not be able to do deferred imitation. On the other hand, if event sequences can be learned through observation and activated by means of an automatic process such as priming, then amnesics might be successful. It is just possible that imitating a simple event sequence is similar to a stem-completion task in which adults study a list of words and then are asked to complete three-letter word stems with words from the list. Amnesics cannot do this task because they cannot recall the words (Graf et al., 1984). However, when no explicit instructions are given to use the words on the studied list, and participants are simply asked to report the first words that come to mind, amnesics tend to use the studied words for their stem completions to the same degree as do normal adults (Warrington & Weiskrantz, 1974). The words on the list have been activated (primed) sufficiently for the patients to produce them over the various other possibilities. If amnesic patients could imitate events in the same way, the argument that deferred imitation requires recall would be considerably weakened.

We carried out such a test (McDonough et al., 1995). We devised eight three-action event sequences, some causally structured and some arbitrary in sequence, that mimicked our baby tests but were appropriate for adults. For example, in one sequence the Bernoulli effect (in which an object is captured by a stream of air) was demonstrated by turning on a hair dryer, placing an inflated balloon in the airstream, and rotating the dryer to the side until the balloon, hovering to the side, finally fell. In another sequence we folded a piece of paper in half, cut off its corners, and drew a star on it. We followed as closely as possible the procedure we used with infants. The main difference was the use of verbal instructions. However, to make the imitation tasks as similar as possible to the uninstructed conditions of infant research, we presented the imitation tasks to the adults in the guise of distractor tasks presented in the context of verbal recall tasks. Amnesic patients and control subjects were given a list of words to remember, followed by the props for each event. They were told that this was a distractor task and that they could do whatever they liked with them (thus providing a baseline performance measure for the event sequences). Then they were asked to recall the words. Next they were told they would be asked to recall the words later, and we modeled the sequences for them, explaining that this was another distractor task. They were then asked to recall the words again. Following recall, we read the list once more, explaining that they would be asked to recall the words the following day. On the next day, after a recall test for the words, the participants were again handed the props to do with what they wished, again under the guise of its being a distractor task. This condition served as an instructionless event recall condition such as we used with infants. It could be considered a priming task similar to those that have been found effective with amnesic patients. Immediately afterward, we explicitly asked the participants to reproduce the event sequences we had shown them the day before. This was an instructed event recall condition.

If amnesic patients can carry out deferred imitation solely by priming, they should be successful in the instructionless condition but fail in the deliberate recall situation. On the other hand, if priming is insufficient to mediate deferred imitation, they should do equally poorly in both instructed and instructionless conditions compared with control subjects, indicating that recall is required. The results did not support a priming explanation. The amnesic patients could not produce the action sequences in either the instructed or uninstructed control conditions, whereas the control subjects were good at both. It seems clear that deferred imitation cannot be carried out by repetition priming but indeed does require the ability to recall.

The Nature of Preverbal Recall and Infantile Amnesia

The various experiments described in this chapter make clear that beginning most likely around 6 months of age preverbal infants can recall events they have observed. None of the experimental data, however, provides any evidence for spatiotemporal dating of these memories. Indeed, it seems somewhat unlikely that when an observed event comes to mind at a later time the infant is also aware of when or where it happened. Spatiotemporal dating is not required for recall; many adult recall memories do not include this kind of information (especially when they are from the distant past), and we must work out their time and place by various reconstructive processes. By age 2, verbal recall protocols suggest some awareness of when and where events being recalled took place (e.g., Nelson & Ross, 1980), but this issue has not been systematically studied, so there is little precise information available. For example, we do not know when spatiotemporal dating begins to happen or whether all recallable events include the spatiotemporal context but the context is merely forgotten more rapidly in infancy. We also do not know whether these early recall memories are autobiographical. When infants return to the laboratory and spontaneously reproduce an event they observed there the day or month before, they may or may not remember "I did that!" or "I saw you do that." It may be only that the event itself comes to mind, not the personal connection, the "impression of I-ness" (Claparède, 1951). If so, the information is still explicit but not autobiographical, a distinction captured in Tulving's (1985) distinction between autonoetic and noetic remembering. Unfortunately, I haven't a clue how to test this in pre-verbal infants.

A lack of spatiotemporal dating could partially account for the phe-nomenon of infantile amnesia, in which we can no longer remember events that happened in the preverbal period. Some early memories may actually survive, but without being dated or given a context, they are unapt to be produced by a request for one's earliest memories.[4] Never-theless, even though some such memories apparently survive, the pre-ponderance of evidence is that they are relatively rare. The classic expla-nation has been that infants are unable to lay down declarative memories in the first place, but as we have seen, this is not true at least from 6 months onward. Not only are declarative memories laid down from an early age but also they can be retained throughout the entire period that later becomes inaccessible (Bauer & Wewerka, 1995; Fivush & Ham-mond, 1990). Another common explanation for infantile amnesia (and one that does seem to be at least partially responsible) is that it is not an encoding or storage failure but a retrieval failure. As we become more and more verbally dependent over the years, it becomes more difficult to find the correct retrieval route to nonverbal memories (Nelson, 1978).

The many data about infant conceptualizations described in this book suggest still a third factor, related to the mismatch of nonverbal en-coding and attempts at verbal retrieval. Some infantile amnesia may be due to the overgenerality of the concepts infants use to encode the events of their lives. The lack of specificity of the conceptualizations formed at the time of encoding must make for serious retrieval problems at a later date. Imagine if you conceptualized an event of petting a dog in the supermarket only as touching an animal in an indoor place. Even if some perceptual information survives, retrieval should be difficult. Insofar as you encoded the dog as an animal, not as a dog, and the market only as a building, these encodings would not necessarily make contact with the rich network of knowledge about dogs and markets you would later use when engaging in retrieval.[5] The earlier the experience, the more general its conceptualization is apt to be, and therefore the more difficult the retrieval process should be as well. Furthermore, if the delay interval stretches well beyond infancy, there is a greater likelihood of a mismatch between the encoding conceptualizations and current ones. Along with greater dependency on verbal retrieval, this mismatch might account for young children's still being able to remember events they experienced in infancy that they can no longer retrieve as adults.

In addition, Nelson (1994) and Nelson and Fivush (2000) proposed that autobiographical memory, in the sense of memory for specific episodes that is maintained over long periods of time, is related to the experience of talking to other people about them. Parents take the disjointed productions of young children recalling the past and shape them into narratives. Children gradually learn this art, and sharing their narrative memories with others consolidates them (as presumably does retelling them to oneself). These authors suggested it may be this kind of reinstatement that builds the personal life history we call autobiographical memory. Before this kind of verbal interchange between parents and children begins, there are apt to be relatively few of the reinstatements that increase the likelihood of long-term recall.

We have seen in this chapter ample evidence for recall of the past in the first year of life. As I have suggested throughout, we do not know exactly when this ability begins to emerge, although current data suggest around 6 months of age. Given the evidence for a conceptual system developing at least by this age, such a result should not be surprising. The lower limit on the ability to recall should be as much conceptually related as age related. In the view presented in this book, a conceptual system is a declarative system and its hallmark is access to consciousness. Therefore, it is possible we will find that, to the extent they have established a conceptual store, even younger infants can consciously recall the past. At the same time, as Nelson and Fivush (2000) suggested, sustained autobiographical memory may be dependent on language and the storytelling it allows. Language also aids in conceptual differentiation, which should not only help make recall more detailed but also, as discussed in the next chapter, play a role in bringing the global concepts of the preverbal infant into closer conformity with the community they share.

I I

Language Acquisition

. . . in which the focus shifts from continuity in development to a major source of change, namely language. First, I discuss how global concepts of objects become refined as words for them are learned. Then I return to the relational concepts discussed in chapters 4 and 5 in the context of image-schemas. Most of the chapter is devoted to relational concepts of containment and support, including data relating preverbal and verbal understanding of space. Relational concepts are of particular interest because, in contrast to object nouns, relational words vary greatly from language to language and show the greatest potential for language to influence the growing conceptual system. This topic leads to a brief discussion of the meanings created by image-schemas that provide an entree into learning syntactical forms.

. . . the innateness of language does not relieve one of the obligation of having to learn it. . . . (Gleitman and Gleitman, 1997)

Object Concepts and Words

The most crucial aspect of the relation between preverbal concepts and words is that language is mapped onto concepts and not onto perception or sensorimotor schemas. This is particularly obvious in the case of relational terms, as I discuss in the next section, because relations are not directly given in perceptual displays and so it is clearer that they must be contributed by the mind. In contrast, I used to assume that learning names for objects might be possible on the basis of associative learning without having to call on the meaning of the objects in question. The assumption was that it is relatively easy to learn names for things because one can point to them, and so there is the opportunity for ostensive learning of a kind that does not exist for relations. One can point to a dog but can't point unambiguously to containment and can't point at all to the past. For nouns, the story goes, all one needs is something like Markman's (1991) whole object assumption, and the child should be in business. The parent points to a dog and says, "Dog"; the child learns the word *dog*. I have gradually come to understand that this enticingly simple procedure is insufficient.[1]

In such an account, a word is mapped onto an object with a particular perceptual appearance, but that is only half the story, no matter what the word refers to. Words do double duty, having both sense and reference (Frege, 1952). Unfortunately, it is not uncommon to equate words with concepts on the basis of reference alone, which can give a misleading picture of the newly verbal child's conceptual and semantic systems. When a child calls a dog "dog," we cannot assume that the sense (meaning) of the word matches an adult's. To be sure, the word refers to a specific object that may agree with the adult referent. But it is mapped onto a conceptual meaning, and so even for learning nouns, perception accompanied by ostension is not enough. The perception is interpreted, and it is the interpreted meaning that supports semantic learning as much as, if not more so than, the perceptual appearance of the object being named. As we have seen in the case of dog, for instance, the first meaning for the child is more like land animal than like dog, and so the child's understanding and use of the word *dog* differ from that of an adult speaker. The gulf between the precision of adult language and the globality of many preverbal concepts suggests that there will be a good many mismatches—in particular, overextension of word meanings.

Overextension of early nouns is a common occurrence. Children go through a period in the second year when many of their first-learned words are given too broad a meaning. Eve Clark (2001) estimated that up to 40% of the first 100 words are overextended, even if only for a short time. Some of this overextension appears to be the result of having to make do with a limited vocabulary when trying to communicate with others, and some of it appears to be due to making comments on the relationship of one thing to another, including categorical membership (Rescorla, 1980). However, at least some of it seems to be due to an uncertain assignment of the extension of the word. That is, when a young child uses the word *dog* to label a cow, it may be due to a lack of clarity as to what the difference is between them. As discussed in chapter 6, such lack of clarity does not have to do with perceptual confusion: An 18-month-old can easily categorize dogs as perceptually different from cows. But we call Chihuahuas and Saint Bernards by the same name, so the fact of differing appearance is not sufficient to predict how things will be labeled. It would not be surprising if 18-month-olds thought that *dog* could be applied to different-looking animals, especially to the extent they do not know anything else about how they differ. Thus, the difference in the child's extension of the term may result from a different assumption about its meaning. At the same time, one would expect that whatever is assumed about the meaning of a word, confusions would not cross global domain boundaries, and indeed this is what is found (Gelman, Croft, Fu, Clausner, & Gottfried, 1998; McDonough, 2002a).

Production data alone make it difficult to determine whether overextension results from uncertainty about the exact intension of a word, from an attempt to make an analogical comparison, or from an inability to retrieve a known word when needed. Comprehension data are needed to clarify the error. There are fewer comprehension than production studies of this phenomenon, but several that have been conducted show comparable rates of overextension (Behrend, 1988; McDonough, 2002b). The fact that almost as many words are understood too broadly as are used too broadly suggests that a great deal, if not most, of overextension is actually due to uncertainty about the boundaries of the concepts to which the adult words refer. McDonough studied comprehension in a paradigm in which distractor items were drawn from the same superordinate category, as well as from different superordinate categories, thus allowing a finer comparison of mistakes in comprehension than in most previous studies. Her data indicate that even at 2 years of age, children are unclear about the extension of many words in the animal, vehicle, food, and clothing categories. Overextensions were rare across domain boundaries but occurred frequently within domains, averaging about 29% in both comprehension and production tests. For example, when asked to point to a dog among several pictures, they tended first to point to a dog but then included a fox. They hardly ever pointed to an item from another global category. This result is not a question of earlier versus later acquired names (*dog* being earlier than *fox*), because the same thing happened when they were asked to point to a fox. It seems that 2-year-olds know what a typical dog looks like and what a typical fox looks like and tend to pick a prototypical example first. What they are uncertain about is the extension of the names. A likely reason for this is lack of conceptual differentiation between dogs and foxes, planes and rockets, or cakes and pies.[2]

At this relatively late age, uncertainty about a word's extension may occur only for similar-appearing items. By age 2, children are beginning to acquire a shape bias in noun learning (Jones & Smith, 1993), as they learn that new nouns are apt to be associated with different shapes. So they may no longer extend the word *dog* to a cow, but the overall similarity between a dog and a fox is enough to make them uncertain as to whether the same word should apply. It appears that differentiated meaning is required to limit such words correctly—a set of facts that clearly differentiates dogs from foxes or cakes from pies. Waxman, Shipley, and Shepperson (1991) made a similar point in their study of 3-year-olds learning subordinate categories of dogs, grapes, and fish. When the labels for these categories were accompanied by identifying information, the subcategories were learned much faster. Three-year-olds already know the proper extension of basic-level words such as *dog* and *grape*, having learned a good deal about the relevant categories. McDonough's data come from 2-year-olds, who at this younger age know less about the differences between dogs and other mammals or between grapes and other kinds of food. As the inductive generalization data described in chapter 8 show, up until about age 2, infants are often unclear about the differences among various animal and plant kinds, and they may need help in fleshing out "basic-level" concepts such as dog or fox. Parents do this kind of teaching in many ways, including using a superordinate term to identify new "basic-level" labels, saying things like "This is a fox. It's an animal" (Callanan, 1985; Shipley, Kuhn, & Madden, 1983). This labeling strategy places the referent of a new term in a known conceptual class. In this way even language conspires to build a hierarchical conceptual system. Here a class of a given level of generality is being used to place a new, smaller class into the right area of conceptual space.

Even though parents sometimes use superordinate terms to clarify new basic-level ones, such labels are still infrequent in speech. Therefore, one should expect superordinate terms to be relatively late in acquisition. One of the few studies relating mothers' and children's use of superordinate terms (Nelson, Hampson, & Kessler Shaw, 1993) found that mothers did occasionally use the terms *animal*, *toy*, and *food* to refer to generic classes when interacting with their 20-month-olds, albeit much less frequently than more specific terms, and that *animal* and *toy* occurred in the children's speech, although *food* did not. Other superordinate names occur so rarely in daily language (for example, *vehicle*), that one would expect them to be very late acquisitions indeed.

Learning differentiated labels for an undifferentiated concept such as animal or land animal surely helps expand the early conceptual system, nudging it toward the nuances that adult language conveys. But we need to be careful not to assume that the early words, even when applied to the correct referents, match the adult sense of the terms. This is a well-known point (made by Vygotsky, for example; see chapter 9). Nevertheless, when we hear children using a "basic-level" term correctly, it is enticing to assume that it maps both reference *and* sense onto a "basic-level" concept. But as we have seen, such concepts are slowly developing achievements, in many cases not achieved until some time after the child has begun to talk. The child learns both *dog* and *fox*, but why are two words being used? Is it that a fox goes out on a chilly night and prays for the moon to give him light? These are things the child might learn from listening to adults talk (or sing) to them. It seems likely that the language parents use—most of it "basic level" in nature—is a major contributor to development of "basic-level" concepts, rather than such concepts being responsible for early language understanding.

Giving objects different labels is one good way of drawing young children's attention to differences that they may have seen but not noticed (Balaban and Waxman, 1997). It can even make them attend to a task (such as match-to-sample) in a different way than they otherwise would. Waxman and Hall (1993) found that labeling the objects for 15- to 21-month-olds in a match-to-sample task tended to increase taxonomic choices, as opposed to thematically related ones (in which the match is a functional or associative relation, such as baby and bottle or bird and nest). However, this is not always the case (Bauer & Mandler,

1989). Our data suggested that children in this age range are more prone to attend to categorical relations when faced with an object match-to-sample task than somewhat older children. Because many of our young participants were preverbal, we used reinforcement to provide the match-to-sample instructions: We showed the infants several simple examples and a correct and incorrect match to each and then cheered a lot when they produced the correct response. However, we found it easier to convey the right idea when the match was a taxonomic rather than a thematic one. Infants as young as 16 months knew the thematic relations we were using, but they were more likely to spontaneously match the target object to a like category than to a related theme. This result may have happened because many of the "like" categories were the *same* category to the youngsters, for example, brush and comb, or bed and crib.

Relational Concepts and Words

If even nouns are not learned on the basis of perception and ostension alone, a fortiori it must be true for relational terms, whether those be grammatical affixes, prepositions, or verbs. One cannot unambiguously point to containment, contact, or support or to acts of joining or disappearance. It is also more difficult than in the case of nouns to see how children could learn relational terms at all if they did not have some conception of the relations involved beforehand. It does not seem possible for language to teach perception without any conceptualization at work (although ignoring conceptualization has been a common procedure, especially in some connectionist approaches). If infants had no notion of a particular spatial relation, they would have to keep in memory a running list of situations in which the word was applied, because at this point they would have no knowledge whatsoever of what the word refers to. They would have to keep track of events, perhaps widely distributed in time, in which the mysterious word was used and, in their mind's eye, so to speak, compare them all to abstract what they had in common. A most unlikely scenario!

Surprisingly, then, given the large body of work on language acquisition, until recently there was little work on relational conceptualizations in the preverbal period. Once again, this neglect by psychologists was at least partly due to the prominence of Piaget's theory, which assumed that preverbal infants do not yet have a conceptual system. Linguists, on the other hand, typically did assume that to learn language, perhaps especially its relational aspects, it needs to be mapped onto a conceptual base. The result of this gap between fields was lip service paid to the idea that to learn language requires a conceptual system, but with few attempts to detail its nature.

Studies of early language acquisition suggested that concepts of actionality, objecthood, agency, and location were at work (e.g., Brown, 1973). But many developmental psychologists translated these concepts into sensorimotor schemas, ignoring the fact that even for Piaget sensorimotor schemas were not concepts. It didn't help that he opined that early words were merely sensorimotor schemas themselves, or at least no more than a transition between sensorimotor schemas and concepts (Piaget, 1951). Thus, in many accounts various sensorimotor achievements, such as using a means to achieve an end (for example, removing a cover to reach a hidden object), using a tool, or stringing beads to match a pattern, were posited to be related to language acquisition.

This approach came to an optimistic culmination by attempting to correlate language acquisition with Uzgiris and Hunt's (1975) scales of infant sensorimotor accomplishments (e.g., Bates, Benigni, Bretherton, Camaioni, & Volterra, 1979). Unfortunately, these scales, like the Gesell scales before them, were not so much theoretically derived as consisting of a set of tasks based on Piaget's and others' observations of what most infants can do at various ages. Another way of describing them is to say that they do not in principle differentiate conceptual and motor skills. Examination of these scales shows that early items tend to involve sensorimotor skills and later items become a mixture of sensorimotor and conceptual processes. As a result, the concepts onto which language is being mapped tended to remain relatively unspecified, and it was not clear which linguistic function each of the scales was to support. Not surprisingly, then, the line of research that attempted to correlate the Uzgiris and Hunt scales with individual differences in language acquisition did not turn out to be very informative, and this line of research petered out (see Bates, Thal, & Marchman, 1991; Bloom, Lifter, & Broughton, 1985).

As discussed in chapter 2, sensorimotor schemas are action-control structures and not an appropriate form of representation onto which language can be mapped. For example, two of the earliest grammatical morphemes learned in English are the prepositions *in* and *on*. Assume for the sake of argument that the child about to learn these prepositions has no concepts of containment, contact, or support, only schemas that control actions such as pouring milk into a cup or putting a toy down on a table. These schemas *use* variables of containment, contact, and support in the sense that they monitor whether the cup is filling up or the toy is making contact with the table with the right amount of force. But these variables are context-bound; they haven't been isolated from the action stream and so are not flexible units of thought (Mandler, 1994). Sensorimotor schemas allow components of familiar events to signal what will happen next; in that respect, they are indexical. But they do not allow independent access to their parts for purposes of denotation or to enable the infant to think without the sensorimotor activity taking place (Karmiloff-Smith, 1986). In short, sensorimotor schemas, like perception, are procedural, not conceptual, knowledge.

In an otherwise admirable attempt to model learning words for spatial relations, Regier (1995) made the traditional assumption that words are mapped onto perception itself. But as I discussed in chapter 5, that is insufficient; an interface between continuous perception (or action) and language is needed, something that will allow an analog–digital transformation. Until perceptual meaning analysis parses events into discrete notions, there aren't units of meanings onto which relational language can be mapped. In the formulation offered in chapters 4 and 5, analysis of analog perceptual displays leads to image-schematic meanings that can then be used to understand discrete words. Image-schemas, as we saw, are spatial abstractions. They have an analog character, but they also have some of the characteristics of propositional representations in that they form discrete meaning packages that can be combined productively both sequentially and recursively with other image-schemas. For this reason, they provide an excellent medium to bridge the transition from prelinguistic to linguistic representation. An 18-month-old child hearing "Your shirt is in the dresser" will already have had a year's experience in analyzing one thing as being in another. A single image-schema can be used to join the two objects in a familiar relation. Hence, even though "in" cannot be pointed to, it can nevertheless be added to the semantic system.

Languages, like concepts, make categorical distinctions, and the question is how they come together. In languages that use prepositions to express spatial relations, the distinctions made are often binary or trinary oppositions, and when further subdivisions are made, they still tend to be relatively few in number.[3] Languages vary as to what exactly goes into these packages, and these the child must learn from listening to the language. But whatever partitions a language proffers, they will be interpreted within the framework of the underlying meanings represented by nonverbal image-schemas. That is, some of the work required to map spatial knowledge into language has already been accomplished by the time language acquisition begins. Children do not have to consider countless variations in meaning suggested by the infinite variety of perceptual displays with which they are confronted; meaningful partitions have already taken place. We saw examples of this packaging in the work by Quinn (in press) on learning concepts of above and below. At 3 months of age, infants perceptually differentiate a single object as above or below a line, but it takes a few more months before they make this kind of judgment about sets of heterogeneous objects. Although speculative, such a finding suggests that it takes developmental time to form abstract notions of above and below that are independent of the objects that instantiate the relation. Achieving this kind of abstract representation—one that ignores the concrete details of the objects involved—may be required before spatial relations can be mapped into language.

Without a conceptual interface, language learning models can become unrealistic. In some cases, only associating labels with images is modeled (e.g., Plunkett & Sinha, 1992). Although this kind of connectionist model does a good job of capturing many of the procedural pattern-learning aspects of language learning, it pretty much bypasses meaning. In a related approach, Regier's (1995) structured connectionist model learns how to perceive simple spatial relations in the context of naming them as a speaker of a particular language would. Learning takes place with positive feedback with respect to the categories of a particular language. But this can be only half the story. One's native language does provide information about understanding situations in terms of particular words. On the other hand, infants learn a great deal about spatial relations *before* they begin to understand spoken language. Therefore, they must be able to form spatial concepts without the benefit of a language parsing the world for them. They do not wait to learn relations such as "tight-fitting contact" until language teaches them. Preverbal infants do not get a "Hurrah" when they observe that their diapers are too tight or notice Cheerios spilling out of a bowl when it is knocked over.

To get around this problem of prior knowledge being needed, Regier built into his model a number of constraints that sound very much like image-schemas. Indeed, it was from the image-schema literature that he determined what constraints might be needed. So his model interprets visual scenes in terms of landmarks and trajectors following paths. It computes spatial features such as contact and containment, and it divides the scenes it observes into parts corresponding to source, path of motion, and end state. These divisions seem quite sensible, but in Regier's model they are innate parts of the visual system. At this state of our knowledge, we don't know whether notions such as PATH, BEGINNING-OF-PATH, END-OF-PATH, CONTAINMENT, and so forth are part of our inherited mental architecture or whether they are integral aspects of perception. Some of them may well be, but notice that this approach makes no allowance for concept formation. There are only perception and words— no meanings. The Regier baby sees space in certain innate ways but doesn't have any *concepts* about space until learning language. That places a vast burden on language—one that I doubt it can bear. To me it makes much more sense that the constraints built into Regier's language learning model are learned conceptions, constructed via perceptual meaning analysis. This allows the system not only to learn language but also to think. And it is concepts that enable one to learn more than one language and/or translate one language into another.

More recently, Regier and his colleagues have been analyzing differences between spatial concepts and spatial words (Crawford, Regier, & Huttenlocher, 2000; Regier & Carlson, 2002), and they conclude there are some major differences between the linguistic and nonlinguistic categorization of space. For example, Crawford et al. provide data suggesting that a verbal label like "above" uses the vertical axis as a prototype. People judged a stimulus on the vertical axis to be a better example of "above" than one off the vertical axis to the quadrant on either side. In contrast, this same axis seems to act as a boundary in non-linguistic spatial organization. The same people tended to reproduce the location of a stimulus as farther away from the vertical axis than its actual position, that is, toward the center of the quadrant in which it had appeared. The status of nonlinguistic spatial organization remains unclear in this formulation, but it appears to be opposed to the notion that nonlinguistic spatial schemas are formed prior to language acquisition and later become labeled linguistically. Regier (1997) suggested that because I say that language is mapped onto preexisting schemas that the structure of linguistic spatial categories should directly reflect the structure of nonlinguistic spatial categories. But that doesn't follow from what I have said. We know that languages differ, so that would not be a sensible point of view. What I have said is that language is mapped onto meanings, and not only can these be combined in a variety of ways but also language can highlight some aspects at the expense of others. Most concepts, such as animal, for instance, consist of more than one meaning. In the case of linguistic spatial categories, these can be more coarsely coded than the image-schemas contributing to understanding them. Thus, one can have a category of containment that does or does not include reference to the way an object fits into a container. Korean includes reference to degree of fit; English does not. But as we will see later in this chapter, preverbal infants have both notions: containment and tightness. Therefore, a language could combine the notions or express them separately; either way, children should find the words learnable.

Preverbal Spatial Concepts and Semantic Primitives

An approach to language learning in the 1970s was to assume that there were semantic universals to help with the process (E. Clark, 1973a; H. Clark, 1973). Semantic universals were proposed by Bierwisch (1967) and Postal (1966) to account for the features that differentiate contrasting relational terms in various languages. These universals apparently were considered to be innate, and what needed to be learned was how a given language packages them. Linguists did not spend much time worrying about how to characterize the background of these universals, typically merely assuming that they reflect the cognitive and perceptual structure of the organism. H. Clark (1973) went into more detail, specifying that these universals reflected the perceptual properties to which children are sensitive, such as reference lines and planes. Thus, he took an approach similar to Regier's, discussed previously: Language gets mapped onto perception, which, uninfluenced by anything conceptual, is the source of the universal commonalities found in various languages.

E. Clark (1973a) added an important developmental refinement to the hypothesis of universal semantic primitives, which she called the semantic feature hypothesis, and extended it to include nouns as well as relational words. This hypothesis was that children begin to identify the meaning of a word with only one or two semantic features rather than the whole combination of meaning components in the adult's version. Gradually, the child adds more features of meaning to the lexical entry of the word until eventually it reaches the adult's interpretation. Clark, too, took a perceptual view of how these features might be initially acquired, although it was not always obvious how perception could deliver some of the features she discussed (e.g., such as "young" as a feature for an early meaning of brother). In general, both Clarks tended to equate perception and conception, so they could move easily from talking about perceptions of planes or verticality to "perceiving" youth or maleness.

E. Clark used the phenomenon of overextension as evidence for her view that initially children use too few features to give meaning to a word. Originally, she emphasized perceptual features—for example, aspects of shape such as four-leggedness—as the root cause of the overextension in meaning. (More recently, she has included conceptual features as well and thus takes a position closer to the point of view espoused in this book, in which I emphasize conceptual overgeneralization. I discuss Clark's, 2001, newer views later.) For the noun overextensions, the primitive features Clark (1973a) posited were perceptual ones, such as shape, size, taste, smell, and movement. For relational terms, the primitives were assumed to be the semantic universals of Bierwisch and Postal. However, Clark attempted to order these in terms of their generality, which she hypothesized would also predict order of acquisition of the relational words that they comprise. So, for example, in learning the meanings of the words *before* and *after*, she claimed that children first learned that both words have to do with time, then that they have to do with temporal sequence, and still later that they vary in priority. These primitives form a kind of hierarchy with time at the top, which can be divided into simultaneous or sequential, with sequential divided into prior or not.

In a study on the acquisition of the English terms *in*, *on*, and *under*, Clark refined the semantic feature hypothesis to include behavioral biases (E. Clark, 1973b). She found that from 1½ to 2½ years, children often interpreted *on* or *under* to mean "in" and sometimes *under* to mean "on." Clark argued that learning a word for containment is easier than some other spatial terms because of children's predilection to put objects inside containers rather than on them or, in the case of supporting surfaces, to place objects on the surface rather than under it.

This work was carried out before most of the experimental research on preverbal infants' understanding of concepts of containment and support, which would undoubtedly have modified the way it was couched. Even without preverbal evidence, however, the semantic feature hypothesis began to be seriously criticized by the end of the 1970s, in part because the data on young children's acquisition of relational terms frequently did not follow its predictions (Richards, 1979). For example, *in* is not always acquired before *on*, nor *before* acquired before *after*. Carey (1982) also challenged the theory on theoretical grounds. She made the important distinction between a meaning component being definitionally primitive and developmentally primitive, pointing out that these need not be the same. Semantic analyses of the adult lexicon often use sophisticated and theory-laden concepts unlikely to be in the new language learner's repertoire. The young child cannot have the same understanding of *brother* as an adult without knowing something about biological relations or understand the word *buy* without some appreciation of money. This would make it seem unlikely that language acquisition could depend on the universals uncovered by linguistic analyses of the adult lexicon.

On similar bases, as well as cross-cultural analyses of language acquisition, Bowerman (1996) also rejected the notion of semantic primitives. Bowerman suggested that recent evidence on the language specificity of children's learning in various languages argues against the hypothesis that children start out by mapping spatial words onto prepackaged notions of space. She argued further that even if there are preverbal spatial notions, perhaps represented by image-schemas as I have suggested, that there would have to be a very large number of them to account for all the distinctions that various languages make. Although she conceded there might be such a large number of preverbal spatial image-schemas, they would still be of little help in language acquisition, given that young children extend their first spatial morphemes mainly on the basis of the native language they are learning, not on universal principles.

This position, however, both underestimates the importance of image-schemas in preverbal thought and overestimates the role that language plays in its own acquisition. First, as discussed at the beginning of this section, it does not seem possible to learn language (other than rote pattern learning) without conceptual understanding of some sort. That means we require developmental primitives, whether learned or innate, and these must be universal, because children of all cultures learn language and all languages talk about similar kinds of events and relationships. As Carey noted, however, developmental primitives need not be the same as the semantic primitives that have been proposed to underlie the various spatial distinctions language makes. "Primitive" for new language learners means the concepts with which they begin to interpret their native tongue. There is absolutely no guarantee that their primitives will match the components of relational words found in adult usage. Indeed, semantic analyses of early speech suggest that early word meanings often miss obligatory meanings in the adult language, as Clark (1973a) emphasized.

Second, it is not clear that there need be a vast number of developmental primitives, and in any case infants could easily have learned a good many by the time they begin to learn language. When one looks at the spatial notions that are expressed in various languages, for the most part the number is not large. In English, for example, Landau and Jackendoff's (1993) analysis indicates only about 90 prepositions exist, and many of these are minor variants on each other, such as *in* and *inside* or *beneath* and *under.* In addition, some of them are late acquisitions in children's vocabulary. About 20 prepositions appear to cover most of the spatial relations commonly expressed in daily speech. We are simply not talking about a large number of notions, even taking all languages into account. Learning to take the shape of the container into account when learning containment terms in the Mayan language Tzeltal (Brown, 1994) may add only a slight burden to the child's task. One thing we have learned in the past decade is just how much about the world preverbal children are learning. Why should six kinds of shapes defeat them when learning to talk about containment (if they even learn all these terms at once, which seems somewhat unlikely)? Given the fact that in most languages a few spatial terms are learned first and the variants follow over a period of months to years, Bowerman's argument loses much of its force. One of the virtues of a mechanism of perceptual meaning analysis is that it allows the acquisition of new distinctions at any time that careful analysis of perceptual information is carried out. Language does not just teach facts about foxes and chilly nights; as we have seen, it also directs attention to detail, and analyses of new details go on for years—in some cases throughout life.

Third, Bowerman was concerned that preverbal image-schema representations of various spatial relations cannot provide a principled basis for the productivity of spatial terms. However, her own many acute analyses of the linguistic errors that children make show that the productivity they display is not based exclusively on the semantics of the language they are learning (Bowerman, 1996). Furthermore, learning language is only one of the tasks facing infants. They need representation for many other things as well. Image-schemas are independent of language; positing them was required by our finding extensive conceptual activity in infants, not because of concern with learning language. From my point of view, their use in language learning was a serendipitous extra. On the other hand, to say that language itself constructs the spatial concepts of an individual child has problems of its own. As discussed later, Bowerman's own data show that Dutch children have difficulty with the word *uit* ("out"), which, she suggested, leads them to use a *nonlinguistic* concept to make sense of the various (seemingly conflicting) relations that *uit* covers. A preverbal concept is being used to interpret a difficult linguistic term, which accounts for the way the term is extended. In sum, one can no more say that language teaches the first spatial concepts than one can say that the first spatial concepts make children learn a language other than the one they hear. We simply have to accept that there is a complex interaction between preverbal concepts and the specifics of the language being learned.

I sympathize with Bowerman's concern that the primitives that have been proposed are usually designated in a particular language (typically English), and although authors insist that they do not intend their primitives to be identical with the meanings of words in the language in which they write, "it is not clear what they do intend them to mean. Each language offers a different idea of what some candidate primitive is, and the child must discover this view" (Bowerman, 1996, p. 425). I agree that it is vital to specify primitives in more detail than has often been done and to distinguish developmental from semantic primitives. But at this stage of research, I think we have every reason to be optimistic about finding developmental primitives that are common to all language learners. The data we have collected, described in the next section, give some examples of what such notions look like. That these notions will diverge as different languages are learned does not mean that it is unimportant to understand the preverbal conceptual repertoire that supports language learning. Otherwise, language acquisition will forever remain mysterious. We need to understand why some linguistic expressions like *on* are easy and why others like the Dutch *aan* are more difficult (see later). That means we need a cooperative effort between research on infant conceptual development and language development.

When I first began to specify a few developmental spatial primitives, using image-schema terminology as a representational format (Mandler, 1992a), my view was in agreement with Bowerman (1987) that there are two important aspects of the role of meaning in learning to talk that must be solved before one can claim to have an adequate model of language acquisition. The first is a plausible theory of where children's meaning representations come from, and the second is how they are used to facilitate language learning. I theorized that the answer to the first requirement is that analysis of perceptual information creates image-schema meanings. The answer to the second is that they underlie the necessary concepts, particularly for relational terms that otherwise would be impossible for the young child to learn. This view does not imply that infants will rigidly assume predetermined meanings for every spatial term they hear. They have lots of spatial concepts but are flexible in terms of accepting the way that languages package them.

As Bowerman (1989) and Bowerman and Choi (2001) have documented, languages vary as to how they treat containment and support relations. English makes a binary distinction between *in* and *on*. Even though these map apparently effortlessly onto the CONTAINMENT and SUPPORT image-schemas described in chapter 5, the semantics of *in* and *on* refer to more than containment and support and have many nuances that children certainly do not learn all at once. Obviously, they do not understand abstract uses of *on* such as "on my honor," let alone whether to say "in this view" versus "on this view." (I still don't know which of these is "correct.") But even for concrete examples of support described by *on*, there is a range of variation and restrictions. For example, the word *on* implies support with contact but has both prototypical limitations as well as less prototypical extensions. In the prototypical case, the supporting surface is rigid, the supported object is smaller than the surface, and the supported object is not attached to the surface (Kemmer, in preparation). At the same time, the term is extended radially in a number of ways; for example, a handle on a pan is attached and does not rest on a surface, and a balloon on a string is attached but not supported.

We have little empirical data on the role that adult semantic prototypes play vis-à-vis acquisition, but I assume that it is the prototypical usage of these prepositions that infants hear most frequently and that are most likely to fit with their preverbal conceptions of relations such as containment and support. This would suggest that it is the prototypical meanings they learn first, although this is by no means guaranteed. Much early learning seems to consist of forming "islands" (Tomasello, 1992, 2000) in which the initial learning is not nearly as general as adult usage. Tomasello coined this term to refer to early verb learning, in which various syntactic properties are used with one verb but not a similar one, suggesting local learning of how a given verb operates rather than a more general and abstract understanding of various syntactic structures. It is possible that a similar situation applies to prepositional learning. It might be that a particular child acquires a reasonably comprehensive usage of *in*, while still restricting *on* to certain imitated phrases.

Spanish speakers typically use *en* for both the English prototypical meanings of *in* and *on*. The lack of a distinction here should not cause young language learners any particular difficulty. They can use *en* to talk about an even wider variety of containment, contact, togetherness, and support relations than can be done with a single word in English. Dutch, on the other hand, divides *on* into two kinds of support relations. *Op* is used to express horizontal support and also for certain kinds of nonhorizontal support, as in a poster glued to a wall. *Aan* is used to express a variety of other support relations in which only part of an object is attached to a supporting surface, as in a picture hanging on a wall. It typically, although not invariably, implicates downward force. This is a more sophisticated distinction (what Bowerman, 1996, calls *projective attachment*) and seems much less likely to be part of a preverbal infant's conceptual reper-toire. Not surprisingly, then, Bowerman (1998) reports that young Dutch learners tend to make errors when using this term. (Such errors need not occur in the first usage of a term. To the extent that children learn com-monly used, fixed phrases, confusion among the various uses of *on* might not be evident until the child attempts to describe a new situation.)

Bowerman (1998) also reports work with Gentner in which they in-vestigated whether some ways of classifying space are more "natural" than others. They used the extent to which languages agree in their se-mantic classification of a domain as an indicator of naturalness. Strong cross-linguistic agreement suggests uniformity in the way human beings conceptualize a domain nonlinguistically, and rare categories suggest other sources, including historical accident such as cultural and linguistic mingling. Bowerman and Gentner hypothesized that cross-linguistically common spatial semantic categories should be learned more easily and with fewer errors than rare ones. They tested some categories in English that are common in many languages and some Dutch categories that are rare. In an elicited production experiment with English- and Dutch-speaking children aged 2½ to 6 years, their predictions were strongly confirmed. The Dutch children had particular difficulty with Dutch cross-linguistically rare categories, and their errors reflected more com-mon cross-linguistic ways of classifying. Such a finding indicates once again the importance of nonlinguistic spatial conceptions in early lan-guage acquisition. The most common cross-linguistic ways of classifying are apt to have their basis in the kinds of concepts that preverbal infants develop about space and that influence how they begin to interpret the language that is spoken to them.

Another example of Bowerman and Gentner's point might be work by Brown (2001) on children learning spatial vocabulary in Tzeltal. This language uses an "uphill-downhill" system of spatial description (de-rived from the general slope of the land in the mountainous part of Chi-apas, Mexico, where this language is spoken) to specify relations on both the vertical and horizontal axes. According to Brown, children show the influence of language-specific semantics as early as they begin to use the "up-down" vocabulary, using the words with land slope meanings as well as with vertical meanings. But these spatial terms enter the vocabu-lary rather late, beginning to appear around age 2, and are relatively restricted in their first usage. Furthermore, errors in the verbs associated with this system in both comprehension and production (using verbs meaning to ascend or descend with respect to the local slope of the land rather than the overall slope) still occur as late as age 7 or 8. In some sense these difficulties are minor. After all, Tzeltal children do manage to learn this system—otherwise, it would have disappeared! My point is only that these distinctions are not easy for infant language learners because the concepts involved are more complex than those needed to learn spatial terms in most languages (and may require wider ranging experiences than Tzeltal infants usually have).

In addition to the difficulties with *aan*, Bowerman (1996) describes the difficulty Dutch children have, as mentioned earlier, with the word *uit* ("out"). Adult speakers of both English and Dutch make a systematic distinction between actions of "removal from containment" (*out/uit*) and "removal from surface contact" (*off/af*). English-speaking children master this distinction quite readily, presumably because it is consistently made. However, adult Dutch speakers have one noncanonical usage of *uit*, which is to remove clothing from the body, so one takes a shoe "out of" a foot. That is, they do not use the expected term for removal from surface contact, but surprisingly the term for removal from containment. Bowerman suggests that for Dutch adults the clothing use of *uit* seems to be stored as a separate sense. But young Dutch learners apparently try initially to construct a single meaning for *uit* that includes both removal from containment and removal from the body. The only meaning consistent with both uses is "removal" itself, which sanctions the use of *uit* for taking objects off surfaces. As a result, young Dutch children massively overextend *uit* to removal in general. This means, of course, that the children must have a nonlinguistic concept of removal; otherwise, they could not make this productive construction.

Similarly, children learning English overextend *open* to many acts of separation, whereas Korean children don't. English *open* is a large category, whereas Korean breaks opening actions into about six categories on the basis of distinctions in the physical properties of the objects acted on. Bowerman (1998) suggests that a single word for many related opening actions encourages the young language learner to generalize broadly, even to overgeneralize, whereas when hearing these same events distinguished by different words, "the impulse to generalize is checked."

Although English, Dutch, and Spanish differ somewhat in the way they package containment and support relations, these are nevertheless expressed by prepositions that are used quite generally with many different verbs, so that children hear them in a great many situations. In addition, using the prepositions alone, as children do in the one-word stage of language production, is often sufficient to convey what they want to say. There are languages, however, that have no all-purpose prepositions equivalent to English *in* or *on* and express spatial meanings primarily by means of a variety of motion verbs (and sometimes by nouns such as *top surface* or *interior*). Korean is one of these, and as Choi and Bowerman (1991) documented, it presents a somewhat different task for the young language learner. In Korean there is a verb *nohta* that means "to put loosely on a surface," a distinction not unlike the prototypical meaning of the English preposition *on*. However, there is a verb *kkita* that means roughly "to fit tightly together," as in putting a ring on a finger or a cork in a bottle, thus cutting across the English usages of *in* and *on*. There is another verb *nehta* that means roughly "to put loosely into (or around)," again cutting across the English prepositions *in* and *on*.

My interpretation of this three-way split is that the language provides a distinction between things going in or things going on but supersedes this distinction in the case in which the thing going in or on results in a tight fit (as in a cassette tape going into its case or a lid being snapped onto a container). Choi and Bowerman (1991) noted that these distinctions do not give Korean children any difficulty, in that the word for "fit tightly together" (*kkita*) is one of the first words they learn. Nevertheless, they do make some mistakes. For example, one of the secondary features of tight fit expressed by *kkita* is that the objects should be three-dimensional. Another word, *puuchita*, is used for juxtaposing flat surfaces, such as putting a flat magnet on a refrigerator door. Yet Korean children are apt to overextend *kkita* to the case of putting flat surfaces together. This is another example of the incomplete entries in the semantics of children's first words. Tight fit is the crucial conceptual component; the dimensionality of the objects involved is secondary.

Bowerman (1989) and Choi and Bowerman (1991) suggested that the Korean spatial terms cast doubt on containment and support as privileged spatial primitives that can be mapped directly into language. They proposed that language learners do not map spatial words directly onto nonlinguistic spatial concepts but instead that children are sensitive to the structure of their input language from the beginning. At the same time, they noted that how children figure out language-specific spatial categories remains a puzzle. Although I agree that their data provide strong evidence that young children are sensitive to the structure of their language from *the beginning of language learning*, the mapping is only a puzzle if we assume that *in* and *on* are the only kinds of spatial analyses of containment and support that have been carried out prior to that. "From the beginning" is ambiguous. If it means from the beginning of language learning, it is quite possibly correct; if it means from the beginning of concept formation, it is clearly incorrect. Yet it is the latter interpretation that has commonly been made of their writing. For example, Regier (1997) describes Bowerman's work as saying that:

> . . . although Korean and English have cross-cutting spatial
> categories, Korean-learning and English-learning children
> acquire their early spatial terms in ways that reflect the native
> language, rather than any underlying prelinguistic concepts—
> and do so at the same early age. Thus, rather than simply at-
> tach labels to large pre-individuated spatial concepts such as
> containment or support, children seem to actually *build* their
> spatial categories in response to linguistic input. This evidence
> suggests that the child's hypothesis space is not constrained by
> the large conceptual partitions that Mandler proposes. (p. 214)

Needless to say, I disagree rather thoroughly with this quote. First, what is a "hypothesis space" if not a set of concepts? Second, I do not believe that preverbal infants have made only "large conceptual partitions." Although many object concepts are broad, preverbal spatial concepts often seem to be rather small. Notions such as PATH are quite general, but notions such as BEGINNING-OF-PATH or CONTACT are more discrete. Third, of course, Korean-learning and English-learning children acquire spatial terms in ways that reflect their native language. They are, after all, learning either Korean or English, not Esperanto. But I cannot imagine how children could learn *any* language without some conceptualizations of the subject matter being talked about. They certainly build their *semantic* categories on the basis of the language they are hearing, but that is done in the context of their preverbal *conceptual* categories. On (in?) this view, the child hearing *in* across all instances of containment being talked about interprets *in* to mean containment, whereas the child hearing *nehta* for instances of loose containment and *kkita* for instances of tight containment, interprets these terms to mean loose containment and tight containment, respectively. (It is unknown whether the use of *nehta* for loose encirclement is a later accomplishment for Korean children, but I would predict so.) This situation is roughly the same as Spanish children learning *en* to refer to both containment and support, versus English-speaking children having to learn different words to refer to these two concepts.

It may well be that *in* and *on* appear as early as they do in English because of their status as separate morphemes, their frequent usage, and their relatively straightforward mapping onto two simple image-schemas. Korean children in the one-word stage cannot get by with *in* and *on* because these all-purpose morphemes do not exist in their language. Because children add only a few words at a time in the early months of language production, Korean children express only some of the many usages that English-speaking children manage with their more general *in* and *on*. One of the words they do use is *kkita*. A word expressing the same idea of fitting tightly does not appear in English samples of early speech, because there is no single morpheme in the language to express it. However, this does not mean that English children do not have such a concept until a later stage, when they begin to combine several morphemes together. I hypothesized (Mandler, 1992a) that this is an easy word for Korean children to learn because its meaning reflects the kinds of spatial analyses that preverbal infants everywhere are carrying out. "To fit tightly" (or, for that matter, "to fit loosely") does not seem to be an unduly difficult notion for infants who are engaged in analyzing many kinds of containment and support relations. As the data summarized in the next section show, along with the work of Spelke and Hespos (2002) mentioned in chapter 5, this is indeed the case.

I have no doubt that Korean infants learn about containment and support as much as do infants who will learn English as their native tongue. Even though in Korean containment may seem to take second place to expressing whether objects fit together tightly or loosely, as in *nehta* referring to any kind of loose containment or encirclement without designating which object is in or around, this surely does not mean that containment is less important in Korean thought. When asked for a prototypical example of *nehta*, Koreans use loose containment as their example, rather than loose encirclement (Soonja Choi, personal communication, April 2001). There would appear to be certain relations that are salient to humans everywhere; just because a language does not emphasize them does not make the concepts disappear or even become unimportant.

Some Preverbal Spatial Concepts: The Case of In, On, and Fit Together

In an attempt to resolve some of these issues, McDonough, Choi, Bowerman, and I studied the beginning stages of learning several spatial terms in Korean and English (McDonough, Choi, Bowerman, & Mandler, 1998). In our first experiment, we examined the onset of comprehension of spatial terms in Korean and English (Choi, McDonough, Bowerman, & Mandler, 1999). By 18 months, children learning English begin to understand the terms *in* and *on*, and children learning Korean begin to understand the comparable terms in Korean. As mentioned earlier, the spatial terms in the two languages don't match. Whereas English gets by with a two-way split between any kind of containment and any kind of support, Korean commonly uses three terms (although it makes other related distinctions, such as different verbs for putting on clothes). These are *kkita*, meaning "fit together tightly" (as in putting a finger in a ring or a ring on a finger), *nehta*, meaning "put in or around loosely" (as in putting an apple in a bowl or a ring loosely around a stake), and *nohta*, which means "to put something loosely on a surface," as in putting an apple on a table.

We used a looking paradigm in which two films are presented with a single audio input and measured whether 14- to 23-month-olds tended to look at the film that matches the sound. So, for example, when a film of putting a book onto a stack of other books was shown along with a film of putting a book into a tight-fitting case, the English audio would say, "Look! Where is she putting it in?" The comparable Korean audio would say, "Look! Where is she tight-fitting it?" This is a situation in which both English and Korean children should look at the same film if they understand the terms used. Another pair of films might show tossing a ring into a basket and a ring being put tightly on a pole. The same audios would be used again, the English audio saying, "Look! Where is she putting it in?" and the Korean audio saying, "Look! Where is she tight-fitting it?" In this case, however, the English- and Korean-reared children should look at different films. The English-reared children should look at the film showing the ring going loosely into the basket, whereas the Korean-reared children should look at the film showing the ring going tightly on the pole. We filmed a number of different examples of these relationships, a few of which, along with the terms for them in English and Korean, are illustrated in Figure 11-1. As can be seen there, the relationships expressed by *in* and *on* in English do not overlap, whereas the term *kkita* (meaning "fit tightly together" in Korean) includes a subset of the meanings of both of the English terms.

The data were not reliable until 18 months (Choi et al., 1999). From 18 to 23 months, both English-learning and Korean-learning children looked appropriately at the films that matched the spatial terms of their language. Why should this be the case? One might speculate that language itself was teaching the relevant concepts—that infants had no notion of containment or tight-fittingness, let alone how they might relate to each other, until they heard language being used in consistent ways that made them notice these relationships and begin to understand them.

Clearly, however, these data tell only part of the story. One cannot stop here and conclude that because as early as children understand spatial terms, they do so in a language-specific way that language is teaching the concepts involved. After all, we did not get reliable comprehension data until 18 months. From the point of view of an infancy researcher, that is positively middle-aged! As discussed in chapter 5, we know that infants have learned a great deal about containment and support much earlier than 18 months. Perhaps they have learned a lot about tightness as well. Clearly, we need to find out whether infants younger than 18 months have the concepts relevant to learn both the English and the Korean distinctions. In this case, the Korean distinctions are of greater interest because there are more of them. Both containment and support can be tight or loose (or alternatively one can have a category of fit that supersedes either containment or support). So in this particular comparison, what we

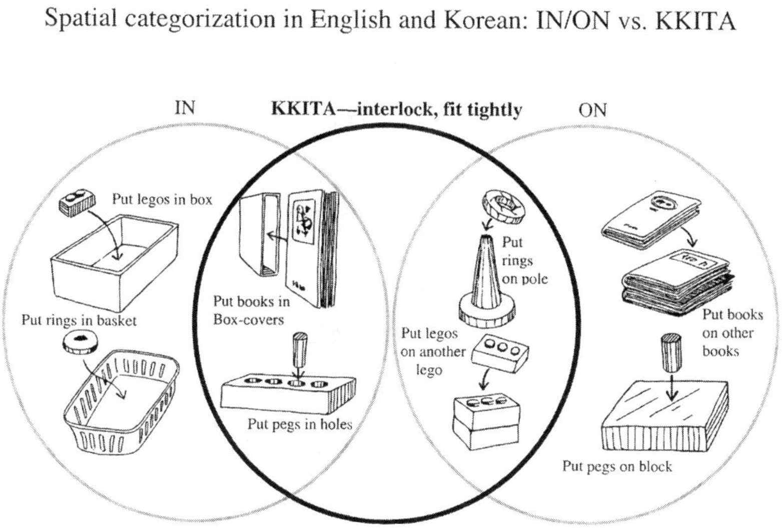

Spatial categorization in English and Korean: IN/ON vs. KKITA

Figure 11-1. Showing how the Korean term *kkita* intersects the English terms *in* and *on*. Reprinted from McDonough et al. (2003) with permission from Elsevier.

most need to know is whether all infants make a tight-loose distinction in the preverbal period.

We decided to use a familiarization/preferential looking technique to study this issue (McDonough, Choi, & Mandler, 2003). If preverbal children have learned the components that will be relevant for learning Korean and English, then they should be sensitive to them at an abstract level. That is, what we want to show is that infants respond to containment or tightness per se, not just to a particular instantiation of these notions. (In the Spelke and Hespos work on tight- versus loose-fitting containment discussed in chapter 5, only one or two objects at a time were considered.) We added a number of films to those used in the first experiment. We varied the objects, their colors, and their features as much as possible, so that infants would have to generalize across objects to the relation itself that was being expressed in the films.

We studied 9- to 14-month-olds in order to cover a reasonable age range before the onset of comprehension of spatial terms in either language (which the previous experiment indicated was 18 months). First, we looked at infants from English-speaking families and contrasted tight containment relations with loose support relations. We recognized that this procedure confounded the two variables of interest (containment versus support and tight versus loose), but we needed to be sure that the technique would work. No one had shown responsivity to such abstract variables at these ages, and these two contrasts were the most clear-cut from the previous study. We familiarized the infants with either a series of tight containment relations (such as a book being put into a slipcover) or a series of loose support relations (such as a hand placing a toy soldier on a stepladder). Then we tested them by showing a new example of the familiarized relation with an example from the other category.

The results are shown in Figure 11-2. During the test phase, the 9-month-olds preferred to look at the familiarized relation, whether that was "tight-in" or "loose-on." The 11-month-olds looked more at the novel relation, but the data were quite variable and the difference was not significant. The 14-month-olds showed a significant preference for the novel relation. Thus, by 14 months the infants clearly were sensitive to the abstract relations under study. Of equal interest was the fact that 9-month-olds also were sensitive to the relations but preferred to look at the familiarized one. This, combined with the gradual shift over age to a preference for the novel, suggested to us that the 9-month-olds might still be in the process of constructing these concepts, or at least were currently involved in analyzing them.

We also gave English-speaking adults the same test (also shown in Figure 11-2). We gave them virtually no instructions other than to look at the films. During the test phase, the adults showed a small but significant preference for looking at the novel relation, again regardless of which relation they had been familiarized with. Thus, infants performed similarly to the adults in showing responsivity to relations of tight containment and loose support and the ability to contrast them. This, of course, is an implicit measure. We also asked the adults for an explicit judgment. After they had looked at the films, the adults were taken to another room where there were laid out three of the objects they had seen during familiarization and one of the items from the other category that they had seen during the test. The experimenter then demonstrated the appropriate action with each of the objects and asked which item of the four did not belong with the others. On this explicit test, 78% of the adults chose correctly and also gave a correct explanation, always in terms of con-

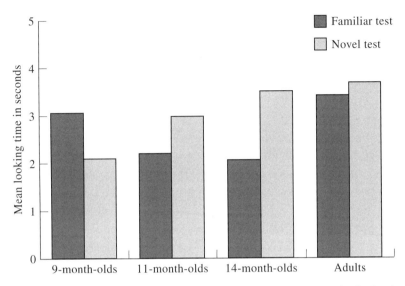

Figure 11-2. Infants learning English gradually shift from a preference for the familiar stimulus to the novel stimulus in a tightly fitting-in versus loosely fitting-on contrast. A smaller but still significant preference for the novel stimulus was found in English-speaking adults. Reprinted from McDonough et al. (2003) with permission from Elsevier.

tainment versus support, none mentioning tight versus loose fit. (This percentage did not vary significantly as a function of whether they had looked longer at the novel relation during the test phase of the previous film procedure.) Thus, the adults not only were responsive to the distinction being tested but also could verbalize what the difference was. (Perhaps the only surprising finding here is that 22% of the adults did not choose the correct answer.)

   Now that we knew the technique was a viable one, we moved to a comparison of even greater import: tight versus loose containment. This comparison is of interest for both infants and adults. For infants, we wanted to know whether they make the distinction at all. Is loose versus tight a contrast they have analyzed? To Laraine McDonough and me (both English speakers), the contrast seemed rather subtle, less so to Soonja Choi, a Korean speaker. Of course, we also needed to check a representative sample of adults, both English and Korean speaking, to see if our intuitions were borne out.

We replicated the experiment just described, this time using tight-fitting and loose-fitting scenes and infants from both Korean- and English-speaking homes, as well as Korean- and English-speaking adults (Mc-Donough et al., 2003). The infants again ranged from 9 to 14 months of age. The test scenes are shown in Figure 11-3. This time, as can be seen in Figure 11-4, infants throughout this age range from both English-speaking and Korean-speaking homes strongly preferred the *familiar* relation rather than the novel one, whether they had been familiarized with tight-in scenes or loose-in scenes. This result surprised us, because it is relatively unusual in the familiarization-dishabituation literature. It suggested to us that the contrast between the two relations was indeed rather subtle, to the extent that when shown a contrast pair, infants tended to continue analysis of the familiarization category. This is not an entirely satisfactory explanation, but in any case, the significant difference in looking at the two categories in the test trials tells us that infants were sensitive to the contrast between tight and loose containment.

The adult data continued this puzzle (see Figure 11-4). Korean adults were just as prone to look at the familiarized relation, whether tight or loose fitting. Perhaps because the relation is subtle, during test trials even the adults tried to confirm the contrast by continuing to examine the familiarized relation. Clearly, however, Korean adults, even though preferring to look at the familiarized relation, distinguished between them in the test trials. These looking time data were mirrored in the oddity task, in which the experimenter acted out the familiarized relation with three objects and the opposite relation with the fourth. The Korean subjects almost all chose the correct object as the odd man out and always gave a correct explanation for it (in some cases more than one verb could be used correctly). In contrast, the English-speaking adults failed to respond differentially on either task. They looked approximately equally at the two types of stimuli in the looking test and chose the odd man out only at chance levels. Furthermore, they rarely gave the correct explanation for their choice even when the choice was correct. Their data indicate that they were not aware of the contrasting relation to which they had been exposed.

These data are of considerable interest for several reasons. First, the entrenched language of the adult speakers clearly influenced both their

Test Scenes

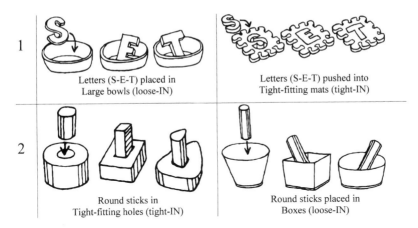

Figure 11-3. The stimuli used to test the contrast between tight-in and loose-in with infants learning Korean and English and with Korean-speaking and English-speaking adults. Reprinted from McDonough et al. (2003) with permission from Elsevier.

implicit and explicit categorizations, at least as far as their first responses are concerned. In this regard, they add to the recent revival of the Whorfian spirit, showing a clear influence of language on thought. However, our data do not speak to the influence of language on problem solving, reasoning, or various other higher order cognitive processes, only to the initial assessment of a situation. One would surely not conclude that American adults cannot use a concept of tight-fit in their reasoning. Nevertheless, I think it is significant that the cultural/linguistic difference was found in both implicit and explicit measures, suggesting a considerable influence of language on the two cultures' initial approach to a particular kind of relation. In this small way, our data agree with the position taken by Levinson (1996), Lucy (1992), and Boroditsky (2001) that language at least superficially affects the thought of adult speakers.

As an aside, I note that our data appear to conflict with recent work by Papafragou, Massey, and Gleitman (2002), who found that the characteristic differences in use of path versus manner verbs in English and in Greek affected how speakers of these two languages describe scenes but

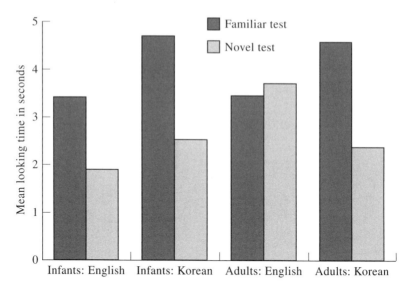

Figure 11-4. Both English-learning infants and Korean-learning infants, as well as Korean-speaking adults, prefer to look at the familiar stimulus. English-speaking adults show no preference. Reprinted from McDonough et al. (2003) with permission from Elsevier.

did not affect how they remembered or categorized the scenes. In contrast, we found categorization to be affected by the languages we studied. However, in their study in at least some cases the path distractors in their categorization tasks violated the underlying conceptualization of the scenes. For example, a path distractor for a picture of a frog jumping into a room was a picture of a frog jumping out of the room. By changing the goal of the figure, this distractor changes the fundamental meaning of the scene and so should be rejected by speakers of *any* language. In contrast, our less dramatic changes may have allowed the effects of language to show up that might be masked when meaning changes too drastically. I agree with Papafragou et al. that whatever effects different languages may have, they cannot change the most fundamental ways that people think.

The second important aspect of our data, and the one of most relevance to this chapter, is that the preverbal infants we studied, whether from Korean- or English-speaking homes, were all sensitive to the contrasting relations of tight versus loose containment, categorizing this difference at an abstract level. Although these data are not complete—for example, we haven't yet studied tight versus loose support—they indicate that the preverbal infants were less biased or more flexible in their approach to categorization of the relations they were shown than were the adults. The data from our various experiments suggest that even by 18 months to 2 years, children may be losing some of this flexibility; at any rate, they have already learned to pay attention to the different distinctions the two languages make.

It is just as interesting that tightness versus looseness is a distinction that infants as young as 9 months make at all, although the data of Spelke and Hespos (2002) suggest that its beginnings are even earlier. It is a distinction that has not loomed large in discussions of universal primitives underlying language. It may be subtle, yet it seems to have as much right to universal status as the more commonly discussed relations of containment, support, contact, and so forth. I predict that research over the next few decades will uncover many such distinctions, quite possibly dozens of them. This is an area crying out for research. The relevant questions have been clearly posed, and we have developed appropriate methods for studying them, so this should be a fascinating and fruitful area of research over the next decade.

Whether various developmental primitives differ in their importance is still another fascinating issue. We obviously do not fully understand the significance of the differential response to the tight-loose contrast versus the containment-support contrast. It should also be noted that we tested only tight versus loose containment. So at this point we do not know whether we were merely testing two types of containment or a broader tightness relation that cuts across containment, possibly including the relation of clothes to the body. We also do not know whether Korean infants respond like American infants to containment per se. That is, we have yet to test whether Korean infants categorize any kind of containment, tight or loose, as different from support (a project Choi is currently investigating). My hunch is that they will. Because infants show little to no comprehension of these spatial relational terms until around 18 months, it seems unlikely that language would have already played a major role in the categorization of these relations as early as 9 months, so I would expect all young infants to perform about the same.

Bootstrapping Into Syntax With Image-Schemas

Both objects and spatial relations can be seen, and so in some sense they are more obvious than grammatical relations, which are truly unobservable. Grammar belongs exclusively to language, not to events; it serves the needs of communication for both production and comprehension in a linear sequential medium (Bates et al., 1991) and indeed may have developed because of those needs (Batali, in press).[4] Nothing comparable to word order of subject, verb, and object exists in events, nor does tense, aspect, mood, or verb transitivity; these are not observables but rather distinctions that aid communication of information about events, such as the thematic roles played by the various objects involved, whether the events took place in the past or present, whether they were completed or not, and so forth. All languages use some combination of morphemes to express aspects of the relations between objects and actions, as well as the perspective of the speaker in relation to the events being described. So we need to ask how infants conceptualize notions that become grammaticized, such as transitive versus intransitive verbs or the past tense. Such grammatical structures must rest on some conceptual basis in order to be used productively. What are infants analyzing about events that enables them to learn syntax in anything other than as a kind of patterning of familiar words?

Psychologists and linguists from a number of different perspectives have discussed the conceptual aspects of early syntactical learning (e.g., Bates & MacWhinney, 1982; Bloom, 1999; Macnamara, 1982; Schlesinger, 1988; Tomasello, 1992), although they vary in how important they consider them to be in learning grammatical structure. Macnamara (1982) suggested that "the child climbs to grammar on a semantic ladder and then kicks the ladder away. Though semantics gets him off the ground, it cannot carry him all the way. Ultimately linguistic rules must take over the initial sortings of words . . ." (p. 134). Schlesinger (1988), on the other hand, doubted that the semantic boat that gets the child to the shore of language understanding will be sunk upon landing, because it can still be helpful in exploring the new territory. I wish to add only a few words to this much discussed topic here, primarily to stress how well the image-schematic preverbal notions discussed in chapters 4 and 5 dovetail with early syntactical learning (Mandler, 1992a; Tomasello, 1992). In line with Macnamara's comment, this is in no sense a claim that preverbal conceptualization accounts for all such learning. As Maratsos (1983) noted, even if formal categories such as "noun" and "verb" begin as representations of objects and actions, they must eventually become defined by the grammatical operations in which they participate.

Furthermore, aside from whatever innate proclivities for language structuring exist and learning how word types function, "conceptless" pattern learning plays an important role. Some years ago, Gleitman and Wanner (1992) suggested that infants use prosodic information to help them discover phrasal boundaries, and Morgan and Newport (1981) showed that without such information adults have trouble learning an artificial language. More recently, Marcus, Vijayan, Bandi Rao, and Vishton (1999) showed that 7-month-olds easily learn a sequential series of syllables, such as *la di la*, which they then generalize to the same pattern applied to new syllables, such as *do si do*, and discriminate from different patterns such as *do si si*. No meaning is required for this sort of learning—only pattern generalization. It is procedural learning, no different in principle from pigeons learning to differentiate patterns in which all the elements are the same or different (see chapter 6). Similarly, Saffran, Aslin, and Newport (1996) showed that 8-month-olds rapidly learned to segment words by responding to the different conditional probabilities of sounds that occurred within and between words in an artificial language. One study with children is particularly interesting because 5- to 6-year-olds picked up these kinds of conditional probabilities from a background speech stream of an artificial language while they were engaged in a coloring task, indicating that this kind of learning does not require attention (Saffran, Newport, Aslin, Tunick, & Barrueco, 1997). Of course, this kind of pattern learning is not exclusive to audition: As we saw in chapter 10, Smith (1984) showed that 5-month-olds learned complexly structured visual sequences in just a few trials. Meaningful rules are not required for these sorts of implicit learning, and they can be implemented easily in computer simulations (Dominey & Ramus, 2000; Kuhne et al., 2000; Sirois, Buckingham, & Shultz, 2000).

In addition to statistical learning, however, early conceptual understanding also gives us clues as to how the new language learner begins to get a toehold on the ladder leading to syntactical understanding. Although grammatical notions are in some sense even more abstract than spatial relations, they do specify a conceptual framework or, as Talmy

(1988) put it, a skeletal structure or scaffolding for the conceptual material that is being expressed. For the simplest kind of declarative sentence, the global domain-level concepts such as animal and vehicle that were used to give meaning to perceptual categories of objects can be useful in beginning to formulate such structures. The image-schemas that give the meaning "animate thing" to dog and cat can also be used to frame sentence structure, that is, to provide the relational notions that allow sentences to be built up. For example, once the meanings are formed for animate objects as things that move themselves and cause other things to move, one has arrived at a simple concept of agent. Similarly, once the meanings are formed for inanimate objects as things that don't move by themselves but are caused to move, one has arrived at a simple concept of patient or object. It may be because the earliest meanings are themselves abstract and relational that abstract linguistic notions such as agent (the doer) and patient (the done-to) can be formed so easily. In any case, the research described in chapters 4 and 5 shows that notions of caused versus uncaused actions, agents and patients, and goals, begin to be formed in the first year.

As we have discussed, what agents do and what is done to patients is crucial to early conceptual interpretation. It is for this reason that verbs in particular are important in the linguistic expression of the structure of events. As Tomasello put it:

> The verb *give*, for example is used to designate an event involving at least three entities with well-defined roles—giver, thing given, and person given to—each of which undergoes a specific change of state. Because conceptual roles such as these are an integral part of verb meaning, the conceptual situations underlying verbs can be seen as providing a kind of "frame" for structuring larger linguistic expressions such as sentences. The semantic structure of verbs thus contains what have been called "grammatical valences," and verbs are therefore responsible for much of the grammatical structure of a language. This obviates the need in many cases for more abstract syntactic principles and rules. . . .The grammatical valences contained in children's first verbs simply "beg" to be completed into sentences. (Tomasello, 1992, pp. 6–7)

Roles such as giver, thing given, and receiver are image-schematic notions that can be seen even in early two-word speech, before the onset of specifically grammatical markings. Semantic properties such as action (or path), agent, location (e.g., end of path), and possession have been claimed to form the defining properties for many early grammatical categories. These are all basic image-schematic notions. Brown (1973), Bowerman (1973), and others analyzed two-word utterances in English-speaking children into the following relational expressions: agent performs action, action gets performed on an object, agent in relation to object, possessor—possessed, action at or to a location or goal of action, object at a location, and attributing something to an object. Appearance and disappearance of objects, as well as their recurrence, were noted as well. With the exception of attribution, these are all PATH notions—emphasizing animates acting on inanimates or aspects of the paths themselves, such as their onset.

Similar comments can be made about the first grammatical markings. Brown (1973) studied a set of 14 grammatical particles as they began to appear toward the end of the second year in three English-speaking children. He followed only a subset of the grammatical forms used, choosing ones that could be scored and that were frequent in parental speech. There are more that might be considered grammatical; for instance, *up* and *down* are early and are one way that English-speaking children typically express types of motion. But for the 14 he studied, the order of acquisition for the first 6 was the following: First came the present progressive (*-ing*). This form expresses an ongoing PATH. The second and third were *in* and *on*, expressing CONTAINMENT and SUPPORT, respectively. The fourth was the plural *-s*, expressing the individuation of objects as one versus more than one. The fifth was the irregular past (*broke, ran*). These irregulars are among the most common past forms in English. The point here is not that the irregular morphemes are learned first but that marking of completed action (END-OF-PATH) is early.

The sixth grammatical particle was the possessive *-s*. It has been suggested that the earliest meaning of possession is END-OF-PATH, in the sense that where objects come to rest is where they belong, and possessors are animate ends of paths (Slobin, 1985; Smiley & Huttenlocher, 1995). From observations of a 2-year-old's use of *my*, I suggested it appeared to be a request for transfer of the item in question from elsewhere to the child (Mandler, 1992a). This usage can be contrasted with children using their own names in conjunction with an item (as in "Jean's book") to express possession in a sense closer to that of adults. This slight misconception of possessive terms may come about because an image-schema of a path from elsewhere to the child has not yet been projected into the social realm. For example, Mills (1985) found that German children sometimes conflate locative and possessive functions, using the German *zu* ("to") to express both going to and belongs to.

The other grammatical particles, coming somewhat later, seem for the most part more like pattern learning pure and simple rather than meaning based, such as the various forms of *be* and the third-person singular -*s*. The regular -*ed* form appeared early, too, as well as the determiners *a* and *the*, but the latter were not necessarily correctly used; whether there was any understanding of their discourse status seems dubious.

Brown did not find the order of acquisition of these morphemes related to phonological salience; for example, the various -*s* particles came in at different times. He suggested that either the meanings varied in difficulty, the number of grammatical aspects required might determine this order of acquisition, or both. For example, -*ing* is fairly straightforward vis-à-vis ongoing activity, but to add the -*be* to it, one has to choose among *is*, *are*, or *am*. Maratsos (1983) suggested the order might be determined by semantic complexity, but ideas about relative complexity are only intuitive. For example, he didn't think that *a* and *the* are any more difficult than *in* and *on*. But *a* and *the* represent discourse functions and so are less likely to be part of infants' conceptual repertoire than basic spatial relations such as *in* and *on*.

Verb acquisition provides another example of the usefulness of image-schemas in understanding language. The first verbs that children learn describe paths of various sorts rather than states. Children don't at first learn verbs like *think* (a mental state) or *sit* (a physical state). Rather, they learn verbs like *fall, run, break*, and *go*. The "shapes" of these paths are represented by image-schemas (Golinkoff, Hirsh-Pasek, Mervis, Frawley, & Parillo, 1995). These specific PATH schemas are more particular than the paths that differentiate animate from inanimate motion but are otherwise similar in kind. Typical examples are *fall*, which specifies a downward path, or *walk*, which specifies a forward horizontal path, but which in both cases leave other details aside. These image-schemas allow children to ignore the details of a given event and so generalize the use of a word from one instance to the next.

There are other aspects of verb learning that seem more abstract and more complex than relations such as containment or verb meanings, and also less intuitively spatial in their meaning, for example, transitive and intransitive verbs. Transitive verbs require two arguments (subject and object) and typically express an agent causing some effect on an object (i.e., caused motion). Intransitive verbs require only an agent and typically express self-motion. Languages vary as to how they differentiate these verb types. In some languages the agent is marked with either a prefix or a suffix, in others the object being acted on is marked, in others the verb itself requires a marker, and in still others there is no marking, but different verbs are required for the same action, depending on whether it is transitive or intransitive (see the example of *open* in Korean, discussed later).

The distinction between transitive and intransitive verbs might seem difficult for a young language learner to pick up. However, to the extent that this grammatical notion reflects image-schemas of animacy, inanimacy, and causality, it shouldn't present the child with undue difficulty. Image-schemas such as ANIMATE MOTION, CAUSED MOTION, AGENT, INANIMATE MOTION, and CAUSED-TO-MOVE-INANIMATE are exactly the kind of meanings needed to master the distinction between transitive and intransitive verb phrases. Abstract though it may be and marked in a variety of ways in different languages, this distinction is universally one of the earliest grammatical forms to be acquired. I assume that the reason for this is that the ideas it expresses are among those that preverbal children have universally mastered by the time language begins.

For example, Korean uses different verb forms for transitive verbs that involve caused motion and for intransitive verbs that involve self-motion (Choi & Bowerman, 1991), two early image-schemas. English doesn't mark these distinctions: We use the same verb to say either that "the door opened" or "Mary opened the door." But Korean uses different words for these two "opens," and Korean children do not confuse them. Indeed, Choi and Bowerman did not find any examples of confusing these two verb forms. So learning this grammatical distinction in Korean appears to rest on a straightforward match between the underlying image-schemas of caused and self-motion and the linguistic distinctions, making learning rapid and easy.

Of course, languages don't always cooperate, and when a language does violate image-schematic notions, we should predict particular errors in acquisition. Dan Slobin (1985) gave an example in the case of transitivity. He pointed out that in early language the child uses transitive marking at first only when talking about someone manipulating objects, as in "John throws the ball." Only later is it extended to less prototypical cases of transitivity, such as "John pushes Mary." Another way of putting this is to say that children first mark transitivity only when talking about an event in which an agent acts on an inanimate object, not when an agent acts on another animate. This kind of underextension error is relatively minor but indicates that a grammatical notion combining several image-schemas in a complex way may require some trial and error before the particular set the language expresses is mastered.

Furthermore, sometimes languages can be so uncooperative as not to express a notion the child wishes to say, so the child invents a form to do so. This is slightly different from the case of Dutch children inventing a usage of *uit* to include any instance of removal. Children can also invent grammatical forms that do not exist at all in the language they are learning. E. Clark (2001) discusses several examples. She calls these forms emergent linguistic categories and distinguishes them from robust categories. This is the distinction between (a) concepts the child tries to express that a language does not grammaticize and for which there are no conventional expressions and (b) concepts that do receive conventional expression in the language. Expressions of emergent categories tend to be fleeting, sometimes lasting only for a few weeks, as the child invents a way to express certain notions the language does not support; robust categories, of course, are not only easily learned but continue to be reinforced by the input. So, for instance, an English-speaking child might for a brief period use different first-person pronouns (*I* and *me*) to express degree of agency, with one of these forms used to express a situation in which the child has control over an action and the other to express less or no control (Budwig, 1989). Another example Clark (2001) gives is the use of different adjectival forms (such as -*y* and -*ed*) to express permanent versus temporary properties of an object. As Clark points out, both of these are notions that appear in many of the world's languages, but not in English.

Many of the grammatical aspects of language seem impossibly abstract for the very young child to master. But when the concepts that underlie them are analyzed in terms of notions that children have already conceptualized, not only does the linguistic problem facing the child seem more tractable but also the types of errors that are made become more predictable. The invention of grammatical forms to express conceptual notions that are salient in a young child's conceptualization of events seems especially informative.

The importance of preverbal concepts to language learning has become somewhat submerged of late by the view that language teaches thought that has begun to dominate the field (see, for example, several of the chapters in Bowerman & Levinson, 2001). The data presented in the previous section make it obvious that there is a potent interaction between preverbal concepts and the particulars of the semantic system being learned. Although it is clear that language-specific semantics begin to be learned fairly early in the acquisition period, the mistakes children make (overextensions, underextensions, and just plain errors) are often not obvious in studies of language production. Unfortunately, production remains the most common measure of language acquisition. We must be careful not to neglect the role played by the learner's comprehension of what is being communicated, which highlights their conceptualizations. If we are ultimately to understand how children learn to express the semantics of their language, we will need to understand the conceptual foundations on which those semantics rest. The value of studying these preverbal concepts is that they give us information about how children discover the patterns of their language and at the same time tell us something about the conceptual resources children bring to bear on the problem. They have the further advantage of helping to disentangle the issues discussed in this chapter, namely, the interaction between the nature of the linguistic input children hear and the conceptual resources they use to make that input meaningful. Overextension and underextension errors and emergent categories help us put these matters in perspective. As Clark (2001) puts it: "because it may be hard to distinguish whether the salience of a robust category stems from its consistent encoding in the input language, from its conceptual basis, or from the combination of the two, emergent categories offer important evidence: their salience can only stem from their conceptual basis since they receive at best minimal support, and at worst no support, in the language children hear" (p. 386). The fact that emergent categories drop out of usage is, of course, another indication of the growing influence that language has in making the child's thought conform to that of the community.

12

Consciousness and Conclusions

. . . in which I revisit memory, categorization, and language acquisition for the purpose of relating consciousness to brain functioning, as well as to re-emphasize the role of consciousness in conceptual development and the importance for infant-adult comparisons of clarifying whether conscious processing is required by a given task. Consciousness is an extensively worked topic these days, but because it is rarely addressed in infancy research, this chapter is a baby step toward filling that gap. This discussion leads to a reprisal of the most important conclusions to be drawn from this book.

[The] dissociation between declarative and nondeclarative knowledge indicates that the parallel brain systems supporting learning and memory differ in their capacity for affording awareness of what is learned.
(Reber & Squire, 1994)

Throughout this book I have alluded to the role of conscious awareness in infant cognitive development. I think most psychologists agree that the distinction between conscious and unconscious processing is important for understanding the adult mind. It is no less important for understanding infancy. The various strands of evidence I have discussed all point to important differences in the way information is processed, depending on whether it is conceptualized by the declarative system or remains unattended and automatically processed. As discussed in chapter 3, unconscious processing is fast, parallel, and unselective, whereas conscious processing is slow, serial, and selective. These differences mean we need to worry about which tasks require infants to engage in conscious interpretation and which do not. Even in studies of adults, this distinction, although accepted, is not always honored. It is respected in the memory field, but in some other areas, such as language processing and perception, it is often not mentioned.

As Piaget's theory emphasized, it matters whether the knowledge being acquired is conceptual knowledge that can be brought to mind and thought about or perceptual/motor knowledge that is inaccessible. Even though we reject his stage theory of knowledge acquisition, we must be careful not to lose that insight. Until we routinely specify exactly what kind of knowledge we are dealing with in a given task we ask infants to perform, we may not be able to answer questions about the processes under study or whether domain-specific or domain-general learning is required.

The defining difference between procedural and declarative knowledge is accessibility to conscious awareness. Many psychologists still resist talking about consciousness, but how can we say we have understood the mind if we cannot address one of its most distinctive characteristics? Fortunately, there is growing interest in consciousness in cognitive science, along with its neural bases (see volume 79 of *Cognition*, 2001). As Jack and Shallice (2001) in that issue pointed out, 30 years ago the attempt to produce a scientific account of consciousness was "a somewhat disreputable exercise indulged in by just a few (such as Mandler, 1975; Posner & Klein, 1973, and Shallice, 1972)." Now, according to Moscovitch (2000): "Having been banished from scientific investigation for nearly a century, the study of consciousness has made a triumphant return and secured a prominent place in research in cognitive neuroscience" (p. 609). It seems that it took the specification of possible loci of conscious processing in the brain to make consciousness respectable at last.

We now know that a great deal of cognitive processing is not conscious. In addition to the examples I have mentioned in this book, such as perceptual priming, learning probabilities of occurrence, perceptual schema formation, and inattentional blindness, there are the following examples: In unconscious perceptual priming (Marcel, 1983), words that are consciously interpreted in one meaning (for example, palm as a tree) also prime other unconsciously aroused meanings (for example, palm of the hand). In blindsight (Weiskrantz, 1997), blind patients report they cannot see a stimulus but are above chance in determining where it is. In hemineglect (Bisiach, 1988; Driver & Vuilleumier, 2001), patients with brain lesions who are unaware of stimuli impinging on one area of the visual field nevertheless show residual processing of these stimuli. As still another example, perceptual judgments of the size of an object can be distorted by visual illusions, but these distortions do not affect accuracy in reaching for it (Aglioti, DeSouza, & Goodale, 1995). In all of these examples, effective visual and/or motor processing is shown to take place completely outside of awareness. A particularly dramatic example is Tony Marcel's (1993) task, in which people are asked to both press a button and say if they see a light presented. When the light occurs at their threshold for detection, they show marked dissociations between what they say and what they do.

Given the importance of the distinction between conscious and non-conscious processing in understanding adult performance, it is a bit surprising that the issue has hardly been raised in infancy research. That is presumably due to the difficulty in measuring conscious awareness in infants. Nevertheless, there are some tasks that we give to babies whose characteristics can be determined from adult research. Insofar as these require conscious processing in adults, they provide a prima facie case for the same kind of processing in infants. I have mentioned several of these throughout this book and will briefly reprise them here with the issue of conscious awareness at the forefront.

Before beginning, I remind the reader that this book concerns whether and when conscious experience is interpreted conceptually. It does not address the issue of experience of sensations or qualia per se—what is sometimes called phenomenality (Block, 2001)—but instead discusses whether a person is consciously interpreting the meaning of something being perceived or consciously recalling a past event. For example, as I discussed in chapter 3, if people are asked to cross out all the vowels in a list of words, they may never become aware of the meaning of the words, even though, of course, they are conscious that they are monitoring the letters. Because they do not attend to the meaning of the words, they are later unable to recall them. On an everyday level, if I am thoroughly attending to what you say, I may well not notice details of your appearance and so will not be able to recall afterward what you were wearing or even if you wore glasses. Priming studies show that such peripheral information is processed, but it does not reach awareness. In all the procedural tasks discussed here, the nonconsciously processed material seems to lack a conceptual interpretation, whereas the consciously processed material is conceptualized.

It is worthwhile re-emphasizing that conscious interpretation of objects and events is a conceptual process. Not all experience is so interpreted. Sensorimotor procedures can be learned and deployed without conceptual interpretation, even though they are consciously (phenomenally) experienced. In addition, of course, much processing that results from conscious interpretation is itself not conscious. For example, we are not aware of the increased activation that is responsible for semantic (conceptual) priming (Marcel, 1983), even though understanding the word or words took place in consciousness. So we must distinguish at least two kinds of consciousness: phenomenal sensations (qualia) and conceptually interpreted awareness of things and events. We may also need to distinguish these two forms of consciousness from reflective consciousness, in which we reflect on our own awareness (e.g., Block, 2001; Marcel, 1993), but such reflection seems unlikely to play much of a role in infant cognition.[1] Conceptualization may be only a subset of conscious processing, but for purposes of understanding the development of conceptual categorization, recall, and language acquisition, the kind of consciousness involved is conceptualized experience, and it is that aspect of consciousness I consider here.

Conscious and Nonconscious Processes in Memory

I begin with memory phenomena, because that is the area in which conscious and nonconscious processing have been most studied and for which we have the most evidence, both psychological and neurological. As discussed in chapters 3 and 10, there is procedural memory (nondeclarative memory), which comes in several varieties, none of which requires explicit, conscious interpretation. Classic examples are Piaget's sensorimotor learning, visual and auditory pattern learning, learning of visual expectations, and both operant and classical conditioning. Declarative memory, on the other hand, allows bringing to awareness a previously experienced event or learned fact about the world. This kind of memory is illustrated by recall and recognition. As discussed in earlier chapters, by recognition

I refer specifically to the conscious awareness of prior occurrence that enables someone to say that a given stimulus has been experienced before. This kind of memory is conceptual in nature and uses brain systems different from those used for procedural memory.

Research to date suggests that the development of visual expectations depends upon striatal structures, and acquisition of conditioned responding depends upon the cerebellum and some of the deep nuclei in the brainstem (Nelson, 1997). These kinds of learning begin early in infancy. In contrast, the ability to recall or explicitly recognize something as having been experienced before depends on a circuit involving medial temporal lobe structures (the hippocampus and surrounding cortices) and higher cortical association areas, including the prefrontal cortex (Mishkin & Appenzeller, 1987; Squire & Zola-Morgan, 1991). Although the medial temporal lobe develops early (Nelson, 1997), the neocortex and its reciprocal connections with the hippocampus develop more slowly (Bachevalier & Mishkin, 1994). The best available evidence suggests that in infants these various components of the declarative memory system begin to coalesce in the second half of the first year (Carver & Bauer, 2001; Carver, Bauer, & Nelson, 2000). Prefrontal cortex in particular appears to serve the function of retrieval of declarative memories, and it is also implicated in recall of temporal order information. One prominent theory of the processes that are involved (Moscovitch, 1995) states that when an event is consciously processed, the medial temporal lobe and related structures bind into the memory trace the neocortical elements that gave rise to the conscious experience in the first place. Thus, assuming the various neural connections are in place, consciousness becomes part of the memory trace itself. At retrieval, then, both consciousness and the content of the event are reactivated.

As discussed in chapter 10, beginning around 9 months of age, infants can recall event sequences they have previously observed. The task that has been used is deferred imitation, which, as we have seen, cannot be accomplished by amnesic adults, providing prima facie evidence that conscious recollection is required to carry out this task. Six-month-olds can reproduce a single act after 24 hours, although this does not require remembering temporal order, which is part of normal memory for most events. It may be, therefore, that recall of ordered events requires some brain development not yet present in 6-month-olds. However, at least by

9 months, infants have developed a declarative memory system that contains some well-organized and long-lasting event representations that can be brought to mind. What about younger infants? Can they also consciously access past experiences from a declarative memory system? At present, we do not have any evidence earlier than about 6 months one way or the other.

Carolyn Rovee-Collier (1997) made a determined but ultimately futile attempt to distinguish implicit and explicit memory in infancy by comparing variables that are thought to affect these two kinds of memory differentially in adults and assessing whether they also differentially affect the two kinds of memory in infancy. She used two operant conditioning tasks and measured retention of the learned response with or without "reinstatement" (that is, reproducing some part of the conditioning environment before retention is assessed). She claimed these tasks measure explicit and implicit memory, respectively. Unfortunately, it is exceedingly difficult to equate these two infant conditioning tasks with the classic tasks measuring implicit and explicit memory in the adult memory literature (for example, stem completion and free recall). In the long run, the only necessary and sufficient condition for the difference has to do with conscious awareness. Rovee-Collier (1997) insists that this requirement is untenable from a developmental perspective, because preverbal infants can't tell us whether they are aware of the past and therefore their consciousness is "solely a matter of philosophical speculation" (p. 469). As an infancy researcher, I understand her frustration in this regard, but nevertheless consciousness is the ultimate criterion of explicit memory. This is why McDonough and I resorted to the study of amnesics—not because we thought that infants were like amnesics (far from it!) but because we could use amnesic performance to show that a nonverbal task such as deferred imitation *requires* conscious awareness of the past. As I discussed in chapter 10, however, at present we have no comparable test to show that conscious awareness of the past accompanies dishabituation to a novel stimulus or retention of conditioned foot kicking. In particular, I cannot see any justification for saying that the retention of a conditioned foot-kicking response—with or without a reinstatement cue—requires conscious awareness. It may be that the only way to test Rovee-Collier's contention that young infants in conditioning tasks are demonstrating conscious memory for a past event is to see if amnesic adults show retention of conditioned foot kicking or fail, as they do on deferred imitation tasks.

Similar kinds of problems have arisen over the years in our understanding of recognition memory in infancy. Because infants respond differently to old and new stimuli, it has often been assumed that there is a straightforward continuum in the development of recognition memory from infancy to adulthood. However, as discussed in chapter 10, we measure recognition in infants by a classic measure of procedural memory (habituation) that does not require awareness, and we measure recognition in adults by a classic measure of declarative memory—namely, by asking them to make a conscious judgment of old or new. This should certainly make us suspicious. We can't conclude anything about a continuum when we use different measures at different points. The continuum that extends from the baby habituation data to the adult is *repetition priming*, or the activation of previously experienced material. This is a classic measure of implicit memory and one that does not require conscious awareness of the past (Squire & Knowlton, 2000). Virtually from birth, babies habituate to stimuli they have repeatedly seen and process the same stimuli on a later occasion more rapidly. The same thing happens with adults; for example, words that have been recently studied tend to be read more rapidly and used spontaneously in stem completion tasks. The difference is that normal adults can say that they have seen the stimuli before, whereas amnesic adults, who show normal priming, cannot (Graf et al., 1984). This is not just a phenomenon of brain damage. Even normal adults, when their meaningful processing of words is disrupted by instructions to look for vowels, look like amnesics in that they cannot recall the words either, in spite of also showing normal priming (Graf, Mandler, & Haden, 1982).

Adult priming tasks are like the habituation–dishabituation or habituation/preferential-looking tasks used with infants in that they show the effects of prior exposure, independently of conscious awareness. Similarly, the galvanic skin response to familiar stimuli has been used to show a continuum in implicit recognition memory in the absence of overt recognition from children to adults (Newcombe & Fox, 1994). What we do not have at this point is evidence of conscious recognition memory in infants younger than about 6 months. Needless to say, I am not suggesting that babies have no declarative memory. On the contrary, the recall data show that they do at least from 6 months of age, and quite possibly earlier. It is just that it is difficult to obtain positive evidence for declarative memory in early infancy when recognition, rather than recall, tests are used.

McKee and Squire (1993) suggested that when a delay is included, habituation/preferential-looking tests do measure explicit memory. Even young infants show the effects of exposure to visual stimuli, typically with a novelty preference (Fagan, 1973), although sometimes after long delays recognition is expressed by a preference for the familiar stimulus (Bahrick, Hernandez, & Pickens, 1997). In the only study I know of to test whether conscious memory might be demonstrated by preferential looking after a delay, McKee and Squire (1993) found that elderly amnesic patients with hippocampal damage who were familiarized with a set of pictures looked longer at new pictures after a delay of 2 minutes, but this novelty effect disappeared by 1 hour. Control subjects looked longer at new stimuli at the 1-hour delay but not after 4 hours. The relatively poor performance of the amnesic subjects suggested to the authors that declarative memory might be involved in this kind of preferential-looking test. However, the study also showed that the looking task was more difficult than an explicit recognition task in which subjects had to point to the new pictures. This is a surprising result, because usually tests of implicit recognition are easier than explicit tests. In addition, the amnesic subjects, although poorer than controls, showed good *explicit* recognition of novel stimuli at an hour delay, even though they did not show longer looking at them. These unusual patterns make the data extremely difficult to interpret.

To further complicate adult–infant comparisons, in young infants novelty preferences may be reflexive or obligatory in nature, which is not the case for older infants or adults. Nelson and Collins (1991) presented familiar and unfamiliar stimuli frequently or infrequently to 6-month-olds. Using event-related potential (ERP) measures, they found that the infants responded as much to the frequency of occurrence of a stimulus as to its familiarity, suggesting that nonspecific novelty detection might play a role in preferential-looking measures. Not until 8 months did ERP data differentiate familiar and novel stimuli regardless of frequency of exposure (Nelson & Collins, 1992). Because the hippocampus may be involved in novelty preferences as well as explicit recognition in infancy,

Nelson (1997) suggested that the form of "explicit" memory that is dependent on the hippocampus early in life differs qualitatively from that observed later in the first year; he calls it "pre-explicit" memory. In sum, preferential looking after a delay is a troublesome measure to interpret if one is interested in its relation to conscious memory. Although it can be used with both infants and adults, it is open to question as to whether the same underlying process is involved. Furthermore, the evidence that it taps declarative memory is dubious. It is unlikely that newborns' or very young infants' preferential looking at a novel stimulus after habituation implies conscious awareness of prior occurrence. As discussed in chapter 10, we are on firmer ground when we use recall as our measure.

Conscious and Nonconscious Processes in Categorization

Categorization is an area of research that I believe has been severely hampered by not making a distinction between procedural and declarative representation. In the adult categorization literature, there are continual arguments over whether categorization is rule based or based on similarity (see, for example, volume 65 of *Cognition*), and these arguments tend to spill over even into infancy studies. Various theories have been proposed and tested in different laboratories using entirely different stimuli—varying from random dot patterns and geometric forms, through disease symptoms and professions, to "things to take on a fishing trip." This hodgepodge of stimuli is like comparing apples and oranges (although, of course, apples and oranges are both fruits—the ambiguity about the nature of categories lurks in our folk beliefs as well as in our scientific ones). It is implausible that identical processes are involved as one moves from categorizing purely perceptual patterns to categorizing complex conceptual knowledge. Indeed, we have seen evidence in this book that the processes are not the same.

As discussed in chapters 6 and 8, there are at least two kinds of categories formed in infancy. First, forming a perceptual category or schema operates beyond the bounds of consciousness. This releases the processor from the bottleneck that consciousness imposes, namely, a restriction to a serial process that handles relatively small amounts of information at a time (G. Mandler, 1975, 2002b). This lack of restriction means that a great deal of information can be processed in parallel. Unfortunately, all too many perceptual categorization studies in infancy have involved either faces or animals (which, of course, also have faces), and we have some reason to believe that faces are processed differently from other stimuli. For example, eyes may automatically attract attention. Nevertheless, even with animals as stimuli, infants rapidly take in a great deal of information in a very few exposures. As one example, Mareschal et al.'s (2002) analysis of young infants' discriminating dogs from cats indicates that many aspects of their faces are encoded in parallel. Because lack of awareness of such schema formation is the case for adults, there is little reason to assume it would be different in infancy. This kind of categorization is part of the visual input system; it is automatic, it does not require attentive processing, and the information it uses is not accessible to consciousness (see chapter 3).

Second, there are conceptual categories, which are concerned with setting up kinds, that is, with formulating the sorts of things that dogs or tables are. Forming a concept is not automatic but rather is a focused and limited process. It appears to be serial in nature, with new information being added bit by bit, rather than accumulating simultaneously. As adults, we do our conscious thinking, planning, and problem solving with the large repertoire of concepts we have built up over the years. However, infants face the task of getting this repertoire started. As they begin to encounter animals, vehicles, furniture, and so forth, they must form some idea of the meaning of these things. I have suggested that through perceptual meaning analysis they consciously analyze what objects are doing. The results of this process—interpretations of the world that suffuse the mind with meaning—are also accessible to consciousness. Because conceptual categories do pass through the bottleneck of consciousness, they are selective. This is one of the reasons that early concepts are broad and missing physical detail.

These two kinds of categories represent procedural and declarative knowledge, respectively, and differ in all the ways that I summarized in chapter 8. Here I merely highlight their characteristics relevant to consciousness and their possible neural underpinnings. The most important difference, as I have repeatedly stressed, is that the contents of perceptual categories are inaccessible to conscious awareness, whereas the contents of concepts are accessible. The claim is that if infants could talk, they could tell you about their concepts, whereas even adults have little knowledge about their percepts. The conceptual knowledge that animals can move themselves, for example, is explicit. We know that this is so by 3 years of age. Massey and Gelman (1988) showed that children of this age are consciously aware that a statue of an animal cannot walk up a hill by itself. They aren't very good at putting this awareness into words—sophistication in explaining one's ideas is a slowly developing skill indeed—but they have no trouble making the judgment that statues of animals can't move themselves, whereas real animals can. We should not be surprised, then, if this awareness is also present when infants do not allow vehicles to eat or sleep. It is not necessary for them to know *why* vehicles don't eat to make the conscious judgment that they do not.

There is by now a great deal of evidence indicating that adults categorize on several very different bases, in some cases responding to perceptual similarity and in other cases to explicit rules. There is also evidence that different neural circuits are involved in categorization tasks based on explicit rules versus those that are based on memory for exemplars (Smith, Patalano, & Jonides, 1998; Ullman et al., 1997). For example, Smith et al. (1998) did a positron-emission tomography (PET) study in which subjects were either in a categorization condition in which they needed to rely on memory for exemplars or in a rule-based condition in which they needed to follow a rule. While they were engaged in these categorization tasks, brain scanning was carried out. The resulting images showed distinct areas of activation involved in the two kinds of categorization, in addition to a number of common areas. In particular, the distinctive areas in the rule condition were in a region of parietal cortex associated with selective attention, as well as in prefrontal cortex, an area associated with applying rules.[2] The common areas and those exclusive to the exemplar memory condition were mostly in the visual cortex.

Smith et al. (1998) noted that it might be difficult to assess whether the memory-based results they found were due to exemplar similarity or prototype similarity. In terms of implicit and explicit processes, this difference matters. Conscious memory for specific instances requires declarative memory and is damaged in amnesia, whereas memory for prototypes is an implicit perceptual process that is spared in amnesia (Kolodny,

1994). However, we still have relatively little hard evidence in most categorization tasks about the extent to which implicit and explicit memory is being used. Furthermore, there is no easy equation to be made between conscious memory for exemplars and exemplar models of categorization (e.g., Nosofsky, 1992). Clearly, work is needed on this issue. Nevertheless, even though we don't know the exact processes used in building perceptual schemas as compared with forming concepts, we do know that different processes and brain regions are involved in different kinds of categorization.

Just as many of the arguments in the adult literature are fading away as it becomes clear that there is more than one basis for categorization, it is to be hoped the same thing will happen in the developmental literature. The failure to recognize that there is more than one basis for categorization has led to superfluous debate. In chapter 6, I described the theory that the first categories are perceptual and at the "basic level" and that only later are superordinate categories learned (Rosch et al., 1976). When we showed that infants form global (superordinate) categories of animals and furniture and in some cases do so before achieving "basic-level" categorization, in order to maintain the traditional view it became necessary to find a perceptual basis to account for our findings. At first, it was suggested that global categorization was also based on the perceptual similarity of animals to each other, but that couldn't account for earlier global categorization because there is less similarity among animals or furniture as classes than among individual animal or furniture kinds. Later it was suggested that rather than there being a "basic-to-global" trend in perceptual development, there is a "global-to-basic" sequence instead (Quinn & Johnson, 2000). Having spent several years doing research showing that there is more than one kind of categorization, each with a different developmental course, I described this turn of the argument as "winning the battle but losing the war" (Mandler, 2000a). It was being proclaimed that, yes, global categories in infancy precede basic-level ones, but this is merely a characteristic of perceptual development, and so there is still no need to talk about anything other than perceptual categories in infancy. To my mind, this is a difficult view to maintain in light of the research discussed in this book. Furthermore, if there is more than one kind of categorization and they have different developmental courses, such an "either-or" question as "Does categorization proceed from a global level to a basic level or from a basic level to a global level?" can't be answered in a sensible way. On the other hand, once the view that there is more than one kind of categorization is accepted, this kind of controversy should disappear.

Conscious and Nonconscious Processes in Language Acquisition

Almost more than any other area, this is a topic in which the distinction between implicit and explicit knowledge is vital but rarely discussed. Consider the work of Marcus et al. (1999), described in the previous chapter, showing that 7-month-old infants easily learn a series of syllables, such as *la di la*, which they then generalize to the same pattern applied to new syllables, such as *do si do*, and discriminate from different patterns such as *do si si*. The authors talk about this as a kind of existence proof for the ability of young infants to learn abstract grammarlike structure. But no linguistic meaning or anything special to language is required for this sort of learning—only the automatic pattern formation and generalization that are typical of the many kinds of procedural learning that take place in infancy. Rule learning is not required for this sort of implicit learning, and as discussed earlier, it is easy to implement in a pattern-learning computer simulation (Sirois et al., 2000). Segmentation of speech sounds and developing expectations about their regularities are also present in nonhuman primates, also suggesting that the mechanisms involved are not specific to the language capacity (Hauser, Newport, & Aslin, 2001).

As discussed in the last chapter, a good deal of learning about grammatical patterns takes place in this way. Expectations are built up about the orders in which word classes appear, without having to attend to the order per se. The work on learning artificial grammars shows that grammatical patterns can be learned without memory for the lexical items involved. For example, Knowlton, Ramus, and Squire (1992) found a dissociation in amnesic patients between explicit memory for presented instances, which was poor, and judgments of grammaticality, which were

as good as for normal subjects. Even in the lexicon, irregular morpholog-
ical transformations, such as *went* being the past tense of *go*, seem to depend on declarative memory, whereas those transformations that are productive, such as the past tense *-ed*, appear to be supported by procedural
knowledge (Ullman, 2001). The rhythms and sequences of speech are exactly the sort of patterns that "come for free" in that they do not require
conscious processing; expectations of regularities are formed automatically. The language learner needs to attend to *went*, but not to *walked*.

Not only is pattern learning sometimes conflated with the acquisition of linguistic meaning but also there is a tendency in the field of word
learning to emphasize referential learning over all else, often overlook-
ing the difference between attaching a label to an object and the meaning of the label. As I mentioned in the last chapter, some connectionist
modeling of language learning makes the assumption that words are
mapped onto perception (e.g., Elman, 1990, 1993), missing the representation of meaning. But if our discussion of language concerns only associations between visual and verbal patterns, the whole issue of conceptual
and semantic meaning has been set aside. We learn not only the familiar
patterns of our language but also what those patterns mean, and nothing
in the patterning of *do si si* or of *determiner noun verb determiner noun* tells
us the conceptual content that is being expressed. Similarly, a child using
the term *dog* to refer to dogs tells us something about reference but not
necessarily about the sense of the term for the child. As we saw, the word
dog can be applied correctly and still have a different meaning for the
child than for the adult.

If we are to untangle the course of language acquisition, it is crucial
to differentiate nonconscious perceptual knowledge of language patterns
from conscious conceptual knowledge of what is being communicated.
Here is a dramatic example, taken from some interesting work that Sue
Carey did 20 years ago (Carey, 1982). She introduced 2- and 3-year olds
to a new color word, *chromium*, and studied their learning of this word.
The children's teacher introduced the term to them in one of several
contexts, such as asking for one of two identical but different-colored
trays: "Give me the chromium tray, not the red one, the chromium one."
A week or more later, they were tested to see whether they had learned
this new color term. All the children knew at least one color term at the
start of this study. About half of them learned the new term from this

exposure, although there were many incomplete meanings. Of interest for present purposes was the contrast Carey made between these data and those of Mabel Rice (1978). All of Carey's participants knew at least one color word, whereas Rice studied children of the same age who had *no* color terms. She tried to teach them *red* and *green*. As many as 2,000 trials, over a period of several weeks, were required for them to learn. As Carey put it, her studies showed that knowing one or two color words is as good as knowing nine or more as far as achieving a fast mapping for a new color word is concerned (Carey, 1982). Carey asked:

> The puzzle is this: What is the hump a child must surmount to learn that first color word? . . . We know that the infant perceives colors and so represents them, and that he can remember them. . . .The concept COLOR is definitionally and developmentally primitive by anybody's account: what is the process of going from COLOR to *color word* and making the latter available as a lexical organizer? No theory of lexical acquisition has even sketched an answer to this question.
> (p. 380)

My answer to the puzzle is that color is primitive only in the sense that encoding it is an automatic *procedure*, available from early in infancy. However, color is *not* accessible to the thinking mind until perceptual meaning analysis takes place. It is only after one or more colors have been consciously noticed and analyzed (for example, by contrasting apples and oranges, or apples and tomatoes) that an explicit concept of color is formed. Only when a color becomes declarative knowledge can children think about it and home in on the appropriate domain when they hear color terms used. Names get attached to declarative knowledge, not procedural knowledge. Perceptual meaning analysis identifies the domain for them, and only after that can they learn the correct mappings (*blue* to blue, *red* to red, and so forth), which takes further time (Shatz & Backscheider, 1999). Thus, even in a domain that seems purely perceptual, explicit conceptual knowledge appears to be required to learn appropriate names.

These are but three areas in infancy research in which it seems to be crucial to know whether nonconscious procedural or conscious declarative knowledge is involved: memory for events, categorization tasks, and language learning. I would suggest there are many more. For example, a still largely unaddressed issue in current research is the status of the knowledge that infants have about objects—not the difference between animals and vehicles, but objecthood itself. The data that Spelke and Baillargeon and their colleagues have collected, showing what infants know about solidity, substance, compressibility, inertia, the effects of gravity, and the like—what is the status of these kinds of knowing? Are these facts that infants can potentially consciously think or "reason" about? Or are they implicit knowledge that affects infants' expectations but not their conscious thought processes?

Work by Hood, Carey, and Prasada (2000) begins to address this issue. They did several experiments with 2-year-olds based on infant experiments done by Spelke, Breinlinger, Macomber, and Jacobson (1992). In one of the Spelke et al. experiments, 4-month-olds were familiarized to an object falling to a stage floor. Then they were shown a shelf placed above the floor. Next, a screen was lowered to hide the display, and the object was dropped again. Then the screen was removed, and the 4-month-olds were shown the object either sitting on the shelf (a possible outcome) or on the floor (an impossible outcome). The infants looked longer at the impossible display. Hood et al. (2000) found that 2-year-olds failed very similar tests, albeit they were asked to point or reach to where they expected the object to be.

Why should this be? I would say this is another example of the differences in processing required by an automatic looking task and one in which a person is asked to predict an outcome. Prediction as a task requirement ("Tell me where you think the object will be") is a conscious conceptual task, requiring activation of a model of the physical world, which is quite different from the procedural knowledge of how the world appears that makes us look longer at impossible displays. To my mind, the Hood et al. finding is no different from the body of research showing that people's perceptual expectations do not necessarily map onto the theories of the world that guide their predictions. Karmiloff-Smith and Inhelder (1974–75) were among the first to point out that this situation can account for U-shaped developmental trends, as children develop explicit theories that do not match their perceptual expectations. Adults, even sophisticated ones, seeing a ball leaving a circular tube at high speed and following a circular trajectory, recognize it isn't correct, but when asked often predict exactly that trajectory (McCloskey & Kohl, 1983). Young children are no different; they recognize that an object launched off a cliff yet falling straight down doesn't look right, yet when asked predict exactly that (Kyeong & Spelke, 1999). A few more experiments of this ilk should help determine if this explanation is correct.

In addition, as I discussed briefly in chapter 11, there also remain questions about the status of the knowledge of spatial relations such as containment, support, attachment, and fittingness. I assume that, like color, these relations must be conceptualized before they can be mapped into language. However, insofar as spatial relations are concerned, to date, we have only part of the story. We saw in chapter 11 that infants are sensitive to these relations before they learn spatial terms, but we do not have perfect evidence that the spatial relations are conceptual, rather than perceptual, sensitivities. Because the data we have come from the same kinds of tests that are used to determine perceptual categorization, the most we can show at present is that the categories that have been formed before spatial vocabulary is learned are quite general, rather than tied to specific objects or contexts. Their abstract character makes them a good candidate for conceptual status but is insufficient by itself to guarantee it, so more work is needed before we can be sure of the exact relationship between conceptualization of space and the acquisition of spatial terms.

In this chapter, as well as throughout this book, I have emphasized the close relationship between conceptual knowledge and consciousness. I have suggested that consciousness is required for concept formation to happen in the first place. I have alluded to the many dissociations that occur between conscious conceptual thought and nonconscious (inaccessible) processing, all of which suggest that nonconscious inaccessible knowledge is not conceptual in nature. It seems clear that knowledge comes in more than one variety. The function of the nonconscious kind appears to be to accumulate perceptual information about the world and to coordinate it with action. The conscious kind of knowledge simplifies the overwhelming amount of incoming information that is being processed, allowing thought to take place. Conscious processing is limited, allowing only a few things to be processed at a time (G. Mandler, 2002b). For adults, this limitation may be seven plus or minus two (Miller, 1956) or more likely five plus or minus two (G. Mandler, 1967). For young children the limitation is smaller, probably something more like approximately three (Worden & Ritchey, 1979), and perhaps slightly less than that in the early months of life (Rose, Feldman, & Jankowski, 2001). In any case, at all ages conscious awareness cuts, reduces, and transforms. It is the transformations that I have emphasized, attempting to show how a conscious, attentive process goes beyond the information given (Bruner, 1973) and produces something different from what the perceptual system alone delivers. It lays down a knowledge system that is derived from perception but is markedly different in its characteristics. Its virtues are that it stores information in such a way as to allow access to past experiences and to enable plans for future ones.

A Few Final Words

I hope I have persuaded the reader that to understand the origins of conceptual thought it is not necessary to adopt a classically framed position of nature versus nurture. We do not have to choose between assuming either that the first concepts are genetically specified or that they are derived solely from environmental input. In contrast, the theory I have proposed is that human infants come with an innately specified analytic mechanism and a few innate biases that are sufficient to derive concepts about the world from perceptual information. It is a reasonable solution in that it has long been generally agreed that all organisms are equipped with a genetic stock of information-processing mechanisms such as associative learning. I have merely added one to a list that in any case may not be long.

Perceptual meaning analysis is a domain-general mechanism that can be applied to any kind of perceptual input and that operates at all stages of life. We may come to rely on it less as we become more language-dependent in our thought, but it remains available for analysis of perceptual information at any age. Of course, there are differences between an infant's and an adult's analyses. Adults not only can apply a large conceptual store to the meaning analyses they carry out but also can couch the output of their analyses in verbal form. The kinds of perceptual information most likely to be analyzed may change with development as well. For example, adults may engage in perceptual analysis deliberately in order to memorize a new face or work a jigsaw puzzle; this would lead them to attend to fine details. Infants don't have such concerns, and so what they analyze is merely what engages their attention.

One innate attentional bias is obvious from the infancy research de-scribed in chapters 4 and 5, and that is the proclivity to attend to paths of motion. I speculated in chapter 4 that this particular bias might be due to a lack of maturity in the foveal visual system early in life that makes static figural detail hard to process. This kind of low-level aspect of the visual system might generate an attentional bias that influences conceptualiza-tion as a side effect. On the other hand, the bias might not have a visual origin but instead be part of an innate bias to use path information to conceptualize events. The data of Bahrick et al. (2002) described in chapter 4, showing an attentional bias toward movement in infants old enough to process figural detail well, seem more consistent with the lat-ter hypothesis. In one sense such a bias seems inevitable; the human world consists of events, and events demand spatial path description. But for infants it would not necessarily have to be that way. It might have been the case that infants first pick out the objects participating in events and concentrate exclusively on physical descriptions of them for their first conceptual achievements. Indeed, this is a conclusion that has some-times been drawn in the literature on infant object recognition. But as we have seen, this is not what happens. Infants see objects, of course, but it is object paths—what the objects are doing—that attract their atten-tion, and by hypothesis their analysis.

There are undoubtedly other biases in what infants attend to that in-fluence their first concepts, although this is a topic that has received rela-tively little attention and so we do not have a lot of information to rely on. One such bias, I have speculated, is a tendency to attend to the beginnings and ends of paths. Such biases may be characteristics of the perceptual sys-tem itself and not unique to perceptual meaning analysis. However, once attention is drawn to the start of motion or to its cessation, the occasion for perceptual meaning analysis exists and, as we saw in chapter 4, leads to concepts such as *agent* and *goal*. It may also be, as in the case of attending to object paths, that these biases are not just side effects of a particular kind of perceptual system. To conceive of a self-starting object as an agent or the end of a path as a goal cannot be characteristics of the perceptual sys-tem itself. Hence, they may represent innate biases of perceptual meaning analysis to interpret paths in a certain way. In either case, these notions seem to differentiate us from many other organisms, even if their percep-tual systems are also attuned to the beginnings and ends of paths.

Other biases that are likely to be part of our innate perceptual system are attention to spatial relations such as containment. Again, little is known about these, but there are some indications that certain spatial relations are more salient than others. In current work being carried out both by Soonja Choi and Laraine McDonough, there are signs that containment relations are more salient than support relations for both infants and adults. Casasola and Cohen (2002) also suggest that infants may have greater difficulty in categorizing support than containment. Is support so ubiquitous a relation that it gets overlooked? This is a promising field of investigation, because if we discover the relations that especially attract infants' attention, this will provide clues to the particular kinds of information most likely to become transformed into concepts.

I hope I have also persuaded the reader that there is more than one way to approach the age-old problem of how concepts can be represented in the mind. The research I have described points to a rich conceptual life before language is learned. It is perfectly possible that this takes place in the absence of language or a symbolic language of thought. The attentional biases that emphasize spatial information, along with a mechanism that outputs accessible spatial descriptions, are sufficient, at least for the kinds of thought infants seem to produce. These descriptions are well represented by image-schemas. Cognitive linguists have claimed for a good many years that the underlying meanings of language are best represented as image-schemas. It is serendipitous (or perhaps to be expected?) that an analysis of preverbal concepts that emphasizes spatial information dovetails with spatial analyses of the meanings that underlie language. Language must be learned by infants who have no language. To the extent that they have already represented concepts in a way that is congenial to linguistic processing, learning is simplified. Another way of making the same point is to note that the shape of language must be determined not only by communicative needs but also by the conceptual nature of the organisms that must do the learning.

It is serendipitous as well that the image-schema format of the concepts that allow language structure to be learned also allows the metaphorical extension of concepts about the physical world to more abstract conceptualizations. This is an advantage of a representational system that mirrors the structure of the world in an abstract way. Abstract mental structures, such as the image-schemas PATH and CONTAINMENT, enable the linking together of a wide range of different experiences that have similar underlying structures. This is what enables analogies across disparate realms to be made, such as a journey through space and a journey through life, or conceiving of comprehension as a "taking in" of knowledge. Such metaphorical thought is ubiquitous in human thinking and can be found even in infants.

I have not said much about metaphorical thought (although see chapter 5) because it is still little studied in infancy. There are a few suggestive pieces of evidence, however, such as Wagner, Winner, Cicchetti, and Gardner (1981), who found that 9- to 13-month-old infants were able to match certain metaphorically linked auditory and visual stimuli not associated in their past experience, such as an upward arrow with an ascending tone or a dashed line with a broken tone (see also Phillips, Wagner, Fells, & Lynch, 1990). And, as discussed in chapter 5, there are various pieces of evidence for analogical thought based on abstract structures, such as the examples Piaget (1951) described in his observations of his 8- to 12-month-old infants learning to imitate; opening and closing the hand in response to observing Piaget blinking his eyes is a clear example. This responsivity to abstract structural commonalities among disparate experiences is the basis of metaphorical thought.

Metaphorical thought may seem far-fetched in relation to the infant mind. But another message from this book is that it is possible to trace a straightforward path from infant concepts to those of the adult. Adult thinking is pervasively filled with metaphor. We can see the roots of this kind of thought in the concepts that infants form. The notion of an agent or doer is already abstract, as are notions of opening and closing, going in or out, making and breaking contact, following a path—all of these notions appear early in life. To move to metaphorical generalizations from these abstract concepts is a small step and one that seems unsurprising, given the kind of analogical learning these underlying representations induce.

Another reason for continuity from infant to adult thought is the global nature of the early concepts. Learning about the kinds of things there are in the world is largely a process of differentiation that is anchored throughout life by the first highly general conceptions, such as animals as self-moving interactors. To the extent that differentiation is the dominant conceptual trend, continuity is assured; conceptual change tends to be organized in terms of what has already been learned. Once one has a concept of animal or furniture, it is easy to add aardvarks or television sets. And as we saw in chapter 9, even if through brain damage one loses knowledge about aardvarks or television sets, knowledge about the fundamental difference between animals and furniture remains.

Needless to say, by emphasizing continuity between the infant and the adult mind, I do not mean to imply that no changes occur. Acquiring a theory of mind, learning to understand and use symbols, and becoming able to reflect on one's knowledge all produce major changes. Although these acquisitions themselves seem to be slow and continuous, the mind afterward is different from what it was before. Language itself brings precision and communication that are markedly greater than what is possible for the preverbal infant. But it is important to view such "stage-like" advances as taking place within a continuous conceptual accumulation. The mechanism of meaning analysis that operates on perceptual information assures a structuring of objects and events that even in infants is recognizably like that of adults.

Finally, I hope also to have persuaded the reader that there are different developmental courses associated with learning consciously attended material and automatic perceptual learning. We found different kinds of processing (parallel versus serial), different rates of learning (fast versus slow), differences in grain (detailed versus global), and differences in the use of the two kinds of information (identification versus understanding). I said in chapter 1 that one could in principle accept a distinction between percepts and concepts yet reject a dual representational system as the way to handle the distinction. However, the whole of this book suggests that such an approach is not viable in the long run. The evidence for different kinds of learning and representation seems overwhelming. There is no need to accept overly simple theories. The human infant shows a remarkable degree of learning power and complexity in what is being learned and in the way it is represented. A theory of the origins of conceptual thought needs to reflect that richness.

Notes

1. Familiarization/preferential-looking is a variant of the standard habituation–dishabituation task, in which infants are habituated to a series of pictures until looking time declines to an asymptote or some predetermined low level; then test trials are given that measure whether the infant looks longer at a new stimulus than at an old one. Longer looking to a new stimulus is called dishabituation. The old and new test stimuli can be presented together or singly on successive trials. It is a useful test, but it does tend to bore babies and make them fussy. In the familiarization/preferential-looking version, a fixed number of habituation trials are given. This is called familiarization. In this variant the experimenter must determine how many presentations are enough for an infant of a given age to encode the objects under study but not so many as to put the baby to sleep. If the number is chosen wisely, the baby remains interested in the test stimuli. After a few months of age, versions using objects tend to interest babies more than picture-looking versions.

2. Formerly I called this process perceptual analysis (Mandler, 1988, 1992a), but for reasons discussed in chapter 4 I have expanded the label.

CHAPTER 2

1. "Perceptually similar" is a slippery notion. There can be perceptual commonalities among some unlikely things, such as that both worms and cars move. This issue is discussed in chapters 6 and 7.

CHAPTER 3

1. The redundancy of this expression is discussed in chapter 1.

2. As discussed in the next chapter, comparison of one stimulus with another plays an important role in forming a concept. Three-month-olds do much less shifting of attention from one stimulus to another than they do even a month later (Colombo, Mitchell, Coldren, & Atwater, 1990; Frick, Colombo, & Allen, 2000), and there is a further large increase in this kind of behavior between 4 and 8 months (Harris, 1973; Janowsky, 1985).

CHAPTER 4

1. Some of the major protagonists were Paivio (1978) and Cooper and Shepard (1978) for the imagists and Fodor (1975) and Pylyshyn (1981) for the propositionalists. Anderson (1978) tried to mediate and was roundly denounced by both sides (Pylyshyn, 1979).

CHAPTER 6

1. The labels, including "genus" and "species," vary from one taxonomist to another; I follow here the labeling used by Berlin et al. (1973).

2. The faces were of men, women, girls, and babies. Although obviously subsumed under the concept of face, it is not clear why these were considered to be basic-level classes.

3. There are no data on generating vehicle names.

4. Because of the ambiguities in the notion of a basic level, in the rest of this book I usually put "basic-level" in quotes. Unfortunately, to communicate with an audience accustomed to the term, it is difficult to avoid entirely.

CHAPTER 7

1. It is not strictly correct to divide vehicles into life-forms the way that animals are so divided, but the data seem so similar that it is a convenient way to describe the tripartite conceptual division that occurs in both realms.

2. *Categorization* was defined as showing runs of sequential touches of items within a category significantly greater than would be expected by chance. The Monte Carlo program used to determine chance length of runs as a function of total number of touches is described in Mandler et al. (1987).

3. Except on the easiest sequential-touching task (one that confounds basic-level similarity and superordinate differences, as in dogs versus cars), we did not get strong categorization with 12-month-olds (Mandler & Bauer, 1988).

4. We tested 7-month-olds only on the animal–vehicle, car–airplane, and dog–fish tasks. The patterns of data at 7 months looked the same as those for the 9- and 11-month-olds but were somewhat more marginal.

5. It would be interesting to study infants who do or do not have a dog or cat in their household as a test of real-world knowledge influencing categorization in the laboratory, but we did not have the chance to do so.

6. We did not submit these data for publication because they consisted only of null effects, but this was one of the experiments that confirmed our decision to avoid pictures and work with objects.

7. Anyone using this technique needs to be aware of this potential pitfall. Jenny Swerdlow developed a scoring manual. A short version of it can be found at my homepage (http://cogsci.ucsd.edu/~jean/).

8. I probably don't need to say this, but just to be on the safe side, I will. Infants' conceptualization of animals is based on the exemplars they have experience with, so a statement such as "All animals start themselves" refers to what infants know, not what the scientist knows.

9. I remind the reader that the converse may also be true. Even very young infants may engage in conceptual categorization. I have not said, as Arterberry and Bornstein (2002) claim, that infants do not form conceptual categories until the second 6 months of life. It is just that we don't yet have the techniques to measure conceptual categorization before that time.

CHAPTER 8

1. Correcting an "ill-formed" event might be considered due to the workings of memory rather than expressing how it should have been performed. Such memory phenomena are ubiquitous and perhaps even more pronounced in children than in adults (Mandler, 1978). However, memory is unlikely to be the cause of the phenomena described here. Imitation was immediate, and infants' memory for events is long lasting and reasonably accurate (see chapter 10).

2. Madole and Oakes (1999) commented that because Meltzoff (1988a) had no trouble getting 9-month-olds to imitate, the difficulty our 9-month-olds had means they had trouble conceiving of an object as a representation of a real-world counterpart. This comment is ill conceived; imitation of an action on a single object such as Meltzoff studied (e.g., depressing a button on a box) is much easier for infants than making two objects interact with each other (e.g., making an animal drink from a cup).

3. It is of interest vis-à-vis the data discussed in chapter 5 that they also found that 14- and 18-month-olds generalized motions such as going up stairs or hopping from one animal to another but significantly less often to a vehicle. Similarly, the infants generalized motions such as sliding or going up a ramp and through the air to land on another ramp from one vehicle to another but significantly less often to an animal.

4. This is not the same as slot filling (Lucariello & Nelson, 1985). According to these authors, the common function of daily events enables infants to form small categories such as things to eat at breakfast, things to eat at lunch, and so forth; these slot-filler categories then require a higher level of abstraction to form the superordinate category of food. My thesis is that the initial conceptual basis is more general than such specific functions, thus laying the foundations for "superordinate" generalizations from the start. However, slot filling such as dividing food into breakfast, lunch, and dinner may be a frequent early form of differentiation.

5. Note that in their studies children were asked whether the representation itself (picture or model) has the properties, for example, whether a doll can actually walk, not whether it *represents* something that can walk.

CHAPTER 9

Portions of the material in this chapter are adapted from Mandler (2002), with permission of Psychology Press.

1. YOT's knowledge was tested by having her point to pictures of named objects. Although her comprehension was generally impaired, there were large differences in her residual comprehension, depending on whether the objects were food, animals, or artifacts. She performed worse on artifacts than on food or animals, but especially badly on indoor artifacts. Other studies of semantic dementia have shown that conceptual loss affects more than verbal information. Visually based semantic matching tasks and object use are also impaired (Hodges, Bozeat, Lambon Ralph, Patterson, & Spatt, 2000).

2. So far as I know he did not study infants, and as discussed in chapter 6, the preschool years are already too old an age to study the first concepts.

3. Interestingly, complexes fail to qualify as concepts because they are like family relations: "In a complex, the bonds between its components are *concrete and factual* rather than abstract and logical, just as we do not classify a person as belonging to the Petrov family because of any logical relationship between him and other bearers of the name" (Vygotsky, 1962, p. 61). It seems possible that Vygotsky here is asserting the inadequacy of concepts based on family or radial structure, two ideas that have become more prominent in current thinking about human concepts (Lakoff, 1987; Rosch & Mervis, 1975).

CHAPTER 10

1. When I once asked a famous memory researcher to define *recall* for me, he hesitated for a while and then said, "It's what recall tests measure." Maybe he was pulling my leg.

2. This situation is the kind that Werker criticized, discussed later in this chapter.

3. Six-month-olds, who are at the lower limit of being able to do any deferred imitation, do show some context effects (Hayne, Boniface, & Barr, 2000).

4. My earliest memory is of this sort—a moderately vivid image in which I fly forward and something red crashes into me. It was purely by chance at a much later age that I happened to describe this scene to my grandmother. She told me that when I was 18 months of age and she was baby-sitting, I was hit while playing on a swing in the park. Before that, I had no idea when or where the scene had taken place.

5. We know from work by Bauer and Dow (1994) that by 16 months infants do remember over a week's delay the specific objects that took part in an event, not just their general class. However, Bauer and Dow measured recognition (choosing from a set of distractors the correct object to use for their imitations), not recall.

CHAPTER 11

1. Simple associative learning can take place, of course, as may happen in the naming games played by mothers and infants (Ninio & Bruner, 1978), but the names so acquired are not necessarily meaning-bearing and may be restricted to the game itself.

2. Interestingly, this finding suggests that 2-year-olds have little compunction about using more than one basic-level label for an item. It would appear that Markman's (1991) hypothesis of mutual exclusivity of word meaning may be induced from experience with language, rather than being an initial hypothesis about language that enables early word learning (Nelson, 1988; but see Woodward & Markman, 1998, for counterarguments).

3. Even in a language such as Korean that uses open-class verbs to express spatial relations, the number of verbs that young children use to talk about these relations is still relatively small (about 10, used over a period of several months; see Choi & Bowerman, 1991).

4. See also Goldin-Meadow, McNeill, and Singleton (1996), for an interesting discussion of the way in which gesture becomes hierarchized and segmented in a linguistic way when it is the sole medium in which communication is carried out.

CHAPTER 12

1. Other distinctions in kinds of consciousness can be made as well, such as autonoetic and noetic awareness (Tulving, 1985). This distinction, associated with the difference between remembering and knowing, as mentioned in the discussion of autobiographical memory in chapter 10, would be a further division of conceptual awareness.

2. There was also distinct activation in supplementary motor cortex, associated with verbal working memory, such as might be expected with rehearsal of verbally expressed rules.

References

Abdi, H., Valentin, D., Edelman, B., & O'Toole, A. J. (1995). More about the difference between men and women: Evidence from linear neural networks and the principal-component approach. *Perception, 24,* 539–562.

Acredolo, L. P., Goodwyn, S. W., Horobin, K. D., & Emmons, Y. D. (1999). The signs and sounds of early language development. In L. Balter & C. S. Tamis-LeMonda (Eds.), *Child psychology: A handbook of contemporary issues.* Philadelphia: Psychology Press.

Aglioti, S., DeSouza, J. F., & Goodale, M. A. (1995). Size-contrast illusions deceive the eye but not the hand. *Current Biology, 5,* 679–685.

Aguiar, A., & Baillargeon, R. (1998). Eight-and-a-half-month-old infants' reasoning about containment events. *Child Development, 69,* 636–653.

Anderson, J. R. (1978). Arguments concerning representations for mental imagery. *Psychological Review, 85,* 249–277.

Anderson, J. R. (1982). Acquisition of cognitive skill. *Psychological Review, 82,* 369–406.

Archambault, A., O'Donnell, C., & Schyns, P. G. (1999). Blind to object changes: When learning the same object at different levels of categorization modifies its perception. *Psychological Science, 10,* 249–255.

Arterberry, M. E., & Bornstein, M. H. (2001). Three-month-old infants' categorization of animals and vehicles based on static and dynamic attributes. *Journal of Experimental Child Psychology, 80,* 333–346.

Arterberry, M. E., & Bornstein, M. H. (2002). Infant perceptual and conceptual categorization: The roles of static and dynamic stimulus attributes. *Cognition, 86,* 1–24.

Arterberry, M. E., Craton, L. G., & Yonas, A. (1993). Infants' sensitivity to motion-carried information for depth and object properties. In C. E. Granrud (Ed.), *Visual perception and cognition in infancy*. Hillsdale, NJ: Erlbaum.

Atran, S. (1990). *Cognitive foundations of natural history*. Cambridge, England: Cambridge University Press.

Bachevalier, J., & Mishkin, M. (1994). Effects of neonatal temporal lobe lesions on visual recognition memory in rhesus monkeys. *Journal of Neuroscience, 14*, 2128–2139.

Bahrick, L. E., Gogate, L. J., & Ruiz, I. (2002). Attention and memory for faces and actions in infancy: The salience of actions over faces in dynamic events. *Child Development, 73*, 1629–1643.

Bahrick, L. E., Hernandez-Reif, M., & Pickens, J. N. (1997). The effect of retrieval cues on visual preferences and memory in infancy: Evidence for a four-phase attention function. *Journal of Experimental Child Psychology, 67*, 1–20.

Baillargeon, R. (1986). Representing the existence and the location of hidden objects: Object permanence in 6- and 8-month-old infants. *Cognition, 23*, 21–41.

Baillargeon, R. (1993). The object concept revisited: New directions in the investigation of infants' physical knowledge. In C. E. Granrud (Ed.), *Visual perception and cognition in infancy*. Hillsdale, NJ: Erlbaum.

Baillargeon, R. (1994). How do infants learn about the physical world? *Current Directions in Psychological Science, 3*, 133–140.

Baillargeon, R. (2000). Reply to Bogartz, Shinskey, and Schilling; Schilling; and Cashon and Cohen. *Infancy, 1*, 447–462.

Baillargeon, R., & DeVos, J. (1991). Object permanence in young infants: Further evidence. *Child Development, 62*, 1227–1246.

Baillargeon, R., & Graber M. (1988). Evidence of location memory in 8-month-old infants in a nonsearch AB task. *Developmental Psychology, 24*, 502–511.

Baillargeon, R., Kotovsky, L., & Needham, A. (1995). The acquisition of physical knowledge in infancy. In D. Sperber, D. Premack, & A. J. Premack (Eds.), *Causal cognition*. New York: Oxford University Press.

Baillargeon, R., Spelke, E., & Wasserman, S. (1985). Object permanence in 5-month-old infants. *Cognition, 20*, 191–208.

Baillargeon, R., & Wang, S. (2002). Event categorization in infancy. *Trends in Cognitive Science, 6*, 85–93.

Balaban, M., & Waxman, S. R. (1997). Do words facilitate object categorization in 9-month-old infants? *Journal of Experimental Child Psychology, 64*, 3–26.

Baldwin, D. A., Baird, J. A., Saylor, M. M., & Clark, M. A. (2001). Infants parse dynamic action. *Child Development, 72*, 708–717.

Barr, R., Dowden, A., & Hayne, H. (1996). Developmental changes in deferred imitation by 6- to 24-month-old infants. *Infant Behavior and Development, 19*, 159–170.

Barsalou, L. W. (1999). Perceptual symbol systems. *Behavioral and Brain Sciences,* *22,* 577–660.

Batali, J. (in press). The negotiation and acquisition of recursive grammars as a result of competition among exemplars. In T. Briscoe (Ed.), *Linguistic evolution through language acquisition: Formal and computational models.* New York: Cambridge University Press.

Bates, E., Benigni, L., Bretherton, I., Camaioni, L., & Volterra, V. (1979). Cognition and communication from nine to thirteen months: Correlational findings. In E. Bates, *The emergence of symbols.* New York: Academic Press.

Bates, E., & MacWhinney, B. (1982). Functionalist approaches to grammar. In E. Wanner & L. Gleitman (Eds.), *Language acquisition: State of the art.* Cambridge, England: Cambridge University Press.

Bates, E., Thal, D., & Marchman, V. (1991). Symbols and syntax: A Darwinian approach to language development. In N. A. Krasnegor & D. M. Rumbaugh (Eds.), *Biological and behavioral determinants of language development.* Hillsdale, NJ: Erlbaum.

Bauer, P. J., & Dow, G. A. (1994). Episodic memory in 16- and 20-month-old children: Specifics are generalized, but not forgotten. *Developmental Psychology, 30,* 403–417.

Bauer, P. J., Hertzgaard, L. A., & Dow, G. A. (1994). After 8 months have passed: Long-term recall of events by 1- to 2-year-old children. *Memory, 2,* 353–382.

Bauer, P. J., & Mandler, J. M. (1989). One thing follows another: Effects of temporal structure on 1- to 2-year-olds' recall of events. *Developmental Psychology, 28,* 441–452.

Bauer, P. J., & Shore, C. M. (1987). Making a memorable event: Effects of familiarity and organization on young children's recall of action sequences. *Cognitive Development, 2,* 327–338.

Bauer, P. J., & Thal, D. (1990). Scripts or scraps: Reconsidering the development of sequential understanding. *Journal of Experimental Child Psychology, 50,* 287–304.

Bauer, P. J., & Wewerka, S. S. (1995). One- to two-year-olds' recall of events: The more expressed, the more impressed. *Journal of Experimental Child Psychology, 59,* 475–496.

Behl-Chadha, G. (1996). Superordinate-like categorical representations in early infancy. *Cognition, 60,* 104–141.

Behrend, D. A. (1988). Overextensions in early language comprehension: Evidence from a signal detection approach. *Journal of Child Language, 15,* 63–75.

Bergson, H. (1911). *Matter and memory.* New York: Macmillan.

Berlin, B., Breedlove, D. E., & Raven, P. H. (1973). General principles of classification and nomenclature in folk biology. *American Anthropologist, 75,* 214–242.

Bertenthal, B. (1993). Infants' perception of biomechanical motions: Intrinsic image and knowledge-based constraints. In C. Granrud (Ed.), *Visual perception and cognition in infancy*. Hillsdale, NJ: Erlbaum.

Bierwisch, M. (1967). Some semantic universals of German adjectivals. *Foundations of Language, 3*, 1–36.

Bisiach, E. (1988). Language without thought. In L. Weiskrantz (Ed.), *Thought without language*. Oxford, England: Oxford University Press.

Bjorklund, D. F. (1995). *Children's thinking* (2nd ed.). Pacific Grove, CA: Brooks Cole.

Block, N. (2001). Paradox and cross purposes in recent work on consciousness. *Cognition, 79*, 197–219.

Bloom, L., Lifter, K., & Broughton, J. (1985). The convergence of early cognition and language in the second year of life: Problems in conceptualization and measurement. In M. Barrett (Ed.), *Single-word speech*. New York: Wiley.

Bloom, P. (1999). The role of semantics in solving the bootstrapping problem. In R. Jackendoff, P. Bloom, & K. Wynn (Eds.), *Language, logic, and concepts: Essays in memory of John Macnamara*. Cambridge, MA: MIT Press.

Bloom, P. (2000). *How children learn the meanings of words*. Cambridge, MA: MIT Press.

Bogartz, R. S., Shinskey, J. L., & Speaker, C. (1997). Interpreting infant looking: The event set x event set design. *Developmental Psychology, 33*, 408–422.

Bomba, P. C., & Siqueland, E. R. (1983). The nature and structure of infant form categories. *Journal of Experimental Child Psychology, 35*, 294–328.

Borgo, F., & Shallice, T. (2001). When living things and other "sensory quality" categories go together: A novel category-specific effect. *Neurocase, 7*, 201–220.

Boroditsky, L. (2000). Metaphoric structuring: Understanding time through spatial metaphors. *Cognition, 75*, 1–28.

Boroditsky, L. (2001). Does language shape thought? Mandarin and English speakers' conceptions of time. *Cognitive Psychology, 43*, 1–22.

Boroditsky, L., & Ramscar, M. (2002). The roles of body and mind in abstract thought. *Psychological Science, 13*, 185–189.

Bower, T. G. R. (1981). *Development in infancy* (2nd ed.). San Francisco: W. H. Freeman.

Bower, T. G. R., Broughton, J. M., & Moore, M. K. (1971). The development of the object concept as manifested by changes in the tracking behavior of infants between 7 and 20 weeks of age. *Journal of Experimental Child Psychology, 11*, 182–193.

Bowerman, M. (1973). *Early syntactic development*. Cambridge, England: Cambridge University Press.

Bowerman, M. (1987). Commentary. In B. MacWhinney (Ed.), *Mechanisms of language acquisition*. Hillsdale, NJ: Erlbaum.

Bowerman, M. (1989). Learning a semantic system: What role do cognitive pre-dispositions play? In M. L. Rice & R. L. Schiefelbusch (Eds.), *The teachability of language*. Baltimore, MD: Paul H. Brookes.

Bowerman, M. (1996). Learning how to structure space for language: A crosslinguistic perspective. In P. Bloom, M. A. Peterson, L. Nadel, & M. F. Garrett (Eds.), *Language and space*. Cambridge, MA: MIT Press.

Bowerman, M. (1998). Report. In *Max Planck Institute for Psycholinguistics annual report*. Nijmegen, The Netherlands: Max Planck Institute.

Bowerman, M., & Choi, S. (2001). Shaping meanings for language: Universal and language-specific in the acquisition of spatial semantic categories. In M. Bowerman & S. C. Levinson (Eds.), *Language acquisition and conceptual development*. Cambridge, England: Cambridge University Press.

Bowerman, M., & Levinson, S. C. (Eds.). (2001). *Language acquisition and conceptual development*. Cambridge, England: Cambridge University Press.

Brown, A. L. (1990). Domain-specific principles affect learning and transfer in children. *Cognitive Science, 14*, 107–133.

Brown, C. (1984). *Language and living things: Uniformities in folk classification and naming*. New Brunswick, NJ: Rutgers University Press.

Brown, P. (1994). The INS and ONS of Tzeltal locative expressions: The semantics of static descriptions of location. *Linguistics, 32*, 743–790.

Brown, P. (2001). Learning to talk about motion UP and DOWN in Tzeltal: Is there a language-specific bias for verb learning? In M. Bowerman & S. C. Levinson (Eds.), *Language acquisition and conceptual development*. Cambridge, England: Cambridge University Press.

Brown, R. (1958). How shall a thing be called? *Psychological Review, 65*, 14–21.

Brown, R. (1973). *A first language: The early stages*. Cambridge, MA: Harvard University Press.

Brugman, C. M. (1988). *The story of over: Polysemy, semantics, and the structure of the lexicon*. New York: Garland.

Bruner, J. S. (1973). *Beyond the information given*. New York: Norton.

Bruner, J. S. (1974–75). From communication to language: A psychological perspective. *Cognition, 3*, 255–287.

Bruner, J. S., Goodnow, J. J., & Austin, G. A. (1956). *A study of thinking*. New York: Wiley.

Budwig, N. (1989). The linguistic marking of agentivity and control in child language. *Journal of Child Language, 16*, 263–284.

Butler, J., & Rovee-Collier, C. (1989). Contextual gating of memory retrieval. *Developmental Psychobiology, 22*, 533–552.

Butterworth, G. (1991). The ontogeny and phylogeny of joint visual attention. In A. Whiten (Ed.), *Natural theories of mind*. Oxford, England: Blackwell.

Callanan, M. A. (1985). How parents label objects for young children: The role of input in the acquisition of category hierarchies. *Child Development, 56*, 508–523.

Campbell, B. A. (1984). Reflections on the ontogeny of learning and memory. In R. Kail & N. E. Spear (Eds.), *Comparative perspectives on the development of memory*. Hillsdale, NJ: Erlbaum.

Caramazza, A., & Shelton, J. R. (1998). Domain-specific knowledge systems in the brain: The animate-inanimate distinction. *Journal of Cognitive Neuroscience, 10*, 1–34.

Carey, S. (1982). Semantic development: The state of the art. In E. Wanner & L. R. Gleitman (Eds.), *Language acquisition: The state of the art*. Cambridge, England: Cambridge University Press.

Carey, S. (1985). *Conceptual change in childhood*. Cambridge, MA: MIT Press.

Carey, S. (2000). The origin of concepts. *Journal of Cognition and Development, 1*, 37–41.

Carey, S. (2001). On the very possibility of discontinuities in conceptual development. In E. Dupoux (Ed.), *Language, brain, and cognitive development: Essays in honor of Jacques Mehler*. Cambridge, MA: MIT Press.

Carey, S. (2002). The origin of concepts: Continuing the conversation. In N. L. Stein, P. Bauer, & M. Rabinowitz (Eds.), *Representation, memory, and development: Essays in honor of Jean Mandler*. Mahwah, NJ: Erlbaum.

Carey, S., & Markman, E. M. (1999). Cognitive development. In B. M. Bly & D. E. Rumelhart (Eds.), *Cognitive science*. San Diego: Academic Press.

Carey, S., & Spelke, E. (1994). Domain-specific knowledge and conceptual change. In L. A. Hirschfeld & S. A. Gelman (Eds.), *Mapping the mind: Domain specificity in cognition and culture*. New York: Cambridge University Press.

Carmichael, L., Hogen, H. P., & Walter, A. A. (1932). An experimental study of the effect of language on the reproduction of visually perceived form. *Journal of Experimental Psychology, 15*, 73–86.

Carver, L. J., & Bauer, P. J. (1999). When the event is more than the sum of its parts: Nine-month-olds' long-term ordered recall. *Memory, 7*, 147–174.

Carver, L. J., & Bauer, P. J. (2001). The dawning of a past: The emergence of long-term explicit memory in infancy. *Journal of Experimental Psychology: General, 130*, 726–745.

Carver, L. J., Bauer, P. J., & Nelson, C. A. (2000). Associations between infant brain activity and recall memory. *Developmental Science, 3*, 234–246.

Casasola, M., & Cohen, L. B. (2002). Infant spatial categorization of containment, support, or tight-fit spatial relations. *Developmental Science, 5*, 247–264.

Chambers, D., & Reisberg, D. (1992). What an image depicts depends on what an image means. *Cognitive Psychology, 24*, 145–174.

Choi, S., & Bowerman, M. (1991). Learning to express motion events in English and Korean: The influence of language-specific lexicalization patterns. *Cognition, 41*, 83–121.

Choi, S., McDonough, L., Bowerman, M., & Mandler, J. M. (1999). Early sensitivity to language-specific spatial categories in English and Korean. *Cognitive Development, 14*, 241–268.

Chromiak, W., & Weisberg, R. W. (1981). The role of the object concept in visual tracking: Child-like errors in adults. *Journal of Experimental Child Psychology, 32,* 531–543.

Claparède, E. (1951). Recognition and "me-ness." In D. Rapaport (Ed.), *Organization and pathology of thought.* New York: Columbia University Press. (Reprinted from *Archives de Psychologie,* 1911, *11,* 79–90)

Clark, E. V. (1973a). What's in a word? On the child's acquisition of semantics in his first language. In T. E. Moore (Ed.), *Cognitive development and the acquisition of language.* San Diego: Academic Press.

Clark, E. V. (1973b). Non-linguistic strategies and the acquisition of word meanings. *Cognition, 2,* 161–182.

Clark, E. V. (1977). Strategies and the mapping problem in first language acquisition. In J. Macnamara (Ed.), *Language learning and thought.* New York: Academic Press.

Clark, E. V. (1983). Concepts and words. In J. H. Flavell & E. M. Markman (Eds.), *Cognitive development: Vol. 3* of P. H. Mussen (Series Ed.), *Handbook of child psychology.* New York: Wiley.

Clark, E. V. (2001). Emergent categories in first language acquisition. In M. Bowerman & S. C. Levinson (Eds.), *Language acquisition and conceptual development.* Cambridge, England: Cambridge University Press.

Clark, H. H. (1973). Space, time, semantics, and the child. In T. E. Moore (Ed.), *Cognitive development and the acquisition of language.* San Diego: Academic Press.

Cohen, L. B., Chaput, H. H., & Cashon, C. H. (2002). A constructivist model of infant cognition. *Cognitive Development, 17,* 1323–1343.

Cohen, L. B., & Strauss, M. S. (1979). Concept acquisition in the human infant. *Child Development, 50,* 419–424.

Cohen, N. J., & Squire, L. R. (1980). Preserved learning and retention of pattern-analyzing skills in amnesia: Dissociation of knowing how and knowing that. *Science, 210,* 207–210.

Collie, R., & Hayne, H. (1999). Deferred imitation by 6- and 9-month-old infants: More evidence for declarative memory. *Developmental Psychobiology, 35,* 83–90.

Colombo, J. (2001). The development of visual attention in infancy. *Annual Review of Psychology, 52,* 337–367.

Colombo, J., Mitchell, D. W., Coldren, J. T., & Atwater, J. D. (1990). Discrimination learning during the first year: Stimulus and positional cues. *Journal of Experimental Psychology: Learning, Memory, & Cognition, 16,* 98–109.

Cooper, L. A., & Shepard, R. N. (1978). Transformations on representations of objects in space. In E. C. Carterette & M. P. Friedman (Eds.), *Handbook of perception: Vol. 8, Perceptual coding.* New York: Academic Press.

Coulson, S. (2000). *Semantic leaps: Frame shifting and conceptual blending in meaning construction.* New York: Cambridge University Press.

Crawford, L. E., Regier, T., & Huttenlocher, J. (2000). Linguistic and non-linguistic spatial categorization. *Cognition, 75*, 209–235.

Csibra, G., Bíró, S., Koós, O., & Gergely, G. (2003). One-year-old infants use teleological representation of actions productively. *Cognitive Science, 27*, 111–133.

Csibra, G., Gergely, G., Bíró, S., Koós, O., & Brockbank, M. (1999). Goal attribution without agency cues: The perception of 'pure reason' in infancy. *Cognition, 72*, 237–267.

Daehler, M. W., Lonardo, R., & Bukatko, D. (1979). Matching and equivalence judgments in very young children. *Child Development, 50*, 170–179.

Deak, G. O., & Bauer, P. J. (1996). The dynamics of preschoolers' categorization choices. *Child Development, 67*, 740–767.

De Haan, M., Johnson, M. H., Maurer, D., & Perrett, D. I. (2001). Recognition of individual faces and face prototypes by 1- and 3-month-old infants. *Cognitive Development, 16*, 659–678.

DeLoache, J. S. (1989). Young children's understanding of the correspondence between a scale model and a larger space. *Cognitive Development, 4*, 121–139.

DeLoache, J. S. (2000). Dual representation and young children's use of scale models. *Child Development, 71*, 329–338.

DeLoache, J. S., & Burns, N. M. (1994). Early understanding of the representational function of pictures: I. Sensitivity to serial, temporal, and abstract structure in the infant. *Language and Cognitive Processing, 15*, 87–127.

Dewey, J. (1960). Qualitative thought. Reprinted in R. J. Bernstein (Ed.), *On experience, nature and freedom: Representative selections.* New York: Liberal Arts Press. (Original work published 1930)

Diamond, A. (1985). The development of the ability to use recall to guide action, as indicated by infants' performance on AB. *Child Development, 56*, 868–883.

Diamond, A. (1990). Developmental time course in human infants and infant monkeys, and the neural bases of inhibitory control in reaching. In A. Diamond (Ed.), *The development and neural bases of higher cognitive functions.* New York: New York Academy of Sciences.

Diamond, A., & Gilbert, J. (1989). Development as progressive inhibitory control of action: Retrieval of a contiguous object. *Cognitive Development, 4*, 223–249.

Diamond, A., & Lee, E. Y. (2000). Inability of five-month-old infants to retrieve a contiguous object: A failure of conceptual understanding or of control of action? *Child Development, 71*, 1477–1494.

Dominey, P. F., & Ramus, F. (2000). Neural network processing of natural language: I. Sensitivity to serial, temporal, and abstract structure of language in the infant. *Language and Cognitive Processes, 15*, 87–127.

Donaldson, M. (1978). *Children's minds.* New York: Norton.

Dorfman, J., & Mandler, G. (1994) Implicit and explicit forgetting: When is gist remembered? *Quarterly Journal of Experimental Psychology: Human Experimental Psychology, 47*, 651–672.

Driver, J., & Vuilleumier, P. (2001). Perceptual awareness and its loss in unilateral neglect and extinction. *Cognition, 79*, 39–88.

Eimas, P. D. (1994). Categorization in early infancy and the continuity of development. *Cognition, 50*, 83–93.

Eimas, P. D., & Quinn, P. C. (1994). Studies on the formation of perceptually based basic-level categories in young infants. *Child Development, 65*, 903–917.

Elman, J. L. (1990). Finding structure in time. *Cognitive Science, 14*, 179–211.

Elman, J. L. (1993). Learning and development in neural networks: The importance of starting small. *Cognition, 48*, 71–99.

Erickson T. D., & Mattson, M. E. (1981). From words to meaning: A semantic illusion. *Journal of Verbal learning and Verbal Behavior, 20*, 540–551.

Fagan, J. F. III. (1970). Memory in the infant. *Journal of Experimental Child Psychology, 9*, 217–226.

Fagan, J. F. III. (1973). Infants' delayed recognition memory and forgetting. *Journal of Experimental Child Psychology, 16*, 424–450.

Fagan, J. F. III, & Singer, L. T. (1979). The role of simple feature differences in infant recognition of faces. *Infant Behavior and Development, 2*, 39–46.

Fantino, E., & Logan, C. A. (1979). *The experimental analysis of behavior: A biological perspective.* San Francisco: Freeman.

Farah, M., & McClelland, J. L. (1991). A computational model of semantic memory impairment: Modality specificity and emergent category specificity. *Journal of Experimental Psychology: General, 120*, 339–357.

Fauconnier, G. (1994). *Mental spaces.* Cambridge, MA: MIT Press.

Fauconnier, G. (1996). Analogical counterfactuals. In G. Fauconnier & E. Sweetser (Eds.), *Spaces, worlds, and grammar.* Chicago: University of Chicago Press.

Fauconnier, G., & Turner, M. (2002). *The way we think.* New York: Basic Books.

Fillmore, C. (1982). Toward a descriptive framework for spatial deixis. In R. J. Jarvella & W. Klein (Eds.), *Speech, place, and action.* New York: Wiley.

Fischer, K. W., & Bidell, T. (1991). Constraining nativist inferences about cognitive capacities. In S. Carey & R. Gelman (Eds.), *The epigenesis of mind.* Hillsdale, NJ: Erlbaum.

Fivush, R., & Hammond, N. R. (1990). Autobiographical memory across the preschool years: Toward reconceptualizing childhood amnesia. In R. Fivush & J. A. Hudson (Eds.), *Knowing and remembering in young children.* New York: Cambridge University Press.

Fodor, J. A. (1972). Some reflections on L. S. Vygotsky's *Thought and language. Cognition, 1*, 83–95.

Fodor, J. A. (1975). *The language of thought.* New York: Crowell.

Fodor, J. A. (1981). The current status of the innateness controversy. In *Representations*. Cambridge, MA: MIT Press.

Fodor, J. A. (1987). *Psychosemantics*. Cambridge, MA: MIT Press.

Folven, R. J., & Bonvillian, J. D. (1991). The transition from nonreferential to referential language in children acquiring American Sign Language. *Developmental Psychology, 27*, 806–816.

Freeman, N. H., Lloyd, S., & Sinha, C. G. (1980). Infant search tasks reveal early concepts of containment and canonical usage of objects. *Cognition, 8*, 243–262.

Frege, G. (1952). *Philosophical writings*. P. Geech & M. Black (Eds.). Oxford: Blackwell.

Frick, J. E., Colombo, J., & Allen, J. R. (2000). Temporal sequence of global-local processing in 3-month-old infants. *Infancy, 1*, 375–386.

Friedman, A. (1979). Framing pictures: The role of knowledge in automatized encoding and memory for gist. *Journal of Experimental Psychology General, 108*, 316–335.

Frye, D., Rawling, P., Moore, C., & Myers, I. (1983). Object-person discrimination and communication at 3 and 10 months. *Developmental Psychology, 19*, 303–309.

Funnell, E., & Sheridan, J. S. (1992). Categories of knowledge? Unfamiliar aspects of living and nonliving things. *Cognitive Neuropsychology, 9*, 135–153.

Garcia, J., & Koelling, R. A. (1966). The relation of cue to consequence in avoidance learning. *Psychonomic Science, 4*, 123–124.

Garner, W. R. (1974). *The processing of information and structure*. Potomac, MD: Erlbaum.

Gelman, R. (1978). Cognitive development. *Annual Review of Psychology, 29*, 297–332.

Gelman, R. (1990). First principles organize attention to and learning about relevant data: Number and the animate-inanimate distinction as examples. *Cognitive Science, 14*, 79–106.

Gelman, R. (1991). Epigenetic foundations of knowledge structures: Initial and transcendent constructions. In S. Carey & R. Gelman (Eds.), *The epigenesis of mind*. Hillsdale, NJ: Erlbaum.

Gelman, R., & Gallistel, C. R. (1978). *The child's understanding of number*. Cambridge, MA: Harvard University Press.

Gelman, S. A. (1988). The development of induction within natural kind and artifact categories. *Cognitive Psychology, 20*, 65–95.

Gelman, S. A. (2003). *The essential child: Origins of essentialism in everyday thought*. New York: Oxford University Press.

Gelman, S. A., Croft, W., Fu, P., Clausner, T., & Gottfried, G. (1998). Why is a pomegranate an *apple*? The role of shape, taxonomic relatedness, and prior lexical knowledge in children's overextensions of *apple* and *dog*. *Journal of Child Language, 25*, 267–291.

Gelman, S. A., & Markman, E. M. (1986). Categories and induction in young children. *Cognition, 23,* 183−209.

Gelman, S. A., & O'Reilley, A. W. (1988). Children's inductive inferences within superordinate categories: the role of language and category structure. *Child Development, 59,* 876−887.

Gelman, S. A., & Wellman, H. M. (1991). Insides and essences: Early understandings of the nonobvious. *Cognition, 38,* 213−244.

Gentner, D. (1983). Structure-mapping: A theoretical framework for analogy. *Cognitive Science, 7,* 155−170.

Gentner, D., & Markman, A. B. (1997). Structure mapping in analogy and similarity. *American Psychologist, 52,* 45−56.

Gentner, D. R. (1988). Expertise in typewriting. In M. T. H. Chi, R. Glaser, & M. J. Farr (Eds.), *The nature of expertise.* Hillsdale, NJ: Erlbaum.

Gergely, G., Nádasdy, Z., Csibra, G., & Bíró, S. (1995). Taking the intentional stance at 12 months of age. *Cognition, 56,* 165−193.

Gibbs, R. W. (1994). *The poetics of mind.* New York: Cambridge University Press.

Gibbs, R. W. (2000). Making good psychology out of blending theory. *Cognitive Linguistics, 11,* 347−358.

Gleitman, L., & Gleitman, H. (1997). What is a language made out of? *Lingua, 100,* 29−55.

Gleitman, L. R., & Wanner, E. (1992). Language acquisition: The state of the art. In E. Wanner & L. Gleitman (Eds.), *Language acquisition: The state of the art.* Cambridge, England: Cambridge University Press.

Goldin-Meadow, S., McNeill, D., & Singleton, J. (1996). Silence is liberating: Removing the handcuffs on grammatical expression in the manual modality. *Psychological Review, 103,* 34−55.

Golinkoff, R. M., Hirsh-Pasek, K., Cauley, K. M., & Gordon, L. (1987). The eyes have it: Lexical and syntactic comprehension in a new paradigm. *Journal of Child Language, 14,* 23−46.

Golinkoff, R. M., Hirsh-Pasek, K., Mervis, C. B., Frawley, W. B., & Parillo, M. (1995). Lexical principles can be extended to the acquisition of verbs. In M. Tomasello & W. E. Merriman (Eds.), *Beyond names for things: Young children's acquisition of verbs.* Hillsdale, NJ: Erlbaum.

Goodwyn, S. W., & Acredolo, L. P. (1993). Symbolic gesture versus word: Is there a modality advantage for onset of symbol use? *Child Development, 64,* 688−701.

Gopnik, A., & Meltzoff, A. N. (1992). Categorization and naming: Basic-level sorting in eighteen-month-olds and its relation to language. *Child Development, 63,* 1091−1103.

Gopnik, A., Meltzoff, A. N., & Kuhl, P. K. (1999). *The scientist in the crib.* New York: Morrow.

Gopnik, A., & Wellman, H. M. (1994). The theory theory. In L. A. Hirschfeld

& S. A. Gelman (Eds.), *Mapping the mind: Domain specificity in cognition and culture*. New York: Cambridge University Press.

Graf, P., & Mandler, G. (1984). Activation makes words more accessible, but not necessarily more retrievable. *Journal of Verbal Learning and Verbal Behavior, 23*, 553–568.

Graf, P., Mandler, G., & Haden, P. (1982). Simulating amnesic symptoms in normal subjects. *Science, 218*, 1243–1244.

Graf, P., Squire, L. R., & Mandler, G. (1984). The information that amnesic patients do not forget. *Journal of Experimental Psychology: Learning, Memory, and Cognition, 10*, 164–178.

Greene, R. L. (1986). Effects of intentionality and strategy on memory for frequency. *Journal of Experimental Psychology: Learning, Memory, and Cognition, 12*, 489–495.

Greenwood, J. D. (1999). Understanding the "cognitive revolution" in psychology. *Journal of the History of the Behavioral Sciences, 35*, 1–22.

Guyau, J.-M. (1988). The origin of the idea of time. Reprinted in J. A. Michon, V. Pouthas, & J. L. Jackson (Eds.), *Guyau and the idea of time*. Amsterdam: North-Holland. (Original work published 1890)

Haith, M. M. (1980). *Rules that babies look by: The organization of newborn visual activity*. Hillsdale, NJ: Erlbaum.

Haith, M. M. (1998). Who put the cog in infant cognition? Is rich interpretation too costly? *Infant Behavior and Development, 21*, 167–179.

Haith, M. M., & Benson, J. (1998). Infant cognition. In D. Kuhn & R. Siegler (Eds.), *Cognition, language, and perception: Vol. 2* of W. Damon (Series Ed.), *Handbook of child psychology*. New York: Wiley.

Haith, M. M., Wentworth, N., & Canfield, R. (1993). The formation of expectations in early infancy. In C. K. Rovee-Collier & L. P. Lipsitt (Eds.), *Advances in infancy research*. Norwood, NJ: Erlbaum.

Hamilton, D. L., & Gifford, R. K. (1976). Illusory correlation in interpersonal perception: A cognitive basis of stereotypic judgments. *Journal of Experimental Social Psychology, 12*, 392–407.

Harnad, S. (1990). The symbol grounding problem. *Physica D, 42*, 335–346.

Harris, P. L. (1973). Eye movements between adjacent stimuli: An age change in infancy. *British Journal of Psychology, 64*, 215–218.

Harris, P. L. (1986). Commentary: Bringing order to the A-not-B error. *Monographs of the Society for Research in Child Development, 51*, 52–61.

Hartshorn, K., & Rovee-Collier, C. (1997). Infant learning and long-term memory at 6 months: A confirming analysis. *Developmental Psychobiology, 30*, 71–85.

Hatano, G., Siegler, R. S., Richards, D. D., Inagaki, K., Stavy, R., & Wax, N. (1993). The development of biological knowledge: A multi-national study. *Cognitive Development, 8*, 47–62.

Hauser, M. D., Newport, E. L., & Aslin, R. N. (2001). Segmentation of the speech stream in a non-human primate: Statistical learning in cotton-top tamarins. *Cognition, 78*, 353–364.

Hawking, S.W. (1998). *A brief history of time.* New York: Bantam.

Hayes, N. A., & Broadbent, D. E. (1988) Two modes of learning for interactive tasks. *Cognition, 28*, 249–276.

Hayne, H., Boniface, J., & Barr, R. (2000). The development of declarative memory in human infants: Age-related changes in deferred imitation. *Behavioral Neuroscience, 114*, 77–83.

Heider, F., & Simmel, M. (1944). An experimental study of apparent behavior. *American Journal of Psychology, 57*, 243–259.

Herrnstein, R. J. (1979). Acquisition, generalization, and discrimination reversal of a natural concept. *Journal of Experimental Psychology: Animal Behavior Processes, 5*, 116–129.

Hespos, S. J., & Baillargeon, R. (2001a). Reasoning about containment events in very young infants. *Cognition, 78*, 207–245.

Hespos, S. J., & Baillargeon, R. (2001b). Infants' knowledge about occlusion and containment events: A surprising discrepancy. *Psychological Science, 12*, 141–147.

Hockley, W. E. (1984). Retrieval of item frequency information in a continuous memory task. *Memory and Cognition, 12*, 229–242.

Hodges, J. R., Bozeat, S., Lambon Ralph, M. A., Patterson, K., & Spatt, J. (2000). The role of conceptual knowledge in object use: Evidence from semantic dementia. *Brain, 123*, 1913–1925.

Hodges, J. R., Graham, N., & Patterson, K. (1995). Charting the progression of semantic dementia: Implications for the organisation of semantic memory. *Memory, 3*, 463–495.

Hofsten, C. von, & Spelke, E. S. (1985). Object perception and object-directed reaching in infancy. *Journal of Experimental Psychology: General, 114*, 198–212.

Holton, G. (1996). *Einstein, history and other passions.* Reading, MA: Addison-Wesley.

Hood, B., Carey, S., & Prasada, S. (2000). Predicting the outcomes of physical events: Two-year-olds fail to reveal knowledge of solidity and support. *Child Development, 71*, 1540–1554.

Hood, B. M., Willen, J. D., & Driver, J. (1998). Adults' eyes trigger shifts of visual attention in human infants. *Psychological Science, 9*, 131–134.

Huttenlocher, J. (1974). The origins of language comprehension. In R. Solso (Ed.), *Theories in cognitive psychology.* Hillsdale, NJ: Erlbaum.

Huttenlocher, J., & Higgins, E. T. (1978). Issues in the study of symbolic development. In W. A. Collins (Ed.), *Minnesota symposia on child psychology, Vol. 11.* Hillsdale, NJ: Erlbaum.

Inhelder, B., & Piaget, J. (1964). *The early growth of logic in the child.* New York: Norton.

Intons-Peterson, M. J., & Roskos-Ewoldsen, B. B. (1989). Sensory-perceptual qualities of images. *Journal of Experimental Psychology: Learning, Memory, and Cognition, 15,* 188–199.

Jack, A. I., & Shallice, T. (2001). Introspective physicalism as an approach to the science of consciousness. *Cognition, 79,* 161–196.

Jackson, S. W. (1979). Matching behavior in the young infant. *Child Development, 50,* 425–430.

Jacoby, L. L. (1983). Perceptual enhancement: Persistent effects of an experience. *Journal of Experimental Psychology: Learning, Memory, and Cognition, 9,* 21–38.

Janowsky, J. (1985). *Cognitive development and reorganization after early brain injury.* Unpublished doctoral dissertation, Cornell University, Ithaca, NY.

Johansson, G. (1973). Visual perception of biological motion and a model for its analysis. *Perception and Psychophysics, 14,* 201–211.

Johnson, M. (1987). *The body in the mind: The bodily basis of meaning, imagination, and reasoning.* Chicago: University of Chicago Press.

Johnson, M. H., & Morton, J. (1991). *Biology and cognitive development: The case of face recognition.* Oxford: Blackwell.

Johnson, M. H., Posner, M. I., & Rothbart, M. K. (1994). Facilitation of saccades toward a covertly attended location in early infancy. *Psychological Science, 5,* 90–93.

Johnson, S., Slaughter, V., & Carey, S. (1998). Whose gaze will infants follow? The elicitation of gaze-following in 12-month-olds. *Developmental Science, 1,* 233–238.

Johnson, S. C., & Sockaci, E. (2000, July). *The categorization of agents from actions.* Poster presented at the International Conference on Infant Studies, Brighton, England.

Jones, S. S., & Smith, L. B. (1993). The place of perception in children's concepts. *Cognitive Development, 8,* 113–139.

Kahneman, D., & Treisman, A. (1984). Changing views of attention and automaticity. In R. Parasuraman & D. Davies (Eds.), *Varieties of attention.* New York: Academic Press.

Karmiloff-Smith, A. (1986). From meta-processes to conscious access: Evidence from children's metalinguistic and repair data. *Cognition, 23,* 95–147.

Karmiloff-Smith, A. (1992). *Beyond modularity: A developmental perspective on cognitive science.* Cambridge, MA: MIT Press.

Karmiloff-Smith, A. (1993). Self-organization and cognitive change. In M. H. Johnson (Ed.), *Brain development and cognition.* Cambridge, MA: Blackwell.

Karmiloff-Smith, A., & Inhelder, B. (1974–75). If you want to get ahead get a theory. *Cognition, 3,* 195–212.

Keil, F. C. (1979). *Semantic and conceptual development: An ontological perspective.* Cambridge, MA: Harvard University Press.

Keil, F. C. (1989). *Concepts, kinds, and cognitive development.* Cambridge, MA: MIT Press.

Keil, F. C. (1991). The emergence of theoretical beliefs as constraints on concepts. In S. Carey & R. Gelman (Eds.), *The epigenesis of mind*. Hillsdale, NJ: Erlbaum.

Keil, F. C. (1998). Cognitive science and the origins of thought and knowledge. In R. M. Lerner (Ed.), *Theoretical models of human development: Vol. 1* of W. Damon (Series Ed.), *Handbook of child psychology*. New York: Wiley.

Kellman, P. J. (1993). Kinematic foundations of infant visual perception. In C. E. Granrud (Ed.), *Visual perception and cognition in infancy*. Hillsdale, NJ: Erlbaum.

Kellman, P. J., & Spelke, E. S. (1983). Perception of partly occluded objects in infancy. *Cognitive Psychology, 15*, 483−524.

Kemmer, S. (in preparation). *Cognitive lexical semantics*. Amsterdam: John Benjamins.

Kessen, W. (1962). "Stage" and "structure" in the study of children. In W. Kessen & C. Kuhlman (Eds.), *Thought in the young child*. Chicago: University of Chicago Press.

Killen, M., & Uzgiris, I. C. (1981). Imitation of actions with objects: The role of social meaning. *Journal of Genetic Psychology, 138*, 219−229.

Klein, P. J., & Meltzoff, A. N. (1999). Long-term memory, forgetting, and deferred imitation in 12-month-old infants. *Developmental Science, 2*, 102−113.

Knowlton, B. J., Ramus, S. J., & Squire, L. R. (1992). Intact artificial grammar learning in amnesia: Dissociations of classification learning and explicit memory for specific instances. *Psychological Science, 3*, 172−179.

Kolodny, J. A. (1994). Memory processes in classification learning: An investigation of amnesic performance in categorization of dot patterns and artistic styles. *Psychological Science, 5*, 164−169.

Kosslyn, S. M. (1980). *Image and mind*. Cambridge, MA: Harvard University Press.

Kuehne, S. E., Gentner, D., & Forbus, K. D. (2000). Modeling infant learning via symbolic structural alignment. *Proceedings of the 22nd meeting of the Cognitive Science Society*. Philadelphia, PA: Institute for Research in Cognitive Studies.

Kyeong, I. K., & Spelke, E. S. (1999). Perception and understanding of effects of gravity and inertia on object motion. *Developmental Science, 2*, 339−362.

Lakoff, G. (1987). *Women, fire, and dangerous things: What categories reveal about the mind*. Chicago: University of Chicago Press.

Lakoff, G., & Johnson, M. (1980). *Metaphors we live by*. Chicago: University of Chicago Press.

Landau, B., & Jackendoff, R. (1993). "What" and "where" in spatial language and spatial cognition. *Behavior and Brain Sciences, 16*, 217−265.

Langacker, R. W. (1987). *Foundations of cognitive grammar* (Vol. 1). Stanford, CA: Stanford University Press.

Langacker, R. W. (2000). Why a mind is necessary: Conceptualization, grammar and linguistic semantics. In L. Albertazzi (Ed.), *Meaning and cognition*. Amsterdam: John Benjamins.

Lassaline, M. E., Wisniewski, E. J., & Medin, D. L. (1992). Basic levels in artificial and natural categories: Are all basic levels created equal? In B. Burns (Ed.), *Percepts, concepts and categories*. Amsterdam: Elsevier.

Legerstee, M. (1992). A review of the animate-inanimate distinction in infancy: Implications for models of social and cognitive knowing. *Early Development and Parenting, 1*, 59–67.

Leslie, A. M. (1982). The perception of causality in infants. *Perception, 11*, 173–186.

Leslie, A. M. (1984). Infant perception of a manual pick-up event. *British Journal of Developmental Psychology, 2*, 19–32.

Leslie, A. M. (1988). The necessity of illusion: Perception and thought in infancy. In L. Weiskrantz (Ed.), *Thought without language*. Oxford, England: Oxford Science.

Leslie, A. M. (1994). ToMM, ToBY, and Agency: Core architecture and domain specificity. In L. A. Hirschfeld & S. A. Gelman (Eds.), *Mapping the mind: Domain specificity in cognition and culture*. New York: Cambridge University Press.

Levinson, S. C. (1996). Frames of reference and Molyneux's question: Crosslinguistic evidence. In P. Bloom, M. A. Peterson, L. Nadel, & M. F. Garrett (Eds.), *Language and space*. Cambridge, MA: MIT Press.

Loftus, G. R., & Mackworth, N. H. (1978). Cognitive determinants of fixation location during picture viewing. *Journal of Experimental Psychology: Human Perception and Performance, 4*, 565–572.

Lucariello, J., Kyratzis, A., & Nelson, K. (1992). Taxonomic knowledge: What kind and when. *Child Development, 63*, 978–998.

Lucariello, J., & Nelson, K. (1985). Slot-filler categories as memory organizers for young children. *Developmental Psychology, 21*, 272–282.

Lucy, J. (1992). *Grammatical categories and cognition: A case study of the linguistic relativity hypothesis*. Cambridge, England: Cambridge University Press.

Mack, A., & Rock, I. (1998). *Inattentional blindness*. Cambridge, MA: MIT Press.

Macnamara, J. (1982). *Names for things*. Cambridge, MA: MIT Press.

Madole, K. L., & Oakes, L. M. (1999). Making sense of infant categorization: Stable processes and changing representations. *Developmental Review, 19*, 263–296.

Mandler, G. (1967). Organization and memory. In K. W. Spence & J. T. Spence (Eds.), *The psychology of learning and motivation* (Vol. 1). New York: Academic Press.

Mandler, G. (1975). *Mind and emotion*. New York: Wiley.

Mandler, G. (1979). Organization and repetition: Organizational principles with special reference to rote learning. In L.-G. Nilsson (Ed.), *Perspectives on memory research*. Hillsdale, NJ: Erlbaum.

Mandler, G. (1980). Recognizing: The judgment of previous occurrence. *Psychological Review, 87*, 252–271.

Mandler, G. (1985). *Cognitive psychology*. Hillsdale, NJ: Erlbaum.

Mandler, G. (1992). Toward a theory of consciousness. In H.-G. Geissler, S. W. Link, & J. T. Townsend (Eds.), *Cognition, information processing, and psychophysics: Basic issues*. Hillsdale, NJ: Erlbaum.

Mandler, G. (2002a). Organization: What levels of processing are levels of. *Memory, 10*, 333–338.

Mandler, G. (2002b). *Consciousness recovered*. Philadelphia: Benjamins.

Mandler, G., & Kuhlman, C. K. (1961). Proactive and retroactive effects of overlearning. *Journal of Experimental Psychology, 61*, 76–81.

Mandler, J. M. (1978). A code in the node: The use of a story schema in retrieval. *Discourse Processes, 1*, 14–35.

Mandler, J. M. (1983). Representation. In J. H. Flavell & E. M. Markman (Eds.), *Cognitive development: Vol. 3* of P. H. Mussen (Series Ed.), *Handbook of child psychology*. New York: Wiley.

Mandler, J. M. (1984). Representation and recall in infancy. In M. Moscovitch (Ed.), *Infant memory*. New York: Plenum.

Mandler, J. M. (1986). The development of event memory. In F. Klix & H. Hagendorf (Eds.), *Human memory and cognitive capabilities*. Amsterdam: Elsevier.

Mandler, J. M. (1988). How to build a baby: On the development of an accessible representational system. *Cognitive Development, 3*, 113–136.

Mandler, J. M. (1990). Recall of events by preverbal children. In A. Diamond (Ed.), *The development and neural bases of higher cognitive functions*. New York: New York Academy of Sciences.

Mandler, J. M. (1992a). How to build a baby II: Conceptual primitives. *Psychological Review, 99*, 587–604.

Mandler, J. M. (1992b, Spring). The precocious infant revisited. *SRCD Newsletter*, pp. 1, 10–11.

Mandler, J. M. (1994). Precursors of linguistic knowledge. *Philosophical Transactions of the Royal Society, 346*, 63–69.

Mandler, J. M. (1996). Preverbal representation and language. In P. Bloom, M. Peterson, L. Nadel., & M. Garrett (Eds.), *Language and space*. Cambridge, MA: MIT Press.

Mandler, J. M. (1997). Development of categorization: Perceptual and conceptual categories. In G. Bremner, A. Slater, & G. Butterworth (Eds.), *Infant development: Recent advances*. Hove: England: Psychology Press.

Mandler, J. M. (1998a). Representation. In D. Kuhn & R. Siegler (Eds.), *Cognition, perception, and language: Vol. 2* of W. Damon (Series Ed.), *Handbook of child psychology*. New York: Wiley.

Mandler, J. M. (1998b). The rise and fall of semantic memory. In M. Conway, S. Gathercole, & C. Cornoldi (Eds.), *Theories of memory II*. Hove, East Sussex, England: Psychology Press.

Mandler, J. M. (2000a). What global-before-basic trend? Commentary on perceptually based approaches to early categorization. *Infancy, 1*, 99–110.

Mandler, J. M. (2000b). Perceptual and conceptual processes in infancy. *Journal of Cognition and Development, 1*, 3–36.

Mandler, J. M. (2002). On the foundations of the semantic system. In E. Forde & G. Humphreys (Eds.), *Category-specificity in brain and mind*. Hove, East Sussex, England: Psychology Press.

Mandler, J. M., & Bauer, P. J. (1988). The cradle of categorization: Is the basic level basic? *Cognitive Development, 3*, 247–264.

Mandler, J. M., Bauer, P. J., & McDonough, L. (1991). Separating the sheep from the goats: Differentiating global categories. *Cognitive Psychology, 23*, 263–298.

Mandler, J. M., Fivush, R., & Reznick, J. S. (1987). The development of contextual categories. *Cognitive Development, 2*, 339–354.

Mandler, J. M., & Johnson, N. S. (1976). Some of the thousand words a picture is worth. *Journal of Experimental Psychology: Human Learning and Memory, 2*, 529–540.

Mandler, J. M., & McDonough, L. (1993). Concept formation in infancy. *Cognitive Development, 8*, 291–318.

Mandler, J. M., & McDonough, L. (1995). Long-term recall in infancy. *Journal of Experimental Child Psychology, 59*, 457–474.

Mandler, J. M., & McDonough, L. (1996a). Drinking and driving don't mix: Inductive generalization in infancy. *Cognition, 59*, 307–335.

Mandler, J. M., & McDonough, L. (1996b). Nonverbal recall. In N. L. Stein, P. O. Ornstein, B. Tversky, & C. Brainerd (Eds.), *Memory for everyday and emotional events*. Hillsdale, NJ: Erlbaum.

Mandler, J. M., & McDonough, L. (1998a). On developing a knowledge base in infancy. *Developmental Psychology, 34*, 1274–1288.

Mandler, J. M., & McDonough, L. (1998b). Studies in inductive inference in infancy. *Cognitive Psychology, 37*, 60–96.

Mandler, J. M., & McDonough, L. (2000). Advancing downward to the basic level. *Journal of Cognition and Development, 1*, 379–404.

Maratsos, M. (1983). Some current issues in the study of the acquisition of grammar. In J. H. Flavell & E. M. Markman (Eds.), *Cognitive development: Vol. 3* of P. H. Mussen (Series Ed.), *Handbook of child psychology*. New York: Wiley.

Marcel, A. J. (1983). Conscious and unconscious perception: Experiments on visual masking and word recognition. *Cognitive Psychology, 15*, 197–237.

Marcel, A. J. (1993). Slippage in the unity of consciousness. In *Experimental and theoretical studies of consciousness* (Ciba Foundation). New York: Wiley.

Marcus, G. F., Vijayan, S., Bandi Rao, S., & Vishton, P. M. (1999). Rule-learning in seven-month-old infants. *Science, 283*, 77–80.

Mareschal, D., French, R. M., & Quinn, P. (2000). A connectionist account of asymmetric category learning in early infancy. *Developmental Psychology, 36*, 635–645.

Markman, E. M. (1991). The whole object, taxonomic, and mutual exclusivity assumptions as initial constraints on word meanings. In S. A. Gelman & J. P. Byrnes (Eds.), *Perspectives on language and cognition*. Cambridge: England: Cambridge University Press.

Massey, C. M., & Gelman, R. (1988). Preschoolers' ability to decide whether a photographed unfamiliar object can move itself. *Developmental Psychology, 24,* 307–317.

McClelland, J. L., & Rumelhart, D. E. (1985). Distributed memory and the representation of general and specific information. *Journal of Experimental Psychology: General, 114,* 159–188.

McCloskey, M., & Kohl, D. (1983). Naive physics: The curvilinear impetus principle and its role in interactions with moving objects. *Journal of Experimental Psychology: Learning, Memory, & Cognition, 9,* 146–156.

McDonough, L. (1999). Early declarative memory for location. *British Journal of Developmental Psychology, 17,* 381–402.

McDonough, L. (2002a). Early concepts and early language acquisition: What does similarity have to do with either? In N. L. Stein, P. Bauer, & M. Rabinowitz (Eds.), *Representation, memory, and development: Essays in honor of Jean Mandler*. Mahwah, NJ: Erlbaum.

McDonough, L. (2002b). Basic-level nouns: First learned but misunderstood. *Journal of Child Language, 29,* 357–377.

McDonough, L., Choi, S., Bowerman, M., & Mandler, J. M. (1998). The use of preferential looking as a measure of semantic development. In C. Rovee-Collier, L. Lipsitt, & H. Hayne (Eds.), *Advances in infancy research* (Vol. 12). Stamford, CT: Ablex.

McDonough, L., Choi, S., & Mandler, J. M. (2003). Understanding spatial relations: Flexible infants, lexical adults. *Cognitive Psychology, 46,* 229–259.

McDonough, L., & Mandler, J. M. (1994). Very long-term recall in infants: Infantile amnesia reconsidered. *Memory, 2,* 339–352.

McDonough, L., & Mandler, J. M. (1998). Inductive generalization in 9- and 11-month olds. *Developmental Science, 1,* 227–232.

McDonough, L., Mandler, J. M., McKee, R. D., & Squire, L. (1995). The deferred imitation task as a nonverbal measure of declarative memory. *Proceedings of the National Academy of Sciences, 92,* 7580–7584.

McKee, R. D., & Squire, L. R. (1993). On the development of declarative memory. *Journal of Experimental Psychology: Learning, Memory, & Cognition, 19,* 397–404.

Medin, D. L. (1983). Cue validity. Structural principles of categorization. In B. Shepp & T. Tighe (Eds.), *Interaction: Perception, development, and cognition*. Hillsdale, NJ: Erlbaum.

Medin, D. L., & Barsalou, L. W. (1987). Categorization processes and categorical perception. In S. Harnad (Ed.), *Categorical perception*. New York: Cambridge University Press.

Medin, D. L., & Heit, E. (1999). Categorization. In B. M. Bly & D. E. Rumelhart (Eds.), *Cognitive Science*. San Diego: Academic Press.

Medin, D. L., Wattenmaker, W. D., & Michalski, R. S. (1987). Constraints and preferences in inductive learning: An experimental study of human and machine performance. *Cognitive Science, 11*, 299–339.

Meier, R. P., & Newport, E. L. (1990). Out of the hands of babes: On a possible sign advantage in language acquisition. *Language, 66*, 1–23.

Meltzoff, A. N. (1988a). Infant imitation and memory: Nine-month-olds in immediate and deferred tests. *Child Development, 59*, 217–225.

Meltzoff, A. N. (1988b). Infant imitation after a 1-week delay: Long-term memory for novel acts and multiple stimuli. *Developmental Psychology, 24*, 470–476.

Meltzoff, A. N., & Moore, M. K. (1977). Imitation of facial and manual gestures by human neonates. *Science, 198*, 75–78.

Meltzoff, A. N., & Moore, M. K. (1983). Newborn infants imitate adult facial gestures. *Child Development, 54*, 702–709.

Mervis, C. B., & Crisafi, M. A. (1982). Order of acquisition of subordinate-, basic-, and superordinate-level categories. *Child Development, 53*, 258–266.

Mervis, C. B., & Mervis, C. A. (1982). Leopards are kitty-cats: Object labeling by mothers for their thirteen-month-olds. *Child Development, 53*, 267–273.

Mervis, C. B., & Rosch, E. (1981). Categorization of natural objects. *Annual Review of Psychology, 32*, 89–115.

Michotte, A. E. (1963). *The perception of causality*. London: Methuen.

Miller, G. A. (1956). The magical number seven, plus or minus two: Some limits on your capacity for processing information. *Psychological Review, 63*, 81–97.

Miller, G. A., & Johnson-Laird, P. (1976). *Language and perception*. Cambridge, MA: Harvard University Press.

Mills, A. E. (1985). The acquisition of German. In D. I. Slobin (Ed.), *The crosslinguistic study of language acquisition* (Vol. 1). Hillsdale, NJ: Erlbaum.

Milner, B., Corkin, S., & Teuber, H. L. (1968). Further analysis of the hippocampal amnesic syndrome: 14 year follow-up study of H. M. *Neuropsychologia, 6*, 215–234.

Mishkin, M., & Appenzeller, T. (1987). The anatomy of memory. *Scientific American, 256*, 80–89.

Morgan, J. L., & Newport, E. L. (1981). The role of constituent structure in the induction of an artificial language. *Journal of Verbal learning and Verbal Behavior, 20*, 67–85.

Moscovitch, M. (1995). Models of consciousness and memory. In M. S. Gazzaniga (Ed.), *The cognitive neurosciences*. Cambridge, MA: MIT Press.

Moscovitch, M. (2000). Theories of memory and consciousness. In E. Tulving & F. I. M. Craik (Eds.), *The Oxford handbook of memory*. Oxford: Oxford University Press.

Moscovitch, M., Goshen-Gottstein, Y., & Vriezen, E. (1994). Memory without conscious recollection: A tutorial review from a neuropsychological perspective. In C. Umiltá & M. Moscovitch (Eds.), *Attention and performance XV: Conscious and nonconscious information processing.* Cambridge, MA: MIT Press.

Movellan, J. R., & Watson, J. S. (2002). *The development of gaze following as a Bayesian systems identification* (Institute for Neural Computation technical report). La Jolla: University of California, San Diego.

Muensinger, K. F. (1938). Vicarious trial and error at a point of choice: I. A general survey of its relation to learning efficiency. *Journal of Genetic Psychology, 53,* 75–86.

Muir, D. W., & Nadel, J. (1998). Infant social perception. In A. Slater (Ed.), *Perceptual development: Visual, auditory, and speech perception in infancy.* Hove, East Sussex, England: Psychology Press.

Mullen, A. M., & Aslin, R. N. (1978). Visual tracking as an index of the object concept. *Infant Behavior and Development, 1,* 309–319.

Munakata, Y., McClelland, J. L., Johnson, M. H., & Siegler, R. S. (1997). Rethinking infant knowledge: Toward an adaptive process account of successes and failures in object permanence tasks. *Psychological Review, 104,* 686–719.

Murphy, G. L. (1982). Cue validity and levels of categorization. *Psychological Bulletin, 91,* 174–177.

Murphy, G. L., & Smith, E. E. (1982). Basic-level superiority in picture categorization. *Journal of Verbal Learning and Verbal Behavior, 21,* 1–20.

Murray, A. D., & Trevarthen, C. (1985). Emotional regulation of interactions between two-month-olds and their mothers. In T. M. Field & N. A. Fox (Eds.), *Social perception in infants.* Norwood, NJ: Ablex.

Myers, N., Clifton, R., & Clarkson, M. (1987). When they were very young: Almost-threes remember two years ago. *Infant Behavior and Development, 10,* 123–132.

Nelson, C. A. (1997). The neurobiological basis of early memory development. In N. Cowan (Ed.), *The development of memory in childhood.* Hove, England: Psychology Press.

Nelson, C. A., & Collins, P. F. (1991). Event-related potential and looking-time analysis of infants' responses to familiar and novel events: Implications for visual recognition memory. *Developmental Psychology, 27,* 50–58.

Nelson, C. A., & Collins, P. F. (1992). Neural and behavioral correlates of recognition memory in 4- and 9-month-old infants. *Brain and Cognition, 19,* 105–121.

Nelson, K. (1973a). Some evidence for the cognitive primacy of categorization and its functional basis. *Merrill-Palmer Quarterly, 19,* 21-39.

Nelson, K. (1973b). Structure and strategy in learning to talk. *Monographs of the Society for Research in Child Development, 38* (Serial No. 149).

Nelson, K. (1974). Concept, word, and sentence: Interrelations in acquisition and development. *Psychological Review, 81,* 267–285.

Nelson, K. (1978). How young children represent knowledge in their world in and out of language. In R. S. Siegler (Ed.), *Children's thinking: What develops?* Hillsdale, NJ: Erlbaum.

Nelson, K. (1985). *Making sense: The acquisition of shared meaning.* San Diego: Academic Press.

Nelson, K. (1988). Constraints on word learning? *Cognitive Development, 3,* 221–246.

Nelson, K. (1993). The psychological and social origins of autobiographical memory. *Psychological Science, 4,* 1–8.

Nelson, K. (1994). Long-term retention of memory for preverbal experience: Evidence and implications. *Memory, 2,* 467–475.

Nelson, K. (2000). Global and functional: Mandler's perceptual and conceptual processes in infancy. *Journal of Cognition and Development, 1,* 49–54.

Nelson, K., & Fivush, R. (2000). Socialization of memory. In E. Tulving & F. I. M. Craik (Eds.), *The Oxford handbook of memory.* Oxford: Oxford University Press.

Nelson, K., Hampson, J., & Kessler Shaw, L. (1993). Nouns in early lexicons: Evidence, explanations, and implications. *Journal of Child Language, 20,* 61–84.

Nelson, K., & Ross, G. (1980). The generalities and specifics of long-term memory in infants and young children. In M. Perlmutter (Ed.), *New directions for child development: Children's memory.* San Francisco, CA: Jossey-Bass.

Newcombe, N., & Fox, N. (1994). Infantile amnesia: Through a glass darkly. *Child Development, 65,* 31–40.

Newport, E. L. (1990). Maturational constraints on language learning. *Cognitive Science, 14,* 11–28.

Nickerson, R. S., & Adams, M. J. (1979). Long-term memory for a common object. *Cognitive Psychology, 11,* 287–307.

Ninio, A., & Bruner, J. (1978). The achievement and antecedents of labelling. *Journal of Child Language, 5,* 1–15.

Nosofsky, R. (1992). Exemplar-based approach to relating categorization, identification, and recognition. In F. G. Ashby (Ed.), *Multidimensional models of perception and cognition.* Hillsdale, NJ: Erlbaum.

Oakes, L. M., Coppage, D. J., & Dingel, A. (1997). By land or by sea: The role of perceptual similarity in infants' categorization of animals. *Developmental Psychology, 33,* 396–407.

Oakes, L. M., Madole, K. L., & Cohen, L. B. (1991). Infants' object examining: Habituation and categorization. *Cognitive Development, 6,* 377–392.

Oakes, L. M., & Tellinghuisen, D. J. (1994). Examining in infancy: Does it reflect active processing? *Developmental Psychology, 30,* 748–756.

O'Regan, J. K. (1992). Solving the "real" mysteries of visual perception: The world as an outside memory. *Canadian Journal of Psychology, 46,* 461–488.

O'Regan, J. K., Rensink, R. A., & Clark, J. J. (1999). Change-blindness as a result of "mudsplashes." *Nature, 398*(6722), 34.

Paivio, A. (1978). The relationship between verbal and perceptual codes. In E. C. Carterette & M. P. Friedman (Eds.), *Handbook of perception: Vol. 8. Perceptual coding*. New York: Academic Press.

Palmer, C. F., Jones, R. K., Hennessy, B. L., Unze, M. G., & Pick, A. D. (1989). How is a trumpet known? The "basic object level" concept and perception of musical instruments. *American Journal of Psychology, 102*, 17–37.

Palmer, S. E. (1975). The effect of contextual scenes on the identification of objects. *Memory and Cognition, 3*, 519–526.

Papafragou, A., Massey, C., & Gleitman, L. (2002). Shake, rattle, 'n' roll: The representation of motion in language and cognition. *Cognition, 84*, 189–219.

Pauen, S. (2000a). Early differentiation within the animate domain: Are humans something special? *Journal of Experimental Child Psychology, 75*, 134–151.

Pauen, S. (2000b, July). *The "animal–ball experiment": A new paradigm to study causal attribution of animate motion in infancy.* Poster presented at the International Society of Infant Studies, Brighton, England.

Pauen, S. (2002). Evidence for knowledge-based category discrimination in infancy. *Child Development, 73*, 1016–1033.

Phillips, R. D., Wagner, S. H., Fells, C. A., & Lynch, M. (1990). Do infants recognize emotion in facial expressions? Categorical and "metaphorical" evidence. *Infant Behavior and Development, 13*, 71–84.

Piaget, J. (1951). *Play, dreams, and imitation in childhood.* London: Kegan Paul, Trench, & Trubner.

Piaget, J. (1952). *The origins of intelligence in the child.* New York: International Universities Press.

Piaget, J. (1954). *The construction of reality in the child.* New York: Basic Books.

Piaget, J. (1976). *The grasp of consciousness: Action and concept in the young child.* Cambridge, MA: Harvard University Press.

Piaget, J., & Inhelder, B. (1971). *Mental imagery in the child: A study of the development of imaginal representation.* London: Routledge & Kegan Paul.

Plunkett, K., & Sinha, C. (1992). Connectionism and developmental theory. *British Journal of Developmental Psychology, 10*, 209–254.

Posner, M. I. (1988). Structures and functions of selective attention. In T. Boll & B. Brayant (Eds.), *Master lectures in clinical neuropsychology and brain function: Research, measurement, and practice.* Washington, DC: American Psychological Association.

Posner, M. I., & Klein, R. M. (1973). On the functions of consciousness. In S. Kornblum (Ed.), *Attention and performance* (Vol. 4). New York: Academic Press.

Postal, P. M. (1966). Review article: Andre Martinet, "Elements of general linguistics." *Foundations of Language, 2*, 151–186.

Poulin-Dubois, D., Lepage, A., & Ferland, D. (1996). Infants' concept of animacy. *Cognitive Development, 11*, 19–36.

Poulin-Dubois, D., & Vyncke, J. (2003). *The cow jumped over the moon: Infants' inductive generalization of motion properties.* Concordia University, Montreal: Unpublished manuscript.

Povinelli, D. J. (2000). *Folk physics for apes.* Oxford, England: Oxford University Press.

Proffitt, D. R., & Bertenthal, B. I. (1990). Converging operations revisited: Assessing what infants perceive using discrimination measures. *Perception & Psychophysics, 47*, 1–11.

Pylyshyn, Z. (1979). Validating computational models: A critique of Anderson's indeterminacy of representation claim. *Psychological Review, 86*, 383–394.

Pylyshyn, Z. (1981). The imagery debate: Analogue media versus tacit knowledge. *Psychological Review, 88*, 16–45.

Quine, W. V. (1977). Natural kinds. In S. P. Schwartz (Ed.), *Naming, necessity, and natural kinds.* Ithaca, NY: Cornell University Press.

Quinn, P. C. (2003). Concepts are not just for objects: Categorization of spatial relation information by infants. In D. H. Rakison & L. M. Oakes (Eds.), *Categories and concepts in early development.* Oxford: Oxford University Press.

Quinn, P. C. (in press). Young infants' categorization of humans versus non-human animals: Roles for knowledge access and perceptual process. In L. Gershkoff-Stowe & D. Rakison (Eds.), *Building object categories in developmental time.* Mahwah, NJ: Erlbaum.

Quinn, P. C., & Eimas, P. D. (1996). Perceptual cues that permit categorical differentiation of animal species by infants. *Journal of Experimental Child Psychology, 63*, 189–211.

Quinn, P. C., & Eimas, P. D. (1997). A reexamination of the perceptual-to-conceptual shift in mental representation. *Review of General Psychology, 1*, 271–287.

Quinn, P. C., & Eimas, P. D. (1998). Evidence for a global categorical representation of humans by young infants. *Journal of Experimental Child Psychology, 69*, 151–174.

Quinn, P. C., & Eimas, P. D. (2000). The emergence of category representations during infancy: Are separate perceptual and conceptual processes required? *Journal of Cognition and Development, 1*, 55–61.

Quinn, P. C., Eimas, P. D., & Rosenkrantz, S. L. (1993). Evidence for representations of perceptually similar natural categories by 3-month-old and 4-month-old infants. *Perception, 22*, 463–475.

Quinn, P. C., & Johnson, M. H. (1997). The emergence of perceptual category representations in young infants: A connectionist analysis. *Journal of Experimental Child Psychology, 66*, 236–263.

Quinn, P. C., & Johnson, M. H. (2000). Global-before-basic object categorization in connectionist networks and 2-month-old infants. *Infancy, 1,*
31–46.

Quinn, P. C., Polly, J. L., Furer, M. J., Dobson, V., & Narter, D. B. (2003).
Young infants' performance in the object-variation version of the above-
below categorization task: A result of perceptual distraction or conceptual
limitation? *Infancy, 3,* 323–348.

Rakison, D. H., & Poulin-Dubois, D. (2001). Developmental origin of the animate-inanimate distinction. *Psychological Bulletin, 127,* 209–228.

Reason, J. T. (1979). Actions not as planned. In G. Underwood & R. Stevens
(Eds.), *Aspects of consciousness.* London: Academic Press.

Reber, P. J., & Squire, L. R. (1994). Parallel brain systems for learning with and
without awareness. *Learning and Memory, 1,* 217–229.

Regier, R., & Carlson, L. (2002). Spatial language: Perceptual constraints and
linguistic variation. In N. L. Stein, P. Bauer, & M. Rabinowitz (Eds.), *Representation, memory, and development: Essays in honor of Jean Mandler.* Mahwah,
NJ: Erlbaum.

Regier, T. (1995). A model of the human capacity for categorizing spatial relations. *Cognitive Linguistics, 6,* 63–88.

Regier, T. (1997). Constraints on the learning of spatial terms: A computational
investigation. In P. L. Goldstone, P. G. Schyns, & D. L. Medin (Eds.), *The
psychology of learning and motivation* (Vol. 36). San Diego: Academic Press.

Rescorla, L. (1980). Overextension in early language development. *Journal of
Child Language, 9,* 321–335.

Ricciuti, H. N. (1965). Object grouping and selective ordering behavior in infants 12 to 24 months old. *Merrill-Palmer Quarterly, 11,* 129–148.

Rice, M. (1978). *The effect of children's prior nonverbal color concepts on the learning of
color words.* Unpublished doctoral dissertation, University of Kansas.

Richards, J. E., & Casey, B. J. (1992). Development of sustained visual attention
in the human infant. In B. A. Campbell, H. Hayne, & R. Richardson
(Eds.), *Attention and information processing in infants and adults.* Hillsdale, NJ:
Erlbaum.

Richards, M. M. (1979). Sorting out what's in a word from what's not: Evaluat-
ing Clark's semantic features acquisition theory. *Journal of Experimental Child
Psychology, 27,* 1–47.

Riddoch, M. J., & Humphreys, G. W. (1987). Visual object processing in optic
aphasia: A case of semantic access agnosia. *Cognitive Neuroscience, 4,* 131–185.

Roberts, K. (1988). Retrieval of a basic-level category in prelinguistic infants.
Developmental Psychology, 24, 21–27.

Roberts, K., & Cuff, M. D. (1989). Categorization studies of 9- to 15-month-
old infants: Evidence for superordinate categorization? *Infant Behavior and
Development, 12,* 265–288.

Rochat, P., Morgan, R., & Carpenter, M. (1997). Young infants' sensitivity to movement information specifying social causality. *Cognitive Development, 12*, 537–561.

Rogers, T. T., & McClelland, J. L. (in press). A parallel distributed processing approach to semantic cognition: Applications to conceptual development. In D. Rakison & L. Gershkoff-Stowe (Eds.), *Building object categories in developmental time.* Mahwah, NJ: Erlbaum.

Rosch, E. (1973). Natural categories. *Cognitive Psychology, 4*, 328–350.

Rosch, E. (1978). Principles of categorization. In E. Rosch & B. Lloyd (Eds.), *Cognition and categorization.* Hillsdale, NJ: Erlbaum.

Rosch, E., & Mervis, C. B. (1975). Family resemblances: Studies in the internal structure of categories. *Cognitive Psychology, 7*, 573–605.

Rosch, E., Mervis, C. B., Gray, W., Johnson, D., & Boyes-Braem, P. (1976). Basic objects in natural categories. *Cognitive Psychology, 3*, 382–439.

Rose, S. A., Feldman, J. F., & Jankowski, J. J. (2001). Visual short-term memory in the first year of life: Capacity and recency effects. *Developmental Psychology, 37*, 539–549.

Ross, G. S. (1980). Categorization in 1- to 2-year-olds. *Developmental Psychology, 16*, 391–396.

Rovee-Collier, C. (1989). The joy of kicking: Memories, motives, and mobiles. In P. R. Solomon, G. R. Goethals, C. M. Kelley, & B. R. Stephens (Eds.), *Memory: Interdisciplinary approaches.* New York: Springer-Verlag.

Rovee-Collier, C. (1997). Dissociations in infant memory: Rethinking the development of implicit and explicit memory. *Psychological Review, 104*, 467–498.

Ruff, H. (1986). Components of attention during infants' manipulative exploration. *Child Development, 57*, 105–114.

Ruff, H. A., & Saltarelli, L. M. (1993). Exploratory play with objects: Basic cognitive processes and individual differences. In M. H. Bornstein & A. W. O'Reilly (Eds.), *The role of play in the development of thought.* San Francisco: Jossey-Bass.

Rumelhart, D. E., & Todd, P. M. (1993). Learning and connectionist representations. In D. E. Meyer & S. Kornblum (Eds.), *Attention and performance XIV: Synergies in experimental psychology, artificial intelligence, and cognitive neuroscience.* Cambridge, MA: MIT Press.

Saffran, E. M., & Schwartz, M. F. (1994). Of cabbages and things: Semantic memory from a neuropsychological perspective—A tutorial review. In C. Umiltá & M. Moscovitch (Eds.), *Attention and performance XV: Conscious and unconscious information processing.* Cambridge, MA: MIT Press.

Saffran, J. R., Aslin, R. N., & Newport, E. L. (1996). Statistical learning by 8-month-old infants. *Science, 274*, 1926–1928.

Saffran, J. R., Newport, E. L., Aslin, R. N., Tunick, R. A., & Barrueco, S. (1997). Incidental language learning: Listening (and learning) out of the corner of your ear. *Psychological Science, 8*, 101–105.

Salapatek, P., & Kessen, W. (1966). Visual scanning of triangles by the human newborn. *Journal of Experimental Child Psychology, 3,* 155–167.

Sameroff, A. J., & Cavanaugh, P. J. (1979). Learning in infancy: A developmental perspective. In J. D. Osovsky (Ed.), *Handbook of infant development.* New York: Wiley.

Saxby, L., & Anglin, J. M. (1983). Children's sorting of objects from categories of differing levels of generality. *Journal of Genetic Psychology, 143,* 123–137.

Scaife, M., & Bruner, J. S. (1975). The capacity for joint visual attention in the infant. *Nature, 253,* 265–266.

Schacter, D. L. (1987). Implicit memory: History and current status. *Journal of Experimental Psychology: Learning, Memory, and Cognition, 13,* 501–518.

Schlesinger, I. M. (1988). The origin of relational categories. In Y. Levy, I. M. Schlesinger, & M. D. Braine (Eds.), *Categories and processes in language acquisition.* Hillsdale, NJ: Erlbaum.

Searle, J. R. (1980). Minds, brains, and programs. *Behavioral and Brain Sciences, 3,* 417–457.

Shallice, T. (1972). Dual functions of consciousness. *Psychological Review, 79,* 383–393.

Shanks, D. R., & St. John, M. F. (1994). Characteristics of dissociable human learning systems. *Behavioral and Brain Sciences, 17,* 367–347.

Shatz, M., & Backscheider, A. G. (1999). *Toddlers create lexical domains: The case of color.* Unpublished manuscript, University of Michigan.

Shipley, E. F., Kuhn, I. F., & Madden, E. C. (1983). Mothers' use of superordinate category terms. *Journal of Child Language, 10,* 571–588.

Siegal, M. (1991). *Knowing children.* Hillsdale, NJ: Erlbaum.

Siegel, L., & Hodkin, B. (1982). Has Piaget led us up the garden path or into the poison ivy? In S. Modgil & C. Modgil (Eds.), *Jean Piaget: Consensus and controversy.* New York: Holt, Rinehart, and Winston.

Siegler, R. S. (1991). *Children's thinking* (2nd ed.). Englewood Cliffs, NJ: Prentice-Hall.

Simon, T. J. (1997). Reconceptualizing the origins of number knowledge: A "non-numerical" account. *Cognitive Development, 12,* 349–372.

Simons, D. J., & Keil, F. C. (1995). An abstract to concrete shift in the development of biological thought: the *insides* story. *Cognition, 56,* 129–163.

Sirois, S., Buckingham, D., & Shultz, T. R. (2000). Artificial grammar learning by infants: An auto-associator perspective. *Developmental Science, 3,* 442–456.

Slamecka, N. J. (1961). Proactive inhibition of connected discourse. *Journal of Experimental Psychology, 62,* 295–301.

Slobin, D. I. (1985). Crosslinguistic evidence for the language-making capacity. In D. I. Slobin (Ed.), *The crosslinguistic study of language acquisition* (Vol. 2). Hillsdale, NJ: Erlbaum.

Smiley, P., & Huttenlocher, J. (1995). Conceptual development and the child's early words for events, objects, and persons. In M. Tomasello & W. E. Merriman (Eds.), *Beyond names for things.* Hillsdale, NJ: Erlbaum.

Smith, C., Carey, S., & Wiser, M. (1985). On differentiation: A case study of the development of the concepts of size, weight, and density. *Cognition, 21,* 177–237.

Smith, C. L. (1979). Children's understanding of natural language hierarchies. *Journal of Experimental Child Psychology, 27,* 437–458.

Smith, E. E., & Medin, D. L. (1981). *Categories and concepts.* Cambridge, MA: Harvard University Press.

Smith, E. E., Patalano, A. L, & Jonides, J. (1998) Alternative mechanisms of categorization. *Cognition, 65,* 167–196.

Smith, L. B., & Samuelson, L. (1997). Perceiving and remembering: Category stability, variability, and development. In K. Lamberts & D. Shanks (Eds.), *Knowledge, concepts, and categories.* East Sussex, England: Psychology Press.

Smith, P. H. (1984). Five-month-old recall of temporal order and utilization of temporal organization. *Journal of Experimental Child Psychology, 38,* 400–414.

Spelke, E. S. (1994). Initial knowledge: Six suggestions. *Cognition, 50,* 431–445.

Spelke, E. S. (1998). Nativism, empiricism, and the origins of knowledge. *Infant Behavior and Development, 21,* 181–200.

Spelke, E. S., Breinlinger, K., Macomber, J., & Jacobson, K. (1992). Origins of knowledge. *Psychological Review, 99,* 605–632.

Spelke, E. S., & Hespos, S. J. (2002). Conceptual development in infancy: The case of containment. In N. L. Stein, P. Bauer, & M. Rabinowitz (Eds.), *Representation, memory, and development: Essays in honor of Jean Mandler.* Mahwah, NJ: Erlbaum.

Spelke, E. S., Philips, A., & Woodward, A. L. (1995). Infants' knowledge of object motion and human action. In D. Sperber, D. Premack, & A. J. Premack (Eds.), *Causal cognition.* Oxford, England: Clarendon Press.

Squire, L. (1987). *Memory and brain.* New York: Oxford University Press.

Squire, L. R., & Knowlton, B. J. (2000). The anatomical bases of memory. In M. S. Gazzaniga (Ed.), *The new cognitive neurosciences* (2nd ed.). Cambridge, MA: MIT Press.

Squire, L., & Zola-Morgan, S. (1991). The medial temporal lobe memory system. *Science, 253,* 1380–1386.

Stanfield, R. A., & Zwaan, R. A. (2001). The effect of implied orientation derived from verbal context on picture recognition. *Psychological Science, 12,* 153–156.

Starkey, D. (1981). The origins of concept formation: Object sorting and object preference in early infancy. *Child Development, 52,* 489–497.

Sugarman, S. (1983). *Children's early thought.* Cambridge, England: Cambridge University Press.

Sweetser, E. (1990). *From etymology to pragmatics: Metaphorical and cultural aspects of semantic structure.* Cambridge, England: Cambridge University Press.

Talmy, L. (1988). Force dynamics in language and cognition. *Cognitive Science, 12*, 49–100.

Tanaka, J. W., & Taylor, M. (1991). Object categories and expertise: Is the basic level in the eye of the beholder? *Cognitive Psychology, 23*, 457–482.

Tomasello, M. (1992). *First verbs*. Cambridge, England: Cambridge University Press.

Tomasello, M. (2000). Do young children have adult syntactic competence? *Cognition, 74*, 209–253.

Tomikawa, S. A., & Dodd, D. H. (1980). Early word meanings: Perceptually or functionally based? *Child Development, 51*, 1103–1109.

Traugott, E. C. (1978). On the expression of spatio-temporal relations in language. In J. H. Greenberg (Ed.), *Universals of human language: Vol 3. Word structure*. Stanford, CA: Stanford University Press.

Tronick, E., Als, H., Adamson, L., Wise, S., & Brazelton, T. B. (1978). The infants' response to entrapment between contradictory messages in face-to-face interactions. *Journal of the American Academy of Child Psychiatry, 17*, 1–13.

Troseth, G. L., & DeLoache, J. S. (1998). The medium can obscure the message: Young children's understanding of video. *Child Development, 69*, 950–965.

Tulving, E. (1985). Memory and consciousness. *Canadian Psychology, 26*, 1–12.

Tulving, E., & Pearlstone, Z. (1966). Availability versus accessibility of information in memory for words. *Journal of Verbal Learning and Verbal Behavior, 5*, 381–391.

Tyler, L. K., Moss, H. E., Durrant-Peatfield, M. R., & Levy, J. P. (2000). Conceptual structure and the structure of concepts: A distributed account of category-specific deficits. *Brain and Language, 75*, 195–231.

Uller, C., Carey, S., Huntley-Fenner, G., & Klatt, L. (1999). What representations might underlie infant numerical knowledge? *Cognitive Development, 14*, 1–36.

Ullman, M. (2001). The declarative/procedural model of lexicon and grammar. *Journal of Psycholinguistic Research, 30*, 37–69.

Ullman, M., Corkin, S., Coppola, M., Hickok, G., Growdon, J. H., Koroshetz, W. J., et al. (1997). A neural dissociation within language: Evidence that the mental dictionary is part of declarative memory, and that grammatical rules are processed by the procedural system. *Journal of Cognitive Neuroscience, 9*, 266–276.

Uzgiris, I. C., & Hunt, J. McV. (1975). *Assessment in infancy: Ordinal scales of psychological development*. Urbana, IL: University of Illinois Press.

Van de Walle, G. (1999, April). *Nine month olds show manual habituation to shared object color*. Paper presented at the Society for Research in Child Development, Albuquerque, NM.

Van de Walle, G. A., Carey, S., & Prevor, M. (2000). Bases for object individual in infancy: Evidence from manual search. *Journal of Cognition and Development, 1*, 249–280.

Veale, T., & O'Donoghue, D. (2000). Computation and blending. *Cognitive Linguistics, 11,* 253–281.

Vygotsky, L. (1962). *Language and thought.* New York: Wiley. (Original work published 1934)

Wagner, S., Winner, E., Cicchetti, D., & Gardner, H. (1981). "Metaphorical" mapping in human infants. *Child Development, 52,* 728–731.

Warrington, E. K. (1975). The selective impairment of semantic memory. *Quarterly Journal of Experimental Psychology, 27,* 635–657.

Warrington, E. K., & McCarthy, R. A. (1987). Categories of knowledge: Further fractionations and an attempted integration. *Brain, 110,* 1273–1296.

Warrington, E. K., & Shallice, T. (1984). Category specific semantic impairments. *Brain, 107,* 829–854.

Warrington, E. K., & Weiskrantz, L. (1974). The effects of prior learning on subsequent retention in amnesic patients. *Neuropsychologia, 12,* 419–428.

Warrington, E. K., & Weiskrantz, L. (1982). Amnesia: A disconnection syndrome. *Neuropsychologia, 20,* 233–248.

Wasserman, E. A. (1995). The conceptual abilities of pigeons. *American Scientist, 83,* 246–255.

Watson, J. (1972). Smiling, cooing, and "the game." *Merrill-Palmer Quarterly, 18,* 323–340.

Waxman, S. R., & Hall, G. D. (1993). The development of a linkage between count nouns and object categories: Evidence from fifteen- to twenty-one-month-old infants. *Child Development, 64,* 1224–1241.

Waxman, S. R., & Markow, D. B. (1995). Words as invitations to form catgories: Evidence from 12- to 13-month-old infants. *Cognitive Psychology, 29,* 257–302.

Waxman, S. R., Shipley, E. F., & Shepperson, B. (1991). Establishing new subcategories: The role of category labels and existing knowledge. *Child Development, 62,* 127–138.

Weiskrantz, L. (1986). *Blindsight.* Oxford, England: Oxford University Press.

Welder, A. N., & Graham, S. A. (2001). The influence of shape similarity and shared labels on infants' inductive inferences about nonobvious properties. *Child Development, 72,* 1653–1673.

Wellman, H. M., Cross, D., & Bartsch, K. (1986). Infant search and object permanence: A meta-analysis of the A-not-B error. *Monographs of the Society for Research in child Development, 51* (Serial No. 214).

Werner, H. (1957). The concept of development from a comparative and organismic point of view. In D. B. Harris (Ed.), *The concept of development: An issue in the study of human behavior.* Minneapolis: University of Minnesota Press.

Werner, H., & Kaplan, B. (1963). *Symbol formation.* New York: Wiley.

Whalen, J., Gallistel, C. R., & Gelman, R. (1999). Nonverbal counting in humans: The psychophysics of number representation. *Psychological Science, 10,* 130–137.

White, P. A. (1988). Causal processing: Origins and development. *Psychological Bulletin, 104*, 36–52.

Wilcox, T., & Schweinle, A. (2002). Object individuation and event mapping: Developmental changes in infants' use of featural information. *Developmental Science, 5*, 132–150.

Willatts, P. (1997). Beyond the "couch potato" infant: How infants use their knowledge to regulate action, solve problems, and achieve goals. In G. Bremner, A. Slater, & G. Butterworth (Eds.), *Infant development: Recent advances.* Hove, East Sussex, England: Psychology Press.

Wilson, N. J. (1986). *An implementation and perceptual test of a principled model of biological motion.* Unpublished master's thesis, University of Pennsylvania, Philadelphia.

Woodward, A. L. (1998). Infants selectively encode the goal object of an actor's reach. *Cognition, 69*, 1–34.

Woodward, A. L. (1999). Infants' ability to distinguish between purposeful and non-purposeful behaviors. *Infant Behavior and Development, 22*, 145–160.

Woodward, A. L., & Markman, E. M. (1998). Early word learning. In D. Kuhn & R. Siegler (Eds.), *Cognition, perception, and language: Vol. 2* of W. Damon (Series Ed.), *Handbook of child psychology.* New York: Wiley.

Woodward, A. L., & Sommerville, J. A. (2000). Twelve-month-old infants interpretation in context. *Psychological Science, 11*, 73–77.

Worden, P. E., & Ritchey, G. H. (1979). The development of the category-recall relationship in the sorting-recall task. *Journal of Experimental Child Psychology, 27*, 384–394.

Wynn, K. (1992). Addition and subtraction by human infants. *Nature, 358*, 749–750.

Xu, F., & Carey, S. (1996). Infants' metaphysics: The case of numerical identity. *Cognitive Psychology, 30*, 111–153.

Young, M. E., & Wasserman, E. A. (1997). Entropy detection by pigeons: Response to mixed visual displays after same-different discrimination training. *Journal of Experimental Psychology: Animal Behavior Processes, 23*, 157–170.

Younger, B. A., & Cohen, L. B. (1986). Developmental change in infants' perception of correlations among attributes. *Child Development, 57*, 803–815.

Younger, B. A., & Fearing, D. D. (2000). A global-to-basic trend in early categorization: Evidence from a dual-category habituation task. *Infancy, 1*, 47–58.

Younger, B. A., & Johnson, K. E. (in press). Infants' comprehension of toy replicas as symbols for real objects. *Cognitive Psychology.*

Zentall, T. R. (2000). Symbolic representation by pigeons. *Current Directions in Psychological Science, 9*, 118–123.

Zwaan, R. A., Stanfield, R. A., & Yaxley, R. H. (2002). Language comprehenders mentally represent the shape of objects. *Psychological Science, 13*, 168–171.

Index of Names

Index of Subjects

abstract concepts, 79, 122,173, 216–217,
220, 303
of containment, 32, 115
in pigeons, 138–139
spatial bases of, 88–89, 108
accessibility, 7–8, 14–15, 21, 49–51,
54–55, 198, 200, 284
affordances, 185
agent concept, 7, 76, 102–108, 249,
276–277, 301, 303
amnesia, 228–229, 238–239, 287–
289, 295
animal concepts. *See also* artifact concepts
breakdown of, 208, 211–212
contrasted with inanimate things, 71,
73, 76, 85–86, 203, 217
contrasted with plants, 205, 217
identifiers of, 166–167
origin of, 85–86, 94–99, 173,
303–304
tripartite division of, 150–151, 158
used for learning grammatical structure, 276
animate-inanimate distinction, 93,
106–197, 156–157, 202–205, 208,
211, 217

A-not-B test, 223–226
artifact concepts
breakdown of, 208, 211–212
contrasted with animals, 93, 125–129,
203–204
indoor vs. outdoor, 203, 205, 207
inductive generalization of, 183–186,
191
learning the functions of, 183–186
shape as identifier of, 89, 167,
185–186
attention. *See also* inattentional blindness
as basis of conscious awareness, 49
to details, lack of, 24, 47, 90, 113,
128, 186, 188, 193–195, 285
and expectations, 57–58
and gaze, 163–164, 306n.2 (chapter 3)
innate biases in, 301–302
to motion, 72–73, 301
required for perceptual meaning
analysis, 68–69, 72
required for recall, 52–53, 57, 285
awareness. *See* consciousness

basic-level concepts
and attention to details, 194